Rev. Cary Gordon speaks and w
who has heard the voice of God
the face of God on the mounta
are convicting, and he burns with a passion for righteousness and
justice to flourish again in our land. In this dark hour, when all hope
for America seems lost, Pastor Gordon holds forth a blazing torch
that lights the way to revival, renewal, and the rebirth of Christian
civilization on this continent.

—REV. JAMIE JOHNSON (ANGLICAN)
VICE PRESIDENT OF WORLD-WIDE MISSIONS
STORY CITY, IOWA

At a time when many Christians are discouraged by activism turned
futile and the American dream transformed into a nightmare...I
heartily recommend Pastor Gordon's book as exactly what American Christians need.

—LT. COL. JOHN EIDSMOE (FREE LUTHERAN CONGREGATIONS)
PASTOR, CONSTITUTIONAL ATTORNEY, AND ADJUNCT PROFESSOR AT
OAK BROOK COLLEGE OF LAW AND
HANDONG INTERNATIONAL LAW SCHOOL
PIKE ROAD, ALABAMA

In the midst of the decay and deterioration of the truths, Constitution, and ideals of our great founding fathers, we find patriots.
Pastor Cary Gordon is one of them. He is completely committed to
teach the American citizen how to become a great patriot.

Cary has done an outstanding job on his new book, *a Storm, a Message, a Bottle*. It is a true map to American redemption. I don't believe
there is a patriot alive or an American citizen whose heart will not
be moved by this writing. The author has done an expert job defining
some of the most difficult and perplexing elements of our country
and government. No matter your level of involvement or knowledge,
it will be a beneficial read. This book is so well crafted and organized
it could actually be used as a textbook in any university, yet some of
the simple, down-to-earth stories he shares are the real bell ringers.

In my years of ministry, I have never seen a book quite like this,
neither have I met a man who cares more about America. I recommend this book to absolutely everyone, especially those of the Christian faith!

— DR. MARK T. BARCLAY (INDEPENDENT)
FOUNDING PASTOR OF LIVING WORD INTERNATIONAL CHURCH
MIDLAND, MICHIGAN

Just as our pulpits led the way in those Great Awakenings of our past that gave birth to our liberty in the first place, liberty will not remain for the next generation without similar revival on the road we're currently on. And that revival will not come until our pulpits are again ablaze with righteousness—that most prophetically perfect combination of truth and grace. America is crying out for another "black-robed regiment" to shepherd her through the narrow gate, and Pastor Cary Gordon is one who raises his hand and says, "Here I am, LORD, send me." I pray for the sake of my children and grandchildren the Lord will raise up 10,000 more like him.

—STEVE DEACE, NATIONALLY SYNDICATED RADIO HOST
PROLIFIC WRITER FOR USA TODAY, POLITICO, TOWNHALL.COM,
BREITBART, CNS NEWS, BUSINESS INSIDER,
AND THE WASHINGTON TIMES
DES MOINES, IOWA

Pastor Cary Gordon, Executive Pastor of Cornerstone World Outreach in Sioux City, Iowa, has meticulously written an outline of what God has given him over the years as he has been called by God to battle for biblical truth on the front lines of our nation.

a Storm, a Message, a Bottle is truth unvarnished, for everyone that cares about the future of our beloved country. It is a challenging read for every Christian leader in America. If you are a Christian, you are a leader, influencing everyone around you. This mind-probing, heartfelt book is intriguing, educational, and inspirational. It is a roadmap detailed in all walks of life to change the culture of our nation and to influence the world.

Pastor Gordon's passion for his family and extended family's future reaches into my house, your house, the church house, the court house and the White House.

—DR. J. ALBERT CALAWAY (ASSEMBLIES OF GOD)
FOUNDER OF TRUTH, VALUES AND LEADERSHIP
INDIANOLA, IOWA

In spite of the difficulties affected by macular degeneration in both of my eyes, I have spent the last three days reading this great book with a high powered magnifying glass. I had to keep going because I was fascinated with what I was reading. I also took the time to compare notes with quite a number of extra biblical references such as the great history of the Jews by Josephus, and other word study dictionaries. I must say I was very impressed with the whole thing. What touched me most was Chapter 6, entitled "The Sin of Libertarianism."

In this particular chapter, Pastor Cary Gordon powerfully argues that the foundation of all civil law and order must be the Word of God.

This then leads to the inevitable conclusion that when men make laws which are contrary to God's Word we must choose to obey God, not man, and disobey those man-created ordinances. There are some good examples of this in our New Testament.

If we are persecuted, threatened, imprisoned or even killed for this, we must stand our ground. I know Pastor Cary and his church, Cornerstone World Outreach, have already come up against some hostile opposition in the courageous stands they have already made in their city over local issues.

This book should find its way into the hands of every pastor, Bible training institution, and every serious student of the kingdom of God.

—Pastor Alan Vincent (Pentecostal)
Outpouring Ministries International
San Antonio, Texas

In this book, a Storm, a Message, a Bottle, Pastor Gordon not only exposes the root of the problem but how to climb out of the pit! I was deeply moved from the very first chapter and challenged by the level of detailed substance presented throughout the work. In particular, once I completed the 12th chapter entitled, "How to Defend Your Nation by Winning Your City," I was absolutely inspired! I can't wait for the rest of you to be able to read this book and be invigorated by it like I am right now! I am not aware of another book written in the contemporary era that has the potential to awaken, motivate, and organize the American church into action! Every pastor who cares about the Word of God and state of America needs to read this book!"

—Pastor Michael Demastus (Church of Christ)
Fort Des Moines Church of Christ
Des Moines, Iowa

Throughout the history of the Christian Church, course corrections on proper theology have been necessary. Corrections usually come via "a pen of a man of God." Such is the case with Pastor Cary Gordon and his book, a Storm, a Message, a Bottle. Antinomianism (against law) is perhaps at its most feverish pitch since the Reformation. Now we have everything from professing Christians to entire denominations that look nothing like the Protestant, Evangelical, Orthodox Church given to us by the giants of the faith from the Reformation era and indeed from the Apostolic era. Consequently, our land and our families are in a free fall while the humanists are capturing nearly every institution that has given us liberty and prosperity using scriptural principles. This book belongs in every Christian home, every church library and needs to be preached from every pulpit in America. With that, God may give us favor and the light of Christianity will shine again.

—Dan Smithwick (Reformed faith)
Founder of Nehemiah Institute
Winter Garden, Florida

Our beloved nation has become comatose with a brand of gospel that is rapidly becoming as salt without savor. As we see our values trampled by a secular parade of libertarian logic, the truth of God's Word is being rendered powerless. True patriots at heart cry out for an end to the seemingly unstoppable moral decay, while it seems the church has flown a white flag of surrender, abdicating to moral relativists who would seek to convince all that God, much less religion, has no place in the public discourse. To all those who cry out for an answer to this moral dilemma and a new awakening in our land, this is the book you have been waiting for!

This thought-provoking, soul-searching work masterfully dismantles shaky pop theology and reassembles on a clear and sure foundation the faith once delivered unto us by our forefathers. With a passion for the truth, Rev. Gordon exposes Satan's web of lies woven into the very fabric of modern thinking. Fasten your seatbelt and hang on, as some of your very own paradigms will be challenged; I assure you by the end of the ride you will be wanting more.

In the 1999 sci-fi film *The Matrix,* the main character, Neo, is given a choice between taking a red pill or a blue pill. Wikipedia explains, "The red pill and its opposite, the blue pill, are pop culture symbols representing the choice between embracing the sometimes painful truth of reality (red pill) and the blissful ignorance of illusion (blue pill)."

This book is the red pill.

I challenge you, the reader, to take the red pill. I dare you not to put this book down until you have thoroughly vetted its pages and let its truths sink deep into your soul. You will never be the same.

—Pastor Douglas Bankson (Independent)
Founder of Victory Church World Outreach Center
Apopka, Florida

a**STORM**
a**MESSAGE**
a**BOTTLE**

a**STORM**
a**MESSAGE**
a**BOTTLE**
A Map to American Redemption

Rev. Cary K. Gordon

CREATION
HOUSE

A Storm, a Message, a Bottle by Cary K. Gordon
Published by Creation House
A Charisma Media Company
600 Rinehart Road
Lake Mary, Florida 32746
www.charismamedia.com

Unless otherwise noted, all Scripture quotations are from the King James Version of the Bible.

Scripture quotations marked AMP are from the Amplified Bible. Old Testament copyright © 1965, 1987 by the Zondervan Corporation. The Amplified New Testament copyright © 1954, 1958, 1987 by the Lockman Foundation. Used by permission.

Scripture quotations marked ASV are from the American Standard Bible. Copyright © 1960, 1962, 1968, 1971, 1972, 1973, 1975, by the Lockman Foundation. Used by permission.

Scripture quotations marked ESV are from the Holy Bible, English Standard Version. Copyright © 2001 by Crossway Bibles, a division of Good News Publishers. Used by permission.

Scripture quotations marked GW are taken from GOD'S WORD®, © 1995 God's Word to the Nations. Used by permission of Baker Publishing Group.

Scripture quotations marked HCSB are taken from the *Holy Bible*, Holman Christian Standard Bible, copyright © 1999, 2000, 2002, 2003, 2009. Used by permission of Holman Bible Publishers, Nashville, Tennessee. All Rights Reserved.

Scripture quotations marked NIV are taken from the Holy Bible, New International Version®, NIV®. Copyright © 1973, 1978, 1984, 2011 by Biblica, Inc.™ Used by permission of Zondervan. All rights reserved worldwide. www.zondervan.com The "NIV" and "New International Version" are trademarks registered in the United States Patent and Trademark Office by Biblica, Inc.™

Design Director: Justin Evans
Cover design by Timothy Hicks of Creative Media Solutions.

Visit the author's website: www.cornerstoneworld.org.

Library of Congress Cataloging-in-Publication Data: 2014953365
International Standard Book Number: PB: 978-1-62998-400-1 / HB: 978-1-62998- 399-8
E-book International Standard Book Number: 978-1-62998-401-8

While the author has made every effort to provide accurate telephone numbers and Internet addresses at the time of publication, neither the publisher nor the author assumes any responsibility for errors or for changes that occur after publication.

First edition

15 16 17 18 19 — 987654321
Printed in Canada

Dedication

Dedicated to a man, like our founders,
who did more than merely pledge his life,
fortune, and sacred honor...a man who,
like Daniel, prayed with his curtains drawn
wide and his windows open...a man who
did not run when the angry lions came.

They hated God's law, and you loved
it with all your heart, mind, soul, and
strength. I will forever cherish the
memory of your celebration on that
Tuesday evening, March 13, 2012, atop
the Regions Bank Building overlooking
the great city of Montgomery, Alabama.

That was the night I saw beaming lights, not
only from the lofty balcony of the Capitol
City Club towering above the Montgomery
cityscape, but shining from the eyes of a
man who just discovered himself vindicated
by both God and his countrymen.

This book is dedicated to my dear friend
and adopted grandfather, Chief Justice Roy
Moore, of the Alabama State Supreme Court.

Even now you remain a lighthouse in
the darkness of our present storm.

Above: Chief Justice Moore and I chortling after hearing the news
of his amazing victory on election night, March 13, 2012.

Contents

Foreword... xv

Introduction..xvii

Prologue   A "Message in a Bottle"...........................xxi

Chapter 1   Where Self-Government Ends

and Another Begins 1

Chapter 2   Generational Conspiracy 19

Chapter 3   Situational Ethics: Cancer of Christianity.......... 38

Chapter 4   Moses: Father of Fascism? 68

Chapter 5   Dividing the Law 96

Chapter 6   The Sin of Libertarianism 121

Chapter 7   Tethered: Internal Conscience

and External Law 140

Chapter 8   Authorized: Fifteen Classes of

Conduct to Forbid 156

Chapter 9   A Global Commonwealth of Nations 195

Chapter 10   Art Thou a King Then? 210

Chapter 11   Duverger Is Lord? 243

Chapter 12   How to Defend Your Nation by

Winning Your City................................. 257

Epilogue   Share Your Treasure.............................. 269

Appendix 1   Appendix of Biblical Law 273

Appendix 2   Jesus's Impact on Politics and Law

in 55 Parables 288

Appendix 3   Troubling Passages Explained 298

Notes..339

About the Author... 357

Contact the Author 359

Foreword

$\mathcal{A}$ T A TIME when many Christians are discouraged by activism turned futile and the American dream transformed into a nightmare, my good friend Pastor Cary Gordon's book comes to us exactly as the title suggests: a *Storm, a Message, a Bottle: A Map to American Redemption.*

As executive pastor of Cornerstone World Outreach in Sioux City, Iowa, Pastor Gordon has stood on the front lines of the culture war, leading Christians into battle against the forces of secularism, state-worship, and immorality, and transforming Cornerstone into a leading conservative Christian bastion in the Upper Midwest United States. He writes in an engaging, conversational style; as I read I can almost hear him preaching the same message from his pulpit.

His book is a rallying cry, warning against the defeatism of cultural retreat on the one hand and too much compromise on the other. His "Appendix of Biblical Law," including his detailed Scripture-based outlines of "Laws of the Self-Interpreting Bible," "Laws of Biblical Worldview," and "Troubling Passages Explained," are by themselves worth many times the price of the book.

I heartily recommend Pastor Gordon's book as exactly what American Christians need: a manual for culture warriorhood and a roadmap to victory!

To Cary:
I am proud to call you my fellow soldier and friend.

Godspeed,

—LT. COL. (RET.) JOHN A. EIDSMOE,
SENIOR COUNSEL AND RESIDENT SCHOLAR
FOUNDATION FOR MORAL LAW

Introduction

*V*ERY FEW PERSONS are genuinely willing to reconsider their hard-core positions on arguments of eschatology.* I believe with absolute certainty that it is quite impossible to carry on *any* fruitful debate on *any* subject of the Bible unless both parties adhere to a functioning standard of interpretive laws through which they are both willing to filter all questions and answers of Christian doctrine. A list of interpretive laws is included in the *Appendix of Biblical Law*, which is found on page 273. None of the laws listed are necessarily original with me, as they are principles taken from the Scriptures themselves, but all were extrapolated and compiled into one place through my personal research. Any failure to give credit for how a particular law has been similarly situated to those described by any other writers should be assumed as unintentional.

Next to each law of interpretation the reader will also find a scriptural reference point. Again, these are given to demonstrate that the laws of interpretation employed by the author were not created by some group of professors lecturing from an "ivory tower." The Bible is—by design of heaven—a self-interpreting work that supplies its own set of interpretive rules by precept and example. It is my hope that all readers, protagonists and antagonists of this teaching alike, will respect the self-interpreting laws of the Bible when conjuring any mental rebuttal and/or rejection of what is declared in this writing. Failing to do so will demonstrate a certain kind of "lazy-believism" that lacks integrity and is judged undeserving of further scrutiny by any serious student of the Holy Word.

With that said, while all Christians love and admire the quotes of

---

* The study of "end times" is known as **eschatology** (from the Greek *eskhatos* meaning "**last things**"), a subject that includes such topics as death, the afterlife, the Second Coming, the Millennial Kingdom, resurrection of the dead, heaven, and hell.

their historic church fathers, brave leaders, and revivalists, the mastery of *other* men's doctrines and *their* brilliant apologetics must take a backseat to something far more important—a functional and biblically supportable list of interpretive laws one can *personally* lean upon as a standard—determining truth from error for *themselves*. With only three exceptions that come to mind, I have *never* met a single Christian (not even a pastor) with a *functional* and *accurate* list of interpretive laws they have honestly and meticulously used in an effort to hash out their *own* doctrinal positions, much less to be used in the criticism of others. In nearly every case where an antagonist could not produce any system of interpretive laws wherewith to justify his dogmatic opinions, in most cases he still could not be convinced against his own cavalierly constructed position. (With this personal experience in mind, I sigh.)

The point is simply this: The contents and style of this book will be considered controversial by many. I may be perceived by the reader at some point as "being too hard" and at another "being too gentle." It is my sincere hope that every reader will carefully weigh the possibility that, despite present human shortcomings and imperfections, what has been shared here is God's own immutable truth.

If the present-day church is to have a constructive reformation of doctrine and behavior, then all believers must embrace laws of interpretation they mutually believe are biblically defensible (laws two opposing sides can read and agree upon) *before* beginning a debate in search of doctrinal purity. If any constructive renewal of Spirit is to take place, they must enjoin two opposing quarrelers who *sincerely* desire truth (and do not merely engage in debate so they can take worldly pleasure in proving themselves to be in possession of a superior intellect).

To do anything less than this is tantamount to two sides attempting to argue about quantum physics, one side arguing in French and the other speaking German, with a moderator who speaks neither language and possesses no comprehension of basic math. The best that could be produced by this comical scenario would be three angry and emotional people who feel "disrespected" after the dust settles from battle.

Before God, I confess I have done my best to adhere to the laws shared in the Appendix, but acknowledge I am fallible and could have failed in some way, somewhere along the road of production. In such an instance, I preemptively beg the reader's pardon and grace. The laws given are those emulated and demonstrated by Jesus Christ, and others during His and other holy men's public ministries. The reader is encouraged to peruse them. It is said that one pastor developed an entire college course on the subject of interpretation after he read them. (Yes, he first read them after he started a friendly disagreement with yours truly.)

The idea here is that any doctrinal position must pass the muster of *every single law* listed. If a position fails to stand up to the scrutiny of even one rule, further investigation is required, and said belief should not be taught with any *justifiable* dogmatism. I believe truth is knowable and absolute. Once absolute truth is found, believers are called upon to be *firmly persuaded* about it, and therefore, *should* be dogmatic about it. Emphatic dogmatism, in such a scenario, is natural, healthy, and necessary. To demonstrate anything less after having truly believed one has apprehended the truth would only prove a void of godly passion in the soul. The dogmatism all must *reject* is the kind some possess without having followed the proverbial "clinical procedures of the laboratory." This kind of dogmatism is righteously branded "annoying white noise," or as Paul described, "a clanging cymbal."

In addition to the laws of interpretation, I have also included a compilation of issue-based worldview laws with corresponding Bible references as a study aid. Appreciation is offered to Rev. J. Chace Gordon for his many hours of work compiling this list. Additionally, I would be remiss if I did not also salute the great and valuable work of Daniel J. Smithwick of Nehemiah Institute.

Beneath the Authority of Jesus Christ,

—REV. CARY K. GORDON

Prologue

A "Message in a Bottle"

*I*N 1784, A shipwrecked Japanese fellow sent a message in a bottle detailing his and forty-three shipmates' situation. The bottle washed ashore and was found by a Japanese seaweed collector one hundred and fifty one years later in the village of Hiraturemura. The town where the bottle was found was the birthplace of the very man who had originally sent the message.[*]

In 1914, a British soldier named Thomas Hughes threw a green ginger beer bottle containing a letter to his wife into the English Channel. Two days later he was killed in combat in France. Eighty-five years into the future (1999), the bottle was found by a fisherman who snared it on the River Thames. Although the intended recipient of the letter had unfortunately died twenty years prior to its discovery, the bottle was delivered to Private Hughes's eighty-six-year-old daughter living in New Zealand.[†]

To my beloved children, and the yet unborn grandchildren, great-grandchildren, and beyond, I devotedly send this "message in a bottle." It has been written with the whole church of God in mind, of course, but it is *specifically* dedicated to you. I hope you will read it by your twenty-first birthday! (It might be too hard to understand if you read it any sooner.) I realize you may find this hard to believe, but the truth is, I have *dearly* loved you—beyond words—even before I have met you. (Some of you will not meet me face-to-face until heaven.) Nevertheless, I think of you often, and wonder who you will become and how you will serve our King Jesus.

If you have not already done so, I beg of you to humble yourself

---

[*] Robert Kraske, *The Twelve Million Dollar Note: Strange but True Tales of Messages Found in Seagoing Bottles* (Nashville, TN: Thomas Nelson, 1977), 30–32.
[†] "Sweet Message in a Bottle," BBC News, May 18, 1999, accessed July 10, 2009, http://news.bbc.co.uk/2/hi/uk/346879.stm.

before God, repent of your sins, change your ways, obey the teachings of Jesus Christ with passion, and embrace salvation on a daily basis so that we can be together for eternity. Hell is real! I don't want you to go there. But you *will* go there if you do not follow Jesus Christ with all your heart, mind, and soul. I tell you this, of course, because... like I said... I love you.

> Tell your children of it, and let your children tell their children, and their children to another generation.
>
> —JOEL 1:3, ESV

If the message I have sent you was not heeded by my own generation at the time of this writing, then you may struggle to understand some of the terms and concepts expressed within its pages. On the other hand, if my message *was* accepted and acted upon by my generation, then you'll just blaze through this without any trouble at all. But, in the case it was not, I must assume that education has probably grown much worse in your time, and you are likely the victim of a continual societal degradation we have already been witnessing in America since the early twentieth century. Even now, the prophetic sixteenth century words of Martin Luther have come to pass in the year of this first printing (2015). He warned, "I'm afraid that the schools will prove the very gates of hell, unless they diligently labor in explaining the Holy Scriptures and engraving them in the hearts of youth."

A legend is told of a man who once spotted a bottle while strolling along a particular beach. Once he retrieved it and noticed the paper inside, he popped the cork to discover what appeared to be a very old and weathered treasure map. The map seemed to indicate a buried treasure was resting just off the shore in the deep waters below. So he acquired a small boat, rowed out to where seemed to be the best location, and dove into the freezing cold waters. After some time passed and he had been thoroughly wearied from fighting a combination of strong current, loss of breath, and the general fatigue of mind and body, he convinced himself that he was the victim of a cruel joke. With a combination of cynicism and frustration, he stuffed the map back inside the bottle, re-corked it, and whipped it back into the waters.

A few days later, the same bottle was found by a more determined soul than the first, who did not so easily give in to the same opposing elements. He swam against the same strong current, faced the same loss of breath and fatigue, but he would not quit. To the amazement of the world, he discovered an astonishing ancient treasure only *inches* away from where the first man had given up. Both men had been fortunate to rest their eyes upon the very same bottle. Both men had held the same information in the grasp of their two hands. Both men had the ability to find a treasure of great price, but only one went on to live the high life. The other, who caught the tale of his neighbor's discovery broadcast on the television news, lived with great regrets.

You too have now received a message. You have seen it with your eyes and now hold it in the grasp of your hands. If, by the time you read this, the ecclesiastical powers of the church have not yet repented and subsequently improved their character, I know you will be facing a cultural struggle much greater than those I ever withstood. Don't be discouraged! No matter what comes against you, remember this: *you are a Gordon!* Whether or not you may carry that name, you all carry my genetics! (I'm chuckling, but I'm still serious.) Since that is true, I know that God has blessed you with courage, strength, love, and a sound mind! You can and you *must* rise above the defiant in your generation. Regardless of what your schools or churches may have failed to teach you, I *believe* in you, because I believe in the power of God's grace. I am reminded of that particular passage, which says:

> Now unto him that is able to keep you from falling, and to present you faultless before the presence of his glory with exceeding joy, To the only wise God our Saviour, be glory and majesty, dominion and power, both now and ever. Amen.
> —JUDE 1:24–25

With the help of a good dictionary, a 1599 Geneva Bible (or a King James Version will suffice, if you don't have one yet), and perhaps a good thesaurus, I know you can wade through this message I have written for you and begin to understand and explore your destiny as a servant of King Jesus. If you are ever startled by what I have penned, recall the words of George Orwell, who wrote, "During times of universal deceit, telling the truth becomes a revolutionary act."

I pray you have been raised by godly parents who are generational thinkers, like I have been. I pray they have passed on to you the important lessons of self-government (self-discipline) and that your childhood has made you a strong, dependable, trustworthy, and faithful adult. I pray your parents followed the example of the father of all our faith—the patriarch Abraham, of whom it was said:

> And the LORD said, Shall I hide from Abraham that thing which I do; Seeing that Abraham shall surely become a great and mighty nation, and all the nations of the earth shall be blessed in him? For I know him, that he will command his children and his household after him, and they shall keep the way of the LORD, to do justice and judgment; that the LORD may bring upon Abraham that which he hath spoken of him.
>   —GENESIS 18:17–19

If your rearing at home was done according to God's Law-Word, then you are ready to learn how and by whom you are necessary, empowered, and authorized to resurrect authentic Americanism. It is time for you to understand how your self-government must now relate to your civil government. Understanding this lesson is of critical importance, as you will soon see, because there is a final government which, just beyond the grave...awaits.

'Til we meet in the Golden City!

Your Father,

                                                        —REV. CARY K. GORDON

Chapter 1

Where Self-Government Ends and Another Begins

URING THE LAST week of school, as a six-year-old first grader, my third child, Jonas, began to behave unusually. Jonas had been coming home daily, telling on himself to his mother, asking her for a spanking. I was not aware of it the first few times it happened. On one occasion in particular, my wife, Molly, had contacted his teacher at school and confirmed that he had in fact disobeyed. Molly spanked him, per his honest request, and alleviated the burden upon his conscience. Later that same evening, he called his teacher at home to apologize.

Now don't misunderstand me when I say that Jonas began behaving unusually. The worst thing his teacher could confirm he had done was talk to his neighbor in class without permission. What I mean by "began to behave unusually" is the coming home and telling on himself part of the story. The day afterward, he came home and did it again, but this time it was more complicated.

Again, Molly contacted the teacher and asked if he had behaved in class, and she replied that he had been delightful and obedient and hadn't caused a single problem at all. Molly was confused, so she asked him to explain what he had done to believe he deserved a spanking, as his teacher did not agree that he had done anything wrong. Jonas squirmed for a bit, and finally said, "I can't really remember, but I think I talked to David when she wasn't looking. I just know I did things today that weren't the right thing to do." At that point, Molly came to me and let me know what had been going on for the past few days, and we both scratched our heads.

I was initially unsure what to do about it, so when Jonas came to me a few hours later to remind me to spank him, I responded, "Well, we'll talk about that later." Honestly, I was trying to brush it off. I didn't want to spank him, and he couldn't even fully remember why he felt he needed a spanking. I thought to myself, *Who are you, and what have you done with my son?*

My wife didn't know it, but I had been praying for Jonas, concerned about him for some time. I was concerned because he was such a compliant and obedient little fellow since birth; I had hardly ever had to spank him. While most parents would brag about that kind of good-natured child, it worried me deeply. I understand that one of the most important duties a father will ever be given is the insight into when and how to break the will of a child when rebellion rises in his or her heart. Most all children require multiple spankings during their childhood rearing—some more than others. All children have rebellion in their hearts, and the crescendo of the rebellion does not necessarily occur at the age of forty-eight when they are finally locked away in a prison somewhere...it occurs at the moment of the age of accountability. When their knowledge of good and evil rises to an epiphany and the sin-nature chains them to a train car rolling on steel rails to hell...that is the moment when a godly father must be vigilant above all other moments. It is true that all parents make mistakes, but this would be the moment when a mistake is unaffordable. The fact that these critical moments of truth are sometimes missed opportunities in child-rearing explains why six children can grow up in the same household, yet two will serve Satan all their days, while the other four will be faithful members of a local church. Two of the six children probably never had their will broken by their father's true love. The moment came, but it was either not recognized or ignored, and the opportunity to shape a lifetime was lost.

A parent must follow the example of Father God in the Garden of Eden. Seize the moment when the forbidden fruit is eaten and the knowledge of good and evil has fully soaked into the child's heart, mind, and soul. Miss that moment, and you can still discipline and shape the behavior of a child into outward compliance, respect, good grades, and sports trophies; but if you fail to break their rebellious sin-nature, when they leave your home for college they will run to sin with haste and find eternal destruction. Politely rebellious children can have lovely flesh, wonderful manners, respected parents...and still have a heathen soul.

All children require a swat on the behind as they learn right from wrong, but what I'm talking about here is a single pivotal moment in time when the human will rises in rebellion to challenge authority, and if it is broken and humbled, it does not ever rise again with the same intensity. Having their will broken in a soulish way by their *earthly* father leaves them in a much better position to eventually present their will someday to their *heavenly* Father.

With my first two children, that monumental moment had been unmistakable. My first and second children were both strong-willed kids, so it was not difficult, with the Holy Spirit's help, to rise to the occasion when that single life-altering moment of defiance occurred.

With Ella, the moment of truth was during her fourth birthday party. She acted awful and selfish, and her mother and I were fit to be tied with the unprecedented rebellion she displayed during her party. It was the weirdest and most terrible birthday memory a child or parent could have. I was thoroughly embarrassed at her behavior in front of our friends and family. Once everyone had left, I calmly took my little daughter who had acted like a pretentious brat downstairs and explained what she had done wrong. Then I spanked her little bottom until I saw the rebellion, resentment, and anger leave her eyes. After the first few smacks, she screamed with anger. So I spanked her again. She responded with more anger. So I did it again. She did not scream out, but she looked at me with fury in her eyes while she cried. So I spanked her again. The rebellion had to be broken.

This was the moment that would determine her future; it would have eternal consequences. It was a battle of the wills. One of us was going to yield to the other. Either I was going to chicken out for fear of being too severe and allow the hate and rebellion to remain inside her, or she would break under the duress of a very sore bottom and look at me with true repentance in her eyes. I was determined that I was *not* going to lose this battle. This was it! I knew it. Finally, having forced me to the brink of my own limits, I knew her will was broken, and my heart was broken along with it.

I held her and wept while she wept. I told her I loved her too much to allow her to have evil in her heart against God. We talked about Jesus on the cross, and we prayed together, asking His forgiveness. From that day forward the child was changed. Though it is possible that I did once or twice, I do not recall ever having to spank her again. Obviously, as with every child, she is maturing in her relationship with Jesus and learning to walk in His ways, but she has always been a ray of sunshine and an absolute delight to her mother and me.

Every child was different. Solomon's moment of truth had to do with his discovery and experimentation with lying about anything and everything. He was about four years old. He even lied about insignificant things. He had discovered a particular sin and was going to work it into every situation he could find to apply it. His lying began suddenly. He was deliberate and constant with it, and it was very obvious and frustrating. It took a few days to find the right moment when it could be broken, and with the Lord's guidance, I broke his human will and watched the rebellion, anger, and resentment leave his eyes. With Solomon, spankings did not seem to break his fascination with lying, so we coined the term "mouth-spanking." We explained to him that every time he lied he would be given a tiny spoon of cayenne pepper hot sauce. "Solomon, if you do wrong with your mouth, we will have to spank your mouth so that it learns not to tell lies." I would prepare him before asking a question by saying, "I am going to ask you something, and it is very important that you only tell me the truth, because I will know if you are lying. Did you draw with your crayon on the kitchen cupboard?" He seemed interested in the pretty red bottle we warned him about, so he lied again as if he *wanted* to taste it.

It only happened one more time the following day. He stopped lying altogether for good. He has always been the most honest and trustworthy child since that day. Sensitive to the Lord. Tender in worship. Caring for others. Respectful to authority. A great delight to his parents.

Jonas, however, was hardly ever in trouble; always compliant and respectful. I hardly ever had to spank him, yet I knew that his delightful little phlegmatic personality maintained a silent will of iron that *had* to be broken; the opportunity had never presented itself. So I had prayed on it and asked for God's help. Jonas was now six. My other two children had received their Garden of Eden confrontations sooner than this. I was concerned about what to do.

When the routine of telling on himself happened yet again the following day, I finally realized in my spirit that God was trying to answer my prayers for Jonas. I knew God was at work, and that my fathering moment was about to present itself. I just didn't know how it was going to play out.

On that partially sunny Wednesday afternoon of May 29, 2013, arriving home at approximately 3:30, Jonas came to greet me in my office. I asked, "How was your day today?"

He responded, "It was good."

I countered, "Did you get in any trouble today?"

He said, "No, I didn't get in trouble."

I told him that was great and that I loved him, and I turned back to my computer to keep working on some things. Finally, he interrupted me. "Dad, I am going to need a spanking, though."

I looked at him with an expression of bewilderment on my face and said, "What? You just told me you had a good day and didn't get into any trouble!"

He said, "Well, I did wrong when my teacher wasn't looking. She just didn't know about it."

I was becoming exhausted with this routine, so I brushed him off a while longer and said, "Well, you and I are going to talk about this in a little while and get it resolved, but let me finish the project I'm in the middle of, and I'll call you in a little later."

After an hour passed, I left my library office to use the restroom, and when I returned to the office I saw a post-it note stuck to the corner of my desk. On it he had written—*Spank Jonas*—as a reminder.

I pulled my phone from my shirt pocket and photographed it for a memory, then I tucked the note (at right) away in my desk for Molly's scrapbook. I had no idea how much I was about to love that little note, but I sensed that God was at work.

Finally, I called him into my office, perplexed. He arrived holding a wooden spoon in his hand. He handed it to me and said again, "I need to be spanked now." I asked him why he believed he deserved a spanking...again. He said, "Because I've been talking when I'm not supposed to at school and my teacher didn't catch me."

I asked, "So why do you come home and ask for a spanking when you did wrong and no one knows but you? What are you afraid is going to happen if you don't tell on yourself and get a spanking?"

Jonas initially responded with three words that I had never heard him say before. It was as if he did not know how to describe what had happened over the past few weeks. I could see on his face a straining for words to explain what he felt. Out came three words:

"My heart changed."

As soon as I heard him utter those three words, I knew that my beautiful little boy had left innocence, taken the forbidden fruit and eaten it. His beautiful spirit was now dead to God. He needed a Redeemer to lift the burden from his tiny soul.

"Jonas, what do you mean when you say your heart changed?"

He answered, "I feel a lot of guilt every day."

I asked, "So why do you keep telling on yourself every day when you get home asking for a spanking? What are you afraid is going to happen if you don't tell on yourself?"

Jonas replied with tears in his eyes, "I know if I don't tell on myself, God will get me for it. I don't want to go to hell."

I took him through the Ten Commandments and helped him see how he had broken them all in his own way. He knew them from memory, so I had him recite them one by one. With each one I asked him connected questions.

"Have you ever told a lie?"

Jonas responded, "Yes, Dad. Everyone lies."

"What do you call someone who lies? A liar. You are a liar to God. Have you ever taken something that wasn't yours?"

He thought for a moment, and said, "I don't remember...probably."

I asked him what would happen if I started throwing stones at our neighbor across the street and wouldn't stop. He understood that I would eventually be arrested by the police and taken to jail. I confirmed that the penalty for breaking man's law was being arrested and locked away in prison. The penalty for breaking God's law was being arrested by the angels, and locked away in eternal hell. I saw the fear and sadness in his eyes as we confirmed that he had already, at the tender age of six years old, broken many of the Ten Commandments. Then, by the grace of God, I took it to the next level. (This was the hard part, so brace yourself while you read.) I told him *sternly* that he *deserved* to go to hell for his sins against God, and that I totally agreed with him, that he *also* deserved to be spanked *severely* for his secret disobedience.

When I informed him that his punishment should be ten whacks (one for each commandment) on his behind with the wooden spoon (a spoon that he brought to me when initially asking to be spanked), and that I further believed they should be *very hard* whacks, he burst into tears and began to cry deeply and loudly. He was very remorseful and afraid. I could see the fear and guilt, and it overwhelmed me with compassionate sorrow. I could hardly bear this confrontation.

Then, while he stood in front of me, nearly paralyzed by my righteous pronouncement of judgment against him, I handed him the spoon, bent over my desk, and instructed him to hit me as hard as he could ten times.

I explained that I would take the spanking for him.

He hesitated. He was confused. I commanded it again and told him to do it hard.

He sobbed while I took his spanking. I made him hit me as hard as he could.

And yes, it hurt.

When the spanking was over, this bizarre turn of events allowed me to explain to my six-year-old what Jesus did on the cross, so he could understand it for the first time in his life. My precious child cried and cried. He closed his eyes and prayed with me. He asked Jesus to forgive him of his sins and be his Savior from now on. Jonas's will was not only broken and contrite; he was gloriously saved by the blood of Jesus Christ. He was forgiven and washed of all guilt—white as snow.

We dried our eyes, ate our dinner quickly, and made our way to the car so we could get to church for family night. It was Molly's and my turn to team teach for the children between the ages of five and twelve. We quickly put on our costumes and began to read our scripts aloud before the service began. Molly and I nearly asked one another at the same time, "Have you read your script yet?" Neither of us had been able to find the time to get prepared for the lesson, so we were nervous about doing a good job.

As soon as we arrived at the church, we scurried back into the green room to get our microphones on and hurriedly read through our unseen scripts. You could have knocked me over with a feather. The lesson we would be teaching hundreds of children that night, taken from a three-year curriculum with around 150 independent lessons, was about the Ten Commandments. Some of the very same remarks I had just made with Jonas in the privacy of my office earlier that afternoon were our talking points for the fun-filled night at church. At one point during the lesson, I actually heard Jonas's little voice from his seat on the front row. He spoke to a child sitting next to him, "This is the same thing my dad told me before we got here!" It was a remarkable "coincidence" all planned out by God. The particular way He answered my prayers and then threw in a dash of providence left me teary for a few days.

Jonas had reached the age of accountability and was burdened by the great eternal weight of his sins. One is tempted to think to themselves, *All the little kid did was whisper in class! That is not a big deal!* Well, how big of a deal is sneaking a bite of fruit? Adam and Eve could tell you about the weight of the "smallest" of sins that lay upon their souls in great shame and fear, couldn't they?

Like Adam, Jonas had supernatural knowledge of his own nakedness and guilt. Unlike Adam, instead of running to hide when he felt the guilt that was so heavy, he was driven by the Holy Spirit through knowledge of the law of God to seek help and relief. Jonas asked for punishment, while Adam and Eve tried to escape it. Jonas knew he deserved it. He was right! The rightful and well-earned condemnation his young and tender heart produced drove him to ask his parents for spankings.

This next part is very important. Don't miss this, because it is right here where you can determine whether or not you've been paganized by this world's awful thinking (or worse...cheap grace heresy!). Just think about the eternal damage I might have inflicted upon him had I told him, "You don't deserve a spanking!" Or worse, had I stupidly said, "Oh, don't be so hard on yourself—everybody makes mistakes! You're a good kid! God loves you just the way you are!"

Parents and pastors, don't destroy the most rare and beautiful opportunities God gives you as a natural and/or spiritual parent to lead your children *to* the cross...*through* the cross...*into* resurrection power and the joy of forgiveness and salvation.

Salvation begins at home. Jonas will make a public confession of Christ when he's ready. Thankfully, he enjoys a church that has rejected the lawless heresies of our day, who will understand the legitimacy of his public confession of faith when it takes place.

My little boy became a living epistle! Jonas is a microcosmic example of the effect the law of God has to draw a whole nation to Christ. There will never again be a national American revival of saints or a great awakening of sinners without a public knowledge of the law of God. What happened to my child has happened to entire tribes, nations, and tongues! It begins with knowledge of the Ten Commandments. Knowledge of God's moral absolutes provides the necessary context for guilt, remorse, and repentance. America could not have had its first two great awakenings without its children memorizing them during the school week, its churched adults hearing them preached on Sundays, and its criminals knowing them to be enshrined as the basis for American jurisprudence in every courthouse.[1] The law of God is the bridge to true repentance and eternal salvation. It is the schoolmaster (see Galatians 3:24) that drives the soul of man to either seek relief from his guilt or hide behind the bushes in shame of his nudity. Without any knowledge of God's law, a wicked man is too dull in the heart and head to be anything less than stupidly proud to stand nude in the sun, boasting of his own pornographic physique.

My point could not be weightier!

From time immemorial, this link between self-government (the sometimes guilty and occasionally innocent conscience of individual persons) and the natural formation of a civil government (what happens when individual persons extend their consciences upon an entire city, state, and nation) has existed.

Like a weather vane pointing from the peak of a gabled roof in response to the wind that pushed it, my son Jonas's behavior indicates the direction where his life is headed, and his behavior is in response to the "pushing" of my parental influence. Human behavior points toward something as certainly as it points away from other things. If a weather vane is pointing north, it must also be pointing *away* from the south. Along similar lines, the vast majority of adults (most especially seasoned school teachers) have at some point mumbled to themselves, "If that child's parents don't start doing their job, the kid's going to end up in prison!" Human behavior points in a particular direction.

Men who are personally enslaved by sin will collectively produce a tyrannical form of civil government. After all, civil government is little more than the extension of the individual conscience upon a community, and in a democracy, it's a contest between whose consciences will rule the day. For this same reason, men who are personally freed from the shackles of sin will have a proclivity toward producing liberty in their civil government. To say it another way, wicked men make wicked governments, and righteous men make righteous governments. Most people know this instinctively, even if they aren't able to articulate it out loud.

My little boy Jonas will someday become a productive citizen defending the common good. I have as much ability to recognize this path as any other man has to determine where his arrow will fly based upon the direction of his aim. I only need to reflect upon his trajectory at six years old to determine this. My son will be a citizen that believes rebellion against tyrants is obedience to God, and rebellion against God is complicity with tyrants. He has been through his personal Garden of Eden and survived to tell the tale. By discovering the path that breaks the enslaving chains of sin and guilt, Jonas is well on his way toward a life of true liberty. Someday, as an adult, his interactions with others in his community will naturally become an extension of his own personal discovery of freedom.

Family government (good parenting) produces self-government—well-disciplined children who then become good citizens who produce stable civil government. These truths of human nature lead us to a very important question:

> At what point does my personal liberty—my self-government—
> reach its end, and the jurisdiction of civil government begin?

Webster's 1828 Dictionary defines the word *inalienable* as "cannot be legally or justly alienated or transferred to another." A government cannot legally or justly transfer its natural rights and corresponding duties to a particular individual. The individual is incapable of the duty connected to such a right. For example, with the exception of the mythical boy from the planet Krypton, one lone man cannot defend a national border by himself. One lone soul cannot ensure domestic tranquility. Similarly, an individual cannot legally or justly transfer to a government his own right and connected duty to experience and express compassion. Can a government cry or laugh? Does a government grieve? Does it feel hope? Can a government dream? No, no, no, and no. A government has no soul. It is not human. It is not biological, and therefore cannot feel anything.

If it is true, as our Declaration of Independence claims, that individual human beings are born with inalienable, God-given rights, would it also be true that civil government *also* has God-given inalienable rights? Because a government is not biological some understandably argue that governments do not have rights, but merely possess powers instead. While it is certainly true that powers are not necessarily the same as rights, in the context of the meaning of the word *inalienable*, I confess I am prone to disagree on this point.

Without tripping over distracting semantic arguments, surely a human has an inalienable right to exist; therefore, we say he possesses a natural right to defend himself. One must assume, then (particularly Christians who believe God both created and authorized government to exist), that a government also has, in a similar sense, an *inalienable* right to exist, and therefore retains a natural right to defend itself as well. It would seem that individuals and the governments they form both have rights, *but where is the line between self and civil government drawn, and by what authority?*

Regardless of who you ask, and whose answers you choose to believe, world history has taught us a lesson. We should have learned by now that inside these two all-encompassing questions (Where is the line between self and civil government drawn, and by what authority?) rests the sole source of countless bloody revolutions, rebellions, usurpations, and coups d'état (maybe a peaceful election or two). Honest men know the opposing answers cannot coexist— they cannot all be right at the same time—so the geopolitical battles continue, most with, and some without bullets.

Rose Wilder Lane once wrote of these warring factions among us, one in particular, which erringly insists it possesses the one and only true answer to these two questions (and consequentially, that all men who offer an opposing view should be exterminated from the face of the earth). We infer from her description the illogical inconsistency of Communism: "...the communist is looking for the Authority that controls men, and taking it for granted that the man does not control himself...A woman does not control her gas-range, it controls her. Does it? Since a communist does not know that individuals control themselves, he sees them as cells in Society, which (he believes) has a Great Spirit that is to the individual what the swarm is to the bee."[2]

Somewhere on the opposite end of the political spectrum (where Communists can't serve their cold, sticky porridge) can be found the "rugged individualist," the so-called Libertarian. Though he is

little more than an intellectual pirate of Christian religious philosophy, he nearly always denies this fact, claiming his political philosophy to be the product of non-religious academic innovation. He does
this, in some cases, because he is overtly dishonest with history, or
at the very least, unappreciative of liberty in its historical context
as the exclusive production of Christian theology (or both). In other
instances, it is perhaps that he (along with other secular humanists of most every stripe in the Western world, be they "Republican,"
"Democrat," or "Independent") subconsciously pilfers the ancient intellectual treasures produced by the Bible literacy of others, in order to
make sense of his own world. As they say, "Nature [and the mind]
abhors a vacuum."

On occasion, in an effort to prove that his concepts of liberty do
not require any religious context to exist, the Libertarian may be
found announcing he is an "atheist Libertarian," loudly espousing
the humanist version of "rights for every man!" But alas, liberty does
not come from nothing! As Bojidar Marinov once put it, "Secular
Libertarianism, by its very rejection of [a] transcendent system of law
and morality...is only an attempt to fight something with nothing;
fighting something with nothing only perpetuates tyranny, it doesn't
produce true liberty in the society."[3]

The Libertarian's denial that his own philosophy cannot exist
outside of the context of divine law expressed through the Judeo-
Christian ethic, is something, ironically, that even Karl Marx (the
political "Prince of Darkness") understood. Indeed, this same man
that Dr. Clarence Manion once described as "prophet of the modern
Socialist-Communist political and economic dispensation"[4] knew that
the origin of "rugged individualism" was Christianity. Marx wrote:

> The democratic concept of man is false, because it is Christian.
> The democratic concept holds that each man is a sovereign
> being. This is the illusion, dream and postulate of Christianity.[5]

Dr. Manion continues:

> One hundred years after Karl Marx thus wrote off the impor-
> tance of the individual human personality in that derisive con-
> demnation of Christianity, Adolf Hitler made his decisive bid
> for the control of Europe on what he represented to be a drive

against Communism. Nevertheless, this is what Hitler said about the inalienable rights of the individual man:

> "To the Christian doctrine of infinite significance of the individual human soul, I oppose with icy clarity the saving doctrine of the nothingness and insignificance of the human being."[6]

At this point in the writing one might ask, "What exactly is an atheist Libertarian? What would he do if he were ever elected to public office?" Allow me to explain. When elected to public office, he is your local neighborhood official who believes, in the words of Walter Block, an atheist Libertarian fellow of Loyola University,[7] "...libertarianism is solely a political philosophy. It asks one and only one question: Under what conditions is the use of violence justified? And it gives one and only one answer: Violence can be used only in response, or reaction to, a prior violation of private property rights."[8]

The Libertarian must lean upon the backdrop of Judeo-Christian philosophy in order to make sense of the world around him. He clings to the eighth commandment of the Decalogue[*] as his "one and only one question" through which all political decisions are allegedly filtered, at the expense of the other nine commands of God, all while denying that the source of his so-called intellectual plagiarism is the Law of God—specifically, the Law declared by whom the Declaration calls "Supreme Judge of the World."

Consequentially, Libertarian apologist Tom Mullen further believes (along with Congressman Ron Paul of Texas, and Professor Walter Block) that "all government action is violent action."[9] Ask him why he believes this, and he will bring up something as seemingly insignificant as a parking ticket and wryly ask, "What happens if you do not pay the ticket?" Next, he will answer his own rhetorical question, "If you don't pay the ticket, and if you continue to refuse to cooperate with the actions of government, you will be punished. Therefore, you see, all government action is violent action, if carried to its logical conclusion." (If you wish to frustrate his lesson, simply ask him to

---

* "Thou shalt not steal" is the **eighth command** of Moses. It is the Judeo-Christian theological basis for the concept of private property ownership given by divine authority. In order to steal, it must be assumed that what is stolen rightfully belongs to another.

explain how awarding the American Medal of Freedom to a celebrated civilian remains consistent with his theory of "violent action.")

Mullen describes this kind of interaction between the Libertarian and a poor ignorant stooge (non-Libertarian) this way:

> **You:** Suppose that I do not wish to participate in Medicare and withhold only that percentage of my payroll taxes that would otherwise go to fund it. In return, I agree not to make use of any of the Medicare benefits. What will happen to me?
>
> **Him/Her:** You will be charged with income tax evasion.
>
> **You:** What if I don't answer the charge?
>
> **Him/Her:** You will be arrested.
>
> **You:** What if I do not agree to submit to the arrest?
>
> **Him/Her:** You will be physically forced to submit.
>
> **You:** And if I resist further?
>
> **Him/Her:** (reluctantly) You will be killed.
>
> **You:** So, you now agree that we are forced to participate in Medicare under the threat of violence, correct?
>
> **Him/Her:** (even more reluctantly) Yes.
>
> **You:** Is there any government tax, law, or regulation that we are not similarly forced to participate in under the threat of violence?[10]

With these thoughts in the backdrop, I think we're ready for development of a little parable in the modern vernacular—one designed to explain the interactions of government in the United States, in a simple way. With the reader's permission, I would like to take my liberty (pardon the pun) and substitute the traditional opening line…"So, a libertarian, a conservative, and a liberal walked into a bar…" with this: "An atheist Libertarian, a Christian Conservative, and a liberal Democrat were elected to office." Are you with me? I think that opening will do nicely for what I have in mind. (Pay particular attention to these three characters, as they will re-emerge on occasion throughout the remainder of this writing to help us digest truths about Christianity's relation to politics.)

Let's say this particular atheist Libertarian is elected to public office. While in office, he is confronted with a bill that necessitates an up or down vote. While his natural instinct is to abstain, or simply vote "present" (go figure), he realizes that no other Libertarian will ever be elected again if each refuses to participate in their respective duties as representatives of the people who went to the trouble of voting for them. He further wishes to avoid the stigma generated by the logical conclusion of his own arguments—that all government action is violent and, as the reasoning goes, should be shunned. He does not relish the thought that the public may discover his Libertarianism is little more than a particular variety of utopian anarchism. (Anarchists wish for a world where no local, state, or federal government exists, and private property is violently defended—and justly defended, they claim ever so piously—in tribal fashion.)

Reluctantly, he chooses to protect the cherished title "Libertarian" and avoid the infamy of the more accurate title "Inconsistent Anarchist," so he decides to participate by offering an up or down vote on a proposed bill. He dutifully reviews the bill and makes the decision to vote "no" on what is a proposed tax increase. He votes this way because it is a clear violation of his secular Libertarian doctrine, which states, "Preservation of absolute private property rights, as it relates to justified use of force, is the single (and only) moral anchor for all political decisions." His decision to vote "no" is perfectly acceptable to most of his constituents, and thankfully, celebrated by his cadre of fellow Libertarian pagans (who, by the way, are still tingling from the surreal experience of having personally witnessed a Libertarian who actually won an election).

As a result of this action, the atheist Libertarian is labeled a "hard-hearted radical" by the liberal Democrat.

The Christian Conservative is also elected to public office. He makes the decision to vote "no" on the same proposed tax-increase as the atheist Libertarian; he too believes it a violation of the sacred principles of private property ownership. He has strong convictions that the proposed tax increase is a violation of God-given (unalienable) private property rights, because it is a violation of the Ten

Commandments, specifically, the eighth commandment, "Thou shalt not steal." His decision to vote "no" is alleged to be "shoving his religion down the throats of the unwilling and unbelieving," and he is publicly "christened" a "theocrat" (no doubt meant as an insult) by the atheist Libertarian and liberal Democrat alike.

The liberal Democrat is also elected to public office. He makes the decision to vote "yes" on the same tax increase. Of course, he will vote "yes" (chortles), because he proposed the tax hike! He did so because he believes, like Karl Marx before him (and from the deepest recesses of his compassionate heart and soul), that the greatest achievement of man is the production of a "benevolent" government, and such Shangri-la is only reached through the redistribution of wealth upon all men in equal sum. This redistribution through confiscation (tax) is the most virtuous act of a government!

He is branded as a "pinko"* by the atheist Libertarian, and a "thief" by the Christian Conservative.

What is the truth? Which one did the right thing? You'll certainly know the answer to that question by the end of this writing. Meanwhile, the fact remains that all three officials applied their own personal *theology* to their decision to vote on a proposed tax increase. If we borrow the definition of "violent action" from the atheist Libertarian, "all government action is violent action," we are left to conclude that all three officials apparently "used illegitimate force" against the will of another faction (particularly from the Democrat's point of view).

Conclusion: All governments of the world, as well as the individuals who operate under their respective umbrellas, are "theocracies." What differentiates between them is found in the answer to the question, as radio host Steve Deace once quipped, "Who is Theo?" Once the identity of "Theo" is discovered, the answer to the next question is of equal and critical significance: "Is 'Theo' righteous enough to produce authentic justice and liberty?"

Rose Wilder Lane so beautifully wrote, "So far as I know, only the American Indians called this intangible Authority [Theo], 'The Great Spirit.' Savages called it 'Tabu.' Spartans called it 'Sparta.' My Dukhagin [Albanian] friends called it the 'Law of Lek.'[11] Many groups

---

* **Pinko** is a critical term coined in America in 1925, originally to describe a person regarded as being sympathetic to Communism. The term has its origins in the notion that pink is a lighter shade of red, a color associated with Communism. Thus pink could describe a "lighter form of Communism."

of communists living in these States call it 'God.' Marx called it 'The Will of the Masses,' and 'The Proletarian State.' Communists in this country [America] now call their authority, 'The Party Line,' and it lives in Moscow."[12]

The goal of this book is to reveal the only true answers that *have* ever and *can* ever bring everlasting liberty, equality, and fraternity to mankind on earth—those answers given long ago by earth's divine Creator. Together, we will discover answers to the twofold question: Where is the line between self and civil government drawn, and by what authority?

In the pursuit of these two answers, we now launch into an exploration of the Creator's intervention in human affairs through both the type and antitype of Moses and Christ.[13]

CHAPTER 1: REVIEW QUESTIONS

Enjoy this quiz at http://peacemakersinstitute.com/smb-quiz.

1. Does an individual human being have an inalienable right to exist?

2. Does an individual human being have a right to defend himself?

3. Does a government have a right to exist?

4. Does a government have a right to defend itself?

5. Does a line exist where the jurisdiction of the individual stops and the jurisdiction of the civil government begins?

6. Did Karl Marx place any value upon the individual human being?

7. Did Adolf Hitler place any value upon the individual human being?

8. Did Karl Marx believe that the source of his arch-nemesis worldview, which had spread the idea that every individual soul had intrinsic sacred value, was Christianity?

9. Did Adolf Hitler believe that the source of his arch-nemesis worldview, which had spread the idea that

every individual soul had intrinsic sacred value, was
Christianity?

10. Does the atheist Libertarian place appropriate value
    upon the existence of civil government?

11. Are all governments of the world actually just varying
    types of theocracies?

12. What is the real question that must be asked of every
    theocracy?

Chapter 2

Generational Conspiracy

$\mathcal{T}$HERE ARE MANY preachers in America today who have read some passages in the New Testament of their Bibles and decided that they believe the Bible writers sent us an important message. That message is the founding filter of everything else young Christians under their instruction will ever learn about God for the rest of their lives. The message is very simple: "Jesus came to rescue man from having to follow the Law of God explained in the Old Testament."

Jesus, they say, came to bring us good news! The word *gospel*, they remind us, comes from the original Greek word *euangelion*, which literally means "good message." Another way of describing the meaning of the word gospel, when one considers that this ancient message was aggressively *publicized* across Palestine through street preaching, is that it should be described as "good *news*."

It doesn't take the congregation attending Sunday school very long to extrapolate from this popular conversation that the "good news" was the replacement for "bad news," which one would assume was all the world had before the "good news" arrived. Naturally, much of the modern church assumes the message of the Old Testament, particularly its so-called rigid, puritanical, and at times, seemingly unreasonable laws were at the heart of that "bad news" that so desperately needed to be replaced with Jesus's "good news."

Once it is understood that the bad news of the Old Testament was replaced with the good news of the New Testament, the Sunday school teachers and pastors of our modern churches often like to refer us to what is called "the fruits of the Spirit" listed in Galatians chapter five, which proclaim:

But the fruit of the Spirit is love, joy, peace, longsuffering, gentleness, goodness, faith, meekness, temperance: against such
there is no law.

—GALATIANS 5:22–23

In another false dichotomy,[*] very similar to the "good news/bad
news" contrast assumed to be the rationale for the division between
the Old Testament and the New Testament, our leaders point out the
final phrase of verse twenty-three: "...against such there is no law."
This is all the evidence that is needed to establish that the nine wonderful fruits of the Spirit (love, joy, peace, longsuffering, gentleness,
goodness, faith, meekness, and temperance) are the "opposite of the
law," because..."against such there is no law." Thus, the student's
evolving archetype of what they believe to be true concerning the
difference between the Old Testament and New Testament deepens
like a piling,[†] and as time passes, their understanding hardens to the
point of being unmovable.

What I've just described is dangerous. It can, and has, immobilized
entire generations in church history, but more on that in a moment.

The teaching continues by instructing all that the fruits of the Spirit
are obviously good things produced by obeying the good news. The
opposite of the fruits of the Spirit are things produced by legalism,
which most assume is related to the teaching of the law from the Old
Testament...which...was...bad news.

They further tell us that neither the church nor society at large
apparently needs the laws of God listed in the Old Testament...folks
just need to see how loving God is, and that is enough! Love, they say,
was listed first in the list of the fruit of the Spirit, and it was listed
first because it is the most important part of the good news. Love,
they claim, is the only law of the New Testament, and they attempt to
prove this belief with a quick read of 1 Corinthians chapter thirteen
(affectionately known as "the love chapter" by most Christians) followed up with one final verse that is perverted by the teacher as the
ultimate proof of this damnably popular lie. And the twist of this otherwise beautiful verse is used to create a mental stronghold of false

---

* A **dichotomy** is when one side of an argument presents two unpleasant, opposite, and extreme alternatives to their opponent, alleging that they are the only
choices open in the matter up for debate, when in fact they are not.

† A **piling** is a deep column of concrete that is poured into the ground to provide
support for a structure.

doctrine that will impair the young Christian and the evangelistic atmosphere of his community, state, and nation for many generations to come. It reads:

> A new commandment I give unto you, That ye love one another; as I have loved you, that ye also love one another. By this shall all men know that ye are my disciples, if ye have love one to another.
> —JOHN 13:34–35

And there you have it. Jesus clearly gave the world only one new commandment, they say, and that single good news commandment encapsulates and replaces all the bad news of the law. Though deeply saddened by the state of the poor mind who wrote it, I did not consider it happenstance that I received this specific message from an acquaintance on a social network on the same day I was preparing this particular chapter: "Old Testament = death, plagues, vengeance! New Testament = forgiveness, love, wants you to call home. Having a kid really mellowed God out."

Don't be too angry with the young person who wrote that statement; he was, after all, only summing up the logical conclusion of what is essentially preached across America every Sunday.

This simpletonian, sophomoric, error-filled founding filter of false doctrine puts a stranglehold on the capacity of the otherwise pliable Christian's mind to ever fully grasp the all-encompassing power of the Great Commission of the church and the true transformative energy of the gospel of Jesus Christ.

You see, if what I keep calling the "founding filter" of Christian training is corrupted, then nothing ever read, studied, and assumed from the Bible will ever be properly comprehended. Like venetian blinds that are adjusted to an angle that partially blocks out the light of the sun on a bright day, a flawed founding filter blocks out the light of God's truth from the mind of the aspiring Christian. The status quo Bible teachers of our spiritually fledgling American churches take this particular flawed paradigm of the gospel's relation to the Old Testament further, and claim that by talking about the law, much less preaching about it, we discourage people from wanting anything at all to do with God.

Consider, for example, the way rigid rules and penalty flags thrown by puritanical referees can suck the joy right out of the living room during Monday night football in front of the big screen. Preaching against sin and teaching the Ten Commandments of Moses just alienates listeners with unnecessary guilt and condemnation. It takes what should be a cheerful and happy experience and makes it frustrating and disappointing.

Speaking of football, I don't know many people who almost religiously enjoy football quite like my father-in-law. He is a quiet and peaceable man on most days. The spectacle of him with his wife and four daughters is what most people probably reference when judging his good nature. Whirlwinds of non-stop, high-speed chattering whoosh through the room as five females explode with energetic and dramatic conversation. I know very well that my father-in-law has wonderful things to contribute to those discussions; it's just that he rarely gets a chance to speak because of all the chattering of his girls. Most of the time he patiently chews his food and listens thoughtfully.

Gary Von Ahsen is a calm, patient, and even-tempered man...that is, until he gets in front of a TV with a very good football game brewing. I have personally witnessed moments of great joy—shouting, cheering, and celebrating—as my father-in-law hollered at his television during the wonderful game of football! In fact, there aren't many other things I've seen my father-in-law more excited about since I first met him about eighteen years ago.

On the other hand, I have also witnessed my father-in-law get really frustrated, disappointed, and even outraged while participating in this American tradition! The good and the bad of the game of football and their corresponding effect upon the people in the stands (or at home watching on TV) reminds me a lot of the alleged differences many modern preachers claim are true between the Old and New Testaments and their effects upon the listeners sitting in the church pews on Sunday morning (or at home watching the preacher on TV).

In Galatians, the fifth chapter, we read a list of nine very positive attributes created by the preaching, hearing, and obedience to the gospel of Jesus Christ. As I consider the particular nuance of love that each of those particular words bring to bear, it reminds me of the most enjoyable and amazing football plays of all time. For example, during the 2005 season, Tyrone Prothro blew everyone's minds when he caught a crazy pass by grabbing the football on the backside of his opponent's head! With the odds against Southern Mississippi, Prothro headed deep into the end zone, tumbling to the ground with his opponent sandwiched between him and the football he had just caught... hitting the ground and flipping upside-down with the other player's head stuck between him and the football! Amazingly, Prothro *never* let go of the football and made what looked like an impossible touchdown! In fact, the refs carefully huddled up and discussed their consensus before finally giving the touchdown signal to the crowd. Instant replay proved their call was right, even though a cursory glance from any distant observer would have thought the swirl of tangled bodies a certain incomplete pass.

When I watched the instant replay of this great moment in football history, I realized how it must have caused so much joy (a fruit of the Spirit listed in Galatians five) for everyone watching who loved Tyrone Prothro and his team!

Then there was that amazing last play of the game, back in 2002, when the Kentucky Wildcats and their fans in the stands thought they had really done it—they believed they had defeated LSU at home, and had gone so far as to already deliver the celebratory Gatorade bath upon their coach, who was standing on the sidelines for his involuntary baptism.

Their celebrations proved premature. When it seemed the game was all but over, LSU quarterback Marcus Randall launched a crazy long pass that seemed to be as far as a man could possibly lob a football, and that outlandish long-shot pass was caught by Devery Henderson for a seventy-four-yard game-winning touchdown!

I realized when I watched that play that I was witnessing the biblical fruit of what Galatians describes as "longsuffering." As those LSU players no doubt observed the Kentucky Wildcats celebrating LSU's supposed defeat on the sidelines, they kept the faith (another fruit of the Spirit) and endured their own suffering to create an amazing comeback upset! The announcers screaming into the television broadcast microphones said they had never witnessed anything so amazing in their lives!

Then, in 2010, Michigan State and Notre Dame battled it out deep into the night and eventually headed into overtime. When it became obvious to everyone watching the game that Michigan State absolutely *had* to go for a field goal in order to tie the game, the Spartans lined up for an attempt at kicking the field goal. To everyone's surprise, the Spartans faked the kick and made a sneaky run right past the Fighting Irish in a touchdown trick that stunned everyone watching the game!

When I saw that play, with the fans roaring loudly, celebrating by running across the field, I reflected on the clever gentleness with which the ball was tossed to a runner who fooled everyone on the field. What happened after that amazing play was full of love, goodness, and peace...lots and lots of peace! (*Ahh.* We crushed them!)

When you reflect on the great moments of the game of football you can understand why the fruits of the Spirit are so wonderful! But then you begin to realize that on the opposite side of every one of those great moments was a negative feeling. Someone was feeling crushed, disappointed, hurt, or angry, because they did not get to enjoy those triumphs.

You begin to realize that the source of all the bad feelings, the negative emotions, the unhappiness, the depression, the darkness, and the gloomy sadness (like back in the old days when the Oklahoma Sooners used to soundly crush the Nebraska Cornhuskers)...this dearly beloved sport is responsible for both the positive and the negative feelings in the game of football!

So, if you'll humor me for a moment, based upon what so many preachers have explained about what they believe the Bible teaches about the "good news" of Jesus verses the "bad news" of Moses, I decided to apply these gospel claims to the exact same problems we see with the flawed game of football.

For example, on September 24, 2012, when the Seahawks were given a 14–12 win, the instant replay proved they did not and should not have won. The entire nation seemed troubled by what many are now calling the worst referee call in NFL history. Once Seahawks wide receiver Golden Tate was pulled from the ground after his controversial touchdown, sports columnist John Jeansonne wrote of the substitute referees responsible for the bad call: "...the replacement zebras' goof on Monday, magnificent though not malicious, nevertheless swindled the Green Bay Packers."[1] The following day, nearly every major national broadcast news network and paper in the United States carried the story of the referees' terrible call. Even people who didn't care anything at all about football and rarely watch the game were discussing the crisis! Why? Because the situation left football fans across America with a sense of injustice. With the best referees out on strike, the temporary replacement referees had violated their purpose, and the all-important concept of fairness was trampled.

(If you'll allow me, I'd like permission to be dramatically facetious...)

I decided right then and there that the game of football, like our world, needed a Savior, of sorts, who could free us all from the bondage of these rules! The realm of football needed someone with the courage to replace those very negative rules that end up crushing all the love, joy, peace, gentleness, goodness, faith, and longsuffering out of the game! Those joy-killing rules, by being so rigid, unbending, negative, and unreasonable, were precisely the root of football's problems! Football had "bad news" that needed to be redeemed with "good news."

I mean, all those perfectly straight white lines painted flawlessly on the grass... measured just exactly so... and all the while everyone knows it is impossible to live up to all these artificial boundaries! My goodness! It is a point of fact that there has never been a single game of football played in the history of the world where anyone actually expected to complete a game without violating a single rule! Why? Because football players are not perfect, and coaches aren't perfect, and human beings aren't capable of being perfect at any time in life, on or off the field! That's why. I mean, this whole thing about rules, rules, rules is so impractical and legalistic! The problem with football perfectly illustrates the problem with human existence. The root of human sadness is legalism! Those darned rules!

So many preachers are continually telling us that God is *not* legalistic, but rather, full of grace; and grace, they say, is what God has decided must *replace* laws, rules, rigid regulations, and mean-spirited penalty flags 'n' such.

So, I have decided to redeem football from the curse of the law... of football!

Imagine with me what it would be like if I could walk onto a field and address two opposing teams, and announce to them that from this day forward, there will only be *one* law that governs the game of football; this *one* law will replace the entire unreasonable, legalistic rule book that they have been using for over two hundred years. Imagine how much joy they would get when hearing that all the disappointments and frustrations connected to the game of football were coming to an end! Those horrific moments when the "legalistic" and "unchristlike" refs told them that, no, they had not obtained a first down, because after measuring, it was clear that the football had stopped less than one inch from that perfectly straight line...well, those moments would only be a memory. "Perfectly straight lines" on a field where imperfect people were expected to measure up to rigid, impossible standards is a thing of the past—so five minutes ago!

"Never fear!" I would proclaim into the microphone, before the National Anthem was sung. "I've come to do away with all those joy-killing rules of bondage and replace all the laws of football with one law that is the greatest of them all...*fairness!*" (Insert unfettered cheering with celebratory tears here.) "That's right! There are no rules, save one. Now throw out all those fun-killers, and go out there on that field and play by the *one new rule* that will save this whole concept of the game of football...*fairness!*"

But there is a problem with this idea, ladies and gentlemen, and it is as silly and preposterous and fairy-landish as the teachings so many preachers have brought the world pitting God's law against grace and love. You see, when the players go onto the field to employ the greatest of all the laws of football...*fairness*...they quickly discover that there is no way to determine what is and is not truly *fair* when everyone on the field has their own private opinion as the standard.

They quickly come to realize that there can only be *one* standard (not a different personal opinion according to every different player on and off the field), and that the only way any team can determine what is and is not *fair,* is if there is a rule book of "football laws" to lean back upon in a dispute. Fairness detached from the laws that determine what is and is not fair...is not fairness at all!

It isn't enough to recognize that *fairness* is of extraordinary importance if there is ever going to be a sport called football. It isn't enough to recognize the truth that fairness is the very most important law of the game of football! There is not a logical and sensible way to show obedience and honor to the concept of fairness without the laws of football as a measuring stick!

The Land of Make-Believe, where Mr. Rogers's Owl speaks to the king named "Friday" (who pops up behind a mesmeric train set), and this doctrine where people claim "all that we need is love—because it's the only law in the universe," are equally absurd! Consider the steeple-crumbling, tectonic plate-quaking irony, in the light of popular doctrinal error, of Jesus Christ's prediction. He asserted that the very cause of why many would fail to walk in love in the last days would be because that generation of people would willfully *reject* God's law!

> ...and because of the abounding of the *lawlessness*, the love
> of the many shall become cold.
> —MATTHEW 24:12, YLT, EMPHASIS ADDED

Apparently, obedience to law keeps love vibrant in the New Testament. This passage has got to be a very frustrating verse to overcome for those who insist upon telling the world that Jesus's love came to replace God's law!

If all the church gives the world is one law—love—and claims that life can be lived by love alone, through some kind of mystical-sounding grace... then the church has not given the world the whole picture of truth. In the absence of truth, the definition of love will be as varied as the opinions of those who decide, for themselves, what they actually believe true love is personally. (Fornicating in the backseat of a car?)

Why will so many be cast into hell, according to the warning of Jesus?

> And then I will declare to them, "I never knew you; depart
> from Me, you who practice *lawlessness*!"
> —MATTHEW 7:23, NKJV, EMPHASIS ADDED

Again, law seems to be very important to Jesus and the Father of heaven. Does it not? He predicts that rejection of God's law will be the primary cause for God rendering an eternal death sentence upon men at the judgment! What is it that Jesus warns us the angels will do to people in His parable of the wheat and tares?

> The Son of Man will send out His angels, and they will gather
> out of His kingdom all things that offend, and those who prac-
> tice *lawlessness*, and will cast them into the furnace of fire.
> There will be wailing and gnashing of teeth.
> —MATTHEW 13:41–42, NKJV, EMPHASIS ADDED

When Jesus publicly confronted the Pharisees, who were known for allegedly being "legalistic" (in the negative sense of the word), does anyone besides me find it just a little curious to realize Jesus was actually angry at them because they were outwardly patronizing to God's law, but inside they were actually full of what Jesus called "lawlessness"?

> Woe to you, scribes and Pharisees, hypocrites! For you are like whitewashed tombs which indeed appear beautiful outwardly, but inside are full of dead men's bones and all uncleanness. Even so you also outwardly appear righteous to men, but inside you are full of hypocrisy and *lawlessness*.
> —MATTHEW 23:27–28, NKJV, EMPHASIS ADDED

Down here on planet earth, staring at the fruits of the Spirit and refusing to acknowledge the authority of life's rigid, inflexible, puritanical, and so-called unreasonable rule book is *not* how we determine what is and is not genuine biblical love! You can't possibly know, with any authority, what love is, unless you have a law of God to fall back upon as the righteous rule book with which to contrast it.

It is every bit as absurd to claim *fairness* could ever replace the legalism of the official NFL rule book, as it is totally incomprehensible to say that Jesus brought love to the world to replace the rationale for Old Testament law. Because the church has embraced this abusive and negligent kind of teaching, the law has been forgotten by Christians, and those kinds of Christians remain in bondage to the very sins they claim they are free from because of an imaginary thing they incorrectly call "grace"! The church has embraced this negligent false doctrine, and therefore the world has not had enough Christians living in it who were capable of applying the standard of God's law to their respective governments!

Our federal government in America has officially rejected the Ten Commandments through judicial activism and the like, specifically, the second table of the law. As a result, there is no true standard our nation can apply in order to determine what is truly right or wrong. Because there is no standard between what is truly right and wrong, it has become almost impossible for our unchurched citizens (who, by definition, construct their personal consciences out of man-made "laws" instead of God's laws) to correctly tell the difference between right and wrong at the level of self-government. As one should expect, if we cannot collectively govern ourselves, how can we expect to collectively govern a nation?

Romans 13 says government exists to punish evil and reward good; I believe the popular, horrible doctrine that claims God's message of love replaced God's message of law is to blame for our national inability to tell the difference between the two.

There is only *one way* for us to straighten out this terrible mess!

As you know, when Moses descended the mount, he had with him two tablets of stone carved by the finger of God. As a child, I assumed God handed Moses two tablets of stone (as opposed to one) for the simple reason that He had such large fingers. It made perfect sense to me. God had huge fingers and was clearly unable to fit all Ten Commandments on one tablet of stone. Had God picked a large enough tablet for his finger to write all ten, it obviously would have been too heavy for Moses to carry. My childhood memories still amuse me.

To borrow words from the apostle Paul, I "put away childish things" and came to realize Father God deliberately divided the law on two tablets for more intelligent reasons. The law was purposely divided physically in that it was carved on two stone tablets. It was divided relationally in the sense of how its message was to be directed. The first table of the law speaks to us as individual persons, and it educates our self-government (self-discipline). The second table of the law speaks to our self-government as well, but it goes on to provide the template of human behavior for all governments of the world, informing all nations how to govern in order to create an atmosphere where liberty can thrive.

In 1785, James Madison, father of the American Constitution, published an article on his views of religious freedom that referenced the first table of the law of Moses, and in the process of his "Memorial and Remonstrance against Religious Assessments," he inadvertently provided the only legal definition of religion that exists in American jurisprudence today (despite the fact that many modern judges claim they are uncomfortable with attempting to legally define religion, because they wish to avoid any connection to the Ten Commandments). Madison writes: "...we hold it for a fundamental and undeniable truth, that religion or the duty which we owe to our Creator and the manner of discharging it can be directed only by reason and conviction, not by force or violence."[2]

Madison's remark, "...religion, or the duty which we owe our Creator...," was a direct reference to the first four of the Ten Commandments, which logically fall into the realm of our self-government, and man cannot be made to comply through any external force. They stem from a choice of the human will. The first four self-governing commands are: 1) Do not worship other gods; 2) Do not worship idols; 3) Do not misuse God's name; 4) Keep the Sabbath holy. These are four items of God's law that fall under the logical jurisdiction of self-government, as they take on a vertical relationship between man and God.

Madison argues, "...The religion then of every man must be left to the conviction and conscience of every man; and it is the right of every man to exercise it as these may dictate. This right is in its nature an unalienable right. It is unalienable, because the opinions of men, depending only on the evidence contemplated by their own minds cannot follow the dictates of other men..."[3]

In contrast with the first four of the Ten Commandments, the final six fall under the category of the duty we owe our fellow man. Thus, the basis of all government is demonstrated in the chronological order by which God delivers the Ten Commandments. In other words, the first command is first for a reason. So on and so forth. As we reach the fifth command, what primarily began as a discussion of the vertical relationship between man and God takes on a freshly horizontal feature. As I said before, the final six commandments are "the duty we owe our fellow man." The second table of the law instructs our civil government thusly: 5) Honor your father and mother; 6) Do not murder; 7) Do not commit adultery; 8) Do not steal; 9) Do not lie; 10) Do not covet. The conclusion is simple and understood by children: True religion must honor the first four commandments; good government must honor the last six. Individual souls—from whence all human governments materialize in the universe—must honor all ten. Self-government begets family government, begets church government, begets city government, begets county government, begets state government, begets national government, begets international governance.

James Madison, father of the Constitution and fourth president of the United States, probably came to understand the vertical and horizontal divisions of the two tables of the law by attending church, but he very well may also have learned it as a legal scholar, by reading Sir William Blackstone's Commentaries on the Law of England (1765–1769). Blackstone's Commentaries played a significant role in the formation of the American legal system. I have little doubt where Blackstone acquired his understanding before creating his landmark publication that made law clear to common men for the first time since the Middle Ages. Most likely, Blackstone learned it by reading how Jesus taught the two distinct divisions of Hebrew law in the Gospel of Matthew:

> Love the Lord [your] God with all [your] heart, and with all [your] soul, and with all [your] mind. This is the first and great commandment. And the second is like unto it, Thou shalt love thy neighbour as thyself. On these two commandments hang all the law and the prophets.
> —MATTHEW 22:37–40, EMPHASIS ADDED

Jesus makes this division very simple and clear. Vertically, with regard to our self-government, instructed by the first table of the law, we are commanded to love God with all our hearts. Horizontally, with regard to civil government, instructed by the second table of the law, we are commanded to love our neighbors as ourselves. Again, in the teaching of Jesus Christ, it is reaffirmed that religion, as Madison put it, is "the duty we owe our Creator." And the second is like unto it, in that it is the duty we owe our fellow man...to love our neighbors.

A preacher once taught it this way: "The whole thing can be put in proper perspective by a little story. Three little girls were talking one day about the restrictions which their mothers placed upon them. The first little girl said, 'My mother lets me cross the street.' The second little girl, not to be outdone, responded, 'That's nothing. My mother lets me play anywhere in the neighborhood that I want to play.' The third little girl, after a few moments' hesitation, timidly added her part to the conversation, 'My mother doesn't let me cross the street. She doesn't let me play anywhere in the neighborhood that I want to play...My mother loves me.' God places certain restrictions upon us because He knows what is for our good and because He loves us."[4]

We live in the same world Jesus did, where a childlike understanding of truth is too complicated for arrogant and unteachable adults. The once-pliable, wet concrete has had time enough to become hard, cold, and nearly unmovable. Oh sure, we have nicer tools than Palestine enjoyed two thousand years ago, but human beings are absolutely the same as they were when Jesus taught amongst the wild fig trees, traveling from city to city along the dusty roads.

> I praise you, Father, Lord of heaven and earth, because you have hidden these things from the wise and learned, and

revealed them to little children. Yes, Father, for this is what you were pleased to do.

—Luke 10:21, niv

We Americans are harangued weekly by poor scholarship bellowing into church microphones. Popular modern-day preachers offer an unbiblical prevailing and accepted message that ever so beautifully pontificates the very lies of lawlessness that Jesus and Paul warned us to avoid. It happens every Sunday in a church near you! "Love is all the world needs!" they smile and shout with a victorious tone! And we are worse because of them. A new generation of Christ-loving, God-honoring, and truly loving believers must reject these false doctrines and their goofy either/or dichotomies and get back to the only true standard by which any man can determine what is or is not true love: God's immutable and everlasting law.

We need the Ten Commandments as our ground zero of absolute truth for our personal lives, of course, but also for those logical tiers of government, which are stabilized, according to natural law, by our own self-government. Family government, church government, city, county, state, federal and international governments find support and stability through proper self-government. Every ordinance created and every personality elected to public office must remain anchored to His divine law! We *must* grasp what American Christians understood, once upon a time, that fairness is to the rule book of football, what love is to the laws of God! We should let Jesus speak for Himself in Matthew chapter five, verses seventeen and eighteen:

> Think not that I am come to destroy the Law, or the Prophets. I am not come to destroy them, but to fulfill them. For truly I say unto you, Till heaven and earth perish, one jot or one tittle of the Law shall not escape, till all things be fulfilled (GNV).

A few rhetorical questions are in order, based upon what Jesus said: 1) Has heaven perished? 2) Has earth perished? 3) Have all things been fulfilled? Since the answers are "no, no, and no," we know the law and the prophets are still necessary for the world in which we live, particularly the legal and political world.

Salvation is more than something given for you personally. It is for the whole world and every single sphere of human influence. Christ has paid for all of humanity with His blood! He has a right to dominate every molecule of our planet from its deepest center point at the core to the furthest star in the night sky. Enough of this small-mindedness that limits Christ's work to merely saving individual souls, and leaving His work there, in a neatly packaged little pine box with the undertaker. Enough with these clever sounding arguments inspired by law-hating demons! Away with it!

As you will come to know with certainty as this reading continues, the Great Commission is so much more than merely getting people ready to die! Thank God!

When a prevailing false doctrine takes hold on a majority living at any one time in history, spiritual drought is always the reprise. This is what I believe America, and the world at large, is facing in my generation. Stagnation, created by false doctrines, springs from the same source—a spirit of lawlessness. We have been warned about this spirit in the New Testament; it takes aim at proper understanding of God's law. Go figure.

> And every spirit that confesseth not that Jesus Christ is come in the flesh is not of God: and this is that spirit of antichrist, whereof ye have heard that it should come; and even now already is it in the world.
>
> —1 JOHN 4:3

> For the mystery of lawlessness is already at work; only He who now restrains *will do so* until He is taken out of the way. And then the lawless one will be revealed, whom the Lord will consume with the breath of His mouth and destroy with the brightness of His coming. The coming of the *lawless one* is according to the working of Satan, with all power, signs, and lying wonders.
>
> —2 THESSALONIANS 2:7–9, NKJV, EMPHASIS ADDED

The most notable demonstration of this generational danger (when a whole generation maintains a faithless and paralyzing doctrinal inclination) is seen in the story of Moses. It is illustrated through his personal story while journeying to the Promised Land and dramatized by the generational fallout that occurred between the very small minority of two lonely men, Joshua and Caleb, and the very large majority of the leaders of their whole nation (numbers well beyond the ten influential spies who disagreed with them). The pitting of these two faithful spies against a massive majority of Hebrew citizens became the tipping point of their national history.

As children, many of us who grew up in church remember singing "ten were bad and two were good," as we learned about the faith of Joshua and Caleb. But by carefully reading the story as adults, we realize just how daunting the situation turned out to be. Upon receiving the report of the first ten spies commissioned by Moses to do reconnaissance in Canaan, the Scriptures tell us that all the people of the *whole nation* cried into the night after hearing the bad and faithless report of the spies. (See Numbers 14:1.) Not only did they cry and murmur against Moses and Aaron (Num. 14:2), their tears of sorrow quickly became tears of anger and violence. By the next morning, when Joshua and Caleb attempted to console and reprove them with words of faith and obedience, the retort from the great majority was to violently stone Joshua and Caleb to death! Had it not been for God's miraculous intervention by choosing to appear before the people in His glory and speak with a thundering voice in their defense, Joshua and Caleb might well have been brutally and painfully killed by a mob.

> But the whole assembly talked about stoning them. Then the glory of the LORD appeared at the tent of meeting to all the Israelites. The LORD said to Moses, "How long will these people treat me with contempt? How long will they refuse to believe in me, in spite of all the signs I have performed among them? I will strike them down with a plague and destroy them, but I will make you into a nation greater and stronger than they."
> —NUMBERS 14:10–12, NIV

God's verdict was rendered against them for *generational conspiracy*. Read it slowly and ask yourself, as you read, if you believe there has ever been a generation of Americans who deserved a similar verdict from the God of heaven.

> Not one of you will enter the land I swore with uplifted hand to make your home, except Caleb son of Jephunneh and Joshua son of Nun. As for your children that you said would be taken as plunder, I will bring them in to enjoy the land you have rejected. But as for you, your bodies will fall in this wilderness. Your children will be shepherds here for forty years, suffering for your unfaithfulness, until the last of your bodies lies

in the desert. For forty years—one year for each of the forty days you explored the land—you will suffer for your sins and know what it is like to have me against you. I, the LORD, have spoken, and I will surely do these things to this whole wicked community, which has banded together against me. They will meet their end in this desert; here they will die.

—NUMBERS 14:30–35, NIV

Antinomianism,* Marcionism,† and all doctrines of demons that fall under the umbrella of what some have called "cheap grace" be damned. To that end, this book has been written. To that end, may the proverbial venetian blinds be lifted, once and for all, and the sanitizing, blazing, and beautiful light of God shine in upon our dark world once again!

Knowledge of the sensibility of the Ten Commandments is not enough. There must be a practical application that extends beyond your own self-government. But there is a strong hindrance to any attempt to harness the virtue of the Ten Commandments and see its benefits in the physical world. The hindrance thrives in most Christians' minds. You see, it is not enough to mentally agree with truth; it must be applied, or it fails. Faith without works is dead, being alone, says James the inspired writer.

What is this hindrance of which I speak? Absolute truth is at war with relativistic truth. Our Bible teachers must do more than reaffirm the validity of God's Ten Commandments; they must begin to give instruction on how to apply them within the realm of politics. So long as Christians live as though they believe "pragmatism" (which is a popular word describing relativistic truth's aggressive war against absolute truth) has any application in the world of politics, the Ten Commandments remain a mystical silliness, patronized with cheap talk on Sundays and aggressively ignored and rejected Monday through Saturday.

Too many silly Christians give lip service to their claim that absolute truth exists in this world but live as though truth is relative when

---

* **Antinomianism** comes from the Greek meaning *lawless*. In Christian theology it is a pejorative term for the teaching that Christians are under no obligation to obey the laws of ethics or morality.

† **Marcionism** was an early heresy led by Marcion, who proposed the first canon of Christian texts. The proposed canon consisted of the Gospel of Luke and several of Paul's epistles; however, Marcion edited the writings by deleting any references that appeared to approve of the Old Testament and the creator God of the Jews. Marcionism thus rejected the Old Testament God, claiming that Jesus represented the true sovereign God who was different from the God of the Hebrew people.

it comes to politics. If truth is absolute, then it is absolute in every layer of the cosmos. If relativism is reality, then no such concept of absolute truth exists. Yet, most Christians—a vast majority at the time of this writing—pretend they can have it both ways. Truth is relative in their politics, but absolute when it comes to a discussion of the Cross. How weird! How strangely pagan of these Christians to live in such a fantasy world! "I believe and live by the Ten Commandments, but I don't require my representatives to do the same" is not a representative government sustained and protected by the reality of absolute truth. Rather, it is similarly situated to a Christian verbally claiming opposition to euthanasia while quietly administering a lethal injection into Lady Liberty's forearm. The confused celebration to follow Lady Liberty's "peaceful homegoing" where the song "God Bless America" is cheerfully sung, and all the who's who take turns reminiscing her greatness, is like that same Christian celebrating over a candlelit dinner with Jack Kevorkian[*] after the deed is done.

A fresh revelation of how the Ten Commandments must be applied to the election process is forthcoming, but not before we carefully and thoroughly expose the mind-binding enemy of the Ten Commandments in your life and in the lives of your family, church, city, state, and nation. The enemy is a dark and sinister evil that chains down the Christian mind, preventing him from putting on the mind of Christ (thinking with a renewed mind like Jesus). His name? "Situational ethics." If it is true that learning to think and process information according to the filter of God's Law-Word is described in the Bible as "taking on the mind of Christ," then let it be very clear at the outset of this study, that using what is called "situational ethics" may as well be coined "taking on the mind of Satan."

May God keep us from becoming like the Hebrews, who angrily sought to crush the skulls of a younger and outnumbered generation who believed God's law should be applied in each and every situation. God save us if we have already become a wicked band of people conspiring against Him—a nation filled with men who are hostile to His immutable law.

Keep reading, pilgrim.

---

[*] **Jack Kevorkian**, commonly known as "Dr. Death," was an American euthanasia activist. He is infamous for publicly championing a terminal patient's alleged "right to die" via physician-assisted suicide. He claimed to have killed at least 130 patients. He was finally convicted of murder in 1999 and sentenced to prison. Unlike his patients, he lived to be eighty-three years old and died of disease.

CHAPTER 2: REVIEW QUESTIONS

Enjoy this quiz at http://peacemakersinstitute.com/smb-quiz.

1. Do some ministers commonly believe that Jesus came to rescue mankind from the law of the Old Testament?

2. Do some ministers create a false dichotomy between the Old and the New Testament as "good" and "bad" news?

3. Are the fruits of the Spirit listed in Galatians 5 the polar opposite of the law?

4. Did Jesus really erase all of God's eternal law and replace it with one single new law?

5. Did Father God "having a kid" really mellow God out?

6. Does talking about the law or preaching sermons from it hinder people from coming to Christ Jesus?

7. Are the rules of football very strict and rigid?

8. Are football players perfect enough to play without violating the rigid, inflexible, and unreasonable laws of football?

9. Could the rule book of football be thrown out and replaced with only one rule of "fairness"?

10. Could the behavioral codes of God be thrown out and replaced with only one rule of "love"?

11. What did Jesus say would abound so much in the last days as the primary cause of agape love "growing cold" in many people's hearts?

12. Was our fourth president, James Madison, who is known as the Father of the American Constitution, likely attending an antinomian church that agreed with Marcionite views of Mosaic Law?

Chapter 3

Situational Ethics: Cancer of Christianity

ONE OF THE most exciting moments in the history of the created universe, from both our perspective and God's, is prerecorded in Revelation chapter 21. This particular passage marks the end of a flawed and, at times, disgraceful human journey, spanning thousands and thousands of years between two points in time.

The first point in time was recorded in Genesis 3:6, when Eve and Adam listened to the deception of Satan and disobeyed God. Sin entered an otherwise perfect world, and perversion, mutation, and distortion began taking place across the earth. At that moment in Genesis 3:6, God's intentions—His plan for this world—were interrupted. His goals for the universe were aggravated. His original purpose for man's partnership in creation was hijacked by the free moral agency of his own creation.

> And when the woman saw that the tree was good for food, and that it was pleasant to the eyes, and a tree to be desired to make one wise, she took of the fruit thereof, and did eat, and gave also unto her husband with her; and he did eat.
> —GENESIS 3:6

The final point in time (the most exciting moment in human history) is recorded in Revelation 21:1–2:

> And I saw a new heaven and a new earth: for the first heaven and the first earth were passed away; and there was no more sea. And I John saw the holy city, new Jerusalem, coming down from God out of heaven...

Between Genesis 3 and Revelation 21, thousands of years of trouble and struggle prevailed! Unfathomable evil has sullied the centuries. But when we read Revelation 21:1–2, this extraordinary human journey, filled with pain, has ended. God's original plan has finally been restored. He and His creation can pick up where they left off so long ago—at the moment just before Eve's initial deception and disobedience.

In fact, at this point in time (Revelation 21:1–2) everything has not only been restored...it's improved! Mankind, for the first time ever, has achieved complete perfection and maturity in his free moral agency! This is the most extraordinarily exciting moment in the history of the universe! What a milestone! What an accomplishment! And for the first time ever, mankind has truly become what he was always meant to be!

Unfortunately, you and I get to live between those two points in time...insert September 16, 2013 (or whatever date you may happen to be reading this book)! As Francis Schaeffer once proposed: "How should we then live?"

This is the Christian story in a nutshell: God's plan was interrupted and temporarily ruined in Genesis 3. It will be completely repaired for Revelation 21. Those who live in between Genesis 3 and Revelation 21 must choose to either accept or reject the single narrow path which Jesus provided—the only choice for a traveler who desires to see heaven!

MORAL LAW

The question all men must ask is this: Is that path fixed or flexible? Is it static or arbitrary? Do men have the authority to build that road themselves, or was the road paved for mankind long ago? Regardless of one's religious persuasion, there are only three possible approaches to the making of moral decisions in life:

1. Legalism: rigid and binding laws and principles under the auspices of God's divine love; truth is absolute.

2. Situationism: agape love is all that really matters; truth is relative.

3. Antinomianism: law is the enemy of liberty—spiritual anarchy is good; truth is relative.

Every human being is an immortal and eternal creature. We will all live forever in one of two places: heaven or hell. We are confronted by the existence of morality (moral law) from the cradle to the grave. Our parents instruct and instill in each of us (to the best of their abilities) a particular standard of conduct as a human being. There are no guarantees that a parent's view of human conduct is correct. We are guaranteed, however, that our parents *were* flawed to some degree. Thankfully, some of us manage to emerge from our childhood with a few acceptable social skills. The rest, from what we can tell, seem to find government jobs.

But it is that code of conduct—the moral law—we must eventually face as adults. At some point we each must reevaluate the code of conduct that was passed to us by our parents and make sure it was the right one. Our immediate concern should be for our own children. God forbid that we should pass along error to the next generation!

Jesus warned every human being that whatever code of conduct we choose to pursue in life, whatever moral law we choose to follow and obey, that path will inevitably lead to one of two places: heaven or hell! Since legalism, situationism, and antinomianism are opposing positions, only one option can be correct. This is our long-term (eternal) consideration.

The most popularly accepted method of applying a personal and public code of conduct is the situationist view! I'm going to go out on a limb and say that (conservatively speaking) probably 90 percent of the modern Western world believes that situationism is the only appropriate approach to morality. I include the modern church in that proportion. Based solely upon this reality—that the situationist approach has tremendous popularity as the intellectual and spiritual basis for determining the difference between right and wrong—it is most likely pure error. Because it is popular, I submit to you there waveth a *large red flag*!

To the Christian, the red flag should be unmistakable because of one simple warning given by Jesus Christ:

> Therefore all things whatsoever ye would that men should do to you, do ye even so to them: for this is the law and the prophets. Enter ye in at the strait gate: for wide is the gate, and broad is the way, that leadeth to destruction, and many there be which go in thereat: Because strait is the gate, and

narrow is the way, which leadeth unto life, and few there be
that find it.

—MATTHEW 7:12–14

Let me paraphrase this warning from Jesus: "The correct path in
life that will lead to heaven...will almost always be the *least popular
choice*." Due to the sin nature within every human, and the dispro-
portionate few that show a willingness to defeat that nature, when
it comes to making moral decisions, Jesus warned that the "popular"
roads were always going to be the roads paved to hell.

So which foundational system should a human being build their
code of conduct upon? Again, there are only three logical choices.
Every rational human being inevitably chooses one. I submit to
you that choosing the proper system doesn't have to be difficult.
Objectively deciphering reality is all that is necessary to lead a man
or woman toward the correct choice. The apostle Paul thought so, as
well, when he wrote:

> God's anger is revealed from heaven against every ungodly
> and immoral thing people do as they try to suppress the
> truth by their immoral living. What can be known about God
> is clear to them because he has made it clear to them. From
> the creation of the world, God's invisible qualities, his eternal
> power and divine nature, have been clearly observed in what
> he made. As a result, people have no excuse. They knew God
> but did not praise and thank him for being God. Instead, their
> thoughts were pointless, and their misguided minds were
> plunged into darkness.
>
> —ROMANS 1:18–21, GW

Paul goes on here to make the biblical case against sexual immorality, among other issues. I find it very interesting that he points to
natural and physical laws, easily observed by any man or woman,
as the chief evidence that men have *no excuses* for their unbelief
in His existence, nor for their rejection of His predetermined moral
standards.

Borrowing the logic of the apostle Paul expressed in the passage we
just read, the best way for a man or woman to decide which system
of morality to choose is for them to accept the truth about their own
identity and origin—demonstrated in *nature* and explained by God's

written Word. If you and I are nothing but a sack of liquid neurons, which interact by electrical sparks, then truth is relative and unknowable. Morality is a persistent and unnecessary obstacle between you and...whatever is or is not your personal definition of "fun."

But if we are more than that—if we are created beings—then truth is absolute and discoverable, life is based upon fixed and unbending principles, and how we respond to those laws of the universe will play a substantial role in determining our eternal state. To put it simply: if the former is true, you can arbitrarily make up your own rules for life and "be true to yourself," as the saying goes. If the latter is true, someone else already made up those rules, and you better get schooled on what they are and follow them.

No surprises...Jesus and Paul were correct!

So which of the three (Legalism, Situationism, or Antinomianism) do I pick? The answer lies in the truth of your created origin! Remember, there is a line drawn in the mind of God between two points in time: Genesis 3 and Revelation 21. Existing between those two points are flawed human beings struggling to live in a way worthy of heaven. Three logical options exist, upon which they must base their code of conduct, and only one is the correct foundation.

You could say that God has two kinds of law in the universe: 1) Physical and natural laws that are so apparent in the universe (those Paul referred to as so brazenly obvious that it removed all excuses from humanity to deny God's existence); 2) Moral and spiritual laws which God reveals to us through His inspired written Word.

Paul reminded everyone in his letter to the Romans that the best place to begin understanding moral and spiritual law was by observing physical and natural law:

> From the creation of the world, God's invisible qualities, his eternal power and divine nature, have been clearly observed in what he made. As a result, people have no excuse.
> —ROMANS 1:20, GW

So let's look at that realm for a moment before we answer the question of man's origin. Once we observe physical reality and couple that with spiritual reality, it makes it much easier to choose the correct foundation for our conduct in this life. Choosing the correct option will make us better parents, better brothers and sisters, better lovers, better neighbors and citizens. It will improve the world we live in!

PHYSICAL LAW

Let's consider physical laws. Natural physical law is universal in nature. It has no prejudice and plays no favorites. It is binding across the globe in all countries. Natural physical law does not change over time; it is consistent throughout all recorded history. To illustrate the narrow and rigid nature of physical truth, author, pastor, and television personality Batsell Barrett Baxter once wrote: "Take for example, God's natural laws which surround us in the universe. God has two kinds of laws: the natural, physical laws that are so apparent in our universe, and the moral, spiritual laws which He reveals to us in His inspired Word. We can learn much about His moral laws by studying His physical laws."[1]

Consider the law of mathematics. The same unchanging and unbending laws that were known and applied by the ancient Egyptians while the pharaohs constructed the pyramids are being used today as we plan for the colonization of Mars. How about the laws of chemistry? They have not changed since the beginning of time! When you mix baking soda with vinegar, it explodes into a messy, smelly foam in every laboratory of the world without consideration of the chemist's personal preferences or feelings. Who could forget the law of gravity? It is the same today that it was when the ancients of the Neolithic age built the astronomical observatory we call "Stonehenge." Gravity is holding me to this floor—right at this very moment—with the same authority that it now constrains the casket of Hugo Chavez in Venezuela. This law of God now regulates every continent and all the seas and oceans of the world. Its legal authority on earth exists outside the scope and authority of mankind and is not subject to our personal interpretations, feelings, or caprice.

The physical, natural laws that govern our universe—those Paul told us to observe—are universal, binding and unchanging for all men at all times. Again, Baxter continues, "...dial six of the seven digits in a normal telephone number correctly, then vary the seventh number just slightly. The result of this minor variation will be that you will find yourself 100 percent wrong in securing the desired person at the other end of the line. Miss just one digit ever so slightly, and you fail completely!"[2]

LEGALISM

What is our conclusion? Paul said that moral/spiritual law was best understood by observation of natural/physical law. Therefore, the Christian accepts that God's standard of human conduct is static and inflexible. We are required to learn His code of conduct, apply it to our daily lives, and obey it entirely. Clearly, the spiritual system of morality that is in harmony with nature's physical laws is the system of righteous legalism, which is based upon the existence of *obtainable* absolute truth.

At this juncture it becomes necessary to distinguish between good and bad legalism. Culturally, the word *legalism* is nearly always used in a negative sense, especially when used as a theological term. In Noah Webster's 1828 *American Dictionary of the English Language*, he made it a point to distinguish between the negative and positive connotations while defining the word *legality*. Webster assigned the *primary* definition of the word as: "Lawfulness; conformity to law." This is *good* legalism. I found it very telling to see how Webster offered his secondary definition of the word. He wrote: "In theology, a reliance on works for salvation."

Let me be extremely clear! When we think of this term apart from popular religious bias—a bias that has undoubtedly been shaped by popular antinomian church culture (I'll further explain the idea of "antinomian church culture" in a moment)—Webster's first definition is what I am attempting to resurrect in this writing. It has been all but lost in the church. It is of utmost importance that every man learn that good and righteous legalism exists. The Christian *must* accept that God's standard of human conduct is *static* and *inflexible*. It is demonstrated and proven in nature. We are *required* to *learn* His code of conduct, *apply* it to our daily lives, and *obey* it entirely. In this way, we must *accept* and *celebrate* the blessed inherent goodness of legalism. We are required to live in conformity to God's unchanging law! With regard to Webster's secondary and negative definition of legality, it is true that no one should rely on works for their salvation.

On October 31, 1517, an enlightened Catholic priest, Martin Luther, openly expressed his disgust and frustration with the clergy, who misled the world by the teaching of indulgences. He nailed his 95 theses to the door of the Castle Church of Wittenberg. The impoverished people (both naturally and spiritually) were taught that they were saved by works—that the purchasing of indulgences was their only hope of redemption. The clergy's purse was getting fatter, and the people were poorer for it as the priesthood peddled lies and exploited the commoners' ignorance.

Luther, desperately wanting the people to absorb and comprehend God's Word for themselves, translated the Bible into the German language. When the people could read for themselves that "the just shall live by faith" and that God did not require celibacy, radical reform began emerging in the nation. Nuns and monks left the abbeys and monasteries and sought to be married, and the people stopped paying for forgiveness! Finally, they were exposed to God's unchanging law!

Martin Luther's Reformation taught the world that living by faith is not living a life of works as a means to redemption, nor is living a life of lawless disobedience. An enlightened people are empowered to live obedient lives that glorify God, conforming to God's law. This was Luther's goal—Webster's good definition of legalism. He despised Webster's negative definition (a reliance on works for salvation), and these feelings were the impetus behind his boldness.

Yesterday, I managed to navigate the day without murdering anyone. I'm certain God was pleased. Earlier this afternoon, I resisted the temptation to drive 120 miles per hour, a violation of Iowa code. I'm sure that pleased God too. In the first instance, remaining in compliance to the command, "Thou shalt not kill," and in the second, refraining from the danger of speeding (a violation of Iowa law), I was not so daft to think I earned heaven, nor should anyone. With that said, how foolish would it be for someone to read my confession of compliance with the law and accuse me of trying to earn heaven through my good works. How equally foolish for critics to accuse me of "preaching works" as a means to "earn heaven" simply for telling others they should comply with these laws too. If you don't think people are that absurd in their antinomian theology, then you haven't tried to carry on a reasonable conversation on this topic in a social network lately.

Do good works earn salvation? Nope. Yet it is just as frightening to know that so many folks believe lawlessness is connected to grace. Men should refrain from relying upon lawlessness as an aid to their salvation, while calling it "grace." Good law exists. Obedience is required. If Webster were alive today, I have no doubt that he would reluctantly change the primary and secondary definitions of this word in order to accommodate our cultural shift *against* God's law.

Nearly everyone in and out of the church has made the negative connotation of the word *legality* the primary definition in their hearts
and minds. Karl Marx is said to have taught that one of the first steps
to taking over a nation was to confuse the meanings of words. I have
no doubt that he learned that from Satan.

The good news is that when we cooperate with the power of grace
in our personal lives, Jesus said in Matthew 11:30 that His yoke is easy
and His burden is light. In other words, "My laws are good laws and
my expectations for you to obey them are only reasonable." Whether
the term *legalism* has become a pejorative[*] and unpopular choice or
not, it is the *appropriate* choice for a Christian who believes in 1) the
goodness of the laws of Christ; 2) His reasonable expectations for our
obedience; and 3) the power of God's grace in our lives to assist us in
the human journey toward heaven.

ANTINOMIANISM

The most radical departure from legalism offers the flawed option of
antinomianism, a position of arbitrary morality that reduces us into a
state of liberty-crushing chaos and suffering. According to Theopedia,
"Antinomianism comes from the Greek meaning *lawless*. In Christian
theology, it is a pejorative term for the teaching that Christians are
under no obligation to obey the laws of ethics or morality."[3] Theopedia
continues, "The first people accused of antinomianism were found,
apparently, in Gnosticism;[†] various aberrant and licentious acts were
ascribed to these by their orthodox enemies; we have few independent records of their actual teachings. In the Book of Revelation 2:6–15,
the New Testament speaks of Nicolaitans, who are traditionally identified with a Gnostic sect, in terms that suggest the charge of antinomianism might be appropriate."[4] In short, antinomianism is anti-law.

SITUATIONISM: MOTHER OF MODERATISM

Despite its overwhelming popularity, fixed between the choices
of legalism (absolute law) and antinomianism (anti-law) lies the

---

[*] **Pejorative** is a word or phrase that has negative connotations or that is
intended to disparage or belittle.

[†] **Gnosticism** is a heresy which is made up of a diverse set of beliefs. It is the
teaching based on the idea of *gnosis* (a Koine Greek word meaning "secret knowledge"), or knowledge of transcendence arrived at by way of internal, intuitive
means. Gnosticism thus relies on personal religious experience as its primary
authority.

indefensible illusion that portions of legalism and antinomianism could be true at the same time. Thus, "situationism" is the popular moral myth of modern times.

If you were able to give the political "baby of moderatism" a maternity test, the birth mother of that poor child riddled with birth defects would be "Mother Situationism." It is popular today in America to claim that being "politically moderate" is the most virtuous solution to America's troubles. They portray what I refer to as "the honest left" and "the honest right" as "extreme positions that should be avoided"! Really? Are you people serious? Then answer me this: What is the "moderate" position, as George Schwartz once put it, "between monogamy and polygamy?"[5]

Leonard E. Read once lamented about the fallacy of the existence of a virtuous political moderatism. He stated, "Aristotle developed the idea of the 'golden mean'... He used the term to describe virtues which consist of an intelligent moderation between the extremes of two opposite vices. One concludes from his reflections that courage lies midway between cowardice and rashness... but, halfway between the theft of a small amount and the theft of a large amount is robbery all the way, no matter how you slice it... there is no virtue in being a 'political moderate.' This position sounds something like the 'golden mean,' but there the resemblance ends. What we have is a confusion of sound with sense. In our day, 'political moderate' is more an excuse for intellectual sloppiness than a guide to moral discipline."[6]

Not unlike the serpent that first beguiled Eve in the Garden of Eden, the heretic Marcion became most infamous in the first century church for best expressing the spirit of antinomianism and situationism in doctrinal form. Theopedia continues, "[Marcion] proposed the first canon of Christian texts. The proposed canon consisted of the Gospel of Luke and several of Paul's epistles; however, Marcion edited the writings by deleting any references that appeared to approve of the Old Testament and the creator God of the Jews. Marcionism thus rejected the Old Testament God, claiming that Jesus represented the true sovereign God who was different from the God of the Hebrew people. Marcion's proposal for a 'New Testament' helped to spur others to respond with other canons that retained the Hebrew scriptures and did not reject Christianity's Jewish heritage. Athanasius, in response to Marcionism, recommended that the Church approve the 27 books which comprise the Christian New Testament [today]."[7]

Francis Schaeffer's question, "How should we then live?" does have a solid and intelligent answer. Marcion avoided the real answer because he did not want to reconcile the "mean and angry" God he saw in the Old Testament with the "kind, happy, and loving" God he insisted upon seeing in the New Testament. The "mean and angry" God of the Jews, and the "kind, happy, and loving" God of the Christians, simply could not be the same. So Marcion worked hard to warp the Scriptures around his personal preferences, conjuring a false dichotomy between the Old Testament and New Testament, just like many modern preachers in our world today. Marcion attempted to create God in his own image, according to his own preferences. Meanwhile, the laws of nature and nature's God tell a very opposite story.

Polycarp, the protégé of the apostle John, patriarch of the first century church and doctrinal archnemesis of Marcion, is said to have confronted Marcion one day when the two men crossed paths in the street of the markets. Polycarp accurately called Marcion a "child of the devil" to his face. Thankfully, the first century church overwhelmingly sided with Polycarp. The opposite spirit seems to have taken hold of the church in our day. It is a prospect I find frightening, when I consider my children, grandchildren, and beyond. Despite Marcion's heresy and his modern disciples, there remains a sensible answer to this man-created dilemma born through rebellion against God's laws. Here it is: we must live according to the fixed standards of human conduct expressed in the Holy Bible and taught by Jesus Christ, who said in Matthew 5:17:

> Think not that I am come to destroy the law, or the prophets: I am not come to destroy, but to fulfil. For verily I say unto you, till heaven and earth pass, one jot or one tittle shall in no wise pass from the law, till all be fulfilled. Whosoever therefore shall break one of these least commandments, and shall teach men so, he shall be called the least in the kingdom of heaven: but whosoever shall do and teach them, the same shall be called great in the kingdom of heaven.

Dr. Batsell Barrett Baxter summarized the battle between the absolute truth of God and the relativistic truth of situationism: "The whole crux of the matter is, 'Who is to be the judge?' Is God, who created the universe, including man, and who knows all of the intricacies of life, better suited to decide what is right behavior in any given situation?

Or is man, who himself is involved in the complexities of life, both as a sinner and through his own emotional involvement, better able to make right decisions about ethical behavior?" Dr. Baxter goes on to answer his own rhetorical question: "...God is better able to know how man ought to behave, for God alone has the grasp of the entire situation and the objectivity to know what is right and what is wrong."[8]

THE QUESTION OF ORIGIN

Now that we've looked at physical/natural laws that exist outside the scope of man's authority, and we face the reality that the same must be true of spiritual and moral law, we must answer the question of our origins: "Who is man?" As we reach John chapter 10, we find that Jesus has just called Himself the Son of God, and all the religious leaders are threatening to kill Him by stoning. In response to their hostility, Jesus quotes Psalm 82:6 and says something that, to this very day, many Christians don't believe about themselves:

> Jesus answered them, Is it not written in your law, I said, Ye are gods? If he called them gods, unto whom the word of God came, and the scripture cannot be broken; Say ye of him, whom the Father hath sanctified, and sent into the world, Thou blasphemest; because I said, I am the Son of God?
>
> —JOHN 10:34–36

(As I write what follows it flows from my earliest memories as a child, hearing a sermon on Creation that caused an epiphany in my life that everyone needs to experience.) Who are you? What amazing potential might be lying dormant within you right now? In Genesis chapter 1, we read the story of creation and we see God's original plan for man revealed!

Now, before we go any further, let's remember the line drawn across world history...a line from Genesis 3:6 to Revelation 21:1. We've answered the question about which foundation is appropriate for human morality while traveling between those two points. Now let's imagine the future, for just a moment. Imagine you and I arrive at the scene as Revelation 21:1 unfolds before our eyes. Let's pretend that no one person reading this book is conspicuously missing from that moment. Okay? When we read the Bible, we discover not only *what* God created, but *how*…and if we look deeper still, we can see the most precious of all revelations…the "*why*" of the universe.

This is important, because understanding what happens after Revelation 21 should profoundly affect all Christians! What are we going to be doing throughout the eternal ages? The answer to this mesmeric question is a critical component necessary to comprehending our calling during this brief moment in the history of the cosmos, between Genesis 3:6 and Revelation 21:1. In other words, what we will be doing *then* will help us know what we are to do *now*! God's view of who you are through Jesus Christ is connected to His plans for you during the eternal ages. Let's explore the wonders of this question further for a moment.

Think with me as we ponder the artistic style and tools used by our Creator in the beginning. In Genesis 1:14, God decided that He wanted *light*, so He spoke it into existence. He spoke *to* something and then the desired result came out of the thing to which He spoke!

Look with me at the pattern God demonstrated in creation. In Genesis 1:14, God spoke *to* the *firmament* and said, "Let the *firmament* bring forth light!" In Genesis 1:20, God decided that He wanted to make fish and whales and all kinds of splendid creatures, and so He spoke them forth. But if you look closely, He spoke *to* the *waters* and said, "Let the *waters* bring forth the fish of the sea"! In Genesis 1:24, God decided to make a category of land-dwelling animals, so He spoke *to* the *dirt* and said, "Let the *dirt* bring forth all living creatures"! In Genesis 1:25, God decided that He wanted to make another category of land animals called beasts, so He spoke *to* the *dirt* again and said, "Let the *dirt* bring forth the beasts of the earth"!

The fascinating thing about all of this is that science has proven that all living creatures contain in their makeup the same chemical compounds that comprise their living environment. Even more fascinating is the fact that if you try to separate that animal (made up of the same elements found within the environment they live) and put them into a different environment…they will die! The physiology of fish is made up of the same compounds found in the water in which they live, and if you remove them from their environment, they will inevitably die!

In verse fourteen, God wanted light, so He spoke to the firmament. Out of the firmament came the gases to form the sun, and if you separate the sun from that gaseous environment, it will die! In verse twenty, God wanted fish, so He spoke to the waters. Out of the waters came the compounds to form the fish, and if you separate the fish from the water environment, the fish will die! In verse twenty-five, God wanted beasts, so He spoke to the dirt. Out of the dirt came the compounds to form beasts, and if you separate the beasts from the dirt environment, the beasts will die!

But then God decided that He wanted a friend...

He longed to communicate with someone...someone with a similar brain capable of similar intelligence...someone with a similar body capable of similar interests...someone with a similar spirit capable of creative power. We all know that God formed Adam out of the dirt, but God *did not speak to the dirt!* In Genesis chapter one, verse twenty-six, when God decided He wanted a glorious friend, the Trinity got together, and God *spoke to Himself!*

> And God said, Let us make man in our image, after our likeness:
> and let them have dominion over the fish of the sea, and over
> the fowl of the air, and over the cattle, and over all the earth,
> and over every creeping thing that creepeth upon the earth.
> —GENESIS 1:26

In this context, the context of God's extraordinary creation, and most especially man as the crown jewel of the universe...Genesis 1:26, Psalm 82, and Jesus Christ raising the issue in John chapter ten all say, with no apology, appealing to your highest personal potential (once you're cleansed from your sins) "ye are gods!" A reference to the very literal truth of man's creative purpose when first given life in Eden. Man and woman were created in the image and likeness of God! The submissive relationship of the creature beneath the greatness of his own Creator, "a little lower than Elohim," where man was created by God, in the image of God, is easily contrasted against the fallacies of Marcion and his modern disciples. (A sermonized fairy tale where man creates God in his own image, according to his own personal preferences, every Sunday morning...Humanism in Christian dress.)

Wow!

As we read (understanding that we will someday literally witness the fulfillment in history of Revelation 21:1), it is as if we are allowed through our imaginations to stand on the edge of the eternal ages with God and picture ourselves wholly perfected, for the first time ever. We still have the power of free choice, but we have learned how to use it flawlessly so that, not unlike God Himself, we will never sin again!

In this amazing moment that will someday occur, we can only begin to understand *who* we are destined to become! And with that understanding, we are better equipped to cooperate with His standard of human conduct—this afternoon, living in the line of historical time drawn between Genesis 3:6 and Revelation 21:1!

Obedience to His predetermined standards of conduct keeps us close to the environment from which we came. He spoke to Himself! Disobedience takes us away from Him, and the further away we get from Him, the sicker we become, until we die! The secular humanist attempts to elevate man to the position of God in his own universe, by suggesting man is capable of creating his own arbitrary and relativistic standards of behavior. Consider the irony: Since you came from a prehistoric slug, morality is whatever you want it to be. You're your own god, so let the hedonism flow like a river!

In contrast, the Christian truth appeals to man's highest and noblest nature—his ability to adhere to a fixed standard of unbending conduct, empowered by grace, and obtained through repentance. The Christian worldview is able to legitimately condemn the logical conclusion of secular and religious humanism: Adolf Hitler, Pol Pot, Genghis Khan, and others.

> When I behold thine heavens, even the works of thy fingers, the moon and the stars, which thou hast ordained, What is man, say I, that thou art mindful of him? and the son of man that thou visitest him? For thou hast made him a little lower than God [Elohim]*̄, and crowned him with glory and worship. Thou hast made him to have dominion in the works of thine hands; thou hast put all things under his feet.
>
> —PSALM 8:3–6, GNV

Most Christians, including their spiritual leaders, have succumbed to a pagan frame of mind used to determine the difference between right and wrong. So long as this dire problem remains hidden behind our cultural status quo, we will continue to stumble through life provoking and receiving completely unnecessary problems, particularly in the realm of politics and law. Situational ethics is a humanist and

---

* **Elohim** is a Hebrew word specifically used as a reference to the supreme *God* of the universe more than 2,300 times in the Bible, according to Strong's Concordance. The 1599 Geneva Bible is more precisely translated in this case, than the King James Version, which misleadingly uses the English word *angels* instead.

pagan false way of morality that is in competition with God's law and at variance with everything our Bible teaches us.

THE GOOD LEGALISM OF CHRIST

One of the greatest myths believed by Christians is that the primary problem with the Pharisees in Jesus's day was "legalism." Look carefully and you'll find that the problem was *not* legalism. The problem was "illegalism." Jesus gave an example of *illegalism* in Matthew 15:6:

> Thus have ye made the commandment of God of none effect by your tradition.

And in Matthew 15:3 Jesus said:

> But he answered and said unto them, Why do ye also transgress the commandment of God by your tradition?

In both cases (there were many others), Jesus criticized the Pharisees for *not* obeying God's law. He scolded them for using tricky and religious sounding traditions as a means to avoid obedience to the absolutes of God's law. Notice how Jesus rebuked the Pharisees for teaching and obeying a *little* of the law, but not teaching and obeying God's law *fully* and *completely*, in this next passage:

> Woe unto you, scribes and Pharisees, hypocrites! for ye pay tithe of mint and anise and cummin, and have omitted the weightier matters of the law, judgment, mercy, and faith: these ought ye to have done, and not to leave the other undone.
> —MATTHEW 23:23

If we read the Bible without filtering it through popular and errant antinomian teachings, we will realize that *God's Law is full of God's grace.* How could anything God gave man be *against* His own grace? Folks, think about it! That is not possible! It is not the provision of God's complete and everlasting law that is our problem; it is our mishandling of it! God gave Moses the spirit of the law and the letter of it. Those who yielded their hearts to its rationale and loved God with all their hearts, minds, and souls were blessed by the spirit of the law. Those who rebelled against the love and grace shown by the spirit of the law were penalized by the letter of it. Reminiscing about the complete work of God's eternal law, which is to say the spirit of the law and the letter of the law, Paul made two remarks that should be interpreted in the light of the other. Here's the first one:

> But we know that the law is good, if a man use it lawfully; Knowing this, that the law is not made for a righteous man, but for the lawless and disobedient, for the ungodly and for sinners, for unholy and profane, for murderers of fathers and murderers of mothers, for manslayers...
>
> —1 TIMOTHY 1:8–9

Here's the second remark:

> Who also hath made us able ministers of the new testament; not of the letter [of the law], but of the spirit [of the law]: for the letter [of the law] killeth, but the spirit [of the law] giveth [eternal] life.
>
> —2 CORINTHIANS 3:6, EMPHASIS ADDED

In the context of these two harmonious verses written by the same man, we see a truth about God's law that was true 1,500 years before Christ was born and remains true right now in our present covenant through Christ. The spirit of the law (love and grace) has *always* been the way of redemption. It has always been—at all times and places throughout history—the only hope a man had of escaping the wrath of God in hell.

If either individuals or nations rebelled against the eternal spirit of the law (which is Christ Himself) then the "letter killeth." This will be expounded upon more as the writing continues, but for now let it suffice to say this: individual people must accept the spirit of the law in order to truly accept Jesus Christ. All who won't accept Christ must have the letter of the law. The spirit of the law gives eternal life, according to Paul. It even gave eternal life in the days of Moses. The letter of the law is designed to punish criminal behavior that endangers those who accept the spirit of it.

Those who teach the subject of New Testament grace, who do not comprehend what I just explained, ironically, have very little grace to offer the world. There is no such thing as grace without law. (Hang in there, you'll understand why before you finish this book. Don't get mad and walk away.)

What is really *against* God's grace? Wait for it... Wait for it...

Finding clever ways to *disobey* eternal divine laws that *never* change. *That* is what is *against* God's grace! "Don't lie!" "Don't commit adultery!" "Don't steal!" "Don't murder!" Folks, Jesus is still saying "don't" from heaven right now at this very moment while you read. He is the God of absolutes!

Ironically, the Jewish culture in which Jesus lived did not share the same proclivity as ours today. Despite the Mosaic infidelity to the spirit and letter of God's law, they were still very much anchored to a moral system of what anyone today would quickly label as "absolutism." We have assumed the word *legalism* to be a negative, villainous evil. Perhaps when you consider the man-created and *uninspired* Mishna- and Talmud-based peripheral laws the Pharisees created and layered on top of the Torah (the *inspired* Old Testament) and that some of those particular ordinances seemed difficult to follow, this attitude against legalism is understandable. However, it is a dangerous error to assume the "legalist" approach to morality is wrong. It is *not* wrong. It *never* has been wrong. It *never will* be wrong. It is just the opposite. Righteous legalism—the *legalism* of Christ (as opposed to *illegalism* of the Pharisees)—connected to God the Father's Ten Commandments, carved by His own powerful finger, is quite necessary for victory in this New Testament life!

Remember, there are only three choices a human being can make with regard to adopting a system of morality to guide him toward his own grave. Legalism is popularly rejected by the mainstream Christians today, but this is not necessarily an indicator that a righteous legalism does not exist, nor does it indicate that righteous legalism is out of harmony with the New Testament. Of the three logical options available to human beings, only *legalism* assumes and requires truth to be absolute. The only other two options, antinomianism and situationism, both assume and require truth to be relative. The three systems of morality are entirely incompatible and cannot coexist! We must make a choice, and we must make the right choice!

In the Jewish culture of Jesus, the law of God was very much correctly assumed to be absolute truth. With that in mind, let us observe Jesus's interaction among those who correctly understood that truth was not relative:

And when he was come into the temple, the chief priests and the elders of the people came unto him as he was teaching, and said, By what authority doest thou these things? and who gave thee this authority? And Jesus answered and said unto them, I also will ask you one thing, which if ye tell me, I in like wise will tell you by what authority I do these things. The baptism of John, whence was it? from heaven, or of men? And they reasoned with themselves, saying, If we shall say, From heaven; he will say unto us, Why did ye not then believe him? But if we shall say, Of men; we fear the people; for all hold John as a prophet. And they answered Jesus, and said, We cannot tell. And he said unto them, Neither tell I you by what authority I do these things. But what think ye? A certain man had two sons; and he came to the first, and said, Son, go work today in my vineyard. He answered and said, I will not: but afterward he repented, and went. And he came to the second, and said likewise. And he answered and said, I go, sir: and went not. Whether of them twain did the will of his father?

—MATTHEW 21:23–31

This is a fascinating text because Jesus posed a question to men leading a culture that, unlike ours, actually accepted God's law as absolute truth. The irony, of course, is that the chief priests and the elders (who according to Jesus, as we'll read in a moment, were on their way to hell) were able to answer Jesus's question correctly, but many folks in our culture today would not do so well. This begs the question: *What chance does our culture have of shunning hell and gaining heaven if we struggle to honor truths that even they understood?*

Whether of them twain did the will of his father? They say unto him, The first. Jesus saith unto them, Verily I say unto you, That the publicans and the harlots go into the kingdom of God before you. For John came unto you in the way of righteousness, and ye believed him not: but the publicans and the harlots believed him: and ye, when ye had seen it, repented not afterward, that ye might believe him.

—MATTHEW 21:31–32

Similarly, I wish to pose just such a question of you, dear reader, based upon the history of what some Jewish leaders faced during the great evil of Nazi Germany's attempt to take over the world. As we look at the experiences of particular Jewish men who faced down death during World War II, which of the following six men, to borrow from Jesus's rhetorical question, "did the will of his father"?

THE LESSONS OF THE JUDENRAETE

According to the Encyclopedia of the United States Holocaust Memorial Museum of Washington DC, "During World War II, the Germans established Jewish councils, usually called Judenraete (sg., Judenrat). These Jewish municipal administrations were required to ensure that Nazi orders and regulations were implemented. Jewish council members also sought to provide basic community services for ghettoized Jewish populations. Forced to implement Nazi policy, the Jewish councils remain a controversial and delicate subject. Jewish council chairmen had to decide whether to comply or refuse to comply with German demands to, for example, list names of Jews for deportation."[9]

As a student of these horrific times, I was particularly struck, during my research, by the fact that each of the particular chairmen of the Judenraete I studied, who officiated over the ghettos in many cities across Europe during the Nazi occupation, more or less faced the exact same moral dilemma. Yet, though they each faced the very same Nazi evil, same Nazi agenda, same Nazi leadership, same Nazi intentions, and same Nazi propaganda... each one of them responded *differently*. Through study of their public remarks and, in some cases, personal diary entries, it became very clear to me that the story of Judenraete provided a very clear demonstration of the futility of pagan situational ethics.

CHAIRMAN JOSEPH PARNES OF LVOV, POLAND

Depicted above: the dead are removed from the street in Lvov.[10]

For example, in the city of Lvov (the Polish pronunciation is Lu voo'f), Poland, the Nazis selected a Jew named Joseph Parnes as the chairman of the Judenraete in the Ghetto they established in November of 1941. When Joseph refused to hand over Jews for deportation to forced labor camps where they would be murdered, he was taken out and killed.

Upon my observation of Joseph Parnes's handling of the great moral dilemma he faced, I encapsulate and eulogize his convictions when facing adversity this way: "Parnes believed that aiding and abetting evil makes one guilty of the evil he assists (an Old Testament sentiment clearly reaffirmed by the Christian New Testament in 2 John 1:4–11). Joseph Parnes demonstrated that a man should never cooperate with evil, even if it means being thrown into a fiery furnace or a lion's den, like the famed Jewish heroes who came before him, namely Shadrach, Meshach, Abednego and Daniel."

CHAIRMAN HENRYK LANDSBERG OF LVOV, POLAND

Parnes's successor was Henryk Landsberg. Henryk was chairman until September 1, 1942, following the last deportations of the tens of thousands of Jews who were deported and exterminated through his cooperation.

The Gestapo publicly hanged Henryk Landsberg in the street, along with the rest of his councilmen (close-up shown on page 57, and crowd looking on below).[11] The situational ethic demonstrated by Henryk Landsberg can be described thusly: "Fully cooperate with merciless and murderous evil and hope that the evil you assist won't eventually mercilessly kill you too."

Sixty-five thousand men, women, and children were murdered in Lvov.

CHAIRMAN ADAM CZERNIAKOW OF WARSAW, POLAND

In Warsaw (the Polish pronunciation is Var sav'ah), Poland, the Nazis selected a Jew named Adam Czerniakow (shown below right)[12] as the chairman of the Judenraete in the Ghetto. It is clear from reading Adam's diary entries that he was a reasonably good man trying very hard to do what was right. After having publicly reassured his own people that rumors of their deportations and murders were untrue—having

believed the Nazis who lied to him—and having finally realized he had been tricked and used as an unwitting instrument of Nazi evil, he chose to commit suicide on July 23, 1942, the day the deportations he had publicly assured his people would *not* happen . . . began to happen. Adam Czerniakow fully cooperated with merciless and murderous evil, in ignorance, because he believed the Nazi propaganda of his captors.

The situational ethic demonstrated by Adam Czerniakow can be described thusly: "If the propaganda makes you happier—choose to believe what is untrue."

A total of 254,000 men, women, and children were deported for extermination at the Treblinka kill center. Another 50,000 were killed in the Ghetto totaling more than 300,000 genocidal murders.

CHAIRMAN MORDECHAI RUMKOWSKI OF LODZ, POLAND

In Lodz (the Polish pronunciation is Wutg), Poland, the Nazis selected a Jew named Mordechai Rumkowski (shown above reading a paper given to him by a Judenraete worker)[13] as the chairman of the Judenraete in the Ghetto. Mordechai urged his people to comply with deportation peacefully and created the concept of "rescue through labor," believing that Jews who worked hard might survive the Nazis' plan for extermination by reducing the number of people being deported. The deportations continued despite his attempts to lessen them.

Rumkowski justified passively allowing some of his people to die (by encouraging them to go to their deaths in an orderly fashion), in the hopes that by feeding the proverbial dragon with *some* innocent citizens, it might perhaps decide not to eat the whole village. The situational ethic demonstrated by Mordechai Rumkowski can be described thusly: "You might survive if you make a deal with the devil and try to outsmart him."

Two hundred thousand men, women, and children were deported and exterminated from this Ghetto. Less than ten thousand survived.

CHAIRMAN MOSHE MERIN OF SILESIA PROVINCE

In Silesia Province of the Prussian kingdom, the Nazis selected a Jew named Moshe Merin as the chairman of the Judenraete in the Ghetto. Moshe waged an all-out war against the Jewish underground, claiming that by showing any resistance to the Germans at all, they were dooming all Jews of the Ghettos to destruction. So in Merin's mind, defensive resistance against offensive Nazi evil was *more evil* than the Nazis. (shown above, an SS officer surveys the destruction of an apartment house on Zumkowa Street, in Bedzin, Poland, on Friday, September 1, 1939. A few months after the photo, this town came under the autocratic authority of Moshe Merin).[14] Merin believed that defensive resistance would increase the intensity of Nazi evil. Merin himself was eventually sent to Auschwitz where he suffered and died.

The situational ethic demonstrated by Moshe Merin can be described thusly: "The only way to obtain peace is to refuse to fight; therefore, total surrender and capitulation of your principles will get you a peaceful 'seat at the table.'"

Reports suggest that about eight thousand men, women, and children were deported from here to be exterminated. Around twenty-eight persons survived.

Chairman Jacob Gens of Vilna, Lithuania

In Vilna (pronounced Vilnus), Lithuania, Jewish Chairman Jacob Gens (shown at left)[15] decided to betray the leader of the Jewish resistance in the Ghetto, Yitzhak Wittenberg. He believed that the only way to survive the Nazis was to maintain economic profitability—proving to be *useful* to the Germans. Jacob sought his own personal gain by more than passive cooperation with the Nazis, but by actively joining them in their efforts to crush his own people. Yitzhak Wittenberg (shown at right)[16] turned himself in after so many of his own community turned against him following the Judas-like leadership of Jacob Gens. Wittenberg was tortured by the Nazis until he died. The situational ethic demonstrated by Jacob Gens can be described thusly: "If you can't beat 'em, join 'em."

Situationism Produces Fraudulent Solutions

So let's review how situational ethics proves itself to be a relativistic and flawed system of morality in opposition to, and competition with true Christian morality, which is based upon the absolute, unchanging and legal nature of God's truths of law. Each of these men faced the exact same ideological quandary. They each faced the same evil, with the same intentions, and disliked their respective circumstances. Yet they each applied a different strategy in the situation, based upon what they assumed to be the most moral and righteous stand against evil. Even when facing one general problem, situationism is more likely to conjure up a large assortment of fraudulent solutions than it is a true remedy.

Here are the six approaches in our case study designed to expose situational ethics, as it was applied during the horrors of the Nazi occupation of Europe. A humanist and pagan system of morality, in competition with God's law and at variance with everything your Bible teaches, is described as follows:

1. Chairman Joseph Parnes: Aiding and abetting evil makes one guilty of the evil he assists. Never cooperate with evil, even if it means a fiery furnace or a lion's den.

2. Chairman Henryk Landsberg: Fully cooperate with merciless and murderous evil and hope that the evil you assist won't eventually mercilessly kill you too.

3. Chairman Adam Czerniakow: If the propaganda makes you happier, choose to believe what is untrue.

4. Chairman Mordechai Rumkowski: You might survive if you make a deal with the devil and try to outsmart him.

5. Chairman Moshe Merin: The only way to obtain peace is to refuse to fight; therefore, total surrender and capitulation of your principles will get you a peaceful "seat at the table."

6. Chairman Jacob Gens: If you can't beat 'em, join 'em.

Situationism makes humanistic love one's absolute, but love without law is like water without a bucket to contain it. Law without love is like having an empty bucket with no access to water. Love without law is nothing more than a path of sensual indulgence.

We Americans now face a great evil that threatens to crush our nation and the anemic churches of our nation along with it. What shall we do? How shall we respond to the spiritual, physical, legal, and political peril that lurks in both the shadows and, even more audaciously, in the light of the noon day sun? We must embrace one of three paths at the outset, and we must choose rightly! Only *one* of these men of the Judenraete was correct in his stand against evil. I propose that until and unless Americans can choose which man was correct in the eyes of God, they are *not* ready to enter the voting booth in any given November and face the "lesser of two evils" our nation has apparently been cursed to endure for the past many decades.

SUBMITTING TO THE THREAT OF CONSEQUENCE

If the path America has followed for the last century continues unin-terrupted by the noisy, inconvenient, and offensive blustering of true modern prophets of God, when faced with that choice again, American voters will acquiesce under the threat of consequences, exactly as did Joseph Parnes's successor, Henryk Landsberg. The world will never know what might have happened if Henryk had rallied the Jews to righteous self-defense, in the spirit of their ancient leader Gideon, inspired by one of the most courageous heroes produced during the Nazi oppression—Chairman of the Judenraete, Joseph Parnes. What we do know is that Henryk made a decision to submit to the threat of consequences, and it only brought his people death, and his own neck (which he cowered in fear to save)...the gallows.

As American Christians continue to submit to the fear of "the greater evil" in almost every election, they only continue the for-ward march of the very evil they most resent, routinely failing the moral test that is set before them on an organized calendar-driven schedule. Situational ethics is little more than "moderate antinomi-anism." It is a pagan way of thinking that is antagonistic to authentic Christianity. It's a method people use when they face an important choice and need to make a decision. It is a humanist procedure that people go through in order to decide the difference between right and wrong, based almost exclusively on the consequences they believe their decision will create. Naturally, this habit so many Americans have of using the false way of situational ethics is based upon the assumption that truth is relative, which means there are allegedly no absolute truths anyone can use as a rock-solid anchor when making important moral decisions.

In a collaborative publication of Resident Genius LLC, Mark Nauroth and Garret Milovich once described this flawed system as follows: "...'right' and 'wrong' are simple mathematical functions of plea-sure and pain. For example, if an action causes more happiness than suffering, it's good; if it doesn't, it's bad. You would think a system of ethics based on math would get pretty consistent results, but it doesn't."[17] And it does not for reasons that *should* be obvious. I mean, what do you do with a guy who gets exquisite pleasure by causing other people pain? Pardon the pun, but that just doesn't "add up."

The most popular incarnation of situational ethics in the political world is often described as "voting for the lesser of two evils." Almost everyone I've ever known, regardless of their political affiliation, has come to believe that voting has always been, remains, and will always be a function of voting for the proverbial lesser of two evils.

The pagan asks himself, "Which of the two evils running for office will produce the least amount of pain?" Then he marks his ballot and leaves the voting booth till the next election.

Every four years, in the month of November, Democrats all over America will enter the voting booth and they will follow their conscience. How? They will look at the two major choices they have for president, and they will ask themselves a simple question: Which of these two candidates is the lesser of two evils? Then they will pick who they believe is the better choice of the two that are highlighted, and they will follow their conscience when making that decision.

Meanwhile, evangelical Christian Republican voters who attend church every Sunday will also enter the voting booth, and they will follow their conscience. How? Exactly the same way as the Democrats did! They will look at the two major choices they have for president, or some other office, and they will ask themselves which of the two choices is the "lesser of two evils." After evaluating who they believe will cause the least amount of pain, they will follow their conscience and make the decision to reward one of two kinds of evil. What's sad? Neither one of them built their conscience out of the materials the Bible commands men to use.

Some November in your future, both Democrats and Republicans, Christians and non-Christians alike will use the false way of situational ethics as a measuring stick to determine the difference between right and wrong, and neither will arrive at their very different conclusions in a Bible-honoring and God-fearing way. Both the churched and the unchurched will enter the voting booth and use the exact same pagan, humanist system of moral judgment to reward one of two candidates they believe will cause the least amount of pain. Both sides of the argument will team up with one evil, in the hopes of defeating a greater evil on the other side. A select few will protest both evils.

This is wrong.

This must change.

There is a pathway outlined in God's Word (and echoed in this writing) for the resurrection of righteous government from among any collection of peoples, races, and tongues, who will listen and obey. The stones of that path toward freedom lay before us, repeated within the pages you hold in your hands. The march toward liberty begins by choosing only one of three options: legality, situation, or chaos. We must choose the legality of nature and nature's God, explained by the recorded revelations of Moses, defended by the extraordinary teachings of Jesus Christ, and catapulted to international heights through His death, burial, and resurrection from the dead.

His divine authority has now been injected into this world of ours. He demonstrated His authority over nature, proving Himself to be "nature's God" when He calmed the storm (power over weather), walked on the water (overwhelmed the laws of physics), raised Lazarus from the tomb after four days of decomposition (conquered the authority of death and the time dimension), and illustrated His divine *partnership* with Moses on the shining Mount of Transfiguration. That mountain, in Matthew 17:1–8, symbolized nothing less than Christ's personal fulfillment and public initialization of spiritual, physical, and moral law—each beneath His authority. This unquestionable authority was granted by the Father's thundering voice from heaven: "This is my beloved Son, in whom I am well pleased; hear ye him."

It is our duty, then, to join Him as loyal *servants* in His presence and covenant *ambassadors* in His absence. This can be done properly only by employing His crown-rights in harmony with physical, moral, and spiritual laws as they have been handed down through our Creator's plan—a plan demonstrated in nature, explained in the Old Testament, and both fulfilled and reaffirmed in the New Testament. What was the final charge given by the Lord Jesus Christ a moment after the shining cloud with Moses and Elisha disappeared before their eyes? He reached down to touch His friends, who were trembling at what they had just seen, and inspired fearless courage within them:

"Arise, and be not afraid!"

The power of His words in the moment imparted something amazing into these men. History proves they became unafraid to face death for the sake of His kingdom. Let this mind be in you which was also in Christ Jesus! Arise, and be not afraid, my friends!

CHAPTER 3: REVIEW QUESTIONS

Enjoy this quiz at http://peacemakersinstitute.com/smb-quiz.

1. Between what two points in time span the interruption of God's perfect plan for the created universe?

2. What is the most exciting point in time prerecorded in the prophetic Scriptures?

3. What is the Christian story in a nutshell?

4. Explain the difference between the only three approaches to making moral decisions in life.

5. What is the most popularly accepted method of determining right from wrong?

6. What two kinds of law exist in the universe?

7. What laws did the apostle Paul teach were necessary to observe before one could accurately understand moral laws?

8. Are natural/physical laws legalistic, situationist, or antinomian in nature?

9. Fixed between legalism and antinomianism lies what indefensible illusion that suggests both legalism and antinomianism could be true at the same time?

10. To whom did God speak when He created man?

11. Were Pharisees "legalists," or rather, "illegalists"?

12. What is the lesson of the Judenraete?

Chapter 4

Moses: Father of Fascism?

ASCISM.

The definition of this particular word didn't arrive in our language until first being coined during the painful revolutions of twentieth-century Europe. I could not find the word *fascist* in my enormous historic 1828 American Dictionary of the English Language authored by Noah Webster. Wikipedia described the word in a way in which some people might characterize the government of ancient Israel, under the leadership of Moses, which I found very interesting.

Wikipedia defines fascism this way: "Fascism is a radical, authoritarian nationalist political ideology. It advocates the creation of a totalitarian single-party state that seeks the mass mobilization of a nation through indoctrination, physical education and family policy. Fascists seek to purge forces, ideas, people and systems deemed to be the cause of decadence and degeneration, and to produce their nation's rebirth based on commitment to the national community based on organic unity, in which individuals are bound together by suprapersonal[*] connections of ancestry, culture and blood. Fascists believe that a nation requires strong leadership, singular collective identity, and the will and ability to commit violence and wage war in order to keep the nation strong. Fascist governments forbid and suppress opposition to the state."[1]

According to Conservapedia (the right-wing Internet response to what is alleged to be the left-wing propaganda produced by Wikipedia), "The name 'fascism' derives from an ancient Roman symbol, the *fasces*, a group of birch rods bundled together with an axe. It symbolizes strength in unity; the rods are weak by themselves but strong when bundled together."[2]

This particular word *fasces* actually was in my 1828 Dictionary

---

[*] **Suprapersonal** means above or beyond what is personal.

and not far from that the curious word *fascinous*, which Webster described as "caused or acting by witchcraft." Perhaps this may lend some explanation for the evil connotation associated with the word *fascism*. I do not know.

Was Moses a self-righteous, cruel "father of fascism?" Did the world need a Messiah to deliver them from dark bondage to this irrational, liberty-crushing legalist? Sadly, if some modern Christians were left to answer these two questions based upon the kind of teaching they often get in the contemporary church they might just as well answer in the affirmative, right along with radical atheists and agnostic secular humanists.

The British Centre for Science Education (BCSE), an organization dedicated to defending science education from the purported perils of Christian creationists, certainly believes Moses was a dangerous fascist! For example, Rousas John Rushdoony, a twentieth-century Calvinist philosopher and theologian, who happened to believe the laws of Moses should be applied to all modern governments, was once described by the BCSE as "a man every bit as potentially murderous as Stalin, Hitler, Pol Pot or anyone else you may want to name amongst the annals of evil...[Rushdoony is] a thoroughly evil man."[3]

A few short years ago on the other side of the Atlantic, after painful election losses in November 2006 that rippled across the United States, particularly across the state of Iowa, the irate chairman of the Woodbury County Republican Central Committee fumed to the local news media, "You've heard of IslamaFascists—I think we now have Christian fascists! What is the definition of a fascist? Not only do they want to beat you, but they want to destroy you in the process...We have elements of the party who are moral absolutists"![4] Chairman Steve Salem, a proud and lurid champion of secularism (which prefers, in his particular case, a hollow Republican branding instead of the Libertarian or Democrat versions of the same thing), went on to lambast the influence of the Conservative Christian right wing as the sole cause of every election failure that cycle.

His bizarre public betrayal of the party to which he was elected and privileged to lead did not bode well for him, particularly in the light of the fact that one of the most "radical," "right-wing," "fascist" Christians in America at that time, Congressman Steve King of Iowa's Fifth District (which encompassed more than all of Steve

Salem's Woodbury County), won his re-election bid by a wide and breezy margin.

Naturally, his public tirade set off a firestorm of Western Iowa styled outrage. The snarky comments (with the tragic Islamic Jihadist attacks of 9-11 still very much in the minds of Midwestern Americans) resulted in his forced removal from office by an over-whelming popular vote of an understandably angry Republican base. The Woodbury County Republicans obviously felt betrayed by their leader's public screed.

Said Salem, "I think that the Republican Party needs to do a huge self-analysis and determine if we are going to learn from our mis-takes or if we are going to repeat the same mistakes ... You just keep making that party smaller and smaller and smaller, and you can't win elections when you don't appeal to a large part of the popula-tion!"[5] (No word yet on whether Salem learned from his mistakes.) One of the chairman's sympathizers, Duane Brown of Correctionville, chose not to use the label "Christian fascists" to describe those who believed like Thomas Jefferson, who said, "Our Saviour ... has taught us to judge the tree by its fruit, and to leave motives to Him who can alone see into them."[6] Instead, in his interview with the local newspaper, Duane referred to the same Christian Republicans of Woodbury County as "cockroaches ... who don't like the light of day shining upon them."[7]

Soon after, another former chairwoman of the Republican Party, Barb Vakulskas, publicly sympathized with the indefensible remarks made by Steve Salem during a local radio broadcast. The host of the show, Randy Renshaw, also seemed bizarrely empathetic toward Steve Salem. The entire episode was incredibly offensive, disre-spectful, and chilling beyond the pale. If our local Republican leader-ship had become so vulgarly secularist and anti-Christian, what might be happening to our party nationally? Few would grasp the weight of this local harbinger until many years later during the colossal failure of Mitt Romney's 2012 attempt to defeat and replace Barack Obama.

As an aside, at the time of this particular firestorm, I had taken no direct interest in the Woodbury County Republican Central Committee. Rest assured, throughout the following twenty-four months from the incident, I worked with other like-minded folks, and our coopera-tive synergy successfully positioned a voting supermajority of God-fearing Christians. With those new recruits' godly leadership, the local Republican Party was positively and peacefully transformed, and the radical secularists were replaced with plenty of election victory celebrations to follow. In the end, Salem's vulgar outburst inspired a greater Christianization of Iowa politics. He was eventually replaced by Chairman Brian Rosener, an unbending, principled, firebrand Christian conservative (or "fascist cockroach," depending upon your paradigm within the Milky Way).

Clearly, there are those among us who believe that Moses and Christ, (as well as their present-day admirers) were/are fascists, so the questions bear repeating: Was Moses a self-righteous, cruel, "father of fascism"? Did the world need a Messiah to deliver them from dark bondage to this irrational, liberty-crushing legalism, or was the Messiah in agreement with Moses? Apparently, in the minds of the political wonks, all the way from England to Woodbury County, Iowa, followers of Jesus are also viewed as fascists, and they are sometimes seen as shadow-loving "cockroaches."

The prophetic connection between the lives of Moses and Christ present an unavoidable problem for moderns who falsely teach that Christ and Moses represented two mutually exclusive and opposing forces of God in the earth. This prophetic connection is referred to as "type" and "antitype" in theological circles. Consider the following remarkable comparisons, and things will quickly become clear:

- Both Moses and Jesus were miraculously saved from infanticide.

- Both Moses and Jesus were born into evil circumstances under evil governmental rulers.

- Both were miraculously commissioned by God; Moses at the burning bush and Jesus in John 8:42.

- Both were discredited by their relatives; Moses in Numbers 12 and Jesus in John 7:1–10.

- Both were rejected by their own Hebrew race.

- Both were willing to forgive those who rejected them.

- Both appeared on the earth after their physical deaths.

- Both fasted for forty days.

- Both demonstrated a supernatural radiance upon their faces; Moses after being on the mountain with God and Jesus on the Mount of Transfiguration.

- Both exercised miraculous control over nature; Moses parted the Red Sea and Jesus calmed the squall at sea.

- Both endured murmurings; Moses in Exodus 16:2 and Jesus in John 7:12.

- Both built a "church." Moses did so according to Acts 7:30–38 and Jesus did so in Matthew 16:18.

- Both were mediators of a covenant; Moses the old and Jesus the new and better.

Every Bible student worth his/her salt knows that Moses's life was a "type of Christ," because the bullet points you just read have been recognized and taught for much of the last two thousand years, right? Since this is true, *why do the same people counterintuitively claim Christ represented the polar opposite of everything for which Moses's life stood?* This does not make any sense, yet it is popularly accepted as a "fact" in many churches today!

Moses was the most influential Hebrew prophet in world history. Echoing this sentiment, Rabbi Yerachmiel D. Fried (a noted scholar of Jewish law, philosophy, and the Talmud) once reminded his followers, in a publication of the Texas Jewish Post, of the teaching of Maimonides.* "Maimonides wrote: 'We believe that Moses was the leader of all prophets. He was superior to all other prophets, whether they preceded him or arose afterwards. Moses attained the highest possible human level. He perceived the Godly to a degree surpassing every human being that ever existed.'"[8]

Besides being granted divine understanding of history as described in his record of the creation story, Moses's greatest prophecy of a future event is recorded in his Book of Deuteronomy:

> The LORD thy God will raise up unto thee a Prophet from the
> midst of thee, of thy brethren, like unto me; unto him ye shall

---

* **Maimonides** (Rabbi Mosheh Ben Maimon) 1135–1204 was a preeminent medieval rabbi. He is today acknowledged as one of the foremost rabbinical arbiters and philosophers in Jewish history, his copious work comprising a cornerstone of Jewish scholarship. His fourteen-volume Mishneh Torah still carries significant canonical authority as a codification of Talmudic law.

hearken...And the LORD said unto me...I will raise them up a Prophet from among their brethren, like unto thee, and will put my words in his mouth; and he shall speak unto them all that I shall command him.

—DEUTERONOMY 18:15, 17–18

When Philip, the disciple of Jesus, testified of his faith to Nathanael, he described Jesus as the fulfillment of Moses's great prophecy:

Philip findeth Nathanael, and saith unto him, We have found him, of whom Moses in the law, and the prophets, did write, Jesus of Nazareth, the son of Joseph.

—JOHN 1:45

Remarkably, the text of John 6:14 declares Jesus to be the fulfillment of the greatest prophecy Moses ever declared:

Then those men, when they had seen the miracle that Jesus did, said, This is of a truth that prophet that should come into the world.

—JOHN 6:14

Luke the Evangelist very clearly compares Moses and Christ in his text of Acts' seventh chapter, when He writes:

This is that Moses, which said unto the children of Israel, A Prophet shall the Lord your God raise up unto you, even of your brethren, like unto me; him [Jesus Christ] shall ye hear.

—ACTS 7:37, GNV, EMPHASIS ADDED

I realize that few people in this world are willing to admit the logical end of their own arguments, and when those ends are pointed out by a protagonist of fundamentalism, like me, they indignantly recoil and protest the charges I make against them. Nonetheless, despite what will likely conjure resentment with the hopes that those who espouse error might become humbly aware of a doctrinal faux pas, I am compelled to point out the logical conclusion of that inconsistent assertion that "Christ represented the opposite of everything for which Moses's life stood." This is perhaps better recognized in the popular cliché, "Christ came to do away with the law." If we take this line of thinking to its logical conclusion, one might be resolved to believe Jesus was the "Antilaw" and therefore, Moses might just as well qualify as some kind of fascist "Antichrist."

I have had my fair share of debates with antagonists on both sides of the millennium. In my experience, I have come to find that if you are a typical premillennialist,* you understand the Book of Revelation predicts a coming Antichrist. So, should we suppose the future Antichrist is the sequel, and Moses was the prequel? If you are a postmillennialist,† you may or may not be further along with your present understanding of the modern application of God's law than the premillennialist, but you're likely guilty of believing something far more outrageous, extra-biblical, and mystical-sounding than a literal rapture of the saints. You are likely waiting for the fallen world to finally throw their hands up and say, "Sheesh! We pagans just can't seem to run a decent government! What a disastrous mess we have made on earth! Let us invite the Christians to come and teach us how to govern rightly!"

Dr. Gary North once wrote, "Postmillennialists can afford to be patient. They understand that the future will bring victory for Christ's church in history."[9] I would be remiss if I did not add that political sloth and the spiritual virtue of patience can be mistaken. Perhaps the postmillennialists I have met could use a healthy dose of nerve.

The former tends to escapism excused by a coming supernatural rapture; the latter tends to escapism via a coming fairy tale offer from exasperated secularist infidels who will someday supposedly clamor for Christians to take over the reins of world governments. (They believe this is possible without a literal return of Christ in all His glory and power, too! Now *that's* what I call blind faith!)

The former (premillennialist) refrains from real-world activism because it is viewed as a "useless distraction from saving souls *before it's too late!*" The latter sometimes rejects real-world activism because they are frightened off by the secularist boogieman who shouts the loathed accusation that passing godly laws in America is the equivalent of "forcing religion down the throat of the unwilling!" In some cases, not wishing to be seen as having some intellectual affinity with leftist anti-religious nonsense, postmillennialists concoct a theological *version* of the "forcing religion down the throat of

---

* **Premillennialists** believe Christ will return just prior to a literal one thousand year reign on the earth.

† **Postmillennialists** do not believe Christ will physically rule on the earth for a thousand years, but instead, will eventually return to judge the world after the earth has been fully Christianized by believers.

the unwilling" accusation. For example, an antagonist minister once argued with me, "Gentleness is a fruit of the Spirit, so we should only preach the gospel when it's requested and welcomed!" (You just can't make this stuff up, folks!) How that theory can be reconciled with the Book of Acts is beyond me. Stephen's final sermon, delivered in Acts 7:59 just before he finally lost consciousness via a stone to the head, comes to mind.

Others go to great lengths to accentuate the fact that their political activism (however faintly realized it may be) is absolutely not any attempt to create some kind of "self-righteous top-down form of Christianized government." OK, I understand that natural law requires decentralized* government for maximum liberty, and we should promote an overwhelming emphasis on decentralized activism to remain in harmony with the Bible, but in response to the ad hominem† attack against "self-righteous top-down" Christian government, I pose this question: Is it morally acceptable to allow the satanic top-down form of humanist government that inevitably defaults in the absence of the so-called self-righteous Christianized version? More specifically, how does one return from America's current form of government (a centralized monstrous quagmire, unhinged from our original founding principles) to a de-centralist's dream—if the federal government (where centralization unfortunately occurs) appears to be anathema‡ in some circles of Christian political activism? I'll put it this way: if one intends to detangle a ridiculous web of fishing line wrapped around a high limb, one must begin his work at the limb, no matter how much he would prefer to vengefully cut the tree down with his bare hands and a sharp axe.

Unsurprisingly, regardless of their bitter eschatological differences, neither extreme accomplishes the full scope of the Great Commission. Both fail the Mark 16:15 command to go into *all* the present (kosmos) world. Instead, they choose to infiltrate only *some* of it. Paradoxically, many churches don't actually go into *any* part of the world at all! Quite the opposite is the case! A very minuscule piece of "the world" infiltrates the pews of the church every Sunday morning at 10 a.m., and it is that very spirit of this world, nurtured in many churches, that much prefers to pit the philosophy of Moses against the philosophy of

---

* **Decentralization** is the process of redistributing or dispersing functions, powers, people, or things away from a central location or authority.
† **Ad hominem** is an attack on the person, instead of the person's arguments.
‡ **Anathema** means something denounced as accursed by authorities.

Christ, in order to go on pretending Jesus came to make the bad man (Moses) stop!

To believe that Jesus and Moses were in any way opposed to each other is a bizarre (albeit strangely popular) contradiction. Truly, Moses was a type of Christ, a shadow cast by the light of the Father shining upon the person of His Son Jesus. When Christ and Moses stood together, face-to-face on the Mount of Transfiguration, they weren't arguing! It is wrong to suggest Christ came to make Moses's life work, inspired by God the Father, moot. Either Moses was a type of Christ or he was not. You cannot have it both ways! Likewise, if Moses received instructions for proper government from Father God at Mount Sinai, and he was a "fascist," then wouldn't that make Jesus Christ the "Son of Fascism"? *Surely this could not be true!*

The Gospels repeatedly show Jesus was frustrated with the Pharisees for inventing clever ways of *getting around* obedience to the divinely inspired laws of Moses, not for promoting an accurate interpretation of Moses's laws and enforcing them in society. Despite the paradoxes created in pulpits today, the fact remains that Jesus promoted the inspiration and eternal nature of the Hebrew civil code in Matthew 5:17–20. Let us read it carefully:

> Think not that I am come to destroy the law, or the prophets: I am not come to destroy, but to fulfil. For verily I say unto you, till heaven and earth pass, one jot or one tittle shall in no wise pass from the law, till all be fulfilled. Whosoever therefore shall break one of these least commandments, and shall teach men so, he shall be called the least in the kingdom of heaven: but whosoever shall do and teach them, the same shall be called great in the kingdom of heaven. For I say unto you, that except your righteousness shall exceed the righteousness of the scribes and Pharisees, ye shall in no case enter into the kingdom of heaven.

It is very important that readers not pervert the significant difference between the first word translated as "fulfill" and the second word used later, which happens to be translated as "fulfilled" in this same passage. Though translated with similar looking *English* words, they are derived from quite different *Greek* words in the original text. Common Marcionite error is made by believing Jesus "fulfilled the law." If this is the definition, then society no longer needs God's civic law pertaining to murder, because Christ's obedience to "Thou shalt not murder" has fulfilled the law. (If *that* were the meaning of this verse, we'd all be forced to admit that since Jesus "fulfilled" the law, it's now OK to murder! This is madness!)

It is *not* the meaning and *could not* be the meaning under any rational circumstances. The very *opposite* is what Christ plainly warns. The use and purpose of the civil law of Moses shall *not* pass away from this fallen world *until heaven and earth pass away.*

Has heaven passed away? No. Has earth passed away? No. So the present use of the civic Mosaic system has not passed away either. Are heaven and earth going to *eventually* pass away at some point during the eternal ages to come? Yes. That is precisely what the prophets predicted for centuries. Christ believed and repeated those same predictions. Someday, the world as we now know it will dissolve and find total renewal under Christ's theocratic rule. Thus, the final word *fulfilled* is from the Greek word *ginomai,* which means to come to pass like a prediction of a future event that finally comes true.

Again, when will the "law and prophets" pass away, according to Jesus? After heaven and earth are passed away. In the meantime, what should be the attitude of those who follow the doctrines of Christ forward in history as it unravels during His "kingdom from heaven"? Jesus said He did not come to destroy the Mosaic system, but to "fulfill" it. Jesus could have said it another way, and it would mean the same thing: "I did not come to destroy the Mosaic system of law, but to *fulfill* My obligations to the law as all men must." He tells us how ministers of the gospel will be judged in the *future* of our present covenant with the following warning:

> Whosoever therefore shall break one of these least commandments, and shall teach men so, he shall be called the least in the kingdom of [from] heaven: but whosoever shall do and teach them, the same shall be called great in the kingdom of [from] heaven.
> —MATTHEW 5:19, EMPHASIS ADDED

Did the apostle Paul believe that Christ specifically completed the purpose of the *ritual* portion of Mosaic religious laws that were prophetic of a coming Messiah (like animal sacrifices, priestly pageantry, food ordinances, special holiday feasts, and circumcision laws)?

Yes, he most certainly did.

Did the apostle Paul believe that Christ abolished the *entire* Mosaic codex (specifically the civic portion founded upon the common sense of the Ten Commandments) from any practical application in the modern world?

No, he absolutely did not.

The command "Thou shalt not commit adultery" was not a prophetic prediction, nor were any of the Ten Commandments. It was divine law made for the world's "lawless," both during the administration of Moses and the times of Jesus around 1,500 years later. It was a code of behavior plainly stated for the world to observe with logically corresponding results and consequences. One of the most blatant purposes of the law was to point all peoples and nations to the one true God!

> Keep therefore and do them; for this is your wisdom and your understanding in the sight of the nations, which shall hear all these statutes, and say, Surely this great nation is a wise and understanding people.
> —DEUTERONOMY 4:6

The commandments were designed for those who would refuse to self-govern by legitimate standards of conscience, thereby requiring external restraint by force of law in order to protect the innocent. The difference between the believer and non-believer was simple during the times of Moses, and the difference remains the same today. Believers would obey the divine laws of society because they loved God and appreciated His gift of liberty and goodness. Non-believers, particularly those who feared getting caught, would obey the laws of society because they feared the consequences of the civil sword. Others too stupid and wicked to keep the law for fear of consequences got what they deserved—punishment.

So civil law, then and today, is *supposed* to reflect eternal realities. Consequences for all wrongs are inevitable. Repent or be damned. Turn or burn. Bow to Christ now in humility, or be forced to bow when He returns in His righteous wrath. Why? Because as a Great Father, God takes His responsibility to love, protect, and bless His children very seriously. The innocent must be protected from the damned, both on earth and in the next life. Punishments for crime exist here on earth. Punishments for eternal crimes exist beyond the grave. There is only one truth; therefore, there is only one true justice.

There is only one *standard* of justice. Any deviation from that standard is unjust and contemptible to God. Civic rulers who do not rule justly and honestly on earth will answer to His wrath as well. Just ask King Herod. (See Acts 12:21–23.)

Again, when did Jesus say the Mosaic Law and prophets would no longer be required on earth? They will no longer be necessary after heaven and earth (as we know them) eventually pass away. Paul emphatically agrees with Christ's clear warning when he echoes Him, writing:

> And we know, that the [Mosaic] Law is good, if a man use it lawfully. Knowing this, that the Law is not given unto a righteous man, but unto the lawless and disobedient, to the ungodly, and to sinners, to the unholy, and to the profane, to murderers of fathers and mothers, to manslayers, to whoremongers, to buggerers, to mensteelers, to liars, to the perjured, and if there by any other thing that is contrary to wholesome doctrine.
>
> —1 TIMOTHY 1:8–10, GNV

Does the world still have lawless people living upon it? Yes, it does. This is the rationale for the existence of civil government, according to Romans 13 in our New Testament, remaining in perfect harmony with the Old Testament. And what should be the standard of such civic government designed to confront and restrain lawless people? The standard was and is the Ten Commandments. Both Jesus and Paul warned that they were designed for handling wicked and sinful society and would not pass away until heaven and earth *first* passed away.

Take notice that in Jesus's remarks of Matthew 5:17–20 it was not the law hindering the people's personal salvations through repentance. It was the bad leadership and usurpation of the proper teaching of the law—embodied by the Pharisees—that Jesus reprimanded. Despite His emphatically lucid claim (above) that He did *not* intend to abolish the present and future use of the Mosaic Law, there are numerous accounts throughout the epistles that appear to say the polar opposite, and with equally unmistakable fervor. For example, consider Colossians 2:13–14:

> And you, being dead in your sins and the uncircumcision of your flesh, hath he quickened together with him, having forgiven you all trespasses; Blotting out the handwriting of

ordinances that was against us, which was contrary to us, and took it out of the way, nailing it to his cross.

Nailing it (the law) to the cross! A very vivid picture enters the mind—a picture of bloody suffering and hammer blows! This is graphic! What is the Bible student to do? Did Jesus trick the Jews so they wouldn't figure out His secret agenda for anti-Mosaic-law-subterfuge, or was Paul perhaps mistaken? Does the Bible contradict itself? Do the neo-atheists* have a legitimate critique against the inspiration of the Scriptures? (Pardon the deliberate melodrama.)

There's no need to panic. Actually, both statements do *appear* to be contradictory, but with careful study they are easily proven complementary. This is true of this and many other similarly situated passages in the New Testament that seem to say Jesus "abolished" the law, but with careful study every passage can be clearly reconciled to Jesus's own blunt claim that He did *not* come to do away with the law. (For more information on this see the section of this book entitled "Troubling Passages Explained.") As to that vivid picture of bloody blows of a Roman hammer—forcefully driving that "irrational, liberty-crushing legalism" into the deep wood of the device of crucifixion—to be executed right along with Christ...well, this is not an accurate picture of what the apostle intends to depict. We've just heard it preached that way far too many times.

WAS CHRIST MURDERED OR EXECUTED?

Two things happened on the cross, depending upon the point of view. First, from heaven's perspective, looking down upon the cross through the eyes of His Father, Christ was properly "executed." On the cross He became all sin and the representative of wickedness. (See Isaiah 53:10–11 and John 10:18.) When God the Father looked away, Christ cried out, "Father, why hast thou forsaken me?"

Secondly, from the earthly perspective of His mother Mary's eyes looking up to the cross, Christ was "murdered" unjustly, for He had never done any wrong deserving of death. (See Acts 2:22–24,

---

* **Neo-atheism** is the severe, shrill disputations of writers who disparage and pretend to refute the truth of the Bible. Unlike their predecessors, they exhibit both a ferocity and antagonism to religion which borders on the manic and seeks to demonize the traditionalist and fundamentalist strains of Christianity and creationism. It also sets forth an excessive zeal for evolution or Darwinism. This is exemplified by Dawkins being known as *Darwin's Rottweiler.*

1 Thessalonians 2:15, and John 19:25–27.) Both parental perspectives were supernaturally true at the same time. A particular *part* of the law—a "hand-written" part—apparently perished on the cross with Him. (We would be remiss if we did not carefully recall that the foundation of the Mosaic Law, first given in two tablets of stone, was not "hand-written" by a man, and there was no ink involved. It was carved by the finger of God!)

WAS THE LAW OF GOD ... MURDERED OR EXECUTED?

So there upon the cross, was the law "murdered" or "executed" with Jesus? Was the law "guilty" or was the law "innocent"? Was the law on trial? If so, what was the verdict? Did Jesus die to change the Father God, because He decided to set the example for the apostle Paul and reject "Mosaic Fascism?" Well, in order to begin answering these questions, we should let the law speak in its own defense. Consider the following testimony:

> The law of the LORD is perfect, converting the soul: the testimony of the LORD is sure, making wise the simple. The statutes of the LORD are right, rejoicing the heart: the commandment of the LORD is pure, enlightening the eyes. The fear of the LORD is clean, enduring forever: the judgments of the LORD are true and righteous altogether. More to be desired are they than gold, yea, than much fine gold: sweeter also than honey and the honeycomb. Moreover by them is thy servant warned: and in keeping of them there is great reward.
> —PSALM 19:7–11

Again, was the law, like Jesus, "murdered" or "executed?" Was the law "guilty" or was the law "innocent"? Perhaps a greater question should be asked. Perhaps the proper question is: "Were *we* guilty, or were *we* innocent?" The answer is obvious, and the Bible could speak no more clearly on whether or not the law was "murdered" or "executed." Jesus, the "perfect," "sure," "right," "pure," "clean," "true and righteous," "sweeter than honey"—Jesus, the living Word—was killed on account of the sins of a guilty world.

THE "LAW OF JEALOUSY" AND CHRIST

Paul, Pharisee of Pharisees, alludes to the Hebrew "Law of Jealousy" found in Numbers 5:11–28 in his letter to the Colossians. When a woman in Israel was suspected by her own husband to have committed adultery—and it had allegedly been kept a secret, leaving no witnesses for a proper court trial—the jealous husband was instructed to bring his wife to the court of God.

With a slight semblance of the shame endured on the cross-bearing path toward Golgotha, the journey between the angry married couple's tent and the tabernacle of the priest was no doubt humiliating. Once there, she participated in a ritual to determine either her innocence or her guilt. The accusations against her were "handwritten" on a piece of parchment, along with the curses of the law listed against the crime of adultery. Then a sponge was taken and used to erase the accusation and curses against her from the parchment. The inky and discolored water of the sponge was squeezed into a cup, and she was made to literally drink ink-stained bitter waters of the handwritten accusations against her. If she drank the bitter poisonous water in the ceremony and it made her sick, she was proven guilty, publicly shamed and collapsed to the ground under the power of the poison. If she drank the water and it did not affect her in a negative way, God intervened and protected her from the toxin, and she was declared innocent of all charges and publicly exonerated by the accusation-free piece of blank parchment.

On the cross, Christ was given a bitter drink from a sponge on the end of a stick. He willingly drank in your guilt. Though He was innocent, He became guilty in our stead, "blotting out the handwriting of ordinances that was against us, which was contrary to us, and took it out of the way, nailing it to the cross." Because He was guilty, the bitter water killed Him. Because He was innocent, He was raised from the dead!

> And the priest shall write these curses in a book, and he shall
> blot them out with the bitter water.
> —NUMBERS 5:23

The law was not crucified. The law was neither "executed" nor "murdered." The law was neither "innocent" nor "guilty." The law was never on trial! Jesus did not die to change His Father in heaven.

The law was the good standard, and the law was satisfied through the execution of Christ, leaving the parchment clean of accusations against mankind. With accusations erased, it was "nailed to the cross" for the entire world to behold—a testimony of innocence for all those who repent and believe upon the work of the Cross.

When Moses prophesied that God would someday raise up another prophet just like himself, He delivered the oracles of Almighty God. The disciples recognized in their own writings that Jesus was the fulfillment of what some today call the "greatest prophecy of Moses." When Jesus emphatically stated that He had no intention of introducing a new religion whose system would, in some way by default, "destroy" the Mosaic Law—that was exactly what He meant. He told the truth! When He further stated that future generations of teachers who undermined the law would be called the "least," and those who carefully instructed others to obey it would be called "greatest" in the heavenly kingdom—it was a promise. Jesus Christ believed in and supported the rule of law. So while we have begun to show the complementary nature of Christ's claim and the Epistles' *alleged* counterclaims, what of the scores of other verses that *appear* to say the opposite of Christ?

THE IRONY OF "UNGRACE"

In a recent correspondence with a Christian political activist, I was asked to consider freshly published allegations from the words of an award-winning Christian author's declarations on grace (and a newly coined word, *ungrace*). These remarks were apparently made in a popular devotional reading that was circulating among the ranks of reformed denominational readers. According to my friend, the author apparently wrote, "I see the confusion of politics and religion as one of the greatest barriers to grace... Politics, which always runs by the rules of 'ungrace,' allures us to trade away grace for power, a temptation the church has often been able to resist."[10] Really? Politics always runs by the rules of ungrace? These particular remarks about grace reflect what seems to be a commonly regurgitated nonsequitur* argument posed by those who, ironically, do not fully comprehend the very subject they wish to champion the loudest.

---

* In a **nonsequitur** argument, the conclusion could be either true or false, but the argument is fallacious because there is a disconnection between the premise and the conclusion.

Suffice it to say, the problems with these arguments against Christian political and legal engagement should be named "legion," not unlike the demoniac of the Gadarenes, for they are many. Can Christians trade away grace in exchange for something carnal and of no spiritual significance? Of course they can. Such has been done for something as insignificant as a warm bowl of soup.[11] Yet on another occasion, the temptation for political world power was successfully fended off by Jesus's wisdom.[12] Is it possible for someone to deify government? Of course it is! (Have you ever heard of a Marxist?) Do these acknowledged possibilities then justify a universal scarlet letter of "ungrace" upon all who eat soup? Likewise, could there be any merit to lobbing the term *ungrace* upon the government officer of whom Christ boasted, "I have not seen so great a faith in my whole nation"?[13] It's what I like to call "potato logic." It goes something like this: A potato has skin. I have skin. What could be more clear? It has been sufficiently proven that I, too, am a potato.

Truly, there is no such either/or scenario where one can only have either grace or power, but not both. Evidently, the two issues of grace and power are not mutually exclusive, for Jesus possessed both at the same time and He told us to strive to be like Him. Additionally, recall that the Grand Sanhedrin, whom Jesus frequently confronted throughout the Gospels, were the equivalent of our legislative, judicial, and executive branches of representative government in America today. *Moreover, careful, conservative analysis of the Gospel record reveals that Jesus spent approximately 52 percent of His public sermons addressing the realm of His own culture's legal and political issues.* (See Appendix on page 288.) In light of these facts, consider the inevitable conclusion: According to the "award-winning" author's narrow view of what is supposedly incompatible with true grace, Jesus was a teacher of "ungrace" more than half the time He taught! Huh? Come again? (If that is true of Jesus, what should be said of John the Baptist?)

One need not merely stop with Jesus, the second member of the Trinity, and His delivery of grace to men, in order to disprove the assertions made by users of the word *ungrace* either. Real grace should be viewed through the totality of the persons of the divine Trinity. What of the Holy Spirit, the third person of the Trinity? What do we learn of His application of grace upon the world at large? Well, in First Corinthians chapter twelve, the apostle takes plenty of time to explain how the Holy Spirit provides divine grace upon willing and cooperative people within the church, for the benefit of everyone else in attendance. Grace is understood to be the delivery vehicle of these good gifts from God. Among the many gifts granted to men, there are two listed that are especially germane to this present discussion upon which I am inclined to place a spotlight. They are described as "administrations" and "governments." This begs the question: If there is a grace for differing administrations and governments *inside* the church, is it really impossible for such grace to find application *outside*, among the lost world where it is needed most?

Apparently, it is more than *possible*—it is *mandated* by God that grace be employed in administrations and governments *outside* the realm of the church, for the benefit of Christians and non-Christians alike. By inspiration of the Spirit, God the Father, first person of the Trinity, resolves this issue in Romans chapter thirteen, verses one through six. It is written:

> Let every soul be subject unto the higher powers. For there is no power but of [Father] God: the powers that be are ordained of [Father] God. Whosoever therefore resisteth the power, resisteth the ordinance of [Father] God: and they that resist shall receive to themselves damnation. For rulers are not a terror to good works, but to the evil. Wilt thou then not be afraid of the power? do that which is good, and thou shalt have praise of the same: For he is the minister of [Father] God to thee for good. But if thou do that which is evil, be afraid; for he beareth not the sword in vain: for he is the minister of [Father] God, a revenger to execute wrath upon him that doeth evil. Wherefore ye must needs be subject, not only for wrath, but also for conscience sake. For this cause pay ye tribute also: for they are [Father] God's ministers, attending continually upon this very thing (emphasis added).

Obviously there is a "grace" from Father God, placed upon *cooperative* men to rule in government! In contrast, history is replete with examples of *uncooperative* rulers as well. It stands to reason that these uncooperative rulers more appropriately wear the newfangled badge "ungrace" than those who seek to glorify God in all things, "whether therefore ye eat or drink or whatsoever ye do" including politics and law.

So whether you eat or drink or whatever you do, do it all for
the glory of God.

—1 Corinthians 10:31, niv

We deduce that pitting the Law of Christ against the Law of Moses is
a logical fallacy incited by teachers of an extrabiblical and whimsical
sort of grace that does not really exist—not in this galaxy, anyway.

Finally, Father God gave grace to His children in the Old Testament
too, yet the divinely inspired civil government of the Hebrews managed to coexist. Psalm 84:8, 10–12 says so, bookended by the term
Lord of Hosts, an idiom referencing God's governance of nations.

> O Lord God of *hosts*, hear my prayer: give ear, O God of Jacob.
> Selah... For a day in thy courts is better than a thousand. I
> had rather be a doorkeeper in the house of my God, than to
> dwell in the tents of wickedness. For the Lord God is a sun and
> shield: the Lord will give *grace* and glory: no good thing will
> he withhold from them that walk uprightly. O Lord of *hosts*,
> blessed is the man that trusteth in thee (emphasis added).

One reason so many Christians seem to think that "grace replaced
law" is that they make the tragic mistake of assuming men must not
have enjoyed grace *before* Christ came to the earth. As illustrated
briefly in the previous verse, this is simply untrue. "The Lord will
give *grace* and glory," declares the confident Old Covenant psalmist!
They further miss the fact that law and grace happily coexisted
throughout the Old Testament dispensation, and people still managed
to get to heaven, by faith. We conclude the existence of God's law does
not hinder salvation either. Our antagonists seem to be confusing the
abuses of law, which aggravate salvation, and the *existence* of law.
They are entirely *separate* issues. It is best that we not confuse them
by "potato logic."

Indeed, grace was available to men and women of faith throughout
the Old Testament. Noah "found grace in the eyes of the Lord."[14]
Joseph, the son of Jacob, "found grace" because "the Lord was with
him."[15] Paul explained to Timothy that "grace was given to us in
Christ before time began."[16] Obviously, God was not hoarding up all
of His grace in heaven, refusing to be gracious to men during the Old
Testament.

In reality, Israel tended to be uncooperative with the grace they had *already* been given, through their own acts of sin and rebellion. When Christ arrived on the scene, it wasn't as if a "graceless world" was suddenly introduced to a brand-new, never-before-seen feature of God (a God who, up until that moment in history, had been really strict and mean-spirited). When He came to the earth, Christ brought the *fullness* of grace uniquely packaged in human flesh. *That* was why His coming was remarkable! Grace had always been shared with the men of antiquity, but it hadn't been given in fullness to any single man until Jesus Christ! His grace was *not* brought to the earth to replace law. Law cannot (nor should it) be replaced! It is an expression of love, and according to both the Old and New Testaments, love is described to be the highest law of all laws! (See Leviticus 19:18, Matthew 22:35–40, and Romans 13:9–10.) Could grace replace love? Of course not! Even if it could, what would be the point? Why would anyone want to replace or do away with love? *If grace could not replace love, we are forced to conclude that grace could not replace law either!*

For further clarification, it is necessary to define and comment on three important Bible terms: First, *sin is defined by the Scripture as "transgression of the law"* in both the Old and New Testaments. The theological definition of sin has not and will never change. *It is permanently defined.* Jesus dying on the cross did not change the definition of sin, nor did His actions change the consequences of committing sins. The only way for men to get to heaven in the Old Testament was by having faith in divine redemption, and the only way to heaven today is faith in divine redemption. Those who claim that persons who lived before Christ were allowed to escape hell through the blood of animal sacrifices have never read and believed the plain language of Psalm 40:6–8 (as well as many other passages in the Old Testament) that explicitly warn that the rituals and rites of Mosaic Law alone (or the regulations of any other covenant before Moses was born) accomplished nothing without redemptive faith in the hearts of those who carried them out. Salvation from sin has always been acquired through redemptive faith in every covenant before and after Calvary.

The prophet Amos equated the sins of Judah with transgressing and even casting away the law of God revealed for their benefits in the Ten Commandments. He rebuked Judah about 820 years before Christ was born.

> Thus saith the Lord, For three transgressions of Judah, and for
> four, I will not turn to it, because they have cast away the Law
> of the Lord, and have not kept his commandments, and their lies
> caused them to err after the which their fathers have walked.
>   —Amos 2:4, gnv

Did Amos give a different definition of sin than the apostle John
when he wrote the following from the city of Ephesus in AD 90? No,
he did not.

> Whosoever committeth sin, transgresseth also the Law: for
> sin is the transgression of the Law.
>   —1 John 3:4, gnv

If we believe it is possible to sin in the New Testament, and we
believe the New Testament correctly defines sin, then we are forced
to acknowledge that the law of God is in play in the New Testament,
else there would be nothing men could transgress, and the definition
of sin given in the New Testament would make no sense at all. *Sin is
transgression of the law.*

Second, the law of God is expressed in the explicit and implicit
statements of the Ten Commandments. Divine law is defined this
way—*law is how love behaves.* Love is the chief law of all God's laws
and the rationale for the Ten Commandments. A violation of God's law
is always an act against God's pure agape love. In the same way that
the definition of sin (given above) was not changed by Jesus's death,
burial, and resurrection, the theological definition of law has not and
will never change. *It is permanently defined.* First Corinthians 13,
which is often called "the love chapter," is in perfect harmony with
the Ten Commandments. In fact, reading 1 Corinthians 13 is a valuable
expression of the very same premise Moses shared when he delivered
the Ten Commandments to the Hebrew children. Moses plainly taught
that love was preeminent and eternal law. In all past, present, and
future covenants, permanently, *law is defined as how love behaves.*

Third, the grace of God is incorrectly defined by so many persons
that we must say what it is *not* before we can accept what it truly *is.*
Those who mistakenly believe grace to be a spiritual blanket of sorts,
designed to cover up the embarrassment of ongoing sins (transgressions of the law) so that God will not be nauseated when He looks

down upon us, have missed a critical piece of Bible knowledge explained by the apostle John:

> And that Word was made flesh, and dwelt among us, (and we saw the glory thereof, the glory of the only begotten Son of the Father) full of grace and truth.
>
> —JOHN 1:14, GNV

Grace cannot be a covering for sin in that instance, because Jesus was full of grace and we all know He had no sin to cover up. Others are mistaken to think that grace in the Old Testament was substantively different from grace in the New Testament, as if grace was a cake and God changed the recipe. But why should anyone believe this? Could the grace of God imparted to Noah in Genesis 6:7–8 be inadequate or in some way flawed? If Noah had cried out to God in a similar way as did the apostle Paul concerning his thorn, should God have answered differently to Noah, saying blithely, "So sorry, Noah. My grace at this time in history is temporarily insufficient. My Beloved Son hasn't yet arrived"? The theological definition of grace has not and will never change. *It is permanently defined.*

Genesis 19:19 tells us that Lot's life, along with his daughters' lives, was quite literally saved by grace. The Hebrew children were given a deposit of God's grace in order to facilitate their prosperous deliverance from Egypt in Exodus 3:21. The wonder of God's grace is experienced in both testaments.

So what is grace? In the scholarly book entitled *Grace Empowerment*, pastor and author J. Chace Gordon said it this way: "There is one predominant Greek word used for grace in the New Testament; *charis.* This word can be defined as 'God's divine influence on the heart and its reflection in life.'"[17] *Grace is defined as God's moral strength shared with man.*

In summary, all three definitions of these foundational ideas have been permanently fixed as eternally unchanging concepts. Heaven and earth may pass away, but His Word shall never pass away. Amen! Sin is transgression of the law, law is how love behaves, and grace is God's moral strength shared with man. This is so incredibly important to understand that I want to state it again and invite you to consider the consequences of getting any of these definitions wrong or misunderstanding one definition's proper interaction with another.

1. Law is how agape love behaves.

2. Sin is transgression of the law.

3. Grace is God's moral strength shared with mankind.

Law and grace have teamed up to defeat sin. Think of the definitions of position 1 and position 3 ganging up on the definition of position 2, sandwiched in the middle. In this way, law and grace team up to defeat sin in the life of any believer. God's moral strength (grace) shared with us allows us to live out how agape love behaves (the law) and conquer sin. Now consider what happens when careless teachers confuse these definitions as well as their proper applications.

Incorrectly pit the correct definition of grace (position 3) against the correct definition of law (position 1), and what do you get? If you believe that God's moral strength shared with you allows you to trounce an eternal code of behavior, you will get bondage to sin and hell.

Incorrectly pit the correct definition of sin (position 2) against the correct definition of law (position 1), and what do you get? If you believe your sin can defeat an eternal code of behavior, you commit crime, and reap punishment here on earth and hell in the next life.

Incorrectly pit the correct definition of law (position 1) against the correct definition of grace (position 3), and what do you get? If you believe following a behavioral code without God's moral strength being shared with you is possible, you will reap the vain works of dead religion and eventually be sent to hell.

As we continue reading the passage mentioned a moment ago from the apostle John's letter, rather than incorrectly pitting grace (God's moral strength shared with man) against law (how love behaves), we should read the accurate meaning of the text. Christ clarified the great, good, and important work of Moses by intervening in human history. He brought the fullness of God's grace (God's moral strength shared with man) to the earth by being its personification and teaching men how to better cooperate with God's eternal grace.

> And the Word became flesh, and dwelt among us, (and we beheld his glory, the glory as of the only begotten of the Father,) *full of grace* and truth...And of his *fullness* we have all received, and *grace* for *grace*. For the law was given by Moses, but *grace* and truth came by Jesus Christ.
> —John 1:14, 16–17, emphasis added

The previous verse *does not* claim the purpose of grace (God's moral strength shared with man) was to eradicate or replace God's law (how love behaves), nor could it imply the rubbing out of Moses's inadequate life's work! Consider the flawed logic necessary to claim otherwise. If it is true, according to many who poorly interpret this passage, that "grace replaced law," then we must also conclude that law needed to be replaced because it was both "ungracious" and "deceitful." Why deceitful? Because the same verse not only says Christ brought grace, but it says He brought "grace and truth." This interpretation is easily shown to be nonsensical. *The law of God was already both gracious and truthful!* Christ bringing the fullness of both was complementary to what God was already doing through Israel, despite their stubborn resistance!

God's law remains eternal and unchanging. In approximately 1534 BC, *Moses merely enjoyed articulating and organizing what had always been eternally true of law in God.* Prior to that particular encounter on the mountaintop, for example, Adam broke God's law—so severely that his sin was imputed upon the entire human race. Yet, as Finis Dake points out, "Adam had no father or mother to honor, no one to commit adultery with and no one to steal from—he owned everything."

We must be very clear about Christ's agenda. Christ came, among other things, to submit to His Father's eternally true inspiration by *obeying* Mosaic Law.[18] He also came to support Moses's integrity of doctrine by *defending* its proper interpretation.[19] Christ came to demonstrate how men were expected to *fully cooperate* with God's grace![20] Christ did not, and could not have come to do away with the law of God and God's expectations for human obedience!

Rev. J. Chace Gordon continues: "In the Old Testament, God had to divinely [personally] intervene into people's lives to bring grace. Now that this authority has been invested in the Church, the Church [in Christ] has become God's divine intervention."[21]

The final nail in the coffin of this poor argument, which wrongly pits the law of Christ against the law of Moses, is the overwhelmingly powerful fact that all ten laws of the Mosaic Decalogue are continued into the New Testament. (Only a minor change is made to the law of Sabbath, with the Chief Apostle requiring the New Testament believer to daily enter into the rest of God. (See Hebrews 4:1–13.) Yet the principle of weekly corporate worship remains on the "first day of the

week" according to Acts 20:7 and 1 Corinthians 16:2.) Consider that
if the following data is true, then the modern expectation that men
obey some particular portion of Mosaic Law could not possibly hinder
them from receiving personal salvation. The New Covenant scriptures on the continuation of the Old Covenant's Ten Commandments
should be compared as follows:

1. Exodus 20:3 with Romans 5:8; 1 Corinthians 13; 1 John
   3:1–4:21

2. Exodus 20:4–6 with Romans 2:22; 1 Corinthians
   5:10; 6:9–11; 8:1–10; 10:7, 19–28; 2 Corinthians 6:16;
   Ephesians 5:5; 1 John 5:21; Acts 15

3. Exodus 20:7 with Acts 26:11; Romans 2:24; Colossians
   3:8; Titus 3

4. Exodus 20:8–10 (not commanded in the New Covenant)

5. Exodus 20:12 with Ephesians 6:2–3; Colossians 3:20;
   2 Timothy 3:2

6. Exodus 20:13 with Romans 13:9; 1 Peter 4:15; 1 John
   3:15

7. Exodus 20:14 with Romans 2:22; 13:9; 1 Corinthians
   6:9–11; Galatians 5:19–21; Hebrews 13:4

8. Exodus 20:15 with Romans 2:21; 13:9; Ephesians 4:28

9. Exodus 20:16 with Romans 13:9

10. Exodus 20:17 with Romans 13:9; 1 Corinthians 5:10–11;
    6:9–11

The bottom line is this: Ignoring the whole Old Testament is so
much easier on one's conscience after one convinces himself that
ignoring it is what God wants him to do, right? For this reason, the
antipolitical Christian antagonists will always fight to reject the
whole law, arguing against "dividing the law" into the two reasonable
categories of 1) "this portion still applies today" and 2) "this portion
no longer applies today." Instead of accepting the truth about the balance of the Bible and God's ongoing plan for modern human governments, the "life-coaches" (in step with the Pied Piper of Hamelin) who

best pipe a mesmeric tune to attract the largest group of "disingenuous repenters" get the biggest book deals.

Not unlike the popular award-winning author mentioned earlier, it seems many Christian leaders have fabricated the perfect three-step program to allure sinful and selfish people into remaining comfortable, well...sinful and selfish. The plan is popular. The plan has worked well. The plan seems to have been financially profitable. The plan is simple: 1) Convince everyone God intends that we throw the whole law out the window; 2) remind everyone that the New Testament alone provides inadequate instructions for the administration of modern governments; and 3) conclude by announcing that after thousands of years on record (where the exact opposite was the case), Father God now has a fresh announcement to make. He has apparently decided to become very *uninterested* in civil government. From now on, therefore, future involvement in politics shall be considered "ungrace." (Jesus decided this stark change of direction for the Trinity, so it seems, after His resurrection was completed...?)

What is the result of this three-step plan so many have embraced? In the world where the term "ungrace" is coined and award-winning authors confuse God's flock, if you happen to consider politics a hobby, then it is considered OK to participate, so long as you don't spend too much time on it. Oh, and since these persons have been told that God and their church feel the activity is unimportant ("proven" with evidence that so little is explained about government in the New Testament), they are enabled to make decisions and form opinions about political issues by making it up as they go along. It's "all under grace," right? (I sigh.)

Walking in what is alleged to be "grace" has been reduced to the following paradigm: "Just focus on being really lovey-dovey and non-confrontational. *That* is the key to success for truly loving Christians! The ability to avoid offense at all costs is the greatest virtue of a real Christlike person, because *that* is how grace works." While there are many problems with these fraudulent ideas, there is one particular issue that you would think would give pause for thought in the minds of Christians: none of the above lovey-dovey non-confrontational mush describes what Jesus ever did or said! I digress.

Far too many Christians have bought into this three-step myth. It was easy to buy into it, too. Many were already politically and culturally apathetic long before some squishy Christian author or itinerant evangelist came along and informed them that their current state of ambivalence and self-centeredness was "God's amazing grace at work in your life." The whole shebang of what amounts to an excessively "personal" salvation, paired with an exaggerated "get-rich-quick" mysticism (usually employed before passing the offering plates and/or chicken buckets) fits in very naturally to the "God doesn't care about human government, so you don't need to either—it's all under grace— let us just love one another" state of egomaniacal cultural vanity.

Consider a final irony fashioned by the very group responsible for coining the strange word *ungrace*. Their accusation has been that those who involve themselves in the culture of politics have traded away grace in exchange for power. In light of what we have shown of their errors, it would appear *they* possess little of either.

The greatest irony of "ungrace?" It, too, is "amazing."

CHAPTER 4: REVIEW QUESTIONS

Enjoy this quiz at http://peacemakersinstitute.com/smb-quiz.

1. Did the world need a Messiah to deliver them from the dark bondage of a liberty-crushing legalist like Moses?

2. What particular insect did Republican activist Duane Brown of Correctionville, Iowa, compare to those same people Republican Chairman of Woodbury County, Steve Salem, had already called "Christian Fascists"?

3. What does the British Centre for Science Education believe to be every bit as potentially murderous as Stalin, Hitler, Pol Pot, or any other historically evil figure?

4. What was the greatest prediction of Moses?

5. When Philip testified of his faith to Nathanael, whom did he describe as the fulfillment of Moses's greatest prediction?

6. What does John the Apostle declare of Jesus Christ in John 6:14?

7. What does Luke the Evangelist's account of Stephen's comment declare concerning Jesus Christ in Acts 7:37?

8. Why do many pre-millennialists refrain from real-world activism? Post-millennialists?

9. Do churches that refrain from engaging politics go into "all" the world, or does the world actually infiltrate them?

10. What is the significant difference between the word "fulfill" and "fulfilled" in the passage of Matthew 5:17–20?

11. What percentage of Christ's public sermons addressed His own culture's legal and political issues?

12. Was the law of God grace-filled and truthful when God gave it to Moses? Define the three terms of grace, law, and sin.

Chapter 5

Dividing the Law

ONE OF THE first martyrs of America was Rev. George C. Haddock, a Methodist pastor. (See portrait, next page.[1]) He was murdered on August 3, 1886, at approximately ten o' clock at night, on the corner of 4th and Water Streets in the very same city where I am today privileged to pastor. He was shot through the neck while walking toward an angry and bellowing political enemy. Specifically, Haddock was shot for mixing his profession of faith with his political activism.

This noble man, who had once dared to cast his ballot on election day, despite the knowledge he would have to walk alone down a Milwaukee street, being hammered with stones thrown by an angry mob. This courageous leader, who sowed seeds of character into the hearts of all who watched him cast his ballot, particularly after being injured by an improvised weapon in the hand of an assailant (who apparently did not feel the rocks thrown by the mob were sufficient). This tender man who had in that same season of his life assisted the temporary escape of a fugitive slave, came to his premature and tragic death on Water Street, having only pastored in Sioux City for a brief time.

Why? He wanted an end to the corruption within Sioux City law enforcement, local kangaroo courts, and a pathetic city council. He wanted justice. He understood that justice could not exist in a society duped to accept relativistic pseudo-truth, for without truth—God's truth—no real justice could exist, and therefore American liberty could not be preserved. The simple solution Haddock offered was to enshrine the laws of God within Iowa and city code, and afterward, to ensure that those laws were actually enforced by the men who were entrusted by the public to wear the badge and carry the gun and billy club.

According to witnesses, after the gun blast, Pastor Haddock took only a few more defiant steps, cried out "oh—oh!" before falling to the ground and bleeding out for what he believed most—that men in any government of the world should not pretend to create "new laws" so much as they should understand the laws their Creator has

already made immutable and everlasting. Haddock's lifelong ministry had strongly stood for the elimination of two great public evils: he wanted the abolition of slavery and bootlegging. In the end, he attained prohibition, but not beneath the high price of his own blood.

Though the present generation seems to have long forgotten him, he was for a brief time in American history a household name, legendary among a whole generation living in those years at the close of the Civil War. Reverend Haddock, along with Presbyterian pastor Elijah Lovejoy,[*] John Brown,[†] and President Abraham Lincoln[‡]—scant one of these four men was mentioned in a conversation without the others being soon added. These four, in their own unique ways, became champions representing courageous faith and justice. (Oh, that God would favor this nation with such preachers as the Methodist Pastor Haddock and the Presbyterian Pastor Lovejoy once again!)

Not surprisingly, Pastor Haddock viewed the exclusion of Mosaic Law from Christian living as theological "liberalism." After his murder, his son, reflecting upon his father's doctrine, wrote that Reverend Haddock did not much appreciate the theological liberalism of his day. "The doctrine of 'sweetness and light' is sentimentalism without virtue. Sweetness without virtue only gives relish to bitterness. There is more genuine sweetness and light in the Gospels than any collection of utterances from the modern school of literary or critical culture. Ernest Renan is sweet, but he isn't true. Jesus is a truer prophet than Matthew

---

[*] **Pastor Elijah Lovejoy** was murdered in 1837 by a mob for printing materials promoting the elimination of slavery.

[†] **John Brown** was hung in 1859 by the authorities for "radical abolitionism."

[‡] **President Abraham Lincoln** was assassinated in 1865.

Arnold," he wrote.* "In Liberalism, as occupying a distinct place in religions, [Rev. Haddock] saw a departure from the deep things of the
Bible and of life. After the beautiful in the world of faith, there is yet
the sublime, the solemn, the terrible. Granting the duty of [love], that
of absolute surrender to God is still imperative. No one can doubt the
value of [love], but that so-called generosity of religious thought which
detracts from the exact requirements of law and emasculates the perfect healthiness of the Gospels is questionable, and far removed from
the real attitude of philosophical Christian [love]. The Mount of Olives
was never designed to shut out the summit of Sinai."[2]

As we uncovered in the previous chapter, Moses predicted the
Messiah would be like himself. Philip, Nathanael, John, and Luke recognized the similarities between Jesus and Moses to be so astonishing
they unanimously declared Jesus Christ the greatly anticipated fulfillment of Moses's legendary prediction. Haddock said it so beautifully:
"The Mount of Olives was never designed to shut out the summit of
Sinai." But that is precisely what many preachers today would lead
the sheep of God astray to believe—that the Mount of Olives should
supposedly blot out the light from the summit of Sinai!

During countless discussions I have heard the objection made that
the law of God is such that we must either apply absolutely every iota
of Old Testament law to civic and religious life or reject every iota
of it from civic and religious life. "The law cannot be divided!" they
insist. They impugn the character and credibility of all who say otherwise, claiming, "Cherry-picking some parts of the law for enforcement today and then leaving others out is dishonest theology!" This
all-or-nothing approach, of course, is unreasonable and nefarious. It
is a popular and all too convenient objection made oftentimes by purveyors of false grace.

The solution to this superficial dilemma (on whether or not the
law of God should be jettisoned by the modern church) presents itself
clearly. Once the Bible student grasps the natural and logical divisions
of the Mosaic Law, between those things considered *ceremonial* and
those things considered *necessary* for public justice in civil government,
understanding comes—or, the light comes on. While some antagonists
(Christians) who take an adversarial role against Christian involvement in politics suggest the Law of God should not be intellectually or

---

* **Renan** was a theologian often criticized for spreading racism, and Arnold was
considered a heretic who denied the miraculous stories of the Bible as having literally occurred, thus, Haddock was no fan of either.

functionally divided, it remains very apparent that the Hebrew civil code did have an understood division in practice and experience, as we will shortly explore and explain in this chapter and beyond.

We already established back in Chapter 2 that the law was *physically* divided by God when handed to Moses, carved upon two separate tablets of stone. Next, we learned that the law was divided *relationally* as the first four commands were *vertical* in their application, and the final six were *horizontal*. As we proceed in this chapter, we will show how the law was also divided *tribally* and *functionally*. (Later in the book we'll cover how the law was divided according to *necessity*.)

Not to be confused with the subject of "dividing the law," as it so happens, the modern church tends to be "divided" into three schools of thought with regard to God's law: 1) Christians who believe political activism is a necessary discipline of true obedient living often embrace the idea that some portions of the Old Testament are still both active and necessary under our present New Testament arrangement; 2) Christians who do *not* believe political activism is necessary, much less appropriate, as a discipline of true Christian living, usually claiming the *entire* Old Testament has been made obsolete by the atonement of Christ, and "should not be divided"; 3) Christians who acknowledge some limited value in political activism and do not wish to be seen for what they truly believe—that Moses was a temporarily anointed fascist whose ideas of government should be shunned today. They often attempt to embrace parts of positions one and two at once. This confused group characteristically suggests "principles of the Old Testament are still important to believers today, but they should only be *spiritually* applied to *individual* persons, not to modern governments."

Here is my summation of these three divisions of thought: The first two are transparent about their beliefs, and the third is either dishonest with themselves, others, or both, in an unintelligent and patronizing attempt to suggest that the other two incompatible positions could be true at the same time.

THE ANTAGONIST'S MOTIVE?

The motive of such antagonists, whether they readily identify themselves as being in the second or third categories, is relatively clear. They provide fragile arguments against "dividing the law" because they wish to prove the *entire* Hebrew law is objectionable for application in the modern world. Here's how the cookie crumbles: If modern *preachers* are correct to distinguish between parts of the Old Testament that still apply and others that do not, then modern *believers* will abide by the portions of the Old Testament law they are taught are applicable. If modern Christians believe that any part of the Old Testament remains relevant, then the dearly loved pet-doctrines of our antipolitical antagonists will be exposed as error. If their pet-doctrines are wrong, then the assumption that they should reasonably expect to keep sinning in their futures, and that such occasional errors are "under grace," is a fallacy. If their plan to sin tomorrow is evil, then they are in trouble with God. If they are in trouble with God, they will feel condemnation. Thus, they work very hard to argue that the *whole* law of God explained in the Old Testament has absolutely no relevance in today's "grace-amazed" church. Again, why is this denial of God's law so important to them? Because they have a sin problem, as do all humans. Consequentially, they have a troublesome battle with the conscience, as we all do at times.

(You know the drill.) After sinning, they feel guilty, just as you do. This is a very bothersome situation, and in contrast with you, I hope, how they have chosen to theologically respond to the situation boils down to this: *They have chosen to believe that the power of God's grace, bestowed through the shed blood of Jesus Christ, is only able to* reduce *sin in the life of a believer. They do not believe it is able to* eliminate *sin in the life of a believer.* Thus, habitual sin should be excused. Guilt and condemnation must be purged, labeled as evil, and neatly replaced with the novocaine of happily imagined innocence. Any spiritual/legal rules of human conduct *perceived* to be "rigid" and "unreasonable" must be ditched so the guilty sinner can feel good about himself once again. The conviction of the Holy Spirit is deliberately confused as "condemnation," allegedly "not from God." Here's the popularly cited verse:

> There is therefore now no *condemnation* to them which are in
> Christ Jesus, who walk not after the flesh, but after the Spirit.
> —ROMANS 8:1, EMPHASIS ADDED

The last half of this verse, of course, is entirely ignored by the antagonist, for it makes the point that those who persist to walk after the flesh and refuse to cooperate with God's Spirit will certainly experience condemnation (and very appropriately so)! The carte blanche claim that "condemnation is not from God" further ignores many other passages that suggest condemnation is often very appropriately authorized by God. What an irony to consider, for example, that proper condemnation is reserved specifically for men who warp the doctrine of authentic grace! Read it here:

> For there are certain men crept in unawares, who were before of old ordained to this *condemnation*, ungodly men, turning the grace of our God into lasciviousness, and denying the only Lord God, and our Lord Jesus Christ.
> —JUDE 1:4, EMPHASIS ADDED

Notice that these false teachers did not necessarily shout, "I deny the Lordship of Christ! He was no doubt a mere man just like me—a fraud!" So what is it that the writer believes is the equivalent of shouting "Christ is a fraud" from a pulpit? They taught a warped version of unbiblical grace, and by doing such, *indirectly* accomplished the equivalent of "denying the only Lord God, and our Lord Jesus Christ." (This is scary, and apparently, award-winning popular stuff—coming to a bookstore and/or church near you!)

This version of what is alleged to be the doctrine of grace, which is strongly forbidden by the Scriptures, is sometimes referred to as "cheap grace" or "hyper-grace." One preacher friend of mind recently referred to it as "greeeeazy grace." To be very clear, cheap grace or "greeeeazy grace" by any other name is nothing more than a pretend grace. It is something that exists in the imagination of a habitual sinner—instigated by an ignorant and/or deceptive teacher. It's the belief in a lie that claims "grace empowers you to live guilt free, despite habitual sin."

In contrast, Bible grace is the divine power of God working in your life enabling you to stop sinning. Cheap grace lies to the sinful woman (like the one who approached Christ) and says, "You can't quit sinning, but God will forgive you anyway, so just walk in grace...it retroactively makes your sins OK." The Master Himself says, "Go and sin no more," providing words of authentic grace.

Cheap grace is nothing new. Paul spent a great deal of time correcting false teachings on grace in the Epistles. (What is wild to me is that modern teachers spend so much time teaching the very same error Paul already went to great lengths to correct.)

I assure you that when Jesus said, "Go and sin no more," it was

because He knew the woman would never be able to sin in that way
again if she would accept His grace in her life. In the end, either we
believe that the blood of Christ was only powerful enough to *reduce*
sin in our lives, or we believe it was powerful enough to *eliminate* sin.
From one of those two positions springs truth; and from the other, a
damning error.

It's like the old farmer who said, "Yesssir...afore I met God...I beat
my wife everaday. Since I got religion, I only beat her once a month!"
True grace is the power of God manifested in your life to never beat
your wife again. (Thank God!)

Yes, of course, everyone is a work in progress so long as we're coop-
erating with a healthy conscience and asking for forgiveness quickly
and humbly when we fall. (See 1 John 1:9.) But our goal should be to
attain a sin-free life sometime *before* we die and not lower the bar
to accept defeat until the sweet bye-and-bye. Some factions of the
modern church have taken the fact that everyone is a work in progress (which is to say we continue to occasionally sin until we reach
full maturity), and they have taught continuing in occasional sin to be
the highest expectation of Christian living. This is heresy! Read carefully! Continuing in sin and excusing it with the sinner's favorite cliché,
"Hey, nobody's perfect!" was not the driving force behind the passion of
Christ on the road to the cross!

So, if you can take your understanding of this group of Christians
who are "grace-amazed" with false doctrines, who misuse Bible verses
to avoid feeling guilt after they continually sin, who are quick to proclaim that condemnation is *not* from God, who commonly apply "Judge
not lest ye be judged!" to any and every situation, who generally hate
to be made to feel bad about *anything* they say or do, and you place
them into a discussion about politics and government—you can begin
to understand the root of their proclivity to fight against involvement
in politics. Any biblical teaching that might cause them to feel bad
about their apathy toward the present condition of their own nation's
legal and political affairs inevitably finds itself in the crosshairs of their
guilt-removing cannons, which fire off against reality.

Their attitude is reduced to this simple view of the Bible and spiri-
tuality: "If the Old Testament law makes *me* feel guilty, ashamed, and
condemned for *my* ongoing *personal* sins (and *that* is wrong!), then
it stands to reason that applying the Old Testament law to the whole

nation would make Americans feel guilty, ashamed, and condemned for *their* ongoing *national* sins—and that must be wrong too!"

The extremism our Christian antipolitical antagonists teach about what they claim to be "grace" is incompatible with the Old Testament. Realizing the irreconcilable differences between their grace teachings and Moses's Old Testament law, they attempt to preserve their bad doctrine Mafia style. The Gambino family* of New York comes to mind. They remove their hats in feigned respect and solitude, while Moses and his double-crossing testimony against them get to "sleep with the fishes." The problem of Moses is "handled" down at the docks, under the moonlight. Cheap-gracers, just like the Gambinos [insert raspy voice with an Italian accent here] don't like people whose testimony could cause them legal problems with unsavory consequences.

The laws of God such men habitually break in both their thoughts and actions are just "too condemning!" The antipolitical antagonist's primary motive for rejecting the "whole law" of God explained throughout the Old Testament is at its root a desperate attempt to avoid condemnation, personally. The ensuing resentment against Mosaic Law's proper application upon modern politics is merely a peripheral casualty of the same false doctrine.

MORE CAUSES OF THEIR CONDEMNATION

Deeper still, they argue against the belief that some portions of God's law remain relevant today in defense of the implied allegation that they are "too passive" and "careless"—"poor stewards" of their own community, state, and nation. Finally, some erroneously claim the use of Mosaic Law in modern government is an act of modern "Judaism" (illegally forcing Mosaic Law upon Gentiles), which all agree is expressly forbidden by the New Testament.

They are wrong on the first count for ignoring conviction of the Holy Spirit who does constrain them to reject theological narcissism and engage the culture they are commanded to reach. They are wrong on the second count for pretending that the application of Mosaic civil law upon modern civil government is the same thing as forcing modern churches to incorporate the ritual laws of Moses into the Sunday morning worship experience. (This, in particular, is a straw-man argument—apples

---

* The **Gambino** crime family is one of the "Five Families" that dominates organized crime activities in New York City, United States, within the nationwide criminal phenomenon known as the Mafia.

and oranges—plain and simple.) Finally, they are either innocently oblivious or they willfully ignore the special segregation of the Hebrew priesthood from the elders of Israel. In essence, they are too late to this debate! The law was already divided long ago! The law was divided physically, relationally, tribally, and functionally. It stands to reason that if the law was divisible in the Old Testament, it must also be divisible in the New.

OF PERSONAL SIN AND PUBLIC CRIME

Notice the tribal division of the law. Did the priestly role (service restricted to the tribe of Levi) primarily provide a means through which the *internal* and *personal* sin of the citizen could be atoned for through religious laws, or did it not? Did the role of an Elder of Israel (typically a non-Levite) primarily provide a means for the punishments of *external* and *public* crimes through civil laws, or did it not? The answers are "yes" and "yes." The law was functionally and intellectu-ally divided in the Old Testament, and these divisions were understood by the New Testament writers. (More on that in a moment.)

Explaining the noticeable difference between the office of the Mosaic magistrate and the Mosaic priest, Professor E.C. Wines, DD, LLD, writes, "Moses took no steps to perpetuate this magistracy in his family, or to leave it as a hereditary honor to his posterity. He did not even seek to confine it within his own tribe. All he desired, in his successor, was a man fit for the office; a man, in whom was the spirit of prudence, courage, and the fear of God … [an] able chief mag-istrate. Joshua, the immediate successor of Moses, was of the tribe of Ephraim; Othniel was of Judah; Ehud, of Benjamin; Deborah, of Naphtali; Gideon, of Manasseh; and Samuel, of Levi."[3]

So while a tribesman from Levi might be called upon by God to enter into *either* the priesthood *or* the office of magistrate, no tribe but Levi, alone, was allowed to enter into the priesthood. It was strictly reserved for the Levites, and in a case of intrusion, brought severe penalties. Clearly, God, Moses, the tribes of Israel, Jesus, and the apostle Paul understood this distinction between the ceremonial and the civil arena of law very well.

Meanwhile, despite the aforementioned misconceptions and objec-tions, simple explanation of the division is easily seen between those portions of the law experienced *within* the tabernacle of worship (ceremonial and religious laws) and those laws that impacted daily life exclusively *outside* the tabernacle of worship. One need not be a scholar to comprehend the difference between the sacrificial law for the cleansing of personal sin and getting clarification from one of the Elders of Israel on the process required for a binding contract needed to complete a sale of cabbage. The atoning sacrifice of a turtledove, for sin, and the proper Mosaic legal procedures for the sale of cabbage are distinguished by the obvious.

Along this line, a remarkably obvious division is made *functionally* between the sacred and the ordinary. To be clear, when I say *sacred,* think of it as a reference to the Hebrew religion, the priesthood, the pageantry, and the general issues stemming from self-government as addressed by the first table of the law. When I say *ordinary,* I am referring to the Hebrew civic life, such as how property was sold, contracts were made, crime was deterred, commerce took place, and other general issues stemming from civil government, which were addressed by the second table of the law.

The sacred part of the Hebrew government as it related to Moses and his church in the wilderness was noticeably theocratic. It was a top-down centralized flow of authority descending upon the Hebrew people. The theocracy* of the priesthood did maintain interposing powers that could be exercised upon the ordinary side of Hebrew life (that realm of non-sacred civil government) in extenuating circumstances where correction was necessary or civil authorities were unable to reach a verdict in the ordinary courtroom. (An example of this is described in the Law of Jealousy covered earlier in Chapter 4. If the civil magistrate could not determine guilt after a husband accused his wife of adultery, he could appeal to the priestly court and invoke the Law of Jealousy.)

It is interesting to note that while the priesthood did have interposing authority (in order to halt any rebellion against God made by the popular will of the people), another check and balance was also anointed by God to protect the Hebrew citizenry from any sinful

---

* **Theocracy** was first coined by Josephus Flavius in the first century to describe the characteristic government for Jews. Josephus argued that while the Greeks recognized three types of government: monarchy, aristocracy, and anarchy, the Jews were unique in that they had a system of government that did not fit into those categories. Josephus understood theocracy as a fourth form of government in which only God and his law is sovereign. Josephus's definition was widely accepted until the enlightenment era, when the term started to collect more universalistic and undeniably negative connotations. In modern times, the term has come to imply a top-down centralized and despotic religious power.

tendency toward despotism that might arise in the priesthood. Dr. Wines writes, "...the prophetical order [prophets] maintained the rights of the people, and formed a powerful barrier against the encroachments of arbitrary power [from the priesthood]."[4]

It is from this particular division of Hebrew life that proper, biblically authorized church government should be imitated. Additionally, the New Testament examples of church government, coupled with the clear and repeated warnings throughout Scripture given against pure democracy, should be heeded and employed. (Civil government *should not* be patterned after this division of *theocratic* Hebrew law.)

The ordinary part of the Hebrew government, as it related to Moses—a head of state—was noticeably republican in style. It was a bottom-up representative type government arising from among the decentralized consensus of the people. This portion of Mosaic governance is associated with modern theonomy[*] today. It is from this particular division of Hebrew life that our American system was originally imitated and all biblically authorized civil governments of the world *should* be imitated. (*Church* government *should not* be patterned after this division of *theonomic* Hebrew law.)

In summary, the *sacred* division of Hebrew government was theocratic, and the *ordinary* division of Hebrew government was theonomic. There is a considerable difference between these two flows of authority, and a seemingly endless sea of confusion between the words *theonomy* and *theocracy.* These two words are wrongly used, suggesting they are interchangeable by those who resent Christian political activism and enjoy the false accusation that "Christians will bring tyranny upon the unwilling." They shriek, "You wanna turn America into a Theocracy like Iran!"

With regard to the ordinary division of Hebrew government, Dr. Wines writes, "...Moses established a commonwealth, rather than a monarchy. On this point, there is scarcely a dissenting voice among all the learned men, who have written upon these institutions... [a particular authority on Hebrew law] says, that 'the form of the Hebrew Republic was unquestionably democratical.'"[5] Wines continues, "...Each of the...tribes formed a separate state, having a local legislature and a distinct administration of justice."[6]

---

* **Theonomy** is a view of Christian ethics most noted for its attempts to show how the ethical standards of the Old Testament are applicable to modern society, including the standing laws of the Old Testament, as well as its general ethical principles. The application of such standing laws are bottom-up and republican in nature.

A modern proclaims: "The entire Old Testament law was merely provided by God to show man how terribly sinful he was! We don't need that anymore because of Jesus!" Such persons fail to carefully review the profundity of Hebrew law. (I am always curious as to how they think building a legal contract under Mosaic Law to sell cabbage would supposedly convict men of sin.)

Evidently, there was and remains an inspired portion of the Hebrew codex that served a practical and utilitarian purpose in Israel, not necessarily connected to their need for redemption, per se, but connected to their need for justice and order. These hundreds of sensible laws served to "decently order" (also a New Testament mandate according to 1 Corinthians 14:40) the nation of Israel for the benefit of their common societal good. They were inspired by God, and they worked beautifully until and unless they were willfully discarded, not necessarily by an act of "God's Sovereign Will," but rejected through Hebrew sin and rebellion against His clearly stated will! Still today, the benefits and blessings for any nation fortunate enough to make wise contemporary application of the Mosaic laws remain largely untapped.

In conclusion, the ceremonial law executed before the high priest of Israel had prophetic implications of the coming Messiah. The laws pertaining to the contractual sale of goods did not. Christ's arrival on earth fulfilled the prophetic nature of the ceremonial law carried out in the pageantry of the Hebrew priests; Christ's earthly ministry did not "fulfill" the non-existent "prophetic implications" of a simple sale of private goods. This natural division between the ritual and civil laws of the Hebrews—the distinction made between the duties of the laity leaders/Elders of Israel and the duties of the Hebrew priesthood—are more compelling and apparent than the feeble quarrels of those who object to "dividing the law." I digress.

The New Testament clearly teaches Christians the divine purpose of civil law. The apostle Paul speaks to the New Testament believer on the issue of how God's divine laws should be applied by all modern civil governments. Jesus addressed the duty of all men to "render unto God" what He requires of them. When Jesus said "render unto Caesar what is Caesar's and render unto God what is God's" (see Matthew 22:21), Caesar was expected to do his duty to God right along with Jim, Floyd, Bill, and Steve. Everyone must "render unto God!" Government must honor God, too! They are not exempt from Christ's commands!

What should be said then of modern-day "Caesars" who attempt to take away what belongs to God by abuse of law? This is precisely what happens in civil government when "good" and "evil" are arbitrarily defined by fallen men, without biblical authorization. This is precisely why the Christian and the Bible are required in order for Caesar (civil government) to comprehend its duty before God.

DOCTRINAL JUJITSU JETTISONS JUSTICE

The conclusion of this reality is as follows: for civil government to possess knowledge of its duty to punish evil and for a proper definition of evil, the Christian and his Bible are required. This fact of New Testament living is unavoidable. (But do not be surprised by the doctrinal jujitsu employed by many mainstream churches, which attempt to say otherwise for reasons we have already uncovered).

In his first letter to Timothy, during a discourse intended to correct Timothy's propensity to miss the personal corrections necessary for salvation (some seemed to believe that external obedience to the law—alone—was enough for salvation), Paul clearly explains two issues: 1) That mere obedience to the Hebrew Civil Code was insufficient for eternal salvation; 2) That the immutable principles of those laws obtained by Moses, from the mouth of God, should continue to be applied by civil society against fifteen specific types of persons, because the principles of divine law remain in perfect agreement with the New Testament law of love. I will devote most of Chapter 8 to thoroughly exploring each of the fifteen types of crimes God's law is necessary to handle, if earth ever wishes to experience true justice, but let's go ahead and read it for general insight right now:

> For the end of the commandment is love out of a pure heart, and of a good conscience, and of faith unfeigned. From the which things some have erred, and have turned unto vain jangling. They would be doctors of the Law, and yet understand not what they speak, neither whereof they affirm. And we know, that the Law is good, if a man use it lawfully. Knowing this, that the Law is not given unto a righteous man, but unto the lawless and disobedient, to the ungodly, and to sinners, to the unholy, and to the profane, to murderers of fathers and mothers, to manslayers, To whoremongers, to buggerers, to

menstealers, to liars, to the perjured, and if there be any other thing that is contrary to wholesome doctrine.

—1 TIMOTHY 1:5–10, GNV

So says verse five, "for the end of the commandment is love out of a pure heart." Another way of saying this could be "the purpose of sacred teaching is to produce agape love." Those false teachers (who were likely Judaizers) had apparently been teaching in an incorrect way that failed to honor the highest law—the very premise of Mosaic Law—love the Lord your God with all your heart, mind, and soul, and love your neighbor as yourself. They contrived to be experts of Mosaic Law while missing the entire premise upon which Moses had based godly Hebrew civilization.

Hear, O Israel: The LORD our God *is* one LORD: And thou shalt *love* the LORD thy God with all thine heart, and with all thy soul, and with all thy might. And these words, which I command thee this day, shall be in thine *heart*...

—DEUTERONOMY 6:4–6, EMPHASIS ADDED

As we have previously discussed earlier in this book, the idea that "New Testament love replaces law" is false and unscriptural. Those who accept that error often stumble over the remarks made in 1 Timothy 1:5, believing Paul in some way authorizes today's Christians to jettison the entire law of God from modern life, but the very opposite is the case.

I once had a reformed seminary student who was very outspoken against theonomic teaching go so far as to claim that the intent of Paul's writings in 1 Timothy 1:1–5 was to show that teaching Mosaic Law was entirely inappropriate for the New Testament church. His antinomian remarks were only slightly worse than his comrade's, who countered (in an attempt to show more moderation than his friend had) that he believed Paul was "OK with individual people having the Ten Commandments written in their hearts, but that it would be wrong to force society to obey them." Apparently the idea of having something "written in your heart" is mystical code language for "we don't need God's law anymore."

Paul, in harmony with Moses and Jesus, clearly instructs that the law preached properly fosters a vibrant agape love. He further echoes the sentiment of Christ that by distancing ourselves from the goodness of the law, love is undermined. Contrast Jesus's doctrine with Paul's given to Timothy:

> ...and because of the abounding of the lawlessness [rejection of God's law], the love of the many shall become cold.
> —MATTHEW 24:12, YLT

> But we know that the law is good, if a man use it lawfully.
> —1 TIMOTHY 1:8

D. Edmond Hiebert expounds upon Paul's remark in verse 8 as follows: "By 'lawfully' he [Paul] means not that which the law permits but that it must be used according to its original spirit and intention. The law itself, because it is law, dictates its lawful use and condemns every abuse as unlawful."[7] The original spirit and intention in which Moses gave the law of God to the Hebrews was...wait for it...wait for it... *love*.

When Jesus said the most important truth was to "love the Lord your God with all your heart, mind, soul, and strength," He was simply quoting Moses, who already said it 1,500 years earlier in Deuteronomy 6:5 and 30:6. Moreover, when Jesus said "the second is like unto it, that we must "love your neighbor as yourself," He was simply quoting Moses, who already said the same thing 1,500 years earlier in Leviticus 19:18. Obviously, this "law of love" was not invented during Jesus's public ministry, and it is neither exclusively nor uniquely a New Testament doctrine.

Paul's comments are not in any way intended to instruct either the Hebrews or Gentile Christians to ignore the practical use and necessity of a righteous civil code, in the name of love. His point is to remind them (and us) that faithless (faith works by love) obedience to civil rules has no eternal value capable of saving a sinner from hell. This is true even if the civil laws were inspired by God. On the contrary, obedience that pleases God must emanate from a faith-filled, repentant heart. No ancient Hebrew who obeyed the Ten Commandments and violated the premise of them all (loving God with all their heart, mind, and soul) went to heaven after they died. Absolutely no one. Hebrews chapter 11 makes it abundantly clear that all the patriarchs in all historic covenants between God and man had gained heaven the same way men must today...by faith. Again, the Bible teaches that "faith worketh by love," in Galatians 5:6. In summary: works don't save us in the New Testament any more than they saved anyone living in the Old

Testament; but once we're saved from hell, by faith, through grace, we employ the required works of obedience to God, which is a natural response of gratitude!

The tendency in modern times to argue that the entire Hebrew law should be absolutely abandoned from New Testament living is the result of what appears to be innumerable errant teachings. We have touched on these teachings, but we cannot continue to take the time to fully address them in this book. It is enough to say this and little more: Each of the three persons that I introduced to you in my little parable during the early pages of this writing rejects Hebrew law for differing reasons. 1) The atheist Libertarian rejects such a concept of government, crying, "It's way too big! It's religious, and it espouses the preemptive use of military force against innocent property owners!" 2) The liberal Democrat rejects Hebrew law, arguing, "It's not big enough! It's too religious! It rejects the progressive tax system, and therefore does not uphold adequate social compassion." 3) Ironically, the typical Christian Conservative rejects the wisdom of Hebrew law, because his pastor told him Jesus came to deliver us from its "strict bondage to exasperating and unrealistic rules." (As they say up in Minnesota, "Uff da!")

A Broad Range of Meaning for "The Law"

The largest amount of (Christian) misunderstanding may well stem from the Bible reader's failure to carefully consider the following facts when attempting to interpret a particular passage of Scripture concerning the law and its proper harmony with the New Testament contract. The phrase "the law" is used in various ways throughout the New Testament. Depending upon the context, it can refer to the following six things:[8]

1. It can refer strictly to the Ten Commandments (as seen in Romans 7:7)

2. It can refer strictly to the Pentateuch—"the law and the prophets" (as seen in Romans 3:21)

3. It can be a reference to the entire Old Testament (as seen in 1 Corinthians 14:21)

4. It can be a simple reference to a moral/legal principle (as seen in Romans 7:21)

5. It can be a reference to Roman civil law (as seen in Romans 7:1–3)

6. It can be a simple synonym of the phrase "works of the law," denoting both Old and New Testament fools who believed their own physical works could earn heaven without a necessary faith in God (as seen in Galatians 3:10–11).

Conclusion: The term *law* in the New Testament has a broad semantic range of meaning. Before making a sweeping charge that the entire Mosaic Law is "irrelevant to modern society," the passage's appropriate context must be carefully deliberated.

Just because we may not necessarily know *how* to apply a particular Old Testament principle of law to the modern world, we are not given the intellectual or spiritual authority to ditch the entire codex as if it were "worthless rubbish." Dr. Gary DeMar writes, "There is a way to apply these seemingly difficult laws, as Jesus demonstrates, even if we don't know how to do it at this moment in time."[9] Our understanding of its genius should not be left to the whims of post-modern "cheap-gracers" or gay activists who love to quote Leviticus as means to denigrate the Jewish foundation of Christianity, forcing us to retreat from the conversation, embarrassed of God the Father's "old-fashioned" and "unreasonable" moral expectations for the world.

LAWS MADE OBSOLETE THROUGH CHRIST

We know from the laws of the New Testament that Christ did, in fact, eliminate some portion of the Old Testament laws. But on what authority can anyone say, as many today claim, that Jesus eliminated the entire thing? We *cannot* do so because the *only specific portions listed in the epistles as "done away in Christ"* are as follows:

1. Circumcision (see 1 Corinthians 7:19 and Galatians 6:15)

2. Food Ordinances (see 1 Corinthians 8:8, Galatians 2:10–13, Romans 14:17 and Colossians 2:16)

3. Special Observances of Days (holidays) (see Colossians 2:16)

    4. Animal Sacrifices (see 1 Corinthians 5:7, Hebrews 2:9,
       John 1:29 and 1 Peter 2:24)

The divine law came from God. In the context of Paul's discussion of 1 Timothy 1:5–10, we infer the institution of law was used *unlawfully* on two parts: 1) By those alleged worshippers of Yahweh who falsely believed salvation could be obtained by mere external obedience disconnected from faith and love; 2) By what must have been the "white elephant in the room" to his contemporary audience—the known evil and tyrannical habits of the Roman imperial machine[10]— of whom those in this setting were intimately acquainted, and whose civic abuses provoked rebellion and resentment among the Jews.[11] No doubt, the Romans (and their puppet regime ventriloquized through King Herod) came immediately to mind in a discussion about "using the law" unlawfully.[12]

However, Moses (and more importantly, God) had always intended for the Hebrew people to correct their *internal* heart motives and walk in love so that penalties of their *external* law breaking might be avoided.[13] One need only glance at the nature of the tenth commandment, "Thou shalt not covet thy neighbour's house, thou shalt not covet thy neighbour's wife, nor his manservant, nor his maidservant, nor his ox, nor his ass, nor any thing that *is* thy neighbour's," to see this truth. Coveting takes place in the heart, where no one but God can see.

In short, deterrence within the jurisdiction of self-government was *obviously the point* of a written expression of (law) civil government. Nevertheless, when the self-governed inevitably failed to deal with themselves in the secret places of their own hearts and minds—evidenced by an outward committal of crime—the same law ignored by the self-governed became fiercely enforced by the civil magistrate. This is precisely as it *should* be in every nation of the world today, if man is ever to enjoy justice and liberty.

OF DOCTRINE AND DITCHES

The problem we face, not unlike that faced by the Jews, who once found themselves under the thumb of Rome, is found in the answer to this question: Are our modern civil laws in harmony with the divine aim of law? Paul said it this way:

The end of the commandment is charity out of a pure heart.
—1 TIMOTHY 1:5

The best and truest method of crime deterrence (sin deterrence) was for the individual Hebrew to exercise obedient living *through faith* in the coming (future) Messiah. Their daily reminder was the warning of the inspired Hebrew Civil Code. In the verse above, the word *commandment* is understood to mean "the commandment preached in the synagogue." Many of the ancient Hebrews, along with Paul's contemporaries, had failed to see the necessity of faith amidst law, and both Jesus and Paul had routinely addressed this catastrophic doctrinal error of the rabbis throughout the record of their public ministries. For example, consider the following:

But he answered and said unto them, Why do ye also transgress the commandment of God by your tradition?
—MATTHEW 15:3

Search the scriptures; for in them ye think ye have eternal life: and they are they which testify of me.
—JOHN 5:39

Therefore by the deeds of the law there shall no flesh be justified in his sight: for by the law is the knowledge of sin.
—ROMANS 3:20

Wherefore the law was our schoolmaster *to bring us* unto Christ, that we might be justified by faith.
—GALATIANS 3:24, EMPHASIS ADDED

Some men came down from Judea to Antioch and were teaching the believers: "Unless you are circumcised, according to the custom taught by Moses, you cannot be saved." This brought Paul and Barnabas into sharp dispute and debate with them. So Paul and Barnabas were appointed, along with some other believers, to go up to Jerusalem to see the apostles and elders about this question.
—ACTS 15:1–2, NIV

The grave error of *modern* Bible teachers seems to be a leap from the extreme of the ancient Hebrews' neglect to maintain personal discipline (self-government) into the equally ruinous and foolhardy neglect of maintaining a righteous civil government (in preference to fixating on their excessively "personal" salvation).[14]

In other words, the error of Israel was obeying law without understanding its implied connection to their personal conscience. The error of modern Christianity is obeying conscience without understanding its implied connection to civil law. How poignant, meanwhile, that the apostle Paul tells the New Testament Christian that he should refrain from unjustified rebellion against government authority, not merely to avoid the threat of government's inevitable duty to punish, but "for conscience sake."

> Wherefore ye must needs be subject, not only for wrath, but also for conscience sake.
> —ROMANS 13:5

All men before and after the Cross are wise to remember God's demand that they heed the voice of their conscience and dutifully practice the discipline of self-government. Civil government and the requirement for a righteous code of law remains every bit as necessary in the New Testament as it was in the Old. Moderns who attempt to dismiss this fact defy more than logic, reason, and experience. They are in doctrinal error, failing to acknowledge the teaching of Romans 13 on the ordained necessity of civil government.

It is a perversion of Paul's teaching to favor a "new ditch" in preference to the old rabbinical ditch. The old rabbinical ditch was addressed by Paul in his letter to Timothy[15] and was embodied in the zealotry of the Judaizers, who advocated the restoration of Mosaic Law (against Rome). However, it lacked proper emphasis on the original purpose of that law given by Moses[16] (self-governed conscience constrained by faith and love, producing repentance), and later offered no regard for the Messianic proofs of Jesus Christ.[17]

The "new ditch" in today's world seems to be squishy love and a neo-faith that advocates wholesale rejection of divine standards in their personal lives, as well as in politics and law. Both ditches are damnable. Neither ditch was the goal of the New Testament writers—or the Old Testament writers, for that matter. One ditch produces fruitless obedience (good laws obeyed without faith); the other results in "fruity" disobedience (bad law allowed in the name of grace).

Pharisees were made infamous by Jesus for inappropriately leading

Israel to believe they could earn heaven through their good works. In essence, they took the law of God and pitted it against the grace of God. To avoid repeating Pharisaical errors, the modern evangelical preacher correctly condemns pitting God's law against God's grace. Most evangelical preachers in our day seem to agree that it is wrong to think we can earn heaven by mere obedience to a behavioral code, but their answer to that abusive danger ends up being every bit as menacing. In the same way that a mirror reflects an image by reversing left and right, many Bible teachers seem to think the way to solve the problem of wrongly pitting law against grace is by wrongly pitting grace against law instead. The men standing in one ditch rebuke those in the other ditch. They have only accomplished displaying the reflected image of the error they dislike. Both extremes yield hell for their hoodwinked minions. If pitting God's law against God's grace is negative legalism, then pitting God's grace against God's law is positive hedonism. As we already covered in the previous chapter, God's moral strength shared with us (grace) allows us to live out how agape love behaves (the law) and conquer sin (transgression of the law). Two goods from God are not at war with one another; they are joined in stunning unity.

Truly, it is error to read Paul's correction to those who don't self-govern by faith and extrapolate from that conversation "civil government has no New Testament value," or "the church has only one duty—to preach and teach Jesus, and any involvement in matters of state is a useless distraction." Such common attitudes expressed in these and other popular clichés were certainly *never* the goal of the apostle when writing to Timothy. (Rest assured, we will discuss this particular passage thoroughly in Chapters 7 and 8.)

Actually, all New Testament writers consistently praise and revere the Hebrew law while simultaneously rebuking the neglect of self-government, which was always the highest purpose of the Hebrew law (even when pointing out the only four specific areas of it "done away in Christ").[18] One need only to read Psalm 51:15–19 to realize that long before Christ was born in Bethlehem, Father God has always despised burnt offerings and animal sacrifices when performed ritually, without any heart and faith connection.

O Lord, open thou my lips; and my mouth shall shew forth
thy praise. For thou desirest not sacrifice; else would I give it:

thou delightest not in burnt offering. The sacrifices of God are
a broken spirit: a broken and a contrite heart, O God, thou wilt
not despise. Do good in thy good pleasure unto Zion: build
thou the walls of Jerusalem. Then shalt thou be pleased with
the sacrifices of righteousness, with burnt offering and whole
burnt offering: then shall they offer bullocks upon thine altar.
—PSALM 51:15–19

The prophet Amos spoke on behalf of the Lord in first person,
proclaiming:

I hate, I despise your feast days, and I do not savor your sacred
assemblies! Though you offer Me burnt offerings and your
grain offerings, I will not accept them, nor will I regard your
fattened peace offerings. Take away from me the noise of your
songs, for I will not hear the melody of your stringed instru-
ments. But let *justice* run down like water, and *righteousness*
like a mighty stream.
—AMOS 5:21–24, NKJV, EMPHASIS ADDED

The common assumption that claims people who lived before the
Cross were saved by works of the law, but now, after the Cross, we are
saved by grace is wrong. There is no verse in the Bible to support the
notion. The illogic that follows this line of thinking is also wrong. It goes
like this: "Since people were saved by works in the Old Testament, but
by the Cross in the New Testament, any use of Mosaic Law during the
age of grace is a return to works under the law." It is wrong in the first
part because no one who has lived in any age since Eden has ever been
"saved by works." It is wrong in the second part because it implies the
existence of good civil law hinders personal salvations. It is wrong in the
third part because, as the logic goes, the existence of bad law must be a
great aid to evangelism. If that were true then we should expect that the
whole world would have come to Christ by now! How often I have heard
the bizarre cliché "What the church needs is some good persecution."
This seems to be commonly assumed as truth among ministers despite
its complete disagreement with the Bible, which says, "…that we might
live quiet and peaceable lives…for this is good and acceptable in the
sight of God…Who will have all men to be saved…"

> I exhort therefore, that, first of all, supplications, prayers, intercessions, and giving of thanks, be made for all men; For kings, and for all that are in authority; that we may lead a quiet and peaceable life in all godliness and honesty. For this is good and acceptable in the sight of God our Saviour; Who will have all men to be saved, and to come unto the knowledge of the truth.
>
> —1 Timothy 2:1–4

Apparently the environment that best suits successful evangelism is that described above as "quiet and peaceable." And why is such a place afforded such a great environment for reaching the lost? Because effective prayers are used to divinely influence political authorities. Politics, kings, and all who possess earthly authority are easily used to thwart peace through satanic influence, if not assisted by the prayers of righteous children of God.

At the time of Christ's visitation to earth, despite the efforts of the ancient prophets like Moses, David, Amos, and many others, Israel was in just such a dead ritualistic state, as Amos described. Jesus responded to Israel's poor condition by defending the original intent of Mosaic Law, and later, the apostle Paul decried the same error of those who became labeled as "Judaizers." How disturbing it is when moderns read Paul's New Testament summary (1 Tim. 1:5–11) of the *continuing* purpose of Old Testament law and manage to deduce that self-government is preferred, so civil law has no New Testament value! At work is some hybridized mutation of antinomian and situation ethics: the influence of those unwashed philosophers who draw their intellectual forte from the spirit of lawlessness.

The message of both Bible Testaments remains clear: Humanity must self-govern as sacredly created individuals. Civil authority is necessary in order to address those who refuse to govern themselves; therefore, both self-government and civil government must abide by the *same standard*, or else there can be no true justice.

From whence can this standard come, if not from the pulpits of the righteous men of God? The bereaved son of America's Martyr—Rev. George Haddock—answers the question:

> [Pastor Haddock's] first business was with his church. But the political world suggested duties which, as a Christian citizen and public speaker, he could not evade. He deemed

the responsibility of the pulpit far-reaching, covering all the moral interests of man, and resolutely refused to confine his labors to any narrow limits... His pulpit was an exalted place, too near the Almighty arm for cowardice... It was his fortress, to be well defended. He dared not shirk its duties... He would not prostitute; but he would not get behind it and make it a mask for inactivity... it was not too sacred for any use that sought the real good of men. He was criticized for this view and his practice; but when he read the false notion that "ministers ought to keep out of politics or other discussions which men of exalted moral theories and low moral conduct are fond of advancing," he simply walked across his platform saying, almost to himself: "Humph! It's too bad about us ministers!"[19]

CHAPTER 5: REVIEW QUESTIONS

Enjoy this quiz at http://peacemakersinstitute.com/smb-quiz.

1. What Christian hero stated that the Mount of Olives was never designed to shut out the summit of Sinai?

2. Did the Hebrew civil code have a logical distinction between the sacred law and ordinary law?

3. Do Christian antagonists against political activism typically believe that Christ's blood can *eliminate* sin in the life of a believer, or do they believe His blood only *reduces* sin?

4. Is there an appropriate condemnation reserved for some teachers who pervert the doctrine of grace? (See Jude 1:4.)

5. The antipolitical antagonist's primary motive for rejecting the whole Hebrew law of the Old Testament is, at its root, a desperate attempt to avoid what on a personal level?

6. Was the sacred part of Hebrew government a top-down centralized flow of theocratic authority?

7. Was the ordinary part of Hebrew government a bottom-up decentralized and republican flow of authority?

8. Should church government be patterned after Moses's ordinary division of government?

9. Should civil government be patterned after Moses's sacred division of government?

10. What six ways, depending upon the context, is the phrase "the law" used in the New Testament?

11. What four divisions of Hebrew law are done away in Christ?

12. The error of Israel was obeying civil law without understanding its implied connection to their personal conscience. What is the error of modern Christianity?

Chapter 6

The Sin of Libertarianism

I BEGIN WITH THIS truth: I see no exemption given to any government (or government official) of the modern age, nor is any alternative or evasive rationalization made available for the exploitation of any contemporary lawmakers or judges, neither is there any suggestion that another path or plan for civil authority might perhaps be a "better" idea than that given by inspiration of the Holy Spirit in the Bible. Modern governments are still required to "render unto God" what belongs to God, just as was Caesar, according to the command of Jesus Christ. (See Matthew 22:21.)

While we may both learn and appreciate the political gems of other non-anointed and generally uninspired men of history as they stumble upon some truths which happen to remain in harmony with the Scriptures, true Christians possess no legitimate argument whereupon they may claim, on one hand, fidelity and obedience to Christ and His "authoritative Word," and on another, fidelity and obedience to the antagonistic views of otherwise clever and talented communicators such as Bastiat, Machiavelli, Milton, or Rousseau.

Herein the problem with much of Christian Libertarianism or so-called Christian Conservatism is revealed. It is exposed and found wanting in the only true answer to the rhetorical question posed in the first chapter of this book: "Where is the line drawn between self and civil government, and by what authority?"

Bastiat,[*] for example, claimed in 1850 that the only purpose of government was to "defend the right of an individual to life, liberty, and property,"[1] yet Bastiat's definition of "liberty" remains at odds with the purpose of government given by scriptural law. Moreover, those who claim subordination to the authority of Scripture understand Bastiat's

---

[*] **Frédéric Bastiat** (1801–1850) was a French economist who promoted free enterprise and opposed government regulation.

assumption to be inferior to the true purpose of government, which is broadly expressed by the beloved physician, Luke, in Acts 17:26–27. According to Luke, the ultimate purpose of government is that men of the God-determined nations (outlined by their divinely drawn borders) "might seek the Lord...and find Him,"[2] and whose purpose is more specifically delineated upon the sacred parchment of the apostle Paul's thirteenth chapter of Romans, as well as his first letter to Timothy, which we shall discuss thoroughly before we finish this book.

Not unlike Luke, in another broad stroke, the apostle Paul pens (in the thirteenth chapter of Romans) that civil government is ordained by God for two general purposes: 1) providing order for society (a reward for the just), as well as 2) the punishment of evil. These particular facts (that God has ordained government to "punish evildoers" and "reward goodness") drives us to face the reality that neither the concepts of "evil" nor "good" can be arbitrarily defined by the whimsical fancies of fallen men. Only God Himself, through His inspired Law-Word, has the authority to define the "evil" He authorizes the same human governments to punish. Only God, through His own testimony (Law-Word) has the authority to define the "good" human governments are authorized to reward.

FREEDOM OR FREUDIAN?

In December of 2007, in an interview with ABC news anchor John Stossel, Congressman Ron Paul, answering the question on his willingness to legalize the "personal freedom" of soliciting prostitution, stated: "I think when you defend freedom, you defend freedom of choice, and you can't be picking and choosing how people use those freedoms. So, if they do things that you don't like, and you might find morally repugnant, uh, I as an individual, I don't make that judgment. So I don't believe government can legislate virtue. I can reject it personally...but my solution comes from my personal choice."[3]

Rep. Ron Paul's remarks, taken in context and at face value, make it abundantly clear that he would not outlaw prostitution, despite his personal objection to it, even at the state level. He concluded his remarks on prostitution with the broad and sweeping statement which would apply to local, state, and federal authority: "Governments can't protect individuals from themselves; otherwise they become a tyrannical state." In this regard, Moses and Christ did not agree with either Mr. Paul's personal definition of "liberty" or his description of what he believes the role of civil government to be, decentralized or otherwise. He is in clear defiance of biblical authority, and his Libertarian political theology substitutes a beautifully gilded cage of sin in the place of true freedom in Christ.

Again, Professor Walter Block, a "plumb-line Libertarian" and self-identified "devout atheist"[4] writes: "In brief, plumb-line Libertarianism is the view that human actions are justified only if they are consistent with private property rights, which are themselves, in turn, defended on the basis of homesteading or voluntary acts such as purchase, gifts, etc. Plumb-line Libertarianism may be defined in terms of pure Libertarian principle: It does not compromise this political-economic perspective, not to curry favor with leftists or rightists. As stated above, it is entirely consistent with this view to make alliances with advocates of these other views, but the plumb-line Libertarian will never confuse his own philosophy with either of these two others. What is the plumb-line position of Libertarianism on libertine acts between consenting adults, such as prostitution, pornography, fornication, gambling, homosexuality, nudism, etc.? Since none of these necessarily involves the use of violence or trespass against private property, all of them should be legal in the full Libertarian society."[5]

Long ago, in 1901, psychoanalyst Sigmund Freud published a book referring to an accidental error in speech (caused by a secret subconscious wish) as "parapraxis." Today, the word has been coined "Freudian slip." What's most disturbing about the many voices in the Libertarian movement is that when they announce their desires to legalize drugs and prostitution, as well as make the case that dangerous tyrants like Iran's Ahmadinejad (whom I once watched lead thousands chanting "death to Israel!") have a right to pursue nuclear weapons,[6] it is *not* a Freudian slip. Their desires are not a secret, subconscious wish that accidentally fell out in a regretful moment. Therefore, we have little elbow room wherewith to feel embarrassed on their behalf. (Did I mention that philosophers like Plato believed atheism was a danger to society and "should be punished as a crime,"[7] or that John Locke, a founder of Western religious liberty and inspirer of our Declaration of Independence, supposed atheists should not be given privileges of full citizenship?[8])

Anyway, with respect to Walter's moral failures, chronicled in his own political writings, I ask the following rhetorical question, ironically, not to Walter, but to the confused Christians who apparently

agree with him: When did "property rights" become the alleged ultimate moral law of the universe (whose transgression merits the
acceptable use of force) and by what (or whose) authority? I don't
believe Walter would be willing to identify the source of absolute
moral authority, as it would unstitch the "plumb-line Libertarian"
political philosophy (which may qualify as a veritable humanist religion, rooted in materialism, and in antagonistic competition with
Christianity, by the way).

ABSENCE OF LAW THEORY

Stemming from the influence of Bastiat's writings (as well as
other enlightenment authors), the modern twist of plumb-line
Libertarianism's view of limited government is sometimes referred
to as the "absence of law theory." According to this theory, the fewer
laws that exist, the better off we will all be as a society. How true
this theory is until one discovers that the absence of law theory of
limited government is indiscriminately applied to both good *and* bad
laws alike. "Every law is 'good' in someone's opinion, and every law is
'bad' in the opinion of someone else! So get rid of them all!" This argument is offered as the justification for an appeal to what is errantly
called "fairness."

The problem, of course, is that this approach to the absence of law
theory assumes the nonexistence of absolute truth (or pretends to
honor only one truth as absolute—private property). Pretending that
truth is "relative" as a justification for deleting both good and bad law
is intolerable when you consider such immutable natural truths demonstrated by gravity, mathematics, physics, procreation, the precision
by which the planets orbit the sun, and many others that remind us
of absolute truth's existence. (And who could forget death and taxes?)
Is liberty enhanced by denying the existence of absolute truth? No, it
cannot be. Without truth, there is no justice. Without justice, liberty
cannot be defended and preserved. Ironically, Bastiat recognized this
fact when he wrote, "Law is organized justice."[9]

Some self-described Christian Libertarians (who are understandably embarrassed by the atheistic appeal of their own politics) are careful to point out that they *do* personally accept natural
law theory as their premise and supposedly do *not* filter all their
political decisions through the single issue of private property. This
disclaimer, however, is nearly always met with a startling paradox.

For example, one "Christian Libertarian" (a high-level deputy campaign manager) once responded to my objections by writing, "I'm a Libertarian, but I believe that my rights come from God, not man. I just don't believe that it is my right to legislate morality. If Christ gives me free will, how can I do any less to my fellow man? My job is to convince through examples and proof, not try to make another fit a prescribed mode of behavior."

In other words, this Christian Libertarian filtered all his political decisions through the single lens of private property, just like his atheist counterparts. He had convinced himself, in a very muddled sort of way, that as long as he was willing to verbally admit his private belief in divine natural law, it was OK to completely ignore the implications of the existence of those laws. His paradigm is equivalent to proclaiming, "I believe in free speech; I just don't think it is right to say so out loud!"

I responded to the logical fallacy with, "It would help move our conversation along if you would be able to explain to me which of the final six of the Ten Commandments you believe to be inappropriate for civil enforcement."

All government—church, self, family, local, county, state, and federal—should be viewed through the lens of natural law (the laws of nature and nature's God). This is particularly true of America. It says so in our organic law, the Declaration of Independence. I pose a loaded question: How does the Libertarian "absence of good law" theory work within the confines of family government?

As a father of four (at the time of this writing, my youngest daughter, Rachael, celebrates her first birthday), I observed that the "laws of nature and nature's God" determined the bedtime for my children. My job as a parent was to recognize when they became visibly grumpy and lethargic. I subsequently "codified" those observations and now "enforce" them every night. Does that make me a "tyrant," forcing my will upon innocent children? Or does it make me a servant and steward of the gift of God that is a child?

I further observed that it took a male and a female genitalia (one man and one woman) to create that child. My job as a citizen was to recognize this institution as one lawfully determined outside the boundaries of human authority; therefore, it (marriage) was subsequently "codified" and should be "prescribed" and "protected" across all nations of the globe. Does this political agenda make me a "tyrant," forcing my will upon unwilling fetish fanatics? Or does that make me a servant and steward of the gift of God that is marriage (an arrangement produced by natural law that is necessary in order to create and rear children)?

Using "potato logic," the antagonist often counters that homosexual attractions occur in nature, so such behavior must also be in line with natural law. It is as if the depth of their understanding of the term *natural law* is merely a fancy way of describing things "occurring on planet Earth." Through this lack of cleverness the advocate of divine natural law is given an opportunity to join the concepts of *divine natural law* with *divine ecclesiastical law*, by responding, "Yes, and murder, perjury, larceny, adultery, and incest 'occur in nature' as well."

Melanchthon[*] pointed out the same failure of Greek philosophers who attempted to develop natural law without connecting it to ecclesiastical law when he wrote, "...for many of their popular ideas express the depraved affections of our nature and not laws."[10] In other words, just because it occurs on planet Earth doesn't make it in harmony with divine natural law; and since law is absolute in society, it stands to reason that a good law must be based upon an absolute truth in order for it to be just and "good."

Divine natural law is only meant by our Creator to be a scaffolding at the foundation of civil law. The proper construction of a mature legal system requires the explanation of natural law provided by divine ecclesiastical law for the production of freedom. Professor Eric B. Rasmusen of Indiana University once described the conundrum created by natural law when God is left out of the equation. He wrote:

> The distinction between divine law and natural law is that natural law can be deduced by man by introspection and observation, but divine law is revealed only by direct communication from God. One question is whether divine law can ever contradict natural law. Or, perhaps a little different: Is a sin evil because God forbids it, or does God forbid it because it is evil?
>
> In considering this question it is useless to think about sins that are forbidden by both natural and divine law, sins such

---

* **Philipp Melanchthon** (1497–1560) was a German reformer, collaborator with Martin Luther, the first systematic theologian of the Protestant Reformation, and an influential designer of educational systems. He stands next to Luther and Calvin as a reformer, theologian, and molder of Protestantism. Almost as much as Luther, he was a primary founder of Lutheranism.

as murder, theft, and adultery (in their traditional, uncontroversial, contexts). Rather, the question becomes important in situations such as the following: Is it okay to divorce a man for wife-beating? Did God really command the Israelites to slaughter Canaanite children? Is it just for people to be damned when they never had a chance to hear the Gospel?

As these examples indicate, the question bears heavily on the fundamentals of Christianity. If God forbids sins because they are evil, we are saying that we have a reason independent from God for thinking something is evil, and that reason trumps any reason we might derive from the Bible or systematic theology. Thus, if we believe that killing children is always wrong, so a good God could not command it, we must either reject God's goodness or reject the books of Genesis (Abraham and Isaac), Joshua (the Canaanites), and Kings (I think—David and the Amalekites).

I think it's important to believe that sins are wrong because God forbids them, not the reverse. Here are some reasons:

1. Otherwise you must reject the reliability of the Bible. This is not just a rejection of inerrancy: you must reject substantial portions, and, implicitly, all of the Bible that refrains from condemning those portions.

2. Because we are all biased when it comes to our own actions, when we are deriving natural law we will tend to exclude our own misdeeds from being called sins.

3. Because we are all culturally biased, when we are deriving natural law we will tend to exclude misdeeds that our own culture allows from being called sins.

4. Otherwise we have in effect replaced God with a higher divinity, the source of natural law, in which case we should move directly to worship of that divinity.

Note that if you are willing to throw out Christianity altogether, these reasons disappear. Indeed, that is the response of some people. They acknowledge, correctly, that the Christian God's law conflicts with what we think is right and wrong in our culture, and they conclude, incorrectly, that He is not God. In effect, our culture is their god.[11]

The antagonist provokes by asking, "So which version of divine ecclesiastical law should society be expected to use? Sharia?" Then a favorite and painfully overused polemic, "Would you be OK with Sharia, or is the First Amendment only for Christians?"

The answer could not be more obvious. Why not use the ecclesiastical law system that has produced more liberty than any other in the history of the world? How about Judeo-Christian law? You know, the system that guided the creation of the American legal system. Is that so unreasonable? Simpler still, we could also ask why not use the only ecclesiastical system that is legitimately compatible with freedom? Is there another religion in history that has produced a civilization with more liberty? Is there another religion in history whose influence has produced the real-world experience of private property ownership, prior to America?

Plato was not a Jew and lived centuries before the birth of Christ, yet he recognized the empty folly of improving a system of justice without a solemn search for a reliable foundation of ecclesiastical law to lean upon. Plato wrote, in his famous work *Second Alcibiades*, "That we must wait patiently until some one, either a God, or some inspired man, teach us our moral and religious duties, and, as Pallas, in Homer, did to Diomed, remove the darkness from our eyes."[12] What great shattering of darkness might Plato have enjoyed had he been born three centuries later to witness the greatest explanation of the ecclesiastical system of Mosaic Law ever known...those doctrines illuminated by Jesus Christ.

Using the same skill of reasoning as Plato, more than two millennia later, Herbert Schlossberg explained, "For if there are wicked statutes, it must mean that there is a law above the statutes by which their wickedness is identified and judged. There is a transcendent principle, a higher law, that relativizes all statutes and all sovereigns."[13]

CHRISTIAN TYRANNY

Finally, the atheist Libertarian, liberal Democrat, and some self-described Christian Conservatives protest, "But if you return us to the way colonial Americans thought of Mosaic Law three hundred years ago, you will bring tyranny, forcing your views upon those who do not believe or agree!" (As if the new ruling class of Darwinian secular humanism is less dangerous than those who are motivated by the ever-perilous and shifty standard of...agape love! Absurdity is too gentle a word.)

In his scholarly work on natural law, Phillip Kayser offered these words concerning the common charge that those who apply the Bible to politics are bringers of statist tyranny:

> It is often assumed that Natural Law alone will provide liberty and justice, whereas if Biblical law is instituted we will once again have religious persecution like that under the Roman Emperors from Constantine onward or like the Inquisition under the Roman Catholic Church.
>
> It is ironic that this charge should be made because it is precisely Natural Law that was the dominant social ethic during the periods of these religious persecutions. Furthermore, if Biblical law had been followed there would not have been such religious persecution. Those who fear bloodshed and tyranny if Biblical law becomes the law of the land either do not understand the nature of Biblical law or have assumed that statism will always be a way of life. But Biblical law is diametrically opposed to statism.
>
> Government is a servant (Rom. 13) not a god. Nowhere in Scripture is the church given the right to bear the sword. Indeed, even in theocratic Israel God guaranteed a degree of religious liberty (or toleration). The Conquest and the herem principle were not standing laws (and thus not normative for most of Israel's history) as a reading of Deuteronomy 20 will make clear. The laws of Israel forbade injustice to the pagan in their midst (Lev. 24:22; Ex. 12:49; Num. 9:14; Deut. 1:16; Jer. 22:3), forbade oppression of the pagan (Ex. 22:21; 23:9; Deut. 24:14,17; 27:19; Jer. 22:3), forbade an abhorrence of the pagan (Deut. 23:7) and commanded love (Deut. 10:18-19) and kindness (Lev. 25:35-38; 19:10,33-34) to the pagans in their midst. Israelites were not to discriminate against the pagans when it came to charity to the poor (Lev. 19:10) or when it came to justice in the courts (Lev. 24:22).
>
> There was to be one standard of law for all. "But the stranger who dwells among you shall be to you as one born among you, and you shall love him as yourself; for you were strangers in the land of Egypt." (Lev. 19:34) All of the above

implies that pagans were allowed to live in Israel unmolested provided they did not blaspheme (Lev. 24:16) or seduce Israelites into false worship. If this degree of religious liberty was allowed during that period of redemptive history (and it was certainly more than was allowed to "infidels" in much of Europe's history under natural law) it is difficult to believe the charges of bloodshed and Inquisition that some would hurl at theonomists.

But let us turn the tables around. In reality, it is natural law [alone without God's law] which is unable to give concrete protective laws to the citizens of a realm.[14]

AMERICAN FOREIGN POLICY

Proverbs 3:27 displays a principle that may have application with regard to Bastiat's Libertarian "absence of good law" theory: "Do not withhold good from those to whom it is due, when it is in the power of your hand to do so" (NKJV). If the power of one pair of hands has divine expectations, what should be said of the synergy found in many united hands? The principle of responsibility must apply to government doing good for "those to whom it is due." (We acknowledge, as well, the implication there will be cases where it is *not* due.)

Dovetailing from the principle of Proverbs 3:27, there are some Christians who cling to the Libertarian movement because of deeply held religious convictions against war and its inevitable atrocities. Directly connected to the single issue of property rights and the use of justifiable force (the sole moral law of the atheist Libertarian), the issue of American foreign policy is broached and labeled as "immoral." I know my Libertarian friends often cite Washington's farewell address as the catalyst of their isolationist views of foreign policy they call "non-interventionism." While I won't take the time to point out that Washington was, by modern liberal standards, a "tyrannical fascist theocrat" like myself, I do think it's important to remember one particular remark he made in that address, beloved of the Libertarian anti-war movement:

> ... The great rule of conduct for us, in regard to foreign nations is in extending our commercial relations, to have with them as little political connection as possible. [Sometimes political connections will be impossible to avoid.] So far as we have

already formed engagements, let them be fulfilled with perfect good faith. [Emphasis added.][15]

Further, Washington gave a clear statement of a higher law for politics than the atheist-Libertarians' sacred "rights of property" when
he also stated, in that very same Declination address:

> [W]here is the security for property, for reputation, for life, if
> the sense of religious obligation desert the oaths...?[16]

I postulate the following: the existence of a sign-post, pond, lake,
river, or ocean has no magical power and does not cause a complete
change in the immutable divine principles and responsibilities that a
particular human (or group of united humans) has for his neighbor[s].
If we ask the not-so-clever "And who is my neighbor?" question again,
Jesus will respond the same way to us as He did to the smarmy lawyer
who first made that particular question famous.

Is there a difference in my responsibility for my own property and
my neighbor's responsibility for his own property? Of course, there
is a jurisdictional difference! That's what makes the command of
Christ and Moses to "love your neighbor as yourself," so profound!
(See Leviticus 19:8 and Matthew 22:40.) Moreover, the number of individuals in a room, in a field, on an island, within confines of a national
boundary (or in the view of a certain Good Samaritan, lying in a ditch
along the road to Jericho) have no power to change the principle either.

Needless to say, God's commands to Old Testament Israel clearly
show that neither He nor Moses were "non-interventionists." But our
rejection of non-interventionism need not exclusively rest upon the
Old Testament. This doctrine of ours must also be tethered to theological conclusions formed in the light of what Christ taught, in harmony with the God of Moses, in His four parables of governmental
conflict given in Mark 3:24–27. What do these four parables reveal?
They teach that all issues of authentic justice apply to and transcend
all governments, whether said government be church, family, self,
local, state, federal, or some proposed international government.

Either by pregnancies or fatal diseases, populations will expand
and contract. Some will grow. Some must shrink. Small villages have
grown to nations, and nations have reduced to small villages by
their own obedience to, or rebellion against, God's law. Technology
may also either advance or regress. I have no doubt we will invent

faster, lighter, and more efficient ways to entertain ourselves from our couches, but the orthodox Christian knows divine principles will remain eternally. They "change not!"

With that said, if it may be appropriate to defend the life and property of our next-door neighbor, then it may also be appropriate to defend the lives and properties of a neighboring nation. The non-interventionism of plumb-line Libertarianism admits no such moral reality, believing that a body of water magically removes his moral obligations to human fraternity, whether or not the neighboring nation is a needless victim of great evil, or the cause of it. (I acknowledge that sometimes it is *not* appropriate to defend a neighbor. Like, for example, when he's committing a crime. I further note it would also be wrong to help a neighbor commit a crime, and both cases apply to a biblical foreign policy.)

While we agree that the opposite extreme of non-interventionism—warmongering—is morally unacceptable, it remains equally true that the doctrine of non-interventionism is based on a foundation of selfishness, so it is equally antithetical to the Christian worldview.

Our mutual humane concerns about who makes the decision to go to war and whether or not that decision is made justly, must be directly tied to four things, or else our concerns, however intense, remain worthless: 1) The necessity of legitimate morality in government; 2) The subsequent rejection of illegitimate "atheist-friendly morality" in government; 3) The impossibility that true morality can exist outside of Christ; 4) The implications of the first three points with respect to biblical law and its necessary application to modern governments, as it must be applied to the text of Romans chapter thirteen, according to deductive reasoning.

With that said, the truth is, our beloved nation has devolved into nothing short of a politically-correct-Fabian-socialist-ideological swamp. Our foreign policy has been a basket case for the last seventy years or more. If we don't get things corrected, and soon, God will allow our well-earned destruction. In the early 1950s, Americans failed to pass the Bricker Amendment* by one vote. Since then, our

---

* In 1953 Senator John Bricker sponsored a constitutional amendment that came to be known as the **Bricker Amendment**. In its original form this proposal would have eliminated much of the automatic incorporation of conventional international law into the national law of the United States, leaving it to the political discretion of Congress or the state legislatures to decide upon the internal enforceability of the international obligations of the United States.

presidents have, like it or not, embroiled us in foreign disputes. Some were worthy, and some were not. Despite our misgivings or agreement with those particular covenants, they have been made, and we are obligated to keep them, even to our own hurt.

Should America be judged by God because of the evil of a majority of voters? Should we be decimated as a nation because of our own sins? This is the question of questions! The answer terrifies me enough to openly reject plumb-line Libertarianism. Here's the answer: God has a measuring cup to determine when that line has been crossed, according to the following passage:

> And also that nation, whom they shall serve, will I judge: and afterward shall they come out with great substance. And thou shalt go to thy fathers in peace; thou shalt be buried in a good old age. But in the fourth generation they shall come hither again: *for the iniquity of the Amorites is not yet full.*
> —GENESIS 15:14–16, EMPHASIS ADDED

Adam Clarke, the sixteenth century protégé of John Wesley, remarked on this particular sixteenth verse with the following commentary: "From these words we learn that there is a certain pitch of iniquity to which nations may arrive before they are destroyed, and beyond which Divine justice does not permit them to pass."[17] The solution to avoid the wrath described in verse 16 could not possibly rest in merely bringing America to a place where "property rights" are considered the legendary "alpha and omega" of all political morality. The very idea leaves me with two opposing and extreme emotions...I could either laugh, or I could cry.

Representative Fisher Ames, one of our founding fathers, in office from 1789–1797, said it this way:

> The known propensity of a democracy is to licentiousness [immorality], which the ambitious call, and the ignorant believe to be, liberty.[18]

WHERE DO HUMAN RIGHTS COME FROM

It is an illogical contradiction for the same man who says, "I believe my rights come from God" to also as firmly proclaim, "I believe civil government is supposed to be a secular institution." The popular attempt to argue both at the same time by overemphasizing valuable things like personal choice and the importance of local control in government is a confusion of sound and sense. It is illogical smoke and mirrors commonly used by self-described Christian Libertarians, and it denies the reality of how the Ten Commandments actually worked as a civil code for forty years under Moses's world-shaping personal leadership.

For this reason, an intellectually honest "secularist" cannot claim any other belief than the assumption that men grant other men rights (though confused and inconsistent *Christian* secularist Libertarians may insist to stay the path of this contradiction). Therefore, secularism, in any wrapping, eventually leads to statism, though the speed at which statism is achieved may vary.

Remember the French "Enlightenment"? That was the birth of a "baby liberty" that grew up to be a monstrous "Madame Guillotine." It was not a bloody mass execution of citizens fomented by statists who sought dictatorship; it was sourced by the failures of "secularist Libertarians" with Maximilien François Marie Isidore de Robespierre at the tip of the revolutionary spear that had unseated the French monarch King Louis XVI declaring France a new democratic republic.

Robespierre was a disciple of the heretic libertarian philosopher Rousseau, who was condemned by Catholics and Protestants alike for claiming that followers of Jesus would not make good citizens. Robespierre elevated Rousseau's wicked teachings to a cultish following after his death, and made deism the official "civil religion" of France.

Specifically, Robespierre and his libertarian followers promoted "natural rights" and "natural law" while calculatingly and consciously rejecting ecclesiastical Christian law (a.k.a. rules from God that can be identified and applied in the legal world) as the backdrop for understanding and justifying their secular version of it.

While shouting "liberty, fraternity, equality!" some estimates say as many as 40,000 citizens were decapitated for "crimes against liberty." The sarcastic idiom "they have an appointment with Madame Guillotine" became a form of public entertainment where brochures were sold highlighting the names of the condemned, as massive crowds looked on during organized public beheadings. Robespierre the libertarian led the Reign of Terror, and encouraged France to let it cleanse them of their enemies. "The government in a revolution is the despotism of liberty against tyranny," he quipped.

Eventually, Europe's most powerful revolutionist found himself screaming at the bottom of the tool of death he so stupidly and wickedly promoted. When his head was severed from his body, France, indeed, was cleansed of at least one monster, and hell's convicts welcomed a new prisoner. The world was cleansed of the most influential leader of secular libertarianism in the history of the French Revolution.

Why did something so similar to the American Revolution result in total tyranny and murderous rampage on the other side of the world from 1793 to 1794? Because if one believes that men grant rights to other men, then he must also accept that men have a "natural right" to take them away. Thank God our founders starkly disagreed with this nonsense. Our Declaration didn't merely cite "nature's law"; it specifically cited "nature and nature's God." Secularism is antagonistic to the organic law of the United States (Declaration of Independence). Secularism denies homage given plainly and blatantly to God in no less than forty-eight state constitutional preambles of these United States, and secularism, in an originalist sense, is incompatible with the sociolegal reality among the thirteen original states, twelve of which *codified the entire decalogue of Moses into American law.*

Note to self, to Democrats, to Repbulicrats, to Independents, to Libertarians, confused antinomian Christians, and Americans in general: making up a fake religion that pays lip service to an unknown God like Robespierre's "Cult of the Supreme Being" accomplishes the same thing as open public atheism—unless, of course, that fake god we conjured up has some specific rules that can be identified and applied in the legal world. Thus, rejecting the application of the Ten Commandments in our system of law whilst clinging to the slogan "In God We Trust" on our fiat currency accomplishes *nothing* beyond making us feel better about the dragon of statist secular government we keep feeding with the corpses of murdered babies.

Don't bore us with secular Libertarian drivel about how we've "learned from Robespierre's historic errors," or assure us that "if only Robespierre had been able to read avowed Atheist Robert Block's erudite expositions on liberty at Lew Rockwell's website, things would have been different in France." At least not until you clean up the curse that has come upon our nation after more than 50,000,000 babies have been "guillotined" since 1973. For all you math whizzes out there...that's about one thousand two-hundred and fifty times more murders than Robespierre. So maybe, just maybe, America needs more than the word "God" on our money. Maybe we need some identifiable and applicable laws from our God.

I know we do. Where's a William Penn that understands "thou shalt do no murder" when you need one?

America needs Jesus Christ, not necessarily old-world Libertarianism that either respectfully patronized, altogether ignored or, in some of the worst cases, attacked the genius of biblical law. The unsuccessful old-world Libertarianism espoused by men as David Hume (1711–1776), Rousseau (1712–1778), Baron d'Holbach (1723–1789), Robespierre (1758–1794), Jacques-André Naigeon (1738–1810) or John Stuart Mill (1806–1873) still fails to provide today's world with the solution for staving off evil. America certainly does not benefit from neo-enlightenment atheist writers like Dr. Walter Block. (I'll give Walter the benefit of the doubt and classify him as one who politely patronizes Christian philosophy.)

Libertarianism, as a movement, is often right about many *superficial* issues. Yes, we understand that private property is extremely important! Yes, we agree that America should not have used the CIA to empower the Iranian Shah Pahlavi in 1953 via "Operation Ajax"! However, Libertarianism is *fundamentally* wrong, because its base rationale falls short of divine truth. As a consequence, Libertarianism undermines the fraternity of man and overemphasizes rugged individualism (at the expense of the natural family, despite the truth demonstrated by nature that a newborn individual cannot survive without exterior parental assistance). As we would expect, Libertarianism further refuses to protect and preserve the natural institution of family, because, as mentioned earlier, it does not really acknowledge divine natural law. Libertarianism, by any stripe, must of necessity promote secularism (which Jesus condemned more than once—think "Herodians").

Dissatisfied with his own father's stoic, cold and emotionless brand of "utilitarian" Libertarianism, John Stuart Mill's 1858 new and improved strand of Libertarianism pronounced, according to historian Alburey Castell, "all human action should aim at creating, maintaining and increasing the greatest happiness for the greatest number of people. Actions are right when they do that; wrong when they do not. A good society is one in which the greatest number of persons enjoy the greatest possible amount of happiness."[19]

The utilitarianism version of nineteenth century Libertarianism, founded by Mill's father and friend Jeremy Bentham, and later polished by the happiness of son John Stuart Mill, is also incompatible with the Christian faith. C.S. Lewis handily refuted the fallacy purported by the secular humanistic bent of Mill's political genre, when he wrote:

> By the goodness of God we mean nowadays almost exclusively His lovingness; and in this way we may be right. And by Love, in this context, most of us mean kindness – the desire to see others than the self happy; not happy in this way or that, but just happy. What would really satisfy us would be a God who said of anything we happened to like doing, "What does it matter so long as they are contented?" We want, in fact, not so much a Father in Heaven as a grandfather in heaven— a senile benevolence who, as they say, "liked to see young people enjoying themselves," and whose plan for the universe was simply that it might be said at the end of each day, "a good time was had by all."[20]

Before his murder, Rev. Haddock rebuked the Libertarians of his post-Civil War era, saying:

> Just as wild beasts enjoy more individual freedom than is possible to tame ones, so the savage man has more personal liberty than man can have in a civilized state, under the restrictions of a constitution and law... And if personal liberty is the chief thing to be considered, then men would be better off without government than with. But if we desire to enjoy the advantages of government and the genuine blessings of freedom, then the object to be held steadily in view is, not personal liberty, but civil liberty. And the difference between the two is as great as the difference between a grapevine growing wild in the forest, clambering unrestrained from tree to tree and bearing small and [bitter] fruit, and the vine of a cultivated vineyard restrained and trimmed and bearing large, luscious grapes.[21]

Now, more than any other time in history, the present Christian generation has the least right to insist upon their own way. No other generation has enjoyed more than six thousand years of divinely inspired hindsight—the lamp in the darkness we call "the Holy Scriptures." So can sincere Christians be "plumb-line Libertarians"? Well, in the same sense that a genuine and very sincere Christian can be unnecessarily flawed and ignorant of the Bible...the answer is yes. But once they are confronted by the truth, if they *remain* a plumb-line Libertarian, they are likely just another rebel/poser wearing an illegitimate label...advocating the same damnable evil that once ruined a great and blessed nation, as described in the final verse of the Book of Judges:

> In those days there was no king in Israel: every man did that which was right in his own eyes.
>
> —JUDGES 21:25

CHAPTER 6: REVIEW QUESTIONS

Enjoy this quiz at http://peacemakersinstitute.com/smb-quiz.

1. Why was Bastiat's claim that the only purpose of government was to "defend the right of an individual to life, liberty, and property" at odds with the purpose of government given by biblical law?

2. What great purpose does the apostle Luke give for civil government according to Acts 17:26–27?

3. What two purposes does the apostle Paul ascribe to God-honoring government according to his letter to the Romans in the thirteenth chapter?

4. Describe the simplistic definition of plumb-line Libertarianism.

5. How does the Libertarian "absence of good law" theory work within the confines of family government?

6. What is potato logic?

7. Divine natural law is only meant by our Creator to be a scaffolding beneath what?

8. The construction of a mature legal system requires explanation of divine natural law provided by what type of law?

9. What did Plato believe was folly when trying to improve a system of justice without first obtaining it as a foundation?

10. Can natural law alone provide liberty and justice?

11. Were God's commands to the Hebrew nation "non-interventionist"?

12. Does law exist to protect unnatural wrongs or natural rights?

Chapter 7

Tethered: Internal Conscience and External Law

*T*HE OVERARCHING AUTHORITY of God's Law-Word is first introduced to *every* newborn human being through the realization of two opposing physical experiences we call pain and pleasure. Despite modern achievements in technology, no infant born into the world in the future year 2500 will arrive with any more measurable abilities than those born 6,000 years ago—naked, innocent, ignorant, and generally upset with its first exposure to the laws of nature and nature's God. Pain and pleasure serve in the development of every human conscience on a childish level. We call the schooling of pain and pleasure the realm of self-government. The lessons of pain and pleasure are sometimes referred to as an initial introduction to "divine natural law."* This introduction to God's law is indiscriminate and binding upon every child born in sin since Eden.

Next, the natural vulnerability of the infant demonstrates that without exterior assistance, the human individual will certainly die. Natural law reminds us that individualism without family brings death. But this requirement for help from without goes beyond mere survival. The experience of pain and pleasure is not enough for proper self-government to be learned, because human experience has proven that these two sensations can be dangerously deceptive. Pleasure can be good, and pleasure can be bad. Pain can be bad, but pain can also be good.

When a child experiences immediate pleasure after having

---

* **Divine natural law** represents the system of laws revealed and enshrined by God within His creation. Since the universe is governed by physical absolutes, man is intuitively capable of assuming moral absolutes must also exist. God is assumed to have the exclusive authority to define good and evil. This is in contrast with proponents of secular/historic natural law who assume man possesses his own exclusive authority to define good and evil.

140

disobediently broken his mother's favorite heirloom vase, he experiences *bad pleasure*. When the shattered pieces are later found behind a couch, he must receive discipline and training from his parent in order to learn to reject *bad pleasures* achieved through immoral actions. When a child finishes whitewashing the old picket fence across the front lawn on a hot summer's day, he experiences *good pleasure* from well-earned compliments on his quality work. A wise parent reinforces that *good pleasure* with praises designed to construct a healthy work ethic in him for the future. In some scenarios the differences between good and bad pleasures are more subtle. An occasional piece of chocolate cake when a birthday is celebrated—*good pleasure*. An unsupervised child eating chocolate cake three meals a day—*bad pleasure*. Discernment between the two requires parenting.

When a youngster crashes his bicycle and scrapes his knees and hands, he experiences bad pain. When a child joins his school soccer team and returns from a rigorous practice run by a strict coach, he will often complain of exhaustion and muscle soreness. It is explained to the child that his pain is temporary and only a sign of successfully building strength and endurance for the coming competitions. This is good pain.

Therefore, natural law provides the infant with a set of parents to guide it in the development of necessary discernment between pain and pleasure. Self-government requires, by necessity, family government. Both self and family governments function as complementary extensions of divine natural law.

CIVIL GOVERNMENT: REWARDS AND PUNISHMENT

As the newborn individual cannot survive or excel without paternal assistance, a portrait of limited governmental federalism* is demon-

---

* **Federalism** is the distribution of power in an organization between a central authority and other more localized units. It involves a covenant between two or more parties where authority is divvied up by jurisdiction. The source of the power can either originate from a superintending central authority and be distributed downward, or the source of the power can originate from the more localized units and be distributed upward. The balance of the power in such arrangements depends entirely upon the contract which binds the parties together. In family government, the distribution of power typically depends upon the maturity of the children. The more successfully a parent trains, the more mature a child becomes. The more mature a child becomes, the less superintending guidance the child requires. This transcendent divine natural law of federalism applies to civil government structures as well. Federalism increases or decreases in direct proportion to the maturity of the civilization.

strated through natural law. In harmony with the lessons of reason and experience, the apostle Paul taught that this "natural law" of pain and pleasure was written into the hearts of men, whether they were "saved by grace" or not.[1] We understand the sensations of pain and pleasure to be harbingers of a larger, more mature picture of the organization necessary for mankind's achievement of the greatest possible good. As the child enters adulthood, pain and pleasure are realized in the "rewards and punishment" offered by the institution of human government. Pain and pleasure teach man to understand rewards and punishment. Self-government trains us toward the adult understanding of civil government. The secular humanist believes civil government to be the greatest end of human accomplishment. The Christian knows this to be untrue. Good citizenship cannot earn heaven. We are admonished by the Creator to seek a "heavenly city" whose builder and maker is God.[2] What then should civil government teach man?

SPIRITUAL GOVERNMENT: HEAVEN AND HELL

As I said earlier, self-government and civil government must abide by the same standard, or else no true justice can exist. The purpose of pain and pleasure in the cradle must remain in harmony with the rewards and punishment of the state through which every pilgrim travels before reaching his own grave. What good is a civil government that misleads men into hell? It is as great an evil as the conscience seared with a hot iron so that it cannot recognize the difference between good and evil.

Archibald Alexander Hodge (1823–1886), a professor of theology at Princeton, said it this way: "If the national life in general is organized upon non-Christian principles, the churches which are embraced within the universal assimilating power of that nation will not long be able to preserve their integrity."[3] Modern preachers who deny the application of this divine standard to civil government are ridiculous and nearsighted teachers of error who require a *public* repudiation for committing a sin of *public* consequence—civil neglect.

Again, DeMar writes, "It has not been until recently that biblical law has been viewed as irrelevant to contemporary society, by non-Christians and Christians alike."[4] I believe there are two primary reasons for this new attitude: 1) prevalent Bible illiteracy among most Americans (whether they are church-attending Christians or not), and unrelated to that common illiteracy, 2) when some small piece of knowledge about what the Mosaic Law actually contains is known, it's usually in the form of ridiculous-sounding sarcastic clichés like, "Do not eat shellfish!" "Do not trim the hair in front of your ear!" "Do not desecrate yourself by touching a dead pig!" "Don't boil a kid (goat) in its mother's milk!"[5] These criticisms are not merely offered by disdainful atheists either. They are nearly as often argued by Christians who regularly attend church. (Something far more sinister, in my opinion, than atheism.)

Since the antagonist believes he has found a handful of rough spots in the Pentateuch, he pretends he has proven it worthy of absolute rejection. If he is to remain consistent, however, he must reject the New Testament as well. Why? Jesus said "eat my flesh" and "drink my blood." Jesus said "pluck out your eyes" and "cut off your hands." So let's all laugh off the Bible and make our own rules. Right? Wrong.

Meanwhile, the fact that the Hebrew codex covers literally thousands of details instructing proper government is either ignorantly unknown or willfully ignored. From contract law to state recognized property rights, from parental authority to military laws of war, from lawful procedures of medical quarantine to the treatment of transnational immigrants, from criminal adjudication to bailments, loans, and pledges…the genius of Mosaic Law remains superior to any system in history.

POPULAR IGNORANCE

E.C. Wines, DD, LLD, president of City University of St. Louis, said it this way back in 1853: "The more the principles of reason…[and] liberty…[possess] men's minds…the more will the polity of the Hebrew commonwealth become an object of…admiration and of imitation. And the more this constitution [Hebrew civil code] is studied, the more will it be recognized…on several points, [it is more advanced] even of the age in which we live."[6] But what modern American, whether he attends a church regularly or not, would know any of this today?

In an October 2010 publication of *Students Living a Mission* (SLAM), columnist Ben Reese laments, "In 2007, Kelton Research polled Americans on their knowledge of the Ten Commandments. Most of the participants couldn't name a single commandment. More people knew the ingredients of a Big Mac than what the 6th Commandment was. Although the poll targeted Americans in general, surveys polling

Christians are not much better. Surely Christians know more about the Bible than hamburgers. Unfortunately, this often is not the case."[7]

Reese went on to cite alarming statistics produced by a 2000 Barna Research survey:[8]

- 92 percent of American families own at least one copy of the Bible

- Only 37 percent of Americans read the Bible weekly

- Only 37 percent of Americans can name all four Gospels

- 12 percent of Christians think Noah's wife was Joan of Arc

- A survey of graduating high school seniors revealed that over 50 percent thought that Sodom and Gomorrah were husband and wife

- A considerable number of respondents to one poll thought that Billy Graham taught the Sermon on the Mount

- 75 percent of Americans believe that the Bible teaches that God helps those who help themselves

It is neither from the ill-formed clichés of modern Christian preachers nor from the overtly anti-Christian antagonists (whether in the form of secularists, communists, socialists, humanists or pro-sodomite debate groups who masquerade beneath the banner of civil rights) that men of integrity should expect to gain a proper attitude and appreciation of the Mosaic system of law.

THE CHIEF APOSTLE SUMMARIZES THE CONTINUING FUNCTION OF CORPORATE LAW

It is from here—the Bible, specifically 1 Timothy 1:5–11—that the Christian is obliged to begin the construction of his concept on where the jurisdiction of self-government should end, and that of civil authority should begin. The apostle summarizes the ever-necessary and continuing use of the divine Hebrew civil code as the standard by which all modern governments will be judged (with expository commentary inserted):

1 Timothy 1:5–11

Verse 5: Now the end of the commandment is charity out of a pure heart, and of a good conscience, and of faith unfeigned:

- The purpose of pastoral preaching (giving *external* commandments) is to provide a clear basis upon which an individual man can regulate himself *internally*. The *private* impact of a *public* sermon on Mosaic Law should produce pure agape love, a good conscience, and uncontaminated faith.

- The necessity of mankind to self-govern according to the standards of truth (commanded by the Creator) remains the goal of God's divine law as it shares the public platform of civil government as well as the private platform of a person's conscience.

- That standard, and *only* that standard, must be identified and enforced by civil authority when men refuse to govern themselves.

- Government enforcement of any principle at variance with God's Word is illegitimate and tyrannical.

- Prioritizing self-government at the expense of righteous civil government is an absurd non sequitur as it denies the relationship clearly shown between civil and self-government, which is demonstrated throughout the entire Old Testament and reaffirmed in the New (specifically restated in verse 5, above).

Verse 6: From which some having swerved have turned aside unto vain jangling;

- The divisive issue of genealogical debates relating to Hebrew law stems from comments made earlier in this context. (See 1 Timothy 5:4.) By fixating on doctrinal arguments related specifically to genealogical debates,[9] which were directly related to legal questions of property ownership, inheritance, private rights, succession ceremony, societal status, and personal economics in general, the more important matters of justice, mercy, and faith were being neglected.

Verse 7: Desiring to be teachers of the law; understanding neither what they say, nor whereof they affirm.

- Emphasizing that *external* obedience to a civil code, while simultaneously neglecting *internal* issues of faith and personal repentance, is a means to gain heaven after death, is impure error.

- To neglect what is most important is to inadvertently suggest that external obedience is all that is necessary in order to earn heaven after death. Such is "vain jangling" nonsense, out of harmony with the obvious teachings of Moses, who penned the very civil code used as the "proof text" of ignorant and unqualified teachers.

Verse 8: But we know that the law is good, if a man use it lawfully;

Verse 9: Knowing this, that the law is not made for a righteous man, but for the lawless and disobedient, for the ungodly and for sinners, for unholy and profane, for murderers of fathers and murderers of mothers, for manslayers,

- Divinely inspired principles of civil government, written and demonstrated by the Hebrews, are very good, but are not enforced against individuals who self-govern according to a conscience built with righteous standards. The law was made for the "lawless"—those who refuse to self-govern by legitimate standards of conscience.

Verse 10: For whoremongers, for them that defile themselves with mankind, for menstealers, for liars, for perjured persons, and if there be any other thing that is contrary to sound doctrine;

Verse 11: According to the glorious gospel of the blessed God, which was committed to my trust.

- The public law, demonstrated by the God of Moses, is *not* made in such a way so as to encourage an illegitimate standard of personal conscience and self-government. They must work in harmony to provide the best atmosphere for proper self-governed liberty to exist. The two issues of external crime and internal conscience are tied together by the final mention of "sound doctrine." Those classes of criminals listed in verse 10 (above) have acted against a wholesome public standard that discouraged them prior to their actions. This provides justification for their punishment.

- In contrast, the doctrines of Bastiat, for example (revered by conservatives and Libertarians), are in direct disagreement with this truth of the Bible. Bastiat preferred the absence of law beyond the point of bodily harm, which denied the eternal purpose of law. All one need do is attempt to apply this flawed theory of civil government to family government (or any other for that matter) to see the error clearly. Are children best served in the absence of rules, except those that forbid them to bite one another? Should those same children be expected to later flourish as adults amidst a government that approaches human conduct in the same way? More than forty Bible writers respond with solidarity, "No and no!"

- Light shines forth amidst the darkness of sin, a two-pronged harmony between the inward conscience and outward civil law. The purest civil code is that which best discourages the personal and individual violation of the self-governed conscience. The most impure (evil) civil code is that which best encourages the personal and individual violation of the self-governed conscience. What could be more clearly demonstrated from the Bible than this? Internal conscience and external civic law must both reflect the same absolute truth to remain legitimate! A best-ordered society is one where con- science and government remain in agreement, based upon the only true fixed standard of truth. (See Romans 13:5 and previous notes on 1 Timothy 1:5, above.)

- Moses's system of law forbade any polytheistic* or pan- theistic† outward act of idolatry. Such religious practices were entirely eradicated under His leadership. Though it is true that most all forms of pagan idolatry at that time routinely inflicted bodily injury upon innocents, it is also true that *some* did not. Yet, Moses did not cherry- pick between which forms of idolatry did inflict physical harm upon others and which did not. He outlawed them all. But he did not pretend to punish or investigate pri- vate opinion by means of civil authority. Thus, Bastiat and Moses (in effect—God) are at variance on where the line must be drawn that shows where self-govern- ment ends and civil authority begins.

- As was briefly mentioned in the previous paragraph, if a foreigner allowed to live among them was privately, in his heart of hearts, a friend of paganism, Moses did not authorize any inquiry into that man's private opin- ions, but he did forbid that such a man use speech as a political action against the law of God, which forbade the act of idolatry. The modern American (unfortu- nately, all three characters from our opening parable: the atheist Libertarian, the Christian conservative, and the liberal Democrat) would reject such a law, claiming it "a violation of religious freedom protected by the First Amendment," but the fundamentalist Christian (as opposed to the typical) knows very well that

---

* **Polytheism** is belief in, or worship of, *multiple gods* or divinities. The word comes from the Greek words poly+theoi, literally "many gods." Most ancient reli- gions were polytheistic.

† **Pantheism** is the view that God is everything and everyone - and consequently that everyone and everything is God.

> participation in demon-inspired false religions are not
> true exercises of liberty.

Moreover, if he also happens to be a careful student of American history, he further discerns that the founders produced the First Amendment for two reasons: 1) To exclusively limit the power of the federal tier of government, in contrast with state government, which was deliberately left unfettered in this particular area; 2) To restrict sectarian strife among competing brands of Christianity at that time.[10]

It was assumed America was a "Christian nation" far beyond the mere cliché moderns are so accustomed to hearing. *Our entire legal system was constructed upon biblical law! The thirteen original states codified the entire Decalogue of Moses, straight out of the Bible.*

Dr. Clarence Manion, former Dean of Notre Dame's School of Law, writes: "More than 200 years after William Penn, the Supreme Court of the United States, deciding the case of the Church of the Holy Trinity vs. the United States asserted that: 'This (the United States) is a religious people. This is historically true. From the discovery of America to this hour there is a single voice making this affirmation.' The decision, then, thoroughly reviews the fundamental documentary history of our country: the Charters, the Commissions, the official Proclamations, and finally the Constitutions of all the States of the Union. The Court then concludes: 'There is no dissonance in these declarations. These are not individual sayings or declarations of private persons; they are organic utterances; they speak the voice of the entire people...There is a universal language pervading them all having but one meaning: they affirm and reaffirm that this is a religious nation.'"[11]

- In the aforementioned example of biblical law as it relates to "religious freedom," you can see where God draws the line to identify the end of self-government and the beginning of civil government. God draws the line between the "lawless" and the "righteous." Striking the divinely determined balance is the only point where authentic liberty can be completely experienced, and it is drawn in a very different place than where Americans are presently willing to abide. This fact of life in modern America (reluctance to obey God in polity) has *not* increased our liberties.

"This case," the judge wrote, "will proceed under Ecclesiastical Islamic Law." So said Circuit Judge Richard Nielsen of Tampa, Florida, in March of 2011.[12] A re-read of the classical Roman poet Publius Vergilius Maro's Latin epic, "The Aeneid," which describes the legendary tale of the "Trojan Horse,"* is in order! Ongoing attempts within this free nation to systematically introduce Islamic "Kadhis Courts" (which is the Islamic precursor to Sharia Law), under the guise of "religious freedom," threatens the American justice system and, as a result, all American liberties. Make no mistake! Kadhis Courts and Sharia Law are wholly incompatible with the American system of constitutional government, because the Islamic system is antagonistic to biblical law, upon which our legal system was thankfully constructed.

Religious freedom, as it was understood in the founding era, proposed the public expectation that citizens should politely tolerate incoming divergent cultures and religions, with the caveats that such incoming religions could *not* be tolerated in the event their tenets threatened the bodily health or general liberty of any other American citizen.[13] Kadhis Courts and Sharia Law in the United States threaten both ... violent Jihadists notwithstanding.

Make no mistake here! (Read slowly if necessary.) America's immigrant Muslim population should be *kindly* tolerated and *politely* extended the freedoms to which they are entitled, but they must be restricted from the covert usurpation of American Constitutional Law just as aggressively as others are restricted from overt acts of physical terrorism! At present, examples of all three characters on the American political stage (whether they be Libertarians,[14] conservatives,[15] or liberals[16]) have shown signs of irrational conformity to this game of Islamic legal and political exploitation, right along with Judge Nielson.

A dire warning is immediately necessary for all Americans: The Muslim will not cease to exploit the secular humanist rationale—what is purported as "religious freedom" in America—as a means to conquer it in strict obedience to the sixth pillar of Islam, which requires legal and political takeover of all nations! Therefore, the Muslim

---

* The **Trojan Horse** was a mythological device used during the Trojan War. It was a large wooden horse on wheels, which was delivered to the gates of Troy as a supposed tribute by the Greeks. Secretly, however, the horse was made hollow and filled with Greek soldiers, who came out at night and opened the city gates to let in the Greek army and attack the city.

should not be allowed to practice his religion on American soil unless and until he is willing to officially denounce an entire hostile portion of his religious obligations (the sixth pillar of Islam), according to the Koran, which reads:

> (V.2:190) *Al-Jihâd* (holy fighting) in Allâh's Cause (with full force of numbers and weaponry) is given the utmost importance in Islâm and is one of its pillars (on which it stands). By *Jihâd* Islâm is established, Allâh's Word is made superior, (His Word being *Lâ ilaha illallâh* which means none has the right to be worshipped but Allâh), and His Religion (Islâm) is propagated. By abandoning *Jihâd* (may Allâh protect us from that) Islâm is destroyed and the Muslims fall into an inferior position; their honour is lost, their lands are stolen, their rule and authority vanish. *Jihâd* is an obligatory duty in Islâm on every Muslim, and he who tries to escape from this duty, or does not in his innermost heart wish to fulfill this duty, dies with one of the qualities of a hypocrite. Narrated 'Abdullâh bin Mas'ûd رضي الله عنه: I asked Allâh's Messenger صلى الله عليه وسلم "O Allâh's Messenger! What is the best deed?" He replied, "To offer the *Salât* (prayers) at their early fixed stated times." I asked, "What is next in goodness?" He replied, "To be good and dutiful to your parents." I further asked, "What is next in goodness?" He replied, "To participate in Jihâd in Allâh's Cause." I did not ask Allâh's Messenger صلى الله عليه وسلم anymore and if I had asked him more, he would have told me more. (*Sahih Al-Bukhâri*, Vol.4, *Hadîth* No.41).[17]

In his exposé on the sixth pillar of Islam, Don Boys, PhD, states:

> Muslim theologians make it very clear that Jihad means holy fighting and speaks of "numbers and weaponry" so that no one would be mistaken as to their obligations. It is disingenuous and dishonest for Muslim clerics to dance around this issue: Do they believe the Koran is a divine book to be obeyed by everyone in everyplace at every time? If a Muslim cleric affirms that he does not believe in holy fighting then he does not believe (or obey) the Koran or he is dishonest. Keep in mind that Mohammed gave Muslims permission to lie if the lie supports Jihad, espionage or to keep peace among the women

in his harem. Every Muslim on earth has the obligation to fight in holy wars in promoting Islam and even to do it with the right attitude! If he does his duty but with some reservations or reluctance, he will die with the qualities of a hypocrite! So, they must fight with gusto or suffer in Paradise.[18]

- The increase of what we shall call "imaginary liberty" must necessarily reduce "genuine liberty." The "imaginary liberty" to practice a religion which overtly and/ or covertly undermines citizen safety and constitutional law in the United States *reduces* religious liberties in the name of "religious liberty." The "imaginary liberty" of a woman's "right to choose," which stems from the "court-granted" (as opposed to "God-given") "right to privacy" eradicates the life—the "genuine liberty"—of the innocent child. This state of American affairs has fostered a culture where liberty has been systematically deleted from our American experience by various means of judicial oligarchy, legislative tyranny, and the mishandling of the executive offices by means of "living constitution" sedition that chaffs at the proof of constitutional intent within the Federalist Papers. What is the "tool of choice" in every case of liberty's erosion? *The pretend ability of sinful human beings to create and grant rights to other human beings.*

- The public law, demonstrated by the God of Moses, was *not* made in such a way so as to encourage an illegitimate standard of personal conscience and self-government. Today, these two separate jurisdictions must work in harmony to provide the best atmosphere for proper self-governed liberty to exist. If any other "liberty" exists, whether by the existence of bad law or the absence of good law, such "liberty" is little more than an invitation into a form of sinful bondage (i.e., pornography, prostitution, homosexuality, adultery, drug abuse, promiscuity, gambling, aborticide, etc.). These are not true liberties! Government fails its divine mission when it condones slavery to such vices (whether actively or passively), because it fails to point the way to "emancipation," which is *only* found in truth. Jesus said, "Ye shall know the truth, and the truth shall set you free."

- As was alluded to on at least two occasions prior to this remark, E.C. Wines explained that under the administration of Moses, "If [a foreigner] was, in his heart, a friend of paganism, Moses did not authorize any legal inquiry into his private opinion."[19] Furthermore, words that were unlawfully spoken in Israel amounted only to the level of high misdemeanor, not treason. Even in America today, though we have strayed from what used to be the case, particular words or expressions of speech remain against the law, despite the misunderstood meanings of our First Amendment.

- The external influence of moral standards in law do not guarantee an internal change in the citizen; but the external influence of immorality enshrined by either the presence of bad law or the absence of good law does guarantee pain and suffering for all individuals at the cost of true liberty.

- Morality in law does eliminate excuses from the individual soul on judgment day. Meanwhile, a government made up of laws that fight against truth (whether passively or actively) does not aid the church mission of evangelism, and therefore violates the broad principle of Acts 17:26–27.

The American sociolegal drift away from God's standard of law over the past two hundred years, as you have just read chronicled throughout this chapter and will see in even greater detail in the chapter to follow, is astonishing. This illustrates why the antinomianism of the libertarian/anarchist movements, in addition to the secularism of both the liberal and conservative movements, each remain distinctively antagonistic toward fundamental Christianity on *many* points. (I acknowledge this is not the case on *all* points.) It is also why the theological versions of antinomianism, which come in a variety of assortments, flavors, and mutations (insisted upon by those who errantly pit the laws of Moses against the law of Christ, and conclude that the church should have nothing to do with politics) is also at odds with the Bible.

The absence of bad law = good. Absence of good law = bad. Bastiat certainly believed the former, yet did not recognize the latter. Meanwhile, Moses, Jesus, Luke, and Paul explained and understood both.

With God's blessing and favor, proper teaching, and through books like the one you hold in your hand, perhaps America can understand once again.

CHAPTER 7: REVIEW QUESTIONS

Enjoy this quiz at http://peacemakersinstitute.com/smb-quiz.

1. What two simple experiences introduce every human to divine natural law as soon as they are born?

2. What external superintending authority is temporarily necessary in order to teach a child the difference between the dangerously deceptive powers of pain and pleasure?

3. Paternal assistance demonstrates what type of limited distribution of power between central and local authority?

4. What should proper civil government teach man?

5. What did Professor Archibald Hodge of Princeton warn?

6. If the antagonist of Mosaic Law believes he has found enough rough spots that justify total rejection of Mosaic Law in modern government, shouldn't he also completely reject the New Testament as well?

7. From where is the Christian obliged to begin the construction of his concept on where the jurisdiction of self-government should end and that of civil authority begin?

8. How many classes of sinners did Paul believe Mosaic Law was designed to punish?

9. Was the public law of Moses designed in such a way so as to encourage an illegitimate standard of personal conscience? Should our system do otherwise?

10. Is the absence of bad law good?

11. Is the absence of good law good?

12. Should the laws of Christ be pitted against the laws of Moses?

Chapter 8

Authorized: Fifteen Classes of Conduct to Forbid

IN CHAPTER 2, I explained that the first table of the law given to Moses by God was "vertical" law. It dealt with self-governance. It spoke to man's private relationship with God. We reviewed James Madison's explanation given to his very young (nine years old in 1785) nation that the first table of the law was not within the realm of civil government's jurisdiction. In contrast, I further explained that the second table was "horizontal" law. It dealt with human-to-human interactions. Today, it forms the basis of all good civil governments of the world. If it is not the officially recognized basis of any particular government in our world, then that government is not good and its evil should be confronted by Christianity until the wrong is righted. Period.

It should be understood by obedient men that any attempt to use civic power to enforce the first table of the law is tyrannical and abusive. All civic authorities who attempt this demonstrate incredulous arrogance by playing equal with God. Moreover, it is also arrogant for civil authority to refuse to involve themselves with the implementation of the second table of the law. It is a rebellious failure for civil government to attempt to act as if some part of the second table is better suited (in their opinion) to have been placed on the first table of the law. "That is a private matter, and not the role of government" is the excuse of rebels. It is a new kind of defacto tyranny. It is dereliction of duty—the tyranny of desertion.

The second table of the law begins by protecting the root of all successful civilizations—marriage. Good government does not pretend to create or authorize marriage. Marriage is outside the purview of mankind, because man is subject to natural laws that pre-exist him. As with the law of gravity, civil government is obliged to recognize

156

marriage's preeminence in nature, protecting and preserving it from ignorant forces. The public consequences for failing to do so cannot be overstated. Marriage, like gravity, does not need protection. It's the fools who trifle with both that can bring down an empire. Thus, the first horizontal law of the second table is, "Honor your father and mother" (see Exodus 20:12).

The marriage institution is the God-authorized gift of creative power handed to human beings. It is the power for a male and female to create immortality. Every child created in the intimacy of sexual intercourse is an endless soul that will inevitably live in either heaven or hell for all eternity. The recipients of life granted by this natural law of procreation are told to honor their parents, personally, and honor the concept of marriage, corporately.

The second law of the second tablet of stone extends this logic to the issue of life itself. While the institution of marriage creates life and the recipient of life is told to honor those who granted it to them, the next commandment states, "Thou shalt not kill" (see Exodus 20:13). In these first two commands of the second tablet, the institution that creates life is protected, and life itself is safeguarded. The logic unfolds more with the addition of the third command on this table of the law. "Thou shalt not commit adultery" is charged to the man and wife.

In summary, the child is told to honor the marriage institution. The citizen is told not to murder the life created by the marriage institution. The husband and wife are told to honor one another within the marriage institution. The first three laws that directly apply to the rationale for civil authority's existence deal with the foundation of civil government, which is family government.

Any modern government that exclusively and erringly claims these first three laws of God are "personal issues" and "not the role of civil government" are in rebellion against God's law. Americans who have bought in to this French Enlightenment malarkey have committed a great sin, and in doing so, helped secularists of all stripes to destroy the America that once was.

Without healthy and stable family government beneath the upper structures of civil authority, there is no basis for private property. Children are born with a sin nature and eventually awaken to the corrupt desire to steal from others. If this sin nature is not crushed by family government (good parenting), the civilization that results over time will no longer experience private property. Once the poorly parented child reaches adulthood, the heightened and inadequately restrained drive of the theft instinct will inevitably institutionalize itself into the act of communal confiscations. The sin nature reaches its pinnacle in the abolishment of privately owned property, and after the theft it is repurposed and labeled as "state-owned." Thus, the tyranny of theft permeates the fabric of all governments where the first three laws of God for government are ignored, abandoned, or rejected, or relabeled as "private matters."

The civil government will either protect the sanctity of marriage and the lives it creates or it will eventually be destroyed by institutionalized theft. In modern times, institutionalized theft has many titles: Communism, Statism, Fascism, Socialism, Marxism, Totalitarianism, Globalism, etc. For these reasons (and many more), the second table of Mosaic Law places the issue of private property as the fourth priority of civil government (and not the first). Once civil government is charged with a responsibility to preserve and protect its own foundation of family government, the fourth commandment declares, "Thou shalt not steal" (see Exodus 20:15).

The final two commandments, "Thou shalt not lie" and "Thou shalt not covet," are similarly situated as those previously mentioned (see Exodus 20:16–17). These final issues of dishonesty and jealousy are sinful tendencies that will criminally jeopardize the acquisition and maintenance of private property in all civilizations. The logic of their position in the flow of the commandments becomes clear when one considers that adultery cannot be committed without some degree of both lying and covetousness, yet it *would* be possible to engage in some form of simple dishonesty or jealousy without committing adultery. The cases of the second table of the law rise and fall together, and with them the civilizations that choose to obey or ignore God's unchanging law.

Ironically, the secular Libertarian philosophy vocally protests institutionalized theft, which is merely the symptom of familial failures. They refuse to give permission for civil government to fulfill its obligations to God's law by protecting and preserving the family government. By doing so, the secular Libertarian guarantees an eventual loss of private property, all while insisting that protection of private property is the loftiest purpose of civil government.

FOUR DIVISIONS OF LAW NO LONGER NEEDED

Those portions of the Hebrew codex that are "done away in Christ" have been done away for a logical reason. Their purpose was accomplished, and they are no longer necessary for the common good of society. 1) Special holidays; 2) Food ordinances; 3) Sacrificial animals, and the rational purpose of; 4) Circumcision laws were very logically done away through the completed work of Christ. All four divisions had served their good and wholesome purpose until they were no longer needed by mankind. In order to show the logic of these four categories of law being those specifically listed as done away in Christ, and also to show the illogic of Him having done away with anything other than those four divisions, I will briefly explain the four categories we have discussed throughout this writing. This should by no means be considered exhaustive, but it should suffice to demonstrate the sensibleness of the New Covenant's impact upon Old Testament law and our present relationship to it.

SPECIAL HOLIDAYS

It is widely accepted by Christian teachers concerning the special holy days (holidays) portion of Old Testament law that all the major holy days of Israel pointed to Christ. Of six major holy days, the first three pointed to Christ's death, burial, and resurrection. The final three pointed to His consummate second coming.

A "For Sale" sign mounted next to a "Will Build To Suit" sign is needed until land is finally sold. Once it is purchased by a new owner, the signs are no longer necessary. All this is true despite the fact that construction has not immediately begun after the transaction was completed. In a similar sense, Christ paid ransom for a universe kidnapped by sin. His return to possess what is rightfully His (and whatever delay in doing so He may find beneficial) has little bearing on His divine property rights and intents. So it stands to reason that the three feasts that point to His consummate return to earth are also done away by the New Covenant, even though they have yet to be realized in history. Even before His death, much less His resurrection, Christ exclaimed from the cross, "It is finished!"

Consider the *Passover*, for example. The Passover both commemorated the salvation of the Hebrew slaves in Egypt, by the blood of the

paschal* lamb, and represented the crucifixion of Christ for the salvation of all who repent. Jesus was literally sacrificed on the Passover
holiday. In 1 Corinthians 5:7 Paul explains:

> For even Christ our Passover is sacrificed for us.

Next, the *Feast of Unleavened Bread* was symbolic of Christ lying
in His grave. He was literally raised from the dead during the celebration of this Jewish festival. Jesus said it this way as He used bread to
symbolize His body broken for us:

> This is the bread which comes down from heaven, that one
> may eat of it and not die. I am the living bread which came
> down from heaven. If anyone eats of this bread, he will live
> forever; and the bread that I shall give is My flesh, which I
> shall give for the life of the world.
> —JOHN 6:50–51, NKJV

The third holy day, the *Feast of Firstfruits,* was fulfilled in Christ
as well. It was during this festival that the Day of Pentecost occurred.
The Holy Spirit was delivered to the New Testament Church in an
extraordinary way on the literal Day of Pentecost, as described in
Acts chapter 2, and the catalyst for the gift of the Holy Spirit was
Christ's "firstfruits" resurrection.

> But now Christ is risen from the dead, and has become the
> firstfruits of those who have fallen asleep. For since by man
> came death, by Man also came the resurrection of the dead.
> For as in Adam all die, even so in Christ all shall be made alive.
> But each one in his own order: Christ the firstfruits, after-
> ward those who are Christ's at His coming.
> —1 CORINTHIANS 15:20–23, NKJV

Again, the previously mentioned three holidays pointed to Christ's
death, burial, and resurrection. The final three are indicative of His
return. While it is acknowledged that those issues associated with
Christ's second coming have not yet been realized in history, the holidays associated with these yet unfulfilled events have been absolved

---

* A **paschal lamb** is one slaughtered and eaten on the eve of the first day of
Passover. Ex. 12:3–11.

from further observance by His initiation of an unstoppable chain of events begun at His triumphal resurrection. In other words, since the price of His blood has been paid, the consummation of all things associated with that purchase is inevitable.

Israel was accustomed to the use of trumpets for making special announcements (see Numbers 10:1–10). Scholarly evidence proves Christ was not born in the dead of winter as today's world is accustomed to believing through the Christmas holiday; rather, He was literally born during the *Feast of Trumpets* and announced by a combination of angels and a blazing star in the night sky. The Feast of Trumpets also pointed toward Christ's judgment against all sinners on the earth. A great announcement of Christ's judging the earth is preceded with the sound of trumpets. This is mentioned in Revelation 8:2. It is no coincidence that the season of His first coming (during the Feast of Trumpets) will be the season of His consummate return to earth. Paul tells us that when Christ returns, a trumpet shall sound.

The *Feast of Tabernacles* was symbolic of the great harvest enjoyed by the Hebrews who obeyed God after leaving Egypt. It also pointed forward in time to the day that God would enjoy the final harvest of the redeemed saints gathered together from the earth through Jesus their Redeemer, mentioned in Revelation 21:3.

The *Feast of Atonement* was celebrated to commemorate the washing away of Israel's sins. It was fulfilled in Christ, who will finally return to cleanse and abolish all sin and corruption from the earth.

FOOD ORDINANCES

It is imperative at the outset to look at this subject with eternal vigilance. When we say that this particular portion of the Hebrew law (the food ordinances) is done away in Christ, it means that we are no longer bound to a particular restricted diet as a New Testament rule of faith and conduct. It does *not* mean, however, that the natural principles of healthy eating and drinking connected to the wisdom of the Hebrew diet have also been discarded. What was or is generally more or less healthy for a human to eat did not necessarily change in a physiological way when Jesus rose from the dead on resurrection morning. Long before Moses was born, God made the distinction between animals He considered "clean" and those He considered "unclean" in the following verses:

Of every *clean* beast thou shalt take to thee by sevens, the
male and his female: but of *unclean* beasts by couples, the
male and his female.
—GENESIS 7:2, GNV, EMPHASIS ADDED

Then Noah built an altar to the Lord, and took of every *clean*
beast, and of every *clean* fowl, and offered burnt offerings
upon the altar.
—GENESIS 8:20, GNV, EMPHASIS ADDED

While Genesis does not explain which animals were clean and
unclean, it is obvious that Noah knew the difference. (A thousand
years later Moses explained the difference, and we'll discuss that in
a moment.) Noah was commanded to take seven pairs of the *clean*
animals, and only one pair of *unclean* animals. This large population
difference between *clean* and *unclean* animals is usually attributed
to the need to make sacrifices to God, but with Moses's explanation
given a thousand years later, we are able to understand that it was
also because the animals called unclean were those that ate other
animals. Moses shows us that the *unclean* animals are all those classified by science as carnivores or omnivores.* Animals that were
considered *clean* were those that consumed a vegetarian diet called
ruminants.† This same logic is extended to the creatures living under-
water and in the air. Predatory birds and fish are *unclean* and vice
versa. The scientific data revealed in recent history overwhelmingly
proves the Hebrew dietary laws to be evidence of remarkable scientific foreknowledge—knowledge only possible by divine inspiration.

It is important to point all this out because this distinction between
clean and unclean was made around one thousand years before
Moses was born. Since that is the case, it is clear that this distinction remains to this day. The New Testament does not forbid us from
choosing a healthy diet. Rather, it merely ends the exclusive distinction given to Israel's dietary laws, as explained to Moses, and it does
so for a very specific reason I will explain in a moment.

---

* A **carnivore** generally means an animal that only eats other animals, as contrasted with an herbivore (plant-eater) or omnivore (animal for whom both plants
and animals are regular and important parts of the diet).
† **Ruminants** are mammals that are able to acquire nutrients from plant-based
food by fermenting it in a specialized stomach prior to digestion, principally
through bacterial actions. The process typically requires regurgitation of fer-
mented ingesta (known as cud), and chewing it again.

Here is a brief explanation for the creation of the dietary laws given to Moses:

> I am the Lord your God, which have separated you from other people. You shall [distinguish] put difference between clean beasts and unclean... Therefore shall ye be holy unto me, for I the Lord am holy, and have separated you from other people that ye should be Mine.
> —LEVITICUS 20:24–26, GNV, EMPHASIS ADDED

There are a few passages popularly cited from the Scriptures as a means to teach that the Hebrew food ordinances were done away in Christ that are particularly inappropriate to prove their expiration. For example, we often hear that Jesus said it was not what went into a man's mouth that defiled him, but what came out of his mouth, sourced by his heart. (See Matthew 15:11–17.) Transliterators of the New American Standard Bible and the New International Version Bible, for example, inappropriately took the Mark 7:19 version of Jesus's remarks described in Matthew 15:11–17, and added the phrase, "In saying this, Jesus declared all foods clean," which is not found in *Textus Receptus.** This is unfortunate and very misleading, particularly when one considers the rule of interpretative law that says, "Interpret the implicit by the explicit." (See Rule 9 based upon principles gleaned in a reading of Matthew 13:10–11, 18–23 in the *Appendix of Biblical Law.*)

Here is why I bring up Rule 9. Jesus's *explicit* statement was nothing more than a reminder to the Hebrew people of Moses's doctrine properly understood, and a rebuffing of the Talmud and Mishnah (non-inspired laws created by Jewish leaders, and not found in the inspired Old Testament/Torah). Jesus was in no way changing the Mosaic food ordinances during these comments. If anything, He was defending the spirit behind them as intended by Father God, who designed them, and Moses, who delivered them to the people.

In his *Gates of Eden* November/December 1997 publication, Dr.

---

* **Textus Receptus** (Latin: "received text") is the name subsequently given to the succession of printed Greek texts of the New Testament which constituted the translation base for the original German Luther Bible, the translation of the New Testament into English by William Tyndale, the King James Version, and most other Reformation-era New Testament translations throughout Western and Central Europe. The series originated with the first printed Greek New Testament, published in 1516.

Daniel Botkin writes concerning this particular textual misunderstanding of Jesus:

> The controversy in this chapter was not over whether or not pork is kosher. The controversy was initiated when the scribes and Pharisees criticized Yeshua's disciples for eating with unwashed hands. The Pharisees believed that *Shibia,* an evil spirit, sat upon the hands at night, and this spirit had to be washed off before eating *(Dake Reference Bible,* 42, fn.r). Jewish beliefs about hand washing are stated in the Talmud:
>
> 1. "A person who despises the washing of the hands before a meal is to be excommunicated" (Ber. 47b).
> 2. "Whoever eats bread without first washing his hands is as though he had sinned with a harlot" (Sot. 4b).
> 3. "Whoever makes light of the washing of his hands will be uprooted from the world" (Sot. 4b).
> 4. "Whoever eats bread without scouring his hands is as though he eats unclean bread' (Sot. 4b)."
>
> These beliefs are rooted in the traditions of men, not in the commandments of God. When Yeshua made His statements that seem to be "declaring all foods clean," He was simply saying that kosher food does not become unkosher if it is eaten with unwashed hands. He was simply disagreeing with the belief that "whoever eats bread without scouring his hands is as though he eats unclean bread." His final statement makes it clear that this was the point He was making: "…but to eat *with unwashed hands* does not defile the man," (See Matthew 15:20).[1]

This is one of a few examples where the Scriptures are sometimes incorrectly used to prove a point in violation of Rule 9 in the *Appendix of Biblical Law,* which I again repeat, "Interpret the implicit by the explicit."

Truly, a straining of various texts in the New Testament is unnecessary to make this point that the Mosaic food ordinances are done away in Christ. Christians do not require any more evidence than what follows in order to dismiss the food ordinances as a New Testament rule of faith.

The Scriptures teach us that in the mouths of two or three witnesses let everything be established. Two witnesses is sufficient.

Three witnesses is more than sufficient. This was a Hebrew principle of law (see Deuteronomy 17:6) that Peter clearly understood and explored in his rooftop vision concerning food ordinances:

> On the morrow as they went on their journey, and drew near unto the city, Peter went up upon the house to pray, about the sixth hour. Then waxed he an hungered, and would have eaten: but while they made something ready, he fell into a trance. And he saw heaven opened, and a certain vessel come down unto him, as it had been a great sheet, knit at the four corners, and was let down to the earth. Wherein were all manner of four footed beasts of the earth, and wild beasts and creeping things, and fowls of the heaven. And there came a voice to him, Arise, Peter: kill, and eat. But Peter said, Not so, Lord: for I have never eaten anything that is polluted, or unclean. And the voice spake unto him again the second time, the things that God hath purified, pollute thou not. *This was so done thrice*: and the vessel was drawn up again into heaven.
>   —ACTS 10:9–16, GNV, EMPHASIS ADDED

It is from here, during Peter's rooftop vision, that we will find sufficient evidence for both the *explicit* command from God ending food ordinances as a rule of faith in our new covenant, and the *implicit* purpose of that *explicit* command is found very clearly presented. "Arise, Peter: kill, and eat!" says the Lord *three* times. (Again, according to Deuteronomy 17:6: "In the mouths of two or three witnesses let everything be established.") This is the *explicit* command.

What is the *implicit* command Peter inferred by the *explicit?*

> And while Peter thought on the vision, the Spirit said unto him, Behold, three men seek thee. Arise therefore, and get thee down, and go with them, and doubt nothing: For I have sent them...And he said unto them, Ye know that it is an unlawful thing for a man that is a Jew, to company, or come unto one of another nation: but *God hath showed me, that I should not call any man polluted, or unclean.*
>   —ACTS 10:19–20, 28, GNV, EMPHASIS ADDED

In contrast with Jesus's previous instructions to His disciples to "go not into the way of the Gentiles" (see Matthew 10:5-7), the previously limited scope of the gospel mission was expanded to a global and multinational enterprise. It is not hard to understand why Peter connected the unclean animals of his vision with the unclean Gentiles who ate them. The prophet Ezra had done the same thing. Ezra connected the uncleanness of Gentiles with their eating habits in his stern warning to the Hebrew people:

> And now, our God, what shall we say after this? for we have forsaken thy commandments, Which thou hast commanded by thy servants the Prophets, saying, The land whereunto ye go to possess it, is an unclean land, because of the filthiness of the people of the lands, which by their abominations, and by their uncleanness have filled it from corner to corner. Now therefore shall ye not give your daughters unto their sons, neither shall ye take their daughters unto your sons, nor seek their peace nor wealth forever, that ye may be strong and eat the goodness of the land, and leave it for an inheritance to your sons forever.
>
> —EZRA 9:10–12, GNV

No wonder Peter was argumentative during his vision on the rooftop! The Torah forbade fellowshipping with unclean pagan people, and Jesus had previously said similarly. The prophet Ezra had been very clear. As opposed to eating the proverbial *badness* of the land, the Israelites were to be separate from the unclean Gentiles and eat the *goodness* of the land!

While I admire Christians who thoughtfully obey the Mosaic dietary laws motivated by a lovingly sincere desire to honor the Lord, I respectfully disagree with the argument that these dietary laws are still in force. While some Christians, like, for example, Dr. Botkin, argue that Peter's rooftop account does *not* abolish the food ordinances as a rule of faith in the New Testament, citing Peter's interpretation of the vision's *implicit* meaning explained in Acts 10:28 ("God hath shown me, that I should not call any man polluted, or unclean."), I do not believe we have the intellectual authority, much less the biblical authority, to *accept* the *implicit* meaning of any text while *rejecting* the reasonable and *explicit* command that provided it.

So long as an explicit text of Scripture can be taken literally, it absolutely should be. This is the case with the message from God in Peter's vision. There is nothing unreasonable or strictly figurative about the explicit command from heaven for Peter to accept formerly forbidden foods. I offer this example: Imagine if I had recently purchased a round-trip ticket on Delta Airlines in order to attend a conference in Dallas, Texas. Suddenly, while resting on a balcony one evening, I received a vision from God and saw a Delta Airlines passenger jet floating down in front of me. The voice of God rang out from behind the jet and said, "Do not board this plane!" It would make perfect sense if I later explained the vision to my wife, saying, "The Lord showed me I am not to attend the conference in Dallas, Texas." In that situation I would have interpreted the implicit by the explicit.

But what if I illogically rejected the *implicit* at the expense of the *explicit*, or vice versa? If I rejected the *implicit* meaning of the *explicit* command, I would wisely cancel my Delta tickets only to foolishly purchase new tickets from *another* airline and continue with my original plans to attend the conference in Dallas, Texas. I might try to justify my disobedience by saying, "Hey, God didn't say I couldn't fly *United* Airlines!" By acting out in such a way, I would be in disobedience to the clear message sent by God.

In contrast to these examples, when we find a statement in the Bible that is metaphorically impossible to take literally, like, for example, Jesus saying He was "bread," or saying He was a "door," then we have the right to accept it as figurative language used for the purpose of pointing to a literal truth. Wouldn't it be absurd if we began bowing down to worship loaves of bread or began saying, "Excuse me, Jesus," every time we opened a door in order to get somewhere?

The point should be clear. Logic dictates that it is not possible to extrapolate an *implicit* meaning from nothing, so an *explicit* meaning is required. The explicit "take, kill, and eat" of the vision was to be taken in harmony with the implicit "call no man unclean on account of what he eats" message from heaven. The two were intrinsically connected and inseparable, and this information, as you'll soon see, was essential for the international spread of the gospel.

If the Gentile people's choice of unclean food was no longer forbidden, then neither was Peter forbidden to keep their unclean company. Until he came under duress in Galatians 2:11–14, Peter had tied those two issues of unclean food and the unclean Gentiles who ate them together. Ironically, there is evidence that Peter vacillated between sometimes obeying the *explicit* meaning of his own vision at the expense of the *implicit*, and vice versa. It apparently depended upon which group he was trying to please at the moment. For this kind of flawed thinking and doctrinal error, Peter would eventually suffer an embarrassing rebuke from the apostle Paul.

> And when Peter was come to Antioch, I withstood him to his face: for he was to be condemned. For before that certain came from James, he ate with the Gentiles: but when they were come, he withdrew and separated himself, fearing them which were of the circumcision. And the other Jews played the hypocrites likewise with him, insomuch that Barnabas was led away with them by that their hypocrisy. But when I saw, that they went not the right way to the truth of the Gospel, I said unto Peter before all men, If thou being a Jew, livest as the Gentiles, and not like the Jews, why constrainest thou the Gentiles to do like the Jews?
> —GALATIANS 2:11–14, GNV

Peter was shown that the food choices associated with the customs of the Gentiles he was commissioned to evangelize were no longer *forbidden*. If that was true, then it connected that he should no longer insist that such Gentiles be forced to adhere to the former Mosaic laws concerning food *after* they were finally brought to the knowledge of Christ. Peter, Barnabus, and others failed to embrace the full scope of this covenant change from God, and were rebuked by the apostle Paul for contradicting that change in front of born-again Gentiles. Had Peter obeyed both the *explicit* and the *implicit* message of his own vision, he might have avoided this rebuke from the apostle.

To be clear, Peter was not told to stop eating or even preferring historically "clean" animals. If you are a New Testament Christian you will do well to remember the age-old reality that some animals are classified by the Bible as "clean" and some are classified as "unclean." This differentiation between animals is connected to the Edenic fall and remains a distinction until the Edenic curse is removed by the Messiah during the Millennial Kingdom and the Eternal Ages to come afterward. The classification between clean and unclean animals was neither created by Mosaic Law nor annulled by Christ. It was merely recognized by Mosaic Law and codified into their national laws as a code of conduct. In the New Covenant, you are free in your liberty through Christ to eat as healthy as you choose, as often as you can, but it is critical to say that you are no longer legally bound by heaven to the dietary laws of the Mosaic covenant.

I have no doubt that we'd all live longer if we would be more careful about heeding the lessons taught by the Mosaic diet, but the release from them was not necessarily because bacon became a great bodily benefit during the resurrection of Jesus Christ, or that iguanas, pigs, and various rodents changed their eating and living habits, thereby becoming a "clean" and healthy New Testament cuisine. This new covenant's divine release from dietary restrictions was quite intentional. Even today, despite our technological advances in shipping and transportation, it is impossible to journey to many places for an extended stay, much less to live there, and maintain an honorably kosher diet.

A couple of years ago, during a brief visit from an orthodox Jewish friend of ours, my family discovered that in order for him to keep the Hebrew food laws, we needed to have special food shipped to our community in advance of his arrival. After carefully reviewing our grocery stores and restaurants, my Jewish friend remarked, "An orthodox Jew could not live in Sioux City and keep the Mosaic dietary obligations without continual problems." Even amidst the prosperity of the Midwestern United States, it is true that in many communities we simply do not have enough kosher food locally available to sustain a proper and enjoyable variety of kosher foods.

If that is the case today, we can imagine the impossibility of taking the gospel to every corner of the earth 2,000 years ago while trying to adhere to the Hebrew dietary codes. The rationale for an abolition of the Mosaic food ordinances is simply this: The church of Jesus Christ for the first century was almost entirely made up of Jews. Had the Jews of the early church not been released from these food restrictions, they would have been unnecessarily hindered from obeying the (Acts 1:8) geographic emphasis of the Great Commission! But it's still important to eat as healthy as you can in order to enjoy a long life, friends!

SACRIFICIAL ANIMALS

Concerning sacrificial animals, we don't need to sacrifice a lamb (or any other animals once required by Mosaic Law) on a stone altar to atone for our sins anymore. Jesus Christ was the lamb slain for the sins of all mankind.

CIRCUMCISION

Circumcision is similarly situated to the expiration of the Mosaic dietary laws. We are not required by the New Testament to participate in this practice, nor are we forbidden to partake in it for the health benefits of doing so. Historically speaking, most males born in Western civilization have been circumcised. All my sons have been circumcised as a matter of reproductive health.

Concerning the many laws surrounding the issue of circumcision, we are no longer required to remove the foreskin of the male penis, as a continual reminder that our entire race (Jews) only exists because of a reproductive miracle in the old bodies of Abraham and Sarah, who became pregnant by supernatural means. Furthermore, we do not require that same sign upon the foreskin of all male reproductive organs to point to a future moment when the greatest reproductive miracle the earth has ever seen would eventually take place...a virgin miraculously impregnated by the Spirit of God with the Son of God, the Messiah of the whole human race.

The purpose of circumcision, on one hand, pointed *backwards* in time to the holy inception of the Jewish race—a people who would have never existed without a miraculous intervention from heaven in their sex organs. Abraham's descendants—the circumcised—were called upon to produce the world's Messiah! Secondly, circumcision's purpose was to point *forward* in time to our Savior's supernatural arrival, and this purpose was also accomplished.

Circumcision law began before Moses was even born, in the covenant of Abraham. From the standpoint that without a reproductive miracle, the Jewish race would never have existed, circumcision, the cutting of the male reproductive organ, was the cornerstone of all Hebrew law to eventually develop. Around 435 years later, when Moses established and formalized Hebrew law, he continued the sacred tradition of Hebrew circumcision passed on from the time of Abraham, and it became the foundational rite of all ceremonial Mosaic Law. Thus, it stands to reason that if Christ fulfilled and abolished the ceremonial law of Moses, this specific law is significant to point out as done away in Christ. As you can see, there are beautiful and logical reasons for each of these particular four divisions of Hebrew law being done away. I digress.

SOME PARTS ARE STILL NEEDED

In the previous chapter, we began viewing instructions from the Chief Apostle to Timothy. The letter was written, among other things, to explain the portions of the law that most certainly *were not* done away in Christ. Dovetailing beautifully with the logic of those things that *were* done away, we are reminded in his letter to Timothy that much of the law remains very needed in our world. It would *not* make any sense to claim it is done away with in Christ, because its purpose has *not* been completed and is still very much needed for the common good of society.

> But we know the law is good, if a man use it lawfully; Knowing this, that the law is not made for a righteous man, but for the lawless and disobedient, for the ungodly and for sinners, for unholy and profane, for murderers of fathers and murderers of mothers, for manslayers, for whoremongers, for them that defile themselves with mankind, for menstealers, for liars, for perjured persons, and if there be any other thing that is contrary to sound doctrine...
>
> —1 TIMOTHY 1:8–10

Does this fallen world still require a just way to handle murderers, thieves, perjurers, abusers, kidnappers, rapists, sexual predators, and cheats? Of course it does. So Father God, Christ and the Holy Spirit, in their infinite wisdom, shared with the apostle Paul why it would *not* be appropriate to mistakenly believe that Christ abolished those portions of the divine law, as it was explained to Moses, that apply to these ongoing issues civilization must continue to confront until Christ's physical reign upon the earth. They are still very much needed.

The antagonist insists that Christ, for some reason, died to abolish the entire law, but they have never been able to explain why! Why would He do such a thing? What would be the point? We can give very logical explanations for the four specific categories of law the New Testament clearly states were completed through the ministry of Christ. It makes perfect sense that their mission in history was fulfilled. It makes absolutely, positively no rational sense at all why one would insist Christ did away with the other areas. Shall we now all become very clever and sophisticated on new and better methods for punishing murderers, thieves, perjurers, abusers, kidnappers, rapists, sexual predators, and cheats? Of course not!

In review, we learned in Chapter 2 that the law of God was intentionally divided *physically* on two tablets of stone. We also learned that the law of God was divided *relationally* through a vertical and horizontal application. Later, in Chapter 5, we saw how the law was divided *tribally* and *functionally*. In this chapter we will solidify the fact that the law is divided according to *need*. The portions no longer needed were done away in Christ. The portions that are still needed remain a vital part of our New Testament. Jesus declared (I paraphrase from Matthew 5:18), "not one jot or tittle of the law shall pass away until the purpose of the law is fulfilled."

What could be more obvious? The purpose of all is not fulfilled, folks.

THE LINE WAS ALREADY DRAWN BY GOD

As was stated in the previous chapter: "Internal conscience and external civic law must both reflect the same absolute truth to remain legitimate! A best-ordered society is one where conscience and government remain in agreement, based upon the only true fixed standard of truth." According to 1 Timothy 1:5–11, the line that distinguishes between where self-government ends and civil government appropriately begins is drawn by the inspiration of the Holy Spirit in the Old and New Testaments; it is summarized by referencing fifteen categories of citizen behavior where God's law is very much needed by our world.

Therefore, *maximum personal liberty* for a citizenry can only be achieved when civil government fulfills its biblical obligations to God; and it is appropriate, in this light, for civil government to enact appropriate penalties against the following issues culled from 1 Timothy 1:5–11, which states the following fifteen classes of conduct to forbid:[2]

1. **Lawless**—Greek: anomos (GSN-<G459>), contempt for law; no rule of moral conduct. Translated "lawless" (1 Tim. 1:9); "without law" (1 Cor. 9:21); "unlawful" (2 Pet. 2:8); "transgressor" (Mark 15:28; Luke 22:37); and "wicked" (Acts 2:23; 2 Thess. 2:8).

"Lawless," in verse 9, is a reference to those who act without lawful control. For example, Daniel 7:24–25 points to a future time when the Antichrist influence will seek to change "times and laws," by which we infer he will make laws contrary to the exclusively Hebrew standard of divinely inspired law among the nations of the world. Daniel's words are recorded as a warning to future generations. It begs the question of our modern lawmakers (and our present preachers in the pulpits), "What spirit motivates you in your work of public lawmaking?" Or in the case of some preachers, "What spirit motivates your 'ecclesiastical law-trouncing?'" The state of affairs in America is no secret—the lawmakers make bad law in direct proportion to deviation from divine law instruction in our churches. Whereas in many churches divine law is passively untaught, in others it is aggressively taught against in the name of alleged "grace." This situation should send chills among Christians, particularly in the light of 1 John 4:3, which warns that the spirit of antichrist "even now already is it in the world."

2. **Disobedient**—Greek: anupotaktos (GSN-<G506>), not under subjection; undisciplined. Translated "disobedient" (1 Tim. 1:9); "not put under" (Heb. 2:8); and "unruly" (Titus 1:6, 10).

This is a reference to disobedience against legitimate authority. Authority is legitimized only through their own submission to divine law. Civil disobedience is *not* forbidden, but encouraged when civil authority strays from the divine and conscience makes such civil disobedience unavoidable.[3]

3. **Ungodly**—Greek: asebes (GSN-<G765>), irreligious (1 Tim. 1:9; 1 Pet. 4:18; 2 Pet. 2:5; 3:7; Jude 1:4, 15).

Law in civil society should restrict exterior acts of irreligion/antireligion. Philosophers like Plato argued that atheism was a danger to society and "should be punished as a crime."[4] John Locke, a founder of Western religious liberty and inspirer of our Declaration of Independence, who wrote the famous *Two Treatises on Government*, argued that atheists should not be given privileges of full citizenship.[5] Consider the tragic and dangerous irony—America now tends to punish public expressions of *faith* with anti-free speech censorship!

It was not until 1961 that the US Supreme Court overturned the laws of state religious tests which refused public elected office to atheists.[6] Up until that time, eight state constitutions refused atheists from public service in elected office.[7] This ruling was a direct violation of states' rights using the incorporation of the Fourteenth Amendment of 1868 (which many believe should be repealed) as a vehicle for violating the original principles of the First Amendment—which forbade *only* the Federal government from sanctioning particular brands of sectarian Christianity.

In contrast to the founding era heavily influenced by Christian faith and Bible literacy, where the irreligious were forbade from office by force of public sentiment and state law, several modern polls show that more than 50 percent of today's Americans would vote for a "well-qualified atheist for president."[8]

4. **Sinners**—Greek: hamartolos (GSN-<G268>), transgressors of law. Translated "sinner" forty-one times and "sinful" (Mark 8:38; Luke 5:8; 24:7; Rom. 7:13).

Divinely inspired principles of civil government, written and demonstrated by the Hebrews, were not made for individuals who self-govern according to a conscience built with righteous standards. The law was made for the "transgressors of law"—those who refuse to self-govern by legitimate standards of conscience. "Transgressors of law" must be punished by the magistrate according to the laws they transgress.

Again, as stated earlier, civil authority exists to punish those who will not govern themselves. A two-pronged harmony between the inward conscience and outward civil law must be maintained for true liberty to exist. A best ordered society is one where conscience and government remain in agreement, based upon the only fixed standard of truth. (See Romans 13:5 and previous notes on 1 Timothy 1:5 above.)

5. **Unholy**—Greek: anosios (GSN-<G462>), totally depraved; the utter opposite of holiness within and without. Only [used] here, and [in] 2 Timothy 3:2.

In contrast with laws made against what is "profane," an act that we infer is committed publicly (explanation is to follow in point #6), the word "unholy" seems to refer to a concealed act of total depravity. In effect, the alleged "right to privacy" created by modern US courts for the purpose of legalizing infanticide, can neither be substantiated by the United States Constitution or biblical law. In contrast to the Scripture's authorization of government to criminalize acts of "private" depravity, we see a continuing slide away from this kind of law today in the United States.

In a publication highlighting the expansion of legalized depravity, David Miller, PhD, writes of Justice Antonin Scalia's mixture of regret and indignation penned in his dissent of the landmark case *Lawrence v. Texas:*

When US Supreme Court Justice Scalia penned the dissenting opinion for his fellow dissenters, Justices Rehnquist and Thomas, in *Lawrence v. Texas*,[9] which made homosexuality a constitutional right, he correctly concluded that if homosexual marriages are to be legalized, no legal/rational basis exists upon which to forbid any other sexual relationship, regardless of the perversity involved:

"State laws against bigamy, same-sex marriage, adult incest, prostitution, adultery, fornication, bestiality and obscenity are likewise sustainable only in light of *Bowers'* validation of laws based on moral choices. Every single one of these laws is called into question by today's decision" (*Lawrence...*, 2003, italics in orig., emp. added).

Scalia added:

This effectively decrees the end of all morals' legislation... [N]one of the above-mentioned laws can survive rational-basis review' (*Lawrence...*, emp. added; cf. Bonney, n.d.). The increasing encroachment of polygamy is a direct manifestation of Scalia's prediction.[10]

Prior to January 1 of 1970, when American state governments first began adopting the European unbiblical theory of "no-fault divorce" in opposition to the precedent of Mosaic Law, divorce was far less rampant in the United States. "No-fault divorce was pioneered by the Bolsheviks following the Russian Revolution of 1917. Before the Revolution, churches, mosques and synagogues defined family life. It was the ecclesiastical law of the various denominations that controlled the family, marriage and divorce. For example, the official registration of birth, death, marriage, and divorce was the responsibility of the church parish. Under these nonsecular laws, divorce was highly restricted (though never completely unavailable, as no major religion in Russia completely disallowed divorce). The 1918 Decree on Divorce eliminated the religious marriage and the underlying ecclesiastical law, by replacing them with civil marriage sanctioned by the state. Divorce was obtained by filing a mutual consent document with the Russian Registry Office, or by the unilateral request of one party to the court. The divorce law under the Bolsheviks did not penalize the husband with alimony, child support or debtor's prison for nonpayment. The two partners were entirely free of legal obligations to each other after divorce."[11]

"No-fault" divorce in the United States originated in the state of California effective January 1, 1970. It was signed into law by then Governor Ronald Reagan, himself a divorcee, and later, the only American President in history, to date, to have been divorced.[12] Harold B. Clark, in his 1944 publication of *Biblical Law*, writes: "Early English and American Law, unlike the Roman law, did not allow divorce, [for the purpose of allowing] another marriage—unless by special legislative dispensation—though it did allow a decree of separation from bed and board for adultery or cruelty. One American state—South Carolina—still adheres to the scriptural injunction, "Those whom God has joined together let not man put asunder." A few states, in an effort to be Scriptural erred on the side of being too strict. Allowing divorce for adultery only was argued "[the statute] is now neither adequate nor appropriate to the life of the community and tends to produce a train of perjury, bigamy and bastardy."[13]

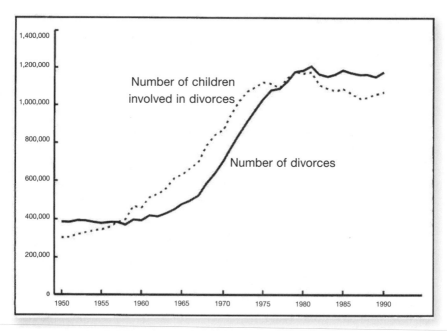

Contrast the "old American" legality of divorce, stemming from biblical law, versus the "new American" legal description of the grounds necessary for receiving a "no-fault" divorce, which is cavalierly referred to as "irreconcilable differences." Findings published by the *Enrichment Journal* on the American rate of divorce show that the (current) divorce rate for first marriages is 41 percent; the divorce rate in America for second marriages is 60 percent; the divorce rate in America for third marriages is 73 percent. Leo Gozich writes: "Over the last 27 years, since no-fault divorce legislation swept across the nation like a tidal wave, America has witnessed a 279-percent increase in the divorce rate; and the fallout for families—Christian and non-Christian—and society has been tragic."[14] The exterior effect of civil law upon society is here clearly illustrated: In 1900, with a family-court legal system patterned after the Mosaic and Christian precedents of law, the divorce rate among *pagans* in the United States was *one half of 1 percent* compared to our present rate of divorce that hovers around the 50 percent mark. A verifiable spike in the divorce rate, directly correlating with the adoption of "no-fault divorce" law, is illustrated by the chart shown on previous page.[15]

6. **Profane**—Greek: bebelos (GSN-<G952>), not fit to attend public worship (1 Tim. 1:9; 4:7; 6:20; 2 Tim. 2:16; Heb. 12:16).

As referenced and contrasted with the *private* act of depravity (in point #5), that which is "profane" has *public* connotations, as one who commits such an act is publicly forbidden from worship in the local church.

Throughout the history of American law, due to the influence of biblical case law, the public act of "profane speech" was appropriately criminalized through much of our national history. Based upon the history of Maryland's blasphemy laws, it was not until the 1930s that American law experienced a final federal intrusion against the sovereign state's right to punish public acts of the "profane." Despite today's revisionist warping of the original intent of the federal government's First Amendment, a very watered-down neo-definition of "illegal profane speech" is still enforced by the FCC on radio and television broadcasts between 6 and 10 p.m. every day in the United States.

> The "Hicklin test" [was] a legal concept stemming from the English case R. v. Hicklin (1868), in English Common Law. Put simply, it stated that a legislature could outlaw anything that "depraves and corrupts those whose minds are open to such immoral influences and into whose hands a publication of this sort might fall."
>
> The test [asked] "whether the tendency of the matter charged as obscenity is to deprave and corrupt those whose

minds are open to such immoral influences." If yes, then such was declared to be obscene. Also, the "Hicklin Rule" looked at the content in question not as a whole, but only in part. In other words, it did not consider the questionable material in relation to whole content. The Hicklin test influenced the courts in the United States until Roth v. United States (1957) when it was superseded [by the Supreme Court.][16]

A contrast of two cities in the state of Virginia back in 2008, further illustrates local attempts to maintain some remnant of biblical law in modern American ordinances. In *Virginia Beach,* a citizen could still be fined $86.00 for a public profane act, whilst the city of *Norfolk* decided (that same year) to suddenly drop its ordinance against public profane acts, claiming the ordinance was suddenly "unconstitutional."

In the case of Paul's letter (1 Tim. 1:9) which empowers human governments to criminalize what is considered "profane," it can be demonstrated, through the history of American law, how anti-Christian "deconstructionism" has slowly untethered American law from its divine biblical authorization. A brief history of American law as it relates to the permission of God for civil authorities to punish that which is (obscene) "profane" follows:

- In 1697, Massachusetts general laws punished blasphemy with up to one year in jail and/or a fine of as much as $300.00.

- In 1838, Abner Kneeland was convicted of blasphemy against Christianity and sentenced to sixty days in prison. When he got out of jail he angrily left Massachusetts and moved to Iowa where he started a "Utopian" village called Salubria. The village fizzled when Abner died in 1844. (Salubria was located close to today's small town of Farmington, Iowa.) Abner was the last US citizen to be imprisoned for blasphemy.

- In 1868, any written text that would corrupt the morals of youth was forbidden by law.

- In 1879, Maryland prohibited public acts of blasphemy. Article 72 Section 189 stated: "If any person, by writing or speaking, shall blaspheme or curse God, or shall write or utter any profane words of and concerning our Saviour, Jesus Christ, or of and concerning the Trinity, or any of the persons thereof, he shall, on conviction, be fined not more than one hundred dollars, or imprisoned not more than six months, or both fined and imprisoned as aforesaid, at the discretion of the court."

- In 1928, Charles Lee Smith became one of the last US citizens to be convicted and fined for blasphemy. He was found guilty by a court of law in the state of Arkansas.

- In 1947, something was considered a violation of obscenity laws in the United States if reading the material caused someone to lust.

- In 1957, anything written without "redemptive social value" was forbidden by law.

- In 1972, the State of Maryland's Court of Appeals suddenly declared blasphemy law "unconstitutional."

- In 1977, the State of Pennsylvania enacted a new anti-blasphemy law. It was not struck down by the District Court until June 30, 2010.

- In 1987, Oregon joined Maryland's earlier 1972 decision to declare its own blasphemy laws "unconstitutional."

- In 1997, the ACLU won against obscenity laws designed to restrict the obscene use of technology, and the terrible decision effectively censored Congress from further attempts to do otherwise.

7. **Patricides**—Greek: patraloas (GSN-<G3964>), those who strike or slay their father.

8. **Matricides** —Greek: metraloas (GSN-<G3389>), those who strike or slay their mother.

9. **Murderers**—Greek: androphonois (GSN-<G409>), those who take any human life contrary to law.

10. **Whoremongers**—Greek: pornois (GSN-<G4205>), male prostitutes.

The Proceedings of the National Academy of Sciences (PNAS) concluded through a 1990 study that there are roughly 23 full-time prostitutes per 100,000 citizens in the present United States, despite the fact that prostitution is illegal in every state except Nevada.[17] This begs the question: How much more prevalent would this illicit industry become in the event that it were legalized?

In 2001, it was estimated that about 292,000 American youth were at risk of becoming victims of commercial sexual exploitation. Approximately 55% of street girls engage in formal prostitution. Of the girls engaged in formal prostitution, about 75% worked for a pimp. Pimp-controlled commercial sexual exploitation of children is linked to escort and massage services, private dancing, drinking and photographic clubs, major sporting and recreational events, major cultural events, conventions and tourist destinations.[18]

About one-fifth of these children become entangled in nationally organized crime networks and are trafficked nationally. They are transported around the United States by a variety of means—cars, buses, vans, trucks or planes, and are often provided counterfeit identification to use in the event of arrest. The average age at which girls first become victims of prostitution is 12–14. It is not only the girls on the streets who are affected—for boys and transgendered youth, the average age of entry into prostitution is 11–13. The lifestyle of such children revolves around violence, forced drug use and constant threats.[19]

Despite current efforts of libertines, Libertarians, and liberals, to further legalize prostitution in the United States—expanding the criminal enterprise beyond the borders of Nevada in defiance to biblical law, masquerading under the banners of "state's rights" or "personal freedom"— staggering facts of criminal abuse to children remain directly associated with the alleged "personal right to pay for and enjoy consensual sex" that make its legalization of great concern to many citizens.

The many issues we have just discussed serve as examples where the biblical authorization of government is substituted for secular/ atheist ideals that incorrectly cloak abusive sins with clear societal ramifications under the false pretense of "liberty." Prostitution, for example, is an abuse of personal liberty that clearly infringes upon the liberties of women and children (as proven above); it is an unhinged Libertarian secularism that further threatens the already fragile institution of the family in the United States, by ignoring biblical law and legal precedents found since the inception of government on the colonial American frontier. Finally, it is an example of how secular Libertarianism masquerades as those who want a return to "originalist American constitutionalism" while actually promoting a further slide *away* from historic jurisprudence and applying the God-scorning "values" of the French Enlightenment that were clearly rejected by contemporary American founders.

The threat that is *greater* than intrusive and unconstitutional federal government is the *pretend* ability of an elected official or government agency to allegedly grant a "right" or "freedom" to another human being. The pretend ability to grant an alleged "right" that has at no time in all of recorded history been granted to men by their Creator, is the ultimate and most powerful enemy of limited government in America today. Prostitution is no more a "right" or "personal choice" than adultery or pedophilia. God's law lists all as crimes. Man-created and/or man-granted rights purported by Libertarianism unchain civil authority from natural law, which is on exhibition through the biblical model of a loving family. (The only greater offense to the natural law of family government is the unnatural mainstreaming of homosexuality—which is also left unfettered by modern Libertarianism in the name of "freedom.")

11. **Sexual perverts**—Greek: arsenokoitais (GSN-<G733>), those guilty of unnatural sexual practices.

For a more detailed explanation, see the information provided within point number 5 (unholy). Suffice it to say the handling of this particular criminal item forbidden by both Testaments is the most popularly cited source of rejection of Mosaic Law by both Christians and non-Christians today. It is often summarized as the assumed "unfair treatment of gay people." For this reason, I will exert special effort to accurately explain the position of Mosaic Law—God's law for the present day—as it should and must relate to those tempted to yield to their unnatural lusts.

"[The term] 'Crime against nature' [was] a legal term used in published cases in the United States since 1814[20] and normally defined as a form of sexual behavior that is not considered natural and is seen as a punishable offense in dozens of countries and several US states. Sexual practices that have historically been considered to be "crimes against nature" include homosexual acts, anal sex, bestiality and necrophilia [sex with the dead]. The term is sometimes also seen as a synonym for sodomy or buggery."[21, 22]

As described earlier in point number 5 (unholy), the ability for American law to properly criminalize any sexual "crime against nature" was suddenly ruled "unconstitutional" by the United States Supreme Court in *Lawrence v. Texas* (2003).

Professor Walter Wink, a promoter of modern theological liberalism at Auburn Theological Seminary, published an article to discredit what he called the apostle Paul's "unambiguous condemnation of homosexual behavior." In response to Paul's letter of Romans 1:26–27 Wink writes: "Paul knew nothing of the modern psychosexual understanding of homosexuals as persons whose orientation is fixed early in life, or perhaps even genetically in some cases."[23] Wink does not stop by merely attempting to discredit the fuddy-duddy and ignorant nature of the inspired New Testament writers, either. Naturally, the Mosaic Law quickly finds its place beneath the heretical antinomian cross hairs of his professorship. Believing himself to have loaded and fired the silver bullet of sexual freedom, Wink blasts: "The Old Testament nowhere explicitly prohibits sexual relations between unmarried consenting heterosexual adults ... "

Later, he poses the argument that the Genesis 19 incident of attempted gang rape in Sodom had nothing at all to do with homosexuality. Apparently, Dr. Wink believes God was angry because the men of Sodom wished to demoralize and humiliate Lot's male guests by treating them like women. It wasn't about homosexual men anally raping heterosexual men, it was about heterosexual men demasculinizing heterosexual men.

Dr. Wink characteristically portrays Levitical law in a deliberate way to leave any biblically uneducated reader under the impression Moses was a horrible and hateful monster of fascism. Under Moses, the poor and innocent persons with a "natural" desire for intercourse with the same sex were savagely executed. Moses was harsh and cruel! The reader is left to suppose that either God was unkind and unjust, or else Moses did not get his ideas from God in the first place. (We must infer that a gentle, pro-gay God sat in heaven, wringing his hands, tolerantly weeping as the dark human tragedy of Mosaic Law brutalized His chosen people.)

Dr. Wink does not miss any opportunity to feed the dragon. We are told by Wink that in Israel, under Moses's leadership, masturbation was tantamount to murder ... lefthandedness was met with repugnance ... a man who dared have sex with his wife during her menstrual cycle was subject to being stoned, strangled, burned, or flogged. What is twisted to sound like a list of horrors nearly takes your breath away. As in most liberal and antinomian criticisms of God—the historical context and rationale of Levitical law that would defend the uprightness of Moses, God, and Scripture, is strategically avoided. (For example, though Dr. Wink would falsely suggest otherwise, husbands were not executed for having sex with their wives during their menstrual cycle. If they were caught and prosecuted in the court of law under testimony of two or three witnesses, the very worst case scenario was exile from the camp. For this reason alone, the requirement for multiple witnesses, it is more likely that it was *never* prosecuted in all of Jewish history.)

Masturbation was *not* tantamount to murder. This may be the most absurd of Wink's contortions, for only moments prior to making this outlandish claim he suggests Mosaic Law never forbade the broad definition of all things considered fornication. (At this point, I roll my eyes. You can't have it both ways, Professor.) Rest assured, there was no death penalty for masturbation. Further, the implied abuse and ridicule of innocent little left-handed children—a scenario any compassionate soul may be tempted to imagine while reading the slog from Wink's unwashed soul—probably did not occur either.)

Wink pretends that a one-size-fits-all punishment was leveled against every infraction against God's law. This is untrue, of course. How quickly and conveniently the critics forget that our common phrase "the punishment must fit the crime" is little more than a derivative of Moses's cliché "an eye for an eye and a tooth for a tooth." In short, Moses's legal system was exceptionally advanced, noble, fair, equitable, and just. Could it be severe when appropriate? Absolutely! If you were to commit incest with a child (Lev. 18:6), you did receive the death penalty. If you were to torture your children by burning them alive as an offering to the demon-god Molech (Lev. 18:21), you did receive the death penalty. (I certainly have no present-day objection to this level of penalty for such evils, by the way.) But let's clarify the issues of severe punishment for a moment.

In ancient Israel, just as it is today, hate was an internal sin that, if left unchecked, would lead to the commitment of murder. Murder brought the penalty of capital punishment if, and only if, one was convicted by two or three witnesses. But hate was not a criminal offense punishable by the magistrate in Israel. Admitting that you hated someone was not a criminal offense punishable by law. Similarly, lust was an internal sin that, if left unchecked, could lead to the commitment of all kinds of forbidden criminal acts. Lust could crescendo as incest, pedophilia, necrophilia, bestiality, homosexuality, or adultery. The outward commitment of these crimes brought the penalty of capital punishment. But lust was not a criminal offense punishable by the magistrate in Israel. A Hebrew citizen who battled with sexual lust, in any form—whether it was incestuous lust, adulterous lust, homosexual lust, heterosexual lust, or lust by any other label—was never uncompassionately dragged across the encampment and burned alive or stoned for having experienced abominable and sinful thoughts! If a teenaged child with raging hormones asked his parent for help, confessing a battle with lustful thoughts and desires, they no more hauled him off and flogged him to death than you would your own beloved children today. Similar points could be made about the connection between internal greed and external theft, etc. Hebrew citizens were warned, however, by the existence of God-inspired criminal statutes that harmful acts of sexual deviancy *in any form* outside the natural marital relationship as ancient Israel understood it, would be met with severe consequences.

Criminal cases where citizens were caught actively engaging in some form of sexual perversion were independently reviewed and tried on a case-by-case basis, much as we do in America today. There was no one-size-fits-all punishment for all crimes big and small. You were considered "innocent until proven guilty" by the mouths of two or three witnesses, much like we enjoy in our present nation. (As has been mentioned throughout this book, much of our present Western civilization, particularly the American legal system we take for granted, are based upon the principles of Mosaic Law.) The scholars seem to understand, as explained by the prolific authority of Hebrew law, Dr. H.B. Clark: "...the fact that a [Mosaic] law prescribes a certain penalty does not preclude the imposition of a lesser punishment. So in the case of Adam, though the prescribed penalty for eating the forbidden fruit was [immediate] death, he was condemned merely to work for a living."[24]

It is a fascinating thing to witness how the very same American humanist who eagerly vilifies the sacred laws of our Bible will (in the same breath) praise and extol the supposed virtues of ancient Greece and Rome—denying the influence of Moses upon American law, while proudly announcing "American law was inspired by the great Roman Empire and Greece!" This is amusing when you recall that, according to the well-known historical record, both Greece and Rome are said to have been far more severe than the law of God carried out by Moses. Clark writes again: "In ancient Greece and Rome, capital punishment was common for even petty crimes."[25] This, in contrast with Moses, whose system of law forced the thief to pay financial restitution for what was stolen.

The modern theonomist is sometimes angrily asked, "Do you support the death penalty for homosexual persons?" Firstly, the biblically correct answer to this question, at face value, is "no," because, like Moses and Christ, we do not believe the government should ever pretend to in any way punish mere thoughts. This scenario belongs to the jurisdiction of self-government. (The outward criminal act confirmed by three witnesses, however, is entirely another issue, and the prosecution of such was as highly unlikely to be proven in court as the married couple copulating during a menstrual cycle, of which we spoke a moment ago.)

The unlikely, even preposterous scenario under which the sodomy crime *could* be legally prosecuted, was *deliberate* and *by design*! Through the existence of this law in Israel, the public at large was strongly warned they should not participate in this form of sexual deviancy. If caught in the bodily act, the physical law would mirror the eternal law of God. A maximum sentence of capital punishment reflected the reality of eternal damnation in the next life—a much more severe consequence than mere physical death. Therefore, to leave any lesser of an impression of its severity in God's eyes to mankind was a true injustice. The issue of judicial discretion where the law prescribes a range of punishments from minimum to maximum verdicts was logically applied by the Hebrew authorities, just as we do in our American courts today. The conscience and the civil law operated upon the same standard of truth, so that true justice could be enjoyed by the Hebrews. Yet, the punishment for this particular crime of sodomy was probably never carried out in the nation's entire history, due to the difficulty of prosecution. In the case of sodomy, the law justly and honorably served as an eternal warning to Hebrew society and the world at large. Civil authorities could only judge external behavior, but the Supreme Judge of the Universe, Jehovah

Elohim, would make eternal judgment against the intents of the heart. Sinners be warned!

Secondly, in response to the hostile and popular question, "Do you support Moses's death penalty for homosexuals?" I would not support the *death penalty* in our modern world for *any* sexually forbidden act, until and unless we *first* reassign the proper range of penalties (with a *maximum* penalty of death for *adultery*).

Here's why I believe my position on properly criminalizing adultery, in particular, is of critical importance to the integrity of Christian theonomy. The authentic marriage, as enshrined by natural law (one man and one woman are required by nature to create a new life), is the standard-setter demonstrating the ultimate divine purpose of human sexuality. If the law of procreation (which men did not make and cannot change) is nature's (God's) sexual standard, then it should be aggressively defended by law as a first priority, as is commanded by the second table of Mosaic Law. Thus, a society that enables and encourages adulterous affairs and high divorce rates has no business executing capital punishment against persons caught in any other form of *substandard* sexual deviancy, until it has first protected the *standard* by which the substandard acts should be righteously measured and judged.

It is unfortunate that the recriminalization of adultery won't be happening in America anytime soon since so many of our present lawmakers are working on their second, third, and fourth marriages. Moreover, some of our religious leaders have fallen into adultery and divorce. Our congregations are overwhelmingly populated by a supermajority of parishioners who are guilty of adultery and divorce. (At this point, the reader may either choose to laugh or cry.) In the light of our sorry condition before God, I would recommend a measurable effort be made to first unscramble the rotten eggs of "no-fault divorce." Adultery should at least have a financial and legal consequence. It is far worse a crime than a simple traffic offense. Courts should begin by not awarding alimony to adulterers. This would be a step in a righteous direction.

The question humanity fails to answer as they review this biblical truth (that adultery should absolutely be entirely recriminalized in America)* is the question of *why* God made adultery a criminal offense in Israel in the first place. It is bizarrely difficult, it seems,

---

* A note to would-be antagonists who wish to claim that Christ's comment, "He that is without sin cast the first stone," was in any way intended to decriminalize adultery: careful study of this passage will prove this assumption to be untrue.

for our modern legal world to properly deal with adultery. Adulterers are treated with more leniency in America than drivers who receive traffic tickets by mail (thanks to the traffic cams); all this despite the fact that the adulterer's crime is a far more serious offense and causes much greater harm to society at large. To compare the evil of adultery to driving 55 mph in a 45 mph zone or failure to completely stop before making a red light right turn is laughable to anyone who has experienced the "never-ending torture of a living death" as it was once described by a parishioner of mine.

While there are many reasons to criminalize adultery, the most blatant is very simple. Beyond the obvious—that God said so—Moses did it because adultery was (and remains) entirely and inexcusably abusive to innocent children who suffered because of it. It may well be a present form of "socially acceptable" child abuse in America, but God does not view it lightly. Parents who engage in it are bad parents in dire need of immediate repentance for sins against their immediate and extended families.

Professor Wink makes this next statement the highlight of his overt agenda to vilify the Old Testament: "Persons committing homosexual acts are to be executed. This is the unambiguous command of the Scripture. The meaning is clear: anyone who wishes to base his or her beliefs on the witness of the Old Testament must be completely consistent and demand the death penalty for everyone who performs homosexual acts."[26] Finally, Wink writes something that is doctrinally accurate, yet in no way offers the rationale for God's criminalization of all forms of sexual deviancy. With regard to Wink's obvious defense of sexual impurity in the name of Christ (I tremble for him), Rev. Haddock of Sioux City once famously quipped: "The best way in the world to determine a man's real religious status is to find out where his sympathies are in a great conflict between opposing forces."

To put it simply, homosexuality remains a crime against nature today because God, Moses, Jesus, and the apostle Paul apparently knew something about it few moderns are willing to presently admit. In short, homosexuality has an alarming link to child sexual molestation, concealed as "helping the young homosexual to come out." It is an abusive behavior that "reproduces" by inflicting abusive behavior upon the young and innocent.

Dr. Peter Sprigg writes:

Homosexual men are far more likely to engage in child sexual abuse than are heterosexuals. The evidence for this lies in the findings that:

- Almost all child sexual abuse is committed by men; and

- Less than three percent of American men identify themselves as homosexual; yet

- Nearly a third of all cases of child sexual abuse are homosexual in nature (that is, they involve men molesting boys). This is a rate of homosexual child abuse about ten times higher than one would expect based on the first two facts.

"*These figures are essentially undisputed.* However, pro-homosexual activists seek to explain them away by claiming that men who molest boys are not usually homosexual in their adult sexual orientation. Yet a study of convicted child molesters, published in the *Archives of Sexual Behavior,* found that '86 percent of offenders against males described themselves as homosexual or bisexual.'[27] This does *not* mean that all, or even most, homosexual men are child molesters – but it does prove that homosexuality is a significant risk factor for this horrible crime.[28]

Dr. Timothy J. Dailey, Senior Fellow at the Center for Marriage and Family Studies of Family Research Council writes: "The Bulletin of the Menninger Clinic, for example, mentions 'seduction' among a list of other possible childhood experiences that could contribute to [homosex] attraction: 'There are a number of factors that occur in childhood which appear to be related to the development of homosexuality in adults. Such conditions as . . . homosexual experiences in childhood; seduction by adult homosexuals.'"[29]

Whether our present-day governments choose to criminalize sexually deviant behaviors or not, both Testaments of the Bible clearly warn that a natural "death penalty" has been irrevocably assigned to such acts. With that said, the truly loving thing to do, in the purest Christian sense, is to warn the would-be offender who is tempted by internal lust. This should be done the same way it was done under God's direction in 1534 BC by codifying serious legal consequences for such outward criminal acts. It is better to do that than to permit the *internal* sinner to pursue *external* evil (all while covering up the truth that his present course of actions will end his life prematurely and unnecessarily).

Ultimately, if we really "hated" homosexuals, we would encourage them to explore and enjoy their sexual fetishes, because the statistics produced by the Centers for Disease Control have shown us their habits will eventually kill them. But if we love them, in a biblical sense, we will tell them they are wrong morally *and* legally, whether they like it or not, and we will offer to help them find victory over their struggles against lust.

Rev. William Tvedt explains it this way:[30]

> I believe death is more than an event, but is more often a force of sin which produces death on multiple levels such as moral, emotional, spiritual as well as physical death. I believe the homosexual claims of a gay lifestyle being a viable alternative should be put to the reality test of statistical information. In so doing, I think we'll find that not only is it not viable, but inescapably under its own death sentence. Allow me to give you [three] clear examples:
>
> 1. Homosexual behavior significantly increases the likelihood of psychiatric, mental and emotional disorders, according to a study in the Netherlands. Youth are four times more likely to suffer major depression, almost three times as likely to suffer generalized anxiety disorder, nearly four times as likely to experience conduct disorder, four times as likely to commit suicide, five times as likely to have nicotine dependence, six times as likely to suffer multiple disorders, and more than six times as likely to have attempted suicide. This research comes from the Netherlands where homosexuality has been accepted and mainstreamed for years, negating the mindset that a lack of tolerance of homosexual behavior and lifestyle produces these psychoses.[31]
>
> 2. HIV/AIDS is rampant in the homosexual community. Epidemiologists estimate that 30 percent of all 20-year-old homosexually active men will be HIV positive or dead of AIDS by the time they are 30.[32] HIV infection rates more than doubled from 1997 to 2000 as safe-sex practices were abandoned. In Los Angeles

and five other major cities, one in 10 young homosexual or bisexual men is infected with HIV.[33]

3. The median age of death for those who regularly engage in homosexual behavior leaned in the direction of less than 50. The data suggest a "20- to 30-year decrease in lifespan because of substantially elevated rates of sexually elevated diseases...cancer and heart conditions, and violence among homosexual men and women."[34]

Reverend Tvedt continues:

The second expression of death after physical death is death to the moral conscience.

"Wherefore God also gave them up to uncleanness through the lusts of their own hearts, to dishonor their own bodies between themselves: Who changed the truth of God into a lie, and worshipped and served the creature more than the Creator, who is blessed for ever. Amen. For this cause God gave them up unto vile affections: for even their women did change the natural use into that which is against nature: And likewise also the men, leaving the natural use of the woman, burned in their lust one toward another; men with men working that which is unseemly, and receiving in themselves that recompense of their error which was meet. And even as they did not like to retain God in their knowledge, God gave them over to a reprobate mind, to do those things which are not convenient; Who knowing the judgment of God, that they which commit such things are worthy of death, not only do the same, but have pleasure in them that do them" (Rom. 1:24–28, 32).

We see Paul's reflection on Sodom and Gomorrah and the homosexuality practiced there that resulted in a reprobate mind or, one could say, a death of their moral conscience (void of moral judgment). Verse 32 says the actions are "*worthy of death.*" It is obviously a judicial statement of the mandate for capital punishment recorded in Leviticus 20:13 and apparently warrants a turning of the soul over to a state of depravity.

The first three expressions of death produced by homosexual behavior being physical, moral and social are minor in comparison to the fourth expression, which is eternal death.

The Scriptures speak of this in no uncertain terms. Those who practice the sin of Sodom and Gomorrah are in danger of eternal death.

"Even as Sodom and Gomorrah, and the cities about them in like manner, giving themselves over to fornication, and going after strange flesh, are set forth for an example, suffering the vengeance of eternal fire" (Jude 1:7).

The context of verse 7 is that of a list of those who suffered eternal judgment culminating with the citing of Sodom and Gomorrah's suffering vengeance of eternal fire. Clearly this is a warning for us today not to practice the sins of Sodom and Gomorrah lest we also suffer the same fate. The Apostle Paul also reinforces with undeniable clarity that those who practice homosexuality will not inherit the kingdom of God.

"Or do you not know that the unrighteous will not inherit the kingdom of God? Do not be deceived; neither fornicators, nor idolaters, nor adulterers, nor effeminate, nor homosexuals, nor thieves, nor the covetous, nor drunkards, nor revilers, nor swindlers, will inherit the kingdom of God" (1 Cor. 6:9–10, NASB).

As Christians, we must not be intimidated by the false charges of hate speech in light of what Paul the Apostle wrote in Colossians 1:28: "Whom we preach, warning every man, and teaching every man in all wisdom; that we may present every man perfect in Christ Jesus." If this is true, it is our responsibility to warn the gay community, that their lifestyle produces physical death, moral death, family death, societal death and finally, eternal death. As we can plainly see from scriptures and scientific research, the odds are against true happiness and fulfillment in the so-called 'Gay Lifestyle.' Our message should not just be a message of warning but also one of hope, repentance and forgiveness to those for whom Christ died."[35]

12. **Slave-traders**—Greek: andrapodistais (GSN-<G405>), kidnappers; those who steal [and make] slaves and sell and buy them, or who hold men for ransom.

It is routinely claimed by progressive historical revisionists in publications across our land that the Christians who founded America, more or less, reviled black people, and therefore (as liberal logic goes), modern Christians are haters of certain kinds of people too—just like the founders were. This is an interesting line of logic, to say the least.

In order for one to study our American history and arrive at this errant conclusion, one must opportunely ignore many points of fact. First, one must overlook the inconvenient records which reveal slavery was introduced to American colonies nearly two centuries *before* the American founders were born, which is to say they very much inherited the evil of slavery.

Next, one must further ignore that a *majority* of our 200 founding fathers *hated* slavery, and publicly decried its anti-Christian evil as a significant justification for the Declaration against England's pro-slavery policies.[36]

Finally, we must also ignore that it was primarily the influence of Quakers, Baptists, Presbyterians, and dozens of other Christian groups and organizations who worked in concert with the pre-dominantly Christian founders toward abolition.[37] In December of 1865, after nearly sixty years without any constitutional amend-ments (approximately two years after President Lincoln's famous Emancipation Proclamation), through the 13th Amendment to the Constitution, the outlawing of slavery in America was completed.

Charles Coulter, an African American copy editor for the Sioux City Journal and Kansas City Star, once argued in a published op-ed that present-day judicial activism was both good and necessary, because after all, it was (allegedly) the catalyst for the freedom to engage in interracial marriage. Yet he failed to mention that, if it had been left up to those same courts a century earlier (1896), the black community at the time of *Brown v. Board of Education* (1954) would have still been enslaved. What's worse, Mr. Coulter's claim was entirely defective, because at the close of the Civil War, it is a matter of public record that *Congress*, not the judiciary, passed laws *against* segregation, but those laws were "struck-down" in 1896 by the activist court in Plessy v. Ferguson.[38]

So when the court finally ended segregation a century later in (1954) Brown v. Board of Education,[39] it wasn't an act of "righteous judicial activism," as Mr. Coulter implied, asserting itself against an evil majority of "racist Christians"—forcing the prejudiced masses to properly evolve into a more "progressive" civilization. It was, in truth, an act of the judiciary correcting its own prior arrogant mis-management of power with what many would argue was an appro-priate reversal.

13. **Liars**—Greek: pseustais (GSN-<G5583>), saying for truth what is known to be false (1 Tim. 1:10; John 8:44–45; Rom. 3:4; Titus 1:12; 1 John 1:10; 2:4, 22; 4:20; 5:10).

14. **Perjurers**—Greek: epiorkois (GSN-<G1965>), those who lie under oath.

15. **Contrarians**—Greek: antikeimai (GSN-<G473> and <G2749>). Those guilty of any vice contrary to sound (legal) doctrine (1 Tim. 1:10; Gal. 5:21).

THE LINE IS DRAWN

Where is the line between self and civil government drawn, and by what authority?

The line is harmoniously drawn in both the Old and New Testaments, by inspiration of our Creator and Author of true government—God the Father! Internal conscience and external civic law must both reflect the same absolute standard of truth to remain legitimate! A best-ordered society is one where conscience and government remain in perfect agreement, based upon the *only* fixed standard of truth.

In other words: If it is required by God for a man not to secretly lust, then it is required by God for civil authority to penalize the outward crescendo of lust we call "adultery." If it is required by God for a man not to secretly hate, then it is required by God for the civil authority to penalize the outward crescendo of hate we call "murder." Thus, civil government in these United States is required to perfectly harmonize with the self-governed citizen. No citizen can be truly self-governed who does not privately submit to God's law in conscience. Therefore, the further the private individual citizen strays from God in his heart, the greater the ratio of public crime and the more speedily the rate of national decay.

According to Romans 13, God has ordained government to "punish evildoers" and "reward goodness." Neither the concepts of "evil" nor "good" can be arbitrarily defined by the whimsical fancies of fallen men. Only God, through His inspired Law-Word, has the authority to define the same "evil" He authorizes human governments to punish. Only God, through His own testimony (Law-Word) has the authority to define the same "good" He authorizes human governments to reward. Therefore, for civil government to possess knowledge of its *duty* to punish evil, and for a proper *definition* of evil, the self-governed Christian and his Bible are required.

CHAPTER 8: REVIEW QUESTIONS

Enjoy this quiz at http://peacemakersinstitute.com/smb-quiz.

1. Was the first table of the law horizontal or vertical in application?

2. Is it tyrannical for civil authority to enforce the first table of Mosaic Law?

3. Is it defacto-tyranny for civil authority to refuse to enforce a part or all of the second table of the law?

4. How do the first three laws of the second table of Mosaic Law protect the root of all successful civilizations?

5. Can man use his own ordinances to defeat gravity or marriage?

6. Can man use his own ordinances to defeat himself by rebelling against gravity and marriage?

7. Can private property survive a culture that does not honor traditional biblical family?

8. Explain the logic of Christ doing away with the special holidays, sacrificial animals, circumcision, and food ordinances of the Mosaic Law.

9. What two arenas of government must reflect the same identical standard of absolute truth in order to remain legitimate?

10. Was admitting the internal sin of hate or lust punishable by a magistrate in Israel?

11. Should adultery be recriminalized in America?

12. What is required in order for civil authority to have a proper definition of good and evil?

Chapter 9

A Global Commonwealth of Nations

S LIBERAL "PROFESSOR of religion" Lee Jefferson (Centre College of Kentucky) once alleged in a Huffington Post article: "There is nothing attributed to Jesus of Nazareth that has anything to do with [homosexuality]. According to the gospels, Jesus never commented on [homosexuality]; that fact certainly bears repeating to anyone criticizing the gay community on Christian grounds."[1] After a painful wrenching of the fundamental laws of Bible interpretation (see Appendix) throughout his defense of New York's decision to create "gay marriage," Professor Jefferson concluded by stating: "So does the Bible have anything to 'say' about gay marriage? The Bible is not specific, literate or even concerned with what we call same-sex orientation or gay marriage.[2]

Interestingly, the good professor did not continue listing the other things Jesus also failed to repudiate. For example, Jesus never directly forbade necrophilia (sexual intercourse with the dead). Yet, it must have been a problem in Jesus's day. I have read that the neighbors of Palestine, the Egyptian pharaohs (who were known to have the most beautiful wives on earth) maintained a curious burial tradition. They would deliberately allow the bodies of their dead wives to rot for three days before turning them over to the undertakers. This was done to ensure the undertaker would not be sexually tempted by her extraordinarily beautiful body.[3] Does that mean necrophilia is perfectly OK, since Jesus didn't hammer away at the "sexual orientation" of the necrophiliacs in the Middle East?

As an aside, would plumb-line Libertarians who reliably support the radical homosexual lobby, in an effort to remain consistent, support the legalization of necrophilia too? This begs many questions. Can a dead body still functionally possess personal property? Surely the stoic utilitarian (like John Stuart Mill's father we discussed at the close of chapter four) would give a heartless "no" to the question of dead bodies and private property, but even if his son, John, reluctantly agreed, what would he say to the necrophiliac, who claimed that this kind of "relationship" was the only way he could "be happy"? Surely today's plumb-line Libertarian could make the case that such an act "does no harm" to the property of the dead body?" Or one might ask the not-so-clever type of liberal question wherewith men of my stature are incessantly regaled:

"How does someone else's necrophiliac orientation harm *your* marriage?"

No doubt, my introduction of the abomination of necrophilia into a political dialogue would send every stripe of Libertarian and liberal into a vocal protest against what they would label as a "vulgar, impractical, and unnecessary topic" during a discussion on liberty. (I know because similar conversations have occurred during my debates with pro-gay activists.) I would respond, calmly: "Oh, you mean to say that one particular divergent sexual habit does not get the same liberty as another? Why ever not? I thought you believed in the *purest* kind of liberty uncontaminated by religion and morality!" The less clever Libertarian/liberal would simply brush me aside by calmly responding: "Of course, necrophilia is perfectly natural and understandable in some situations. Ultimately, it's none of our business." (This is how they alienate themselves from the overwhelming supermajority of observant and understandably repulsed voters. In each case, my mission exposing the fallacy of the existence of any virtuous law outside of God's authority would be successfully accomplished.)

In response to our culture's plethora of liberal "professors of religion" who regurgitate this kind of zany drivel, Dr. Gary DeMar wrote: "Jesus didn't condemn rape (Deut. 22:25–26), sex with animals (Exod. 22:19), sex with a minor, incest (Lev. 18:6–18), abortion (Exod. 21:22–25), kidnapping (Deut. 24:7), arson (Exod. 22:6) or tripping blind people (Lev. 19:14),"[4] yet no biblically literate Christian theist would argue such acts should be legalized by human governments in the modern world! Clearly, neither Jesus nor His disciples found it necessary to spend His limited and valuable time in ministry (a mere three and a half years) restating the entire life work of the prophet Moses, because the foundation (Judaism) upon which Christ built a New Covenant in Palestine was already laid by the God-ordained and anointed patriarchs of Hebrew antiquity.

Consequently, the New Testament references to civil government are understood as given in summary form—relatable reference points deliberately connecting to the previous administration of Moses. In this light, it stands to reason these broad and sweeping truths of government (made in the New Testament) are generally accepted as inadequate, in and of themselves, for governance in the modern world. To be clear, they are *only* inadequate when and if the intended context of the Old Testament is erroneously ignored. In summary, the New Testament brings extraordinary focus and precision to the implementation of Mosaic Law in modern times, because it adds the fresh dimension of Christ's clarifying interpretations and defense of Mosaic Law, which had been long since sullied by the overemphasis of the oral traditions (Mishna) at the expense of the written Torah.[5] (Thank you, Pharisees and Sadducees.)

I postulate this truth: If Israel's mission was to bring the world a Messiah through the pure genetic stock of Adam, promised to come through he and Eve for the purpose of "bruising the serpent's head,"[6] and if the prophet of that same Hebrew nation stated: "The government shall be upon His shoulders,"[7] then the spreading of Mosaic Law to the whole world—a standard-bearing nation of obedient Hebrew believers among worldwide nations of obedient Gentile believers— must also have been part of Israel's divine mission!

Put another way, God's ultimate plan was (and still is) to use Israel as a trend-setting model for what will eventually become a global commonwealth of sovereign nation-states[8] led by one particular nation, set apart by God to lead through demonstration of proper governance and faith, according to His Law-Word. This plan for a commonwealth of sovereign nation-states is precisely what we glean from reading the fourth chapter of Deuteronomy. We will explore the text of Deuteronomy further in just a moment, but before we do so, try to consider these next passages without overspiritualizing them, or immediately dismissing them as "prophetic comments pointing to a glorious millennial kingdom." Humor me for a moment, and consider the fact that when God made the following statements, He intended for such things to *immediately begin* to occur around the world one thousand six hundred years before Christ came to earth. The next verse is the Word of God spoken directly to the pharaoh of Egypt, in the context of God's threats to unleash His wrath against the pagan empire for their resistance!

And indeed, for this cause have I appointed thee [I have raised you up, Pharaoh], to show my power in thee, and to declare my name throughout all the world.
—EXODUS 9:16, GNV

God told Pharaoh, in a manner of speaking: "I'm sending a warning shot to every rebellious human government on this planet, by demonstrating my wrath against your national authority." Later, the Scriptures elaborate on God's global and far-reaching agenda, and the fact that it *began* at the Exodus (not someday when Christ returns) is made very clear. Look at this next passage:

Thou in thy mercy hast led forth the people which thou hast redeemed: thou hast guided them in thy strength unto thy holy habitation. The people shall hear, and be afraid: sorrow shall take hold on the inhabitants of Palestina. Then the dukes of Edom shall be amazed; the mighty men of Moab, trembling shall take hold upon them; all the inhabitants of Canaan shall melt away. Fear and dread shall fall upon them; by the greatness of thine arm they shall be as still as a stone; till thy people pass over, O LORD, till the people pass over, which thou hast purchased. Thou shalt bring them in, and plant them in the mountain of thine inheritance, in the place, O LORD, which thou hast made for thee to dwell in, in the Sanctuary, O LORD, which thy hands have established. The LORD shall reign for ever and ever.
—EXODUS 15:13–18

It is absolutely certain that God's global plan for a commonwealth of nations was *not* going to wait until the millennial reign before it would begin. According to what we just read, it began long ago. Please do not misunderstand this truth, however. We must acknowledge that Jesus's teachings of Matthew chapter twenty-four, in harmony with the Book of Revelation, have made it very clear that God's plan for this global commonwealth will meet continual resistance until Christ physically returns in His wrath. This has certainly been true since the time of Exodus. But what my premillennialist comrades need to embrace is the reality that the political agenda of Father God already started during the Exodus of the Hebrew people. Furthermore, the church must understand that Christ came as a catalyst to His Father's global plan. Jesus did *not* come to shut down His Father's plan, as if it were some old, exhausted coal mine that had seen better days. With these facts in play, look at the conversation between Moses and God that took place several years after the Exodus, and take notice of Moses's concern for the heathen nations:

> And Moses said unto the LORD, Then the Egyptians shall hear it, (for thou broughtest up this people in thy might from among them;) And they will tell it to the inhabitants of this land: for they have heard that thou LORD art among this people, that thou LORD art seen face to face, and that thy cloud standeth over them, and that thou goest before them, by day time in a pillar of a cloud, and in a pillar of fire by night. Now if thou shalt kill all this people as one man, then the nations which have heard the fame of thee will speak, saying, Because the LORD was not able to bring this people into the land which he sware unto them, therefore he hath slain them in the wilderness. And now, I beseech thee, let the power of my lord be great, according as thou hast spoken, saying, The LORD is longsuffering, and of great mercy, forgiving iniquity and transgression, and by no means clearing the guilty, visiting the iniquity of the fathers upon the children unto the third and fourth generation. Pardon, I beseech thee, the iniquity of this people according unto the greatness of thy mercy, and as thou hast forgiven this people, from Egypt even until now. And the LORD said, I have pardoned according to thy word: But as truly as I live, all the earth shall be filled with the glory of the LORD.
>
> —NUMBERS 14:13–21

ESCHATOLOGY PROBLEMS

At this point in the reading we reach an obvious tipping point with regard to people's preconceptions on "end-time prophecy." If you get hung up here, you will miss a grand truth. With that said, I offer everyone a word of caution and a challenge: please do not make a popular mistake and too quickly dismiss this governmental plan for the whole world, relegating it exclusively to "the end of the world when Christ returns." Obviously, as you'll see in just a moment, this plan has already been implemented by God, and whether you believe in the pre-tribulation Rapture or not (for the record ... I do!), the plan we're discussing (a global commonwealth of nations) began long before you

were born, and it is taking place *right now*, under your nose, with or
without your doctrinal consent. Let's continue down this road for a
moment, and address the potentially hazardous issue of eschatology
via a thought-provoking rhetorical question: "When, where, and how
does Christ enjoy His "preeminence" among "thrones, dominions,
principalities and powers?" Is it *only after* His second coming? Or
should this be the obligation of men from the "point of origin?" Are
you ready for the answer? Here it is, written in Colossians 1:16–18
(emphasis added):

> For by Him were *all things created*, that are in heaven, and
> that are in earth, visible and invisible, whether they be
> thrones, or dominions, or principalities, or powers: all things
> were created by him and for him…that in all things *he* might
> have the preeminence.

The answer is all too obvious! God requires *preeminence* from
the point of creation, not the point of conclusion! Dan Smithwick, the
founder of Nehemiah Institute once described it this way: "Christians
must take one of two paths: 1) Learn how to live/survive in *someone
else's civilization* until Revelation 21 arrives; or 2) Learn how to
replace the world's system with *our civilization*, based on obedience
to God's Law Word."

Let's go further. The following three passages make this very clear,
stating: "then you [Israel] shall be a special treasure to me above all
people; for all the earth is mine,"[9] and "that the LORD thy God will set
thee on high above all nations of the earth,"[10] and "in you [Abraham]
all the families of the earth shall be blessed."[11] The global blessing
would be personified in the ministry of the Messiah, and the government would be "upon His shoulders."[12] The New Testament writer, in
Galatians 3:8, reflecting on these very points I have just made concerning the Old Testament mission of Israel, describes it thusly:

> And the scripture, foreseeing that God would justify the hea-
> then through faith, preached before the gospel unto Abraham,
> saying, In thee shall all nations be blessed.

Though easily proven incorrect, I understand that many people
assume Galatians 3:8 is exclusively referring to "spiritual blessings."
I also understand very well how my fellow "pre-tribulation Rapture

teachers" tend to view the previous passages. (You probably instinctively consigned the above-mentioned as exclusively describing the future "millennial kingdom.") OK...the passages certainly do include a description of the coming millennial kingdom, but they do not preclude the timeline between Deuteronomy and the second coming of Christ. I submit to you that pointing to the proverbial "end zone" on a football field, does not give anyone the intellectual right to ignore the existence of the Astroturf that must be traversed in order to arrive there!

Allow me to suggest a plausible scenario...Jesus will (physically) return and He will undoubtedly rule "with a rod of iron," just as the Bible promises, but perhaps that fact was *never* intended to be confused as a license for present-day political passivity. Maybe our team (you and I) are supposed to move the ball closer to the end zone, since we are, after all, the ones on the field playing right now! *Then* (in the future), when we're in proper position, the coach (think Father God) will call that predictable and exciting "time out" (think second coming), and He'll send in our "star player" (think Jesus Christ) to run the play we all know will provide the winning touchdown (think Armageddon)!

You see, the problem I have with most Christians, when it comes to the purpose of this treatise, is not their "strong belief in the ultimate touchdown" predicted to usher in the "greatest team victory of history." The problem I have is the idea that since we have foreknowledge of the Coach's strategy, because He gave it to us during the halftime locker room speech (think four Gospels), it is somehow OK to sit on the sidelines and watch the opposing team stomp us to death (think 2015 and beyond), all while we faithfully and repetitively comfort one another with the Coach's "fantastic halftime speech!"

OK, in case anyone reading is unwilling to let go of these old, debilitating eschatological arguments, I ask you (please?) to allow me the temporary permission to ask some loaded questions, spiced up with what may prove to be necessary sarcasm. 1) If God wanted the Hebrew civil code to positively impact all world governments, why do modern Christians insist the opposite and even deny the obvious impact Hebrew law had upon our own legal foundation in America? (The thirteen original states codified the entire Mosaic Decalogue.)[13] 2) If Israel was commanded to "teach them to thy sons, and thy sons' sons," then isn't it intuitive that this worldwide political program of legal and political influence (setting an example to Gentile nations) was also to continue for many generations? 3) Does the text suggest any generational "end point" where setting such a fine civic example would become "counter-productive" or "repressive" against the message of grace and salvation? 4) Was the Old Testament prophet making more than poetry (for the sake of good Christmas tunes), when he claimed of the coming Messiah "the government shall be upon His shoulders?" 5) Isn't it reasonable to believe that God intends to continue that positive impact today, through the application of Bible truth in modern governments? 6) Do these facts uncover a popular fallacy in modern church doctrine regarding the role of Christians and politics, particularly in America?

All these loaded questions lead to the most important of all rhetorical questions:

7) If Christ supposedly came to eliminate the need for modern nations to emulate Israel's civil code (as is commonly asserted in pulpits today), then what were those Gentile nations God told Israel to set a good example for (before Christ) supposed to have done once Christ arrived? Were they supposed to secularize themselves in the name of "grace"?

How wildly ridiculous would that have been?

THE GLOBAL INFLUENCE OF MOSAIC LAW ACROSS THE THREAD OF HISTORY

A couple weeks ago, my wife and I were enjoying dinner with friends and discussed this very issue of Israel's calling to set a proper example of law and government in the view of the whole world. As we fellowshipped, I was asked an excellent question that just so happened to have a fascinating answer. During the conversation, I had only just made the point (number 7 above) that if our hypergrace antagonists are correct, and Jesus had actually purposed to rid the world of Hebrew law, then the many nations should have secularized themselves in the name of grace once Christ arrived. My friend responded: "What examples of their (Israel) legal and political influence do we see in history before and after the coming of the Messiah?" My immediate response was "America," but I decided, in the present work-at-hand, to mine out some golden nuggets of history, to prove to the modern reader what God has been doing up to our present time, since He began that work in the Exodus around 1600 BC. Understanding what I'm prepared to reveal will deepen your understanding of the modern church's present doctrinal resistance *against* His will for the world. This present resistance is directly connected to our failure to fully embrace the complete nature of the Great Commission.

Suffice it to say that when God told Israel of His global plan to affect the entire world in a positive and helpful way, despite Israel's many faults, they still managed to set a chain of events in motion—a chain of world-shaping events we are still feeling at this very hour. It would literally take a volume of books to fully handle Israel's legal and political impact around the globe, but allow me to very crudely sketch out what God began to do thousands of years ago, in a historical overview of world history.

Along this line of thinking, Professor Wines, president of the City University of St. Louis in 1853, writes, "Moses seems to have been impressed with the conviction that his legislation was destined to exert a commanding influence on the progress of government and civilization. He evidently anticipated that his laws would become known, and would be imitated by other nations... We have plain and certain proofs that these laws were powerfully felt in modifying the religious sentiments, the philosophical opinions, the literary labors, the political maxims, the civil institutions and the moral judgment and practices of mankind."[14]

Mosaic laws were influential upon the Assyrian, Median, Persian, and Egyptian empires. The kings and queens of these world-shaking governments made decrees "recognizing His power and sovereignty in the most explicit terms; commanding all people, nations and languages to praise extol and honor the [Hebrew] King of heaven; and to tremble and fear before Him; and denouncing the most terrible punishments upon such as should dare to speak anything amiss against the God of Israel."[15]

King Nebuchadnezzar (605 BC), King Cyrus (538 BC), King Darius (520 BC) and otherwise pagan world leaders made edicts recognizing the all-powerful God of Israel. Historians tell us of the profound influence of Hebrew law upon Xerxes I (485 BC). (Our own Bible explains how Queen Esther—a Jew—became queen of the Persian Empire in 479 BC.)

About the same time Alexander the Great sought the knowledge he would later employ in a campaign to militarily and politically conquer the whole world, the philosophical minds of his Greek world were at work laying down the logical foundations of philosophy and science upon which all of world history would soon pivot. Socrates mentored

Plato, Plato mentored Aristotle, and Aristotle mentored Alexander the Great. (This generational exchange of ideas took place between 469 BC and 323 BC.) History reveals that all four men (whose lives remain household names—legendary in American society almost twenty-four hundred years later), Socrates, Plato, Aristotle, and Alexander, were each profoundly impacted by the genius of Mosaic Law.

Aristobulus the historian, most famous for his work as a biographer of Alexander the Great, said of Plato: "He followed [Mosaic Law] closely, and diligently examined the several parts thereof."[16] The historian Titus Flavius Clemens humorously referred to Plato the Grecian as "the Hebrew philosopher" and repeatedly charged that "the Greeks stole their chief opinions out of the books of Moses and the prophets."[17]

Professor Wines writes: "Justin Martyr affirms concerning Plato: 'He drew many things from the Hebrew fountains, especially his pious conceptions of God and his worship.'"[18] Numenius, the Greek philosopher, joked: "What is Plato, but Moses atticizing [taking sides with the Athenians]?"[19] It is said of Aristotle, the student of Plato, that he had been taught in frequent exchanges by a wonderful, wise, temperate, and good Jew, whose shared knowledge had made more of an impact upon Aristotle than the other way around.[20] Said Clemens Alexandrinus to Plato, "But as for laws, whatever are true, as also for the opinion of God, these things were conveyed to thee from the Hebrews."[21]

Wines further describes the historical record of Moses's penetrating influence upon world governments: "Hecatuaeus attests the high estimation, in which they [the Hebrew people] were held by Alexander the Great [334 BC]...King Ptolemy Soter [Alexander's successor in 323 BC] entrusted the fortresses of Egypt to [the Hebrew's] hands, believing they would defend them faithfully and valiantly...King Philometer and his famous Queen Cleopatra III [142 BC] appointed [Hebrews] as generals of all their armed forces...King Philadelphus [34 BC]...was delighted with the laws of Moses, pronounced his legislation wonderful, was astonished at the depth of Moses's wisdom and professed to have learned from [Moses] the true science of government."[22]

Cicero (50 BC) is known today as a father of Roman law. He created his famous De Legibus in which he famously informed the world that all concepts of justice and law came directly from God, and he admitted that he borrowed all his concepts of natural law from the Greek philosophers, who, in turn (my readers should now know), borrowed from Moses. Cicero was a champion of the idea that Romans should *return* to their first principles of republicanism. He did so amidst the authoritarian and liberty-crushing foot of Julius Caesar, whose declaration of dictatorship sent Rome descending into the abyss of a centralized totalitarianism. We should all now know that republicanism was the exclusive invention ("discovery from the face of God" are probably better words than "invention") of Moses.

Cicero, who wished for Rome to reject totalitarianism and return to a republic, as prescribed by Moses, was finally killed. His head and hands were cut from his body and nailed to a platform for public display. His tongue was ceremoniously pulled from his head and symbolically stabbed by Antony's wife, Fulvia (with her hairpin), as a sign of revenge against his powers of speech. Forty-three years after Cicero was savagely assassinated, Christ was born in Bethlehem. His life and ministry would shake the world. It was only a matter of time before Christ's message disturbed the powers of the same Roman Empire that had crushed Cicero only one generation prior to His public ministry. (We will dedicate great and careful attention to Christ Jesus's confrontation with governmental powers in the next chapter.) After the ascension of Christ into heaven, the influence of Him and His subordinate predecessor (Moses) continued to change the governments of the world, despite great spiritual and natural resistance. More than seven hundred years after Christ, after the likes of Alexander the Great, who had once (before Christ) built the largest empire in world history, arose King Charlemagne (AD 768). Charlemagne is today known as the "father of all Europe." His political and military prowess gave birth to both the French and German monarchies. Beyond Germany and France, his world-shaking kingdom eventually reunited all of Europe under one vast empire for the first time since the fall of the ancient Romans. According to the renowned historian and clergyman Dr. Gardiner Spring: "...one of the first acts of the clergy under...C harlemagne...was to [codify into public law]...several of the Mosaic laws found in the books of Deuteronomy and Leviticus."[23]

One century later, King Alfred the Great (AD 871) introduced his code of law to the Saxons in an effort to bring positive legal reform to his people. According to author David Pratt: "About a fifth of the law code is taken up by Alfred's introduction, which includes translations into English of the Decalogue, a few chapters from the Book of Exodus, and the so-called 'Apostolic Letter' from Acts of the Apostles

(15:23–29). The Introduction may best be understood as Alfred's med-
itation upon the meaning of Christian law. It traces the continuity
between God's gift of law to Moses to Alfred's own issuance of law to
the West Saxon people."[24]

Reflecting upon Moses's and Jesus's Jewish influence across all of
Europe and its American descendants, including the larger part of
Asia, northern Africa, and beyond, the English historian of the 1840s,
Henry Hart Milman, DD, wrote: "[Moses was] a man who, considered
merely in a historical light, without any reference to his divine inspiration, has exercised a more extensive and permanent influence over
the destinies of his own nation and mankind at large, than any other
individual recorded in the annals of the world."[25]

Not unlike the Jews themselves, in every case of human government
where nations closely followed Mosaic Law, they thrived. In each case of
human government where they began to stray from the divine principles of Mosaic Law, they deteriorated. The rise and fall of world empires
has always been connected to man's submission to the divine laws of
earth's Creator. My dear modern American Christians, this remains true
at this very hour! Nothing in this regard has ever changed! It has only
been more pronounced by the coming of Christ, never lessened.

God's intentions to affect world governments through the demonstration of Mosaic laws began at the exodus of Egypt and successfully and positively shaped Western civilization as we know it today.
Approximately one thousand four hundred and ninety-two years
after Christ ascended into heaven, an explorer named Christopher
Columbus, who was compelled by his Christian faith to spread its
knowledge across the globe, "sailed the ocean blue" in search of a new
world that would eventually become known as "These United States."

America—the nation I now argue in favor of saving from godless
disaster—would become one founded upon the genius of Mosaic and
Christian law—a way of law carried into the eighteenth century by
those faithful Christians who heard the voice of their savior Jesus
Christ, when He warned:

> Whosoever therefore shall break one of these least command-
> ments, and shall teach men so, he shall be called the least in
> the kingdom of heaven: but whosoever shall do and teach
> them, the same shall be called great in the kingdom of heaven.
> —Matthew 5:19

A sentiment of our Lord and Savior apparently acknowledged by Luke the Apostle, who later reminisced as he wrote of God's everlasting law:

> For from ancient generations Moses has had his preachers in every town, for he is read [aloud] every Sabbath in the synagogues.
>
> —ACTS 15:21, AMP

America, in her founding era, would go down in history as a nation who more closely and directly employed Moses's style and character of Republican government than any other since the life and times of Moses himself. In other words, arguably the greatest resurgence of Mosaic Law since the death of its author, more than 3,300 years prior, occurred in the original thirteen colonies under the Declaration of Independence and subsequent ratification of the Constitution of the United States of 1789! As stated earlier in this chapter, thirteen of the original colonies codified the entire Mosaic Decalogue into American law.[26] Taken from the 1776 and 1777 Constitutions of two separate states of Pennsylvania and Vermont, we read:

> Each member [of the legislature], before he takes his seat, shall make and subscribe the following declaration: "I do believe in one God, the Creator and Governor of the universe, the Rewarder of the good, and the Punisher of the wicked."

So we see that God's plan for a global impact to be made through the Hebrew children, that plan that first took shape after the exodus from Egypt, has come to pass across time just as God promised Abraham:

> ...thy seed shall possess the gate of his enemies; And in thy seed shall all the nations of the earth be blessed; because thou hast obeyed my voice.
>
> —GENESIS 22:17–18

Enough said. I believe I have shown, sufficiently, that regardless of your beliefs about end-time events, whether you believe in the Rapture or you demonize the teaching as the "greatest evil of the twenty-first century" (as is the manner of some), there seems to be no "escape clause" wherewith any of us are given license to sit back (or hide away with a stockpile of canned goods in our secret bunker) and allow Satan to control every dimension of life on earth.

We have taken what, for some, has likely been an astonishing journey through world history, chronicling the impact of Moses upon world governments and proving God's success in launching a global plan for proper government modeled by Israel. In the next chapter, let us return to their state just following the great Exodus and reacquaint ourselves with their original mission and its relation to us today.

CHAPTER 9: REVIEW QUESTIONS

Enjoy this quiz at http://peacemakersinstitute.com/smb-quiz.

1. Shouldn't plumb-line Libertarians, who reliably support sodomy, also support necrophilia if they are consistent?

2. How does someone else's necrophiliac orientation harm *your* marriage?

3. How should the New Testament references to civil government be understood? In what form and relating to what previous administration are they given?

4. In addition to bringing the world a Messiah, what other extraordinary mission was a part of Israel's divine mission to the world?

5. Is it true that God's global plan for a commonwealth of nations was supposed to wait until the millennial reign before it would begin?

6. Should Christ have preeminence in all things from the point of creation or from the point of conclusion?

7. Is it reasonable to believe that all nations formerly influenced by Mosaic Law should have responded to Christ's intervention in history by secularizing themselves?

8. Socrates mentored Plato, Plato mentored Aristotle, and Aristotle mentored whom? All were profoundly influenced by whom?

9. God's intentions to affect world governments through the demonstration of Mosaic laws began when?

10. What nation, during its founding era, would go down in history as a nation who more closely and directly employed Moses's style and character of republican government than any other since the life and times of Moses himself?

11. Has God's plan for a global impact to be made through the Hebrew children after the Exodus continued to come to pass as promised long ago to Abraham?

12. Does any legitimate escape clause exist wherewith Christians are empowered to retreat from law and politics?

Chapter 10

Art Thou a King Then?

MODERNS WHO DON'T study the Old Testament think of Israel as a brutish tribe of ancient warmongers on a mission to kill every other non-Jew on the face of the earth. This is terribly wrong! Israel was called upon to decimate particular nations who had succumbed to unrecoverable barbarism. Idolatry was not merely the mistaken belief that a wood-carved totem pole was God. Idolatry, at that time in history, was filled with savage brutality. Innocent virginal children, young adults, and perhaps, in some cases, even the elderly were slaughtered during idolatrous ritual killings. These cultures Israel was commanded to destroy were no longer capable of redemption. They could not be turned toward God's law, and frankly, they were extremely dangerous and had to be punished. But God did not command Israel to "kill the whole world" as some seem to believe. Notice God's instruction to the children of Israel that they should be concerned about the natural (and eternal) state of neighboring nations who needed to see their testimony in civic life. Why? So that such heathen nations would desire to be like them! Israel's mission was to set an international example of proper civil governance under the one true God!

> Behold, I have taught you statutes and judgments, even as the LORD my God commanded me, that ye should do so in the land whither ye go to possess it. Keep therefore and do them; for this is your wisdom and your understanding in the sight of the nations, which shall hear all these statutes, and say, Surely this great nation is a wise and understanding people. For what nation is there so great, who hath God so nigh unto them, as the LORD our God is in all things that we call upon him for? And what nation is there so great, that hath statutes and judgments so righteous as all this law, which I set before

you this day? Only take heed to thyself, and keep thy soul diligently, lest thou forget the things which thine eyes have seen,
and lest they depart from thy heart all the days of thy life: but
teach them thy sons, and thy sons' sons.
                                        —DEUTERONOMY 4:5–9

As established in the previous chapter, Israel's mission was to set
an *international* example of proper governance under the one true
God! Moses did not in any way suggest that this mission should be
delayed until the materialization of the future Messiah (a Messiah
Moses already promised and foretold when he wrote Genesis 3:15). It
is abundantly clear that this campaign of setting a good example of
righteous government—on demonstration for the whole world's benefit—began after the Hebrew exodus from Egypt and long before the
Messiah arrived on the scene. Specifically, God's global plan for good
government began around 1500 BC in the Plain of Moab, near Jericho.
That is when archaeologists inform us that the verses you just read in
Deuteronomy chapter four were likely first written and subsequently
explained by Moses to the Hebrew nation.

THE DEUTERONOMY CHAPTER FOUR MANDATE

There are those who insist to argue that Israel only existed—temporarily—for the purpose of bringing the world a Messiah. In the
light of this discussion, and as thoroughly proven in the last chapter,
their insistence of this falls short of the complete picture. Clearly, the
Messiah Israel was destined to bring the world was intrinsically connected to the issue of good government—something God also desired
for the common good of the whole world. If this particular issue of
government was only a prophetic mention of the coming millennial
reign of the Messiah, as some contend, then Moses's divinely inspired
campaign of Deuteronomy chapter four—setting an international
example of proper governance—does not make any sense at all. What
would have been the point? Moses clearly admonished Israel to set
a good example of government at least one thousand five hundred
years before the Messiah arrived in Bethlehem. Furthermore, this fact
begs the reasonable question: Why would we need to read the Book
of Deuteronomy for instruction on proper government during the
coming millennial reign of Christ, when Christ, the *living word* will be
sitting in the plain sight of us all—seated upon His everlasting throne?

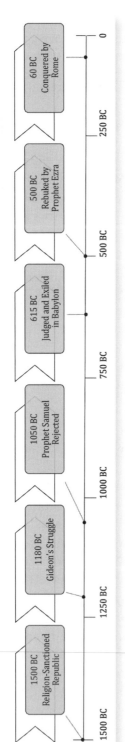

Our conclusion can only lead to one answer: the example and template of all good government is found in our Bible. The Bible—including both testaments—is the guide on government most needed *prior to* the millennium! The Living Word is presently *not* here. He was resurrected from the dead and ascended into heaven, but His written Word certainly remains! Shouldn't we be using it? In reality, many aren't even reading it! Others are fighting to pervert His Word as a means to claim it is presently irrelevant. What a crying shame has tarnished and soiled the present remnant church of the Living God! Our present state of doctrinal affairs is nothing short of an outrage!

I acknowledge the nation of Israel existed in its proper form during a limited time of world history, but we must not fail to recall that her repeated cycles of failure (along with her eventual national demise) came about through her own sin and rebellion against God's ultimate plan. Therefore, the assumption that God's application of His own preferred way for men to govern themselves shared a mutual expiration with the ruin of that particular nation is indefensible and incorrect. Moses ruled Israel for forty short years till his death. After his death, through successive transfers of power to other leaders, the estimated length of Israel's Mosaic government continued approximately 431 years before finally collapsing under the weight of their rebellious noncompliance. Christ did not come to mark the end of Israel's God-given purpose; He came just in the nick of time to salvage what they had rebelliously frittered away through faithless traditions and rebellion. As He said: "Think not that I am come to destroy the law, or the prophets: I am not come to destroy, but to fulfil."[1]

Whether they were able to enjoy their proper religion-sanctioned republic during the life of

Moses (around 1500 BC), struggling to recover their national identity with the help of Gideon (around 1180 BC), tarnished by the introduction of a monarchy in defiance to Samuel's prophetic leadership (around 1050 BC), judged by God and subsequently exiled in Babylon due to their disobedience (around 615 BC), corrupted through their insistent intermarrying with pagans, (rebuked for it by Ezra around 500 BC), or crushed beneath the conquering foot of a Roman imperialism (around 60 BC), God's demand for their obedience to His laws throughout their entangled history, as originally codified by Moses in the beginning, was *never* suspended.

A most startling example of the eternal and immutable nature of God's law and Israel's subsequent responsibility to obey it without excuse-making is demonstrated in Ezra chapters nine and ten. Perspective is brought to the chapter when one considers that Ezra's extremely difficult decision—to uphold Mosaic Law—was taking place more than one thousand years since the death of Moses. Additionally, Ezra's woeful decision to obey Mosaic Law came on the recent heels of seventy years of Babylonian captivity. This particular captivity beneath the control of their pagan masters was fraught with generations of Hebrews intermarrying with Babylonians, giving birth to children and grandchildren, and establishing all the emotional and paternal bonds one might expect. Yet, we find Ezra faithfully commanding Israel to repent of their iniquity and separate from their non-Jewish wives and children. Amidst great suffering and emotional pain, with tears running down his own cheeks, the obedient prophet made the people pledge to obey Mosaic Law:

> Now while Ezra was praying, and while he was confessing, weeping, and bowing down before the house of God, a very large assembly of men, women, and children gathered to him from Israel; for the people wept very bitterly. And Shechaniah...spoke up and said to Ezra, "We have trespassed against our God, and have taken pagan wives from the peoples of the land; yet now there is hope for Israel in spite of this. Now therefore, let us make a covenant with our God to put away all these wives and those who have been born to them, according to the advice of my master and of those who tremble at the commandment of our God; and let it be done according to the law. Arise, for this matter is your responsibility..." Then Ezra

arose, and made the leaders of the priests, the Levites, and all Israel swear an oath that they would do according to this word.
　　　　　—Ezra 10:1–5, nkjv, emphasis added

About five hundred years after Ezra's painful reminder that neither God's laws nor His expectations for men to obey them had changed, Jesus arrived on the scene of Israeli history. Specifically, Christ arrived toward the chronological end of Israel's unraveling as a nation. For approximately three and a half years, He publicly confronted the families of Palestine amidst their Roman dominators. He made it very clear Father God still expected obedient purity from His Hebrew people. Their newfound difficulties in keeping His laws, hindered from the *outside* by Roman authorities and from the *inside* by corrupt teachers of a polluted Judaism, were obstacles of their own doing—to be overcome, not to be excused. Jesus told a rich young ruler that if he wanted to escape hell he should "keep the commandments."

And behold, one came to him and said, Teacher, what good thing shall I do, that I may have eternal life? And he said unto him, Why askest thou me concerning that which is good? One there is who is good: but if thou wouldest enter into life, keep the commandments.
　　　　　—Matthew 19:16–17, asv

Jesus cleansed the Jewish temple while quoting the teaching of the ancient prophet Jeremiah, who wrote:

Don't be fooled into thinking that you will never suffer because the Temple is here. It's a lie! Do you really think you can steal, murder, commit adultery, lie, and burn incense to Baal and all those other new gods of yours, and then come here and stand before me in my Temple and chant, "We are safe!"—only to go right back to all those evils again? Don't you yourselves admit that this Temple, which bears my name, has become a den of thieves? Surely I see all the evil going on there. I, the Lord, have spoken!
　　　　　—Jeremiah 7:8–11, nlt

And He said to them, "It is written, My house will be called a house of prayer. But you are making it a den of thieves!"
　　　　　—Matthew 21:13, hcsb

It was God's law that a man should "honor his father and mother" when the first man on earth, Adam, had no parents to honor and no children old enough to honor him in return. It was God's law when finally carved into stone tablets at the summit of Mount Sinai. It was God's law in Jerusalem while Jesus kicked over tables in righteous anger and indignation, and it is still God's law today!

While the ceremonial/ritual portion of the inspired Hebrew law was annulled through the ministry, death, burial, and resurrection of Jesus Christ, the technical (non-ceremonial) portion of the Mosaic Law, which organized and provided a standard of justice for its citizens, remains the present standard by which all modern governments must be judged. It is true that the Mosaic Law was primarily designed for an agrarian[*] society, so while every single particular law may not find direct application, certainly every principle can. Therefore, Christians who engage in the fields of politics and law should implement every eternal principle of civic law demonstrated in *both* testaments of Scriptures, as often as is possible, for the sake of the greater good of humanity.

We make a mistake when we observe Christ's conversation with Pilate and assume the exchange between them was two men speaking about questions of indictment, guilt and innocence. It was more than that! Pilate questioned Christ to determine whether or not *Christ* was guilty, only to hear an indictment of his own. According to Jesus, Pilate had committed a great sin against God, but those who had delivered Him to Pilate had committed the "greater sin."

> Jesus answered, Thou couldest have no power *at all* against me, except it were given thee from above: therefore he that delivered me unto thee hath the greater sin.
> —JOHN 19:11, EMPHASIS ADDED

When Christ spoke to Pilate of sin and "greater sin" it was the all-powerful voice of Jehovah—the voice that had long ago pierced the air surrounding a burning bush, and instructed Moses to remove his sandals. Some read the above passage and only see Christ confronting the personal sin of Pilate, and the greater sin of Judas Iscariot. But it was more than a guilty verdict against Pilate and Judas, it was an indictment of guilt for crimes committed by two governments against the kingdom of God and Creator. The Lord Christ dubbed

---

[*] Agrarian describes things related to fields, farming, or rural matters.

Roman government the great sinner of nations and the Hebrew Grand Sanhedrin the greatest sinner of nations. No government, before or since, can ever escape His wrath, except by the same means each sinful human soul must embrace escape—repentance, submission, and obedience.

Jesus spent three and a half years walking the roads of Palestine teaching the "gospel of the kingdom." How quickly modern evangelicals seem to forget that the "gospel message" Jesus preached did not have "altar calls" where He encouraged His audiences to walk forward and "ask Him into their hearts." The gospel Jesus preached was the announcement of an impending fulfillment of the Judaic promise of a Messiah who would rule the world. If you think in terms of "Millennial Kingdom," you can better understand this radical Rabbi's exciting messages and His exclusively Jewish audiences.

In fact, as I mentioned in an earlier chapter, careful expository study and research on the fifty-five major parables of Jesus Christ reveal the following data about His public addresses: *A whopping 52.73 percent of Christ's public teachings had deliberate, direct and/ or indirect political/legal connotations that were unmistakable to His contemporary audiences.* These were teachings where Christ related self-governing principles to issues of civil society. Also, 47.27 percent of Christ's remaining public teachings focused upon issues of self-government and its relation to the governance of the spiritual world. (See *Jesus Impact on Politics & Law in 55 Parables* on page 288.)

The old cliché "Jesus didn't talk about politics" is a popular fallacy stemming from a combination of cultural decline, "replacement theology"* (where they tend to completely ignore anything occurring in the Old Testament past Genesis chapter 3), and sometimes, a simple lack of study. The combined impacts of these negative homiletic forces confuse modern church doctrine, weaken the practical impact of the local church in its own community and subsequently fail to achieve the goal of the Great Commission.

Jesus's ministry—His "gospel of the kingdom"—carried with it profound political and legal implications. At the very least, His willingness to publicly engage cultural issues as they specifically related to the dimension of law and politics, made His enemies in government

---

* **Replacement theology**, in its more radical form, maintains that the Jews are no longer considered to be God's chosen people in any sense. This understanding is also known as "Supersessionism." It does not accept a future role for the ethnic and geo-political nation of Israel in the plan of God.

fear Him. This has *never* been in dispute! A conclusion all modern preachers should gather from this fact of His ministerial record is that the modern pulpit that most closely emulates His ministry is the pulpit that will also produce fear in the hearts of abusive and corrupt authorities today. The further the pulpits stray from this standard, the standard of the preaching of Jesus from Nazareth, the more irrelevant and culturally ineffective said pulpits become.

MY KINGDOM IS NOT OF THIS WORLD?

It is no coincidence that the Grand Sanhedrin (the ancient equivalent of our own legislative, judicial, and executive branches of government) conjured evidence against Jesus before the Roman authorities. It is no fluke that He was later mocked with the scarlet robe of a king[2] after His whipping and crowned with thorns as the "King of the Jews."[3]

When directly questioned, "Art thou the King?," Christ answered in the affirmative, offering only one commonly misunderstood caveat; His intentions to "rule the world" would not (initially) come through the force of weaponry and bloodshed upon the unwilling. In order to understand Jesus's answer, we must first properly decipher Pilate's question.

> Then Pilate entered into the judgment hall again, and called Jesus, and said unto him, Art thou the King of the Jews?
> —JOHN 18:33

In other words, Pilate's question implied his concern about a violent uprising against Rome. He might as well have asked, "Are you posing a violent threat to my Roman authority?"

> Jesus answered, My kingdom is not of this world: if my kingdom were of this world, then would my servants fight, that I should not be delivered to the Jews: but now is my kingdom not from hence. Pilate therefore said unto him, Art thou a king then? Jesus answered, Thou sayest that I am a king. To this end was I born, and for this cause came I into the world, that I should bear witness unto the truth. Every one that is of the truth heareth my voice.
> —JOHN 18:36–37

Some mistakenly claim this as the proof-text that Christ supposedly did not have any political or governmental aspirations, and therefore, as the logic goes, neither should we. Nothing could be further from the truth! He so clearly had aspirations that when Pilate asked Him if He was a king for the second time, Pilate's question had already become rhetorical and understood. Jesus obviously did believe He was a king. He said He had a kingdom sanctioned by heaven.

> Jesus answered, Thou sayest that I am a king. To this end was I born, and for this cause came I into the world, that I should bear witness unto the truth. Every one that is of the truth heareth my voice.
> —JOHN 18:37

They further err by suggesting that Christ's response to Pilate was a carte blanche denial that He would *ever* use force. Clearly, Jesus could not have meant this. Jesus had already used force on three separate occasions as He angrily cleansed the temple of money changers with a handmade whip.* Furthermore, He had already made it very clear that a violent and angelic defense was lawfully and righteously within his moral rights to request!

> Thinkest thou that I cannot now pray to my Father, and he shall presently give me more than twelve legions of angels?
> —MATTHEW 26:53

His response was only to show that because His kingdom was from heaven, one that did not suffer the reputed litany of unjust corruptions as Rome (infamous for its brutal imperialization), His methods would first employ the invitation toward hearts and minds. In other words, His intentions to rule the world would not initially come through the force of weaponry and bloodshed upon the unwilling, as was the habit of Pilate's Rome. But make no mistake about it: Jesus did plan to take over the world! He is in the process of doing it right now! His response to Pilate's question, which inferred the meaning (I paraphrase), "Are you posing a violent threat to my Roman authority?," is fully explained throughout the New Testament.

---

* The first time Jesus angrily drove out the money changers was earlier in His ministry according to John 2:15. The second time He cleansed the temple in wrath was on a Friday—the day of His first triumphal entry into Jerusalem recorded in Matthew 21:12. The third cleansing took place on a Monday, according to Luke 19:45.

CHRIST'S THREE-STAGE PLAN TO RULE THE WORLD

Firstly, Jesus would launch His plan to rule the world by willingly shedding *His own* blood, instead of theirs.[4] Secondly, He would rule the world by sending forth ambassadors to it with the message of repentance. (That message of repentance would require a response from all levels of government: self, family, church, local, state, federal, and international, because He was and is truly "Lord of all.") Thirdly, He promised that the time period for this message to the nations of the earth would be limited to a preappointed time already determined by Father God.[5]

Said Jesus Christ to Pilate: "If my kingdom were *from* this world, *then* would my servants [initiate a] fight [with you]."[6] We infer that Jesus meant that if His kingdom had been from this world, it would have behaved as Rome was known to behave; Christ's followers would militarily crush their foes *first* and *then* launch efforts to turn hearts and minds. Since Christ's kingdom did not originate in the fallen world, it would not employ fallen tactics to subdue its enemies. It would employ the exact reverse of the standard operations of kingdom conquests, sending out ample warnings for those resistant to a coming day of reckoning, in an attempt to save as many lives as possible. In the end, there most certainly *would* be violence! We know exactly what the governmental ramifications would have been if Christ had instead launched a military attack upon the soldiers of Rome. Again, Jesus made it a point to say that such an option was within the scope of His authority by reassuring His nervous disciples, saying:

> Thinkest thou that I cannot now pray to my Father, and he shall presently give me more than twelve legions of angels?
>
> —MATTHEW 26:53

But what were the governmental ramifications of His own shed blood? All individuals are called upon to personally repent and self-govern by the law of conscience, instructed by His Law-Word. All subsequent governments (which are little more than the conglomeration of self-governed individuals) are inevitably required to yield to His authority and employ civil government by authorization of Mosaic principles brought into focus through the lens of the New Testament. What will happen if at long last men resist His invitation to yield at the expiration of this generous invitation? They will finally face His delayed wrath.

Wherefore God also hath highly exalted him, and given him a name which is above every name: That at the name of Jesus *every* knee should bow, of things in heaven, and things in earth, and things under the earth; And that *every* tongue should confess that Jesus Christ is Lord, to the glory of God the Father.
                            —PHILIPPIANS 2:9–11, EMPHASIS ADDED

And I saw heaven opened, and behold a white horse; and he that sat upon him was called Faithful and True, and in righteousness he doth judge and make war. His eyes were as a flame of fire, and on his head were many crowns.
                                          —REVELATION 19:11–12

The old promise made to both Abraham and Moses (that the Hebrew children would affect the nations of the world) did not expire in the arrival of Christ; rather, Christ's impact upon all nations became the catalyst of the fulfillment of that ancient promise! The role of Israel was to deliver the world a Messiah and the governments of the world a divine standard of justice in and through His Law-Word. In short, Israel brought salvation for the individual souls of men and divine law for the common good of all human governments.

GOVERNOR JOHN WINTHROP

At this point, there are some who will be tempted to accuse me of suggesting that "America should become some reincarnation of ancient Israel." Let me be very clear: America should be *much more* than a mere reincarnation of Israel. America, along with every other nation of the world, should repent of their rebellious politics that defy God's eternal laws! America should embrace what God has clearly revealed as a means of proper government throughout history (the beginning of this revelation was explained to Israel), recognize His preferences for governance and follow His established instructions. But to suggest that America should become a modern "reincarnation of Israel" falls short, because it ignores the clarifications on God's eternal laws brought through the public ministry of Jesus Christ and the revolutionary inspired books of the New Testament! God doesn't want America to be a reincarnation; He wants America, and all nations of the world...to be truly *Christian*! *It just so happens that in order for us to be truly Christian, Mosaic Law must be properly esteemed and modeled, as it was by Jesus Christ.* Christians who believe what I have just described are sometimes referred to as "theonomists."[7]

Governor John Winthrop (1588–1649), a "theonomist" of Massachusetts Bay Colony, understood God's design for Israel. He believed Israel was specifically called upon by God to demonstrate good government for the benefit of all nations near and far, according to Deuteronomy chapter four, "in the sight of the nations, which shall hear all these statutes." Winthrop no doubt responded to his personal knowledge of the Deuteronomy mandate when he deliberately described the American colonial frontier as "a city upon a hill" with the "eyes of all people...upon us." Let's take a moment and read the closing remarks of Governor John Winthrop's profound theonomic thesis of American government delivered in 1630, on board the good ship Arbella:

> We shall find that the God of Israel is among us, when ten of us shall be able to resist a thousand of our enemies; when he shall make us a praise and a glory, that men shall say of succeeding plantations, "[may] the Lord make it [like] that of New England." For we must consider that we shall be as a city upon a hill. The eyes of all people are upon us. So that if we shall deal falsely with our God in this work we have undertaken, and so cause Him to withdraw His present help from us, we shall be made a story and a by-word throughout the world. We shall open the mouths of enemies to speak evil of the ways of God, and all professors for God's sake. We shall shame the faces of many of God's worthy servants, and cause their prayers to be turned into curses upon us till we be consumed out of the good land whither we are going. [And to] shut this discourse with that exhortation of Moses, that faithful servant of the Lord, in his last farewell to Israel (Deut. 30). "Beloved, there is now set before us life and good, death and evil, in that we are commanded this day to love the Lord our God, and to love one another, to walk in his ways and to keep his Commandments and his ordinance and his laws, and the articles of our Covenant with Him, that we may live and be multiplied, and that the Lord our God may bless us in the land whither we go to possess it. But if our hearts shall turn away, so that we will not obey, but shall be seduced, and [worship] other Gods, our pleasure and profits, and serve them; it is propounded unto us this day, we

shall surely perish out of the good land whither we pass over this vast sea to possess it. Therefore let us choose life that we, and our seed may live, by obeying His voice and cleaving to Him, for He is our life and our prosperity.[8]

By following Israel's example, Winthrop also managed to follow Christ. By following Christ's teaching, he also managed to follow Israel. You see, he knew what we must come to understand in the church today—that the Deuteronomy chapter four mandate had been referenced by Jesus in His Sermon on the Mount, when He preached: "You are the light of the world. A city that is set on a hill cannot be hidden!" Winthrop knew his own government would become a suitable reflection of Israel's righteous example to the world. He believed it would be a true Christian nation implementing God's ultimate plan for all governments, not merely some ill-conceived "reincarnation of Israel" that supposedly "ignored grace" and "ignored Christ," as the modern antagonists like to claim.

Sadly, today's modern Christian authors directly criticize John Winthrop's alleged "misguided blurring of church and state," saying, "They [colonists under Winthrop] assumed that they were the new people of God embarking on a new exodus—an errand in the wilderness—to do theocracy the right way. Today, many American Christians seem to mix up church and state...But the nation of America isn't the people of God; we don't live in a theocracy. The sooner Christians realize this, the sooner the church can make a deeper impact."[9] One can only conclude from this particular author's comments that he mistakenly believes something along the lines of "the purer the secularism the greater the impact of Christianity." Seriously? This is a radical hypothesis conflicting with what is penned by the apostle Paul, in 1 Timothy 2:1–6. Let's read it.

> I exhort therefore, that, first of all, supplications, prayers, intercessions, and giving of thanks, be made for all men; For kings, and for all that are in authority; that we may lead a quiet and peaceable life in all godliness and honesty. For this is good and acceptable in the sight of God our Saviour; Who will have all men to be saved, and to come unto the knowledge of the truth. For there is one God, and one mediator between God and men, the man Christ Jesus; Who gave himself a ransom for all, to be testified in due time.

Paul's instructions given to the predominantly Jewish early church membership (upon whom were granted no privileges of Roman citizenship, much less voting rights) to apply the greatest level of influence they *did* have (the influence of prayer) against the otherwise hostile throws of pagan government, demonstrate how necessary Christian influence upon government was and is still today.

Without the influence of these early Christians doing their best in prayer to halt the powers of darkness being channeled through government, evangelism would otherwise be hindered by the unrestrained pagan government. It was "good and acceptable in the sight of God" that the church experience evangelistic freedom; able to "lead quiet and peaceable life in [unlimited] godliness and [unlimited] honesty."

In this text, it is clear that hostile civil government was understood as a potential hinderer and limiter of peaceable and unlimited godliness and honesty. Why was it important they use the influential power of prayer as a positive godly force in their present state of Roman governmental domination? Because God wanted people to get saved! God desired "all men to be saved, and come unto the knowledge of the truth" (1 Tim. 2:4).

Paul's thought is completed in verse six as he reminds the readers that Christ is Lord of *all*. (We must infer that human governments are included in the definition of the word "all.") Specifically, they were directed by Paul to pray for those in authority, because if and when such leaders were converted and discipled, the umbrella effect upon the whole society would be "good and acceptable in the sight of our Savior."

John Winthrop well knew what Paul had taught Timothy in the passage we just read. Saying "Christ is Lord of all" in some otherworldly and mystical way was little more than a patronizing, passive denial of Christ's literal present-tense lordship—*now.* Winthrop, like Jesus and the apostle Paul, understood the Great Commission commanded more than merely going into all nations; it implied that all nations were equally commanded to conform to the higher laws of God—*now*—through repentance—in response to our heralding the gospel message among them.

Though we know many will inevitably refuse to come to Christ and that the last days will indeed produce perilous times, it was never at any point recommended (or even hinted) that any part of this present fallen world (individuals, whole national governments or otherwise) should wait until Christ finally forced them, at the tip of His sword, to bow and obey to His lordship! In fact, resistant peoples and nations are repeatedly warned throughout the biblical narrative, in both testaments, that refusal of God's *present-tense* lordship in their *present-tense* lives will bring unnecessary and avoidable human suffering in this *present-tense* physical existence. Further, the Bible warns that should one take their rebellion against Christ's *present-tense* Lordship to its greatest extreme, their *present-tense* consequences will quickly convert to *eternal* sufferings in hell. Amidst this reality, we find our own mandate to understand and obey the full scope of the Great Commission.

Our antagonists use the Bible in an impure way. They misuse its beautiful words as justification for removing the proverbial warning sign on the highway which reads: "Bridge Is Out! Do Not Proceed! Extreme Danger!" Why do they believe the sign should be removed? They say "men should be free to keep driving if they want to!" Those who argue to remove the signs are simple purveyors of injustice.

In reality, everyone *should* know that a road sign has never had the magical influence to defeat the horsepower of a V8 engine. The presence of a road sign has never possessed the power to overcome the will of a belligerent driver, but it can offer incentive for the driver to make a good choice. "After all, what if the sign tells me the truth?" he mutters. Should he barrel forward anyway, ignoring the warnings, then all excuses are removed from his defense, right along with society's obligation to feel sorry for the consequences he must face, for justice has been served.

Codifying good and righteous law in a democratic society, where some portion of the population openly resents good law, does not qualify as "forcing religion upon the unwilling." It does not qualify as that any more than Moses's and God's decision to criminalize murder "forced the ancient Hebrews to stop hating." (I would be willing to bet that the day after Moses descended from Sinai with two tablets of stone announcing "Thou shalt do no murder!" someone died at the hands of a homicidal neighbor.) Criminalizing adultery in 2015 America would have no more power to force men to stop lusting for naked women than it did in 1534 BC when Moses forbade it by promising criminal consequences for it. This entire subject of "forcing religion upon the unwilling" is an unintelligent fallacy. The greatest power of any codified law in any civilization of history has never been more than a means to warn a citizen of consequences for his actions. Our antagonists do not really argue in favor of the so-called freedom to reject God. The "freedom to reject God" and the "personal liberties" they pretend to protect are their smoke and mirrors. In reality, they argue in favor of allowing human law to deceive the souls of their neighbors. They fail to love their neighbors as themselves. For this, they are guilty of personally breaking the whole law of God. For fighting against the application of Mosaic Law in modern times, they are guilty of empowering a new kind of Rome—a nation of "great sin." Yet, in the same way Jesus charged the Sanhedrin, our modern religious antagonists commit the "greater sin" than Pilate's Rome.

In 1 Timothy 2:1–6 Paul taught Timothy how to maneuver against a hostile government being used by Satan to hinder successful evangelism. Basically, Paul was giving Timothy in-field advice connected to the Deuteronomy chapter four mandate. (I think it goes without saying that Paul, a former "Pharisee of Pharisees," well understood the Book of Deuteronomy.) Both Paul and Timothy comprehended that Christ's Sermon on the Mount was, among other things, a refreshing reiteration of the Deuteronomy chapter four mandate. As touched upon earlier, the Jewish Christ, speaking to a Jewish audience, proclaimed: "You are the light of the world. A city that is set on a hill cannot be hidden." This was very much a parallel of Moses's related admonition 1534 years earlier, when he also told the Jews, "...this is your wisdom and your understanding in the sight of the nations, which shall hear all these statutes, and say, Surely this great nation is a wise and understanding people" (Deut. 4:6).

THE MISHANDLING OF TRUTH IS NOTHING NEW

The mishandling and overspiritualization of Paul's, Jesus's and Moses's complementary remarks, not unlike the old-world religious criticism of John Winthrop, are nothing new. John Winthrop's understanding of the Deuteronomy chapter four mandate and the Sermon on the Mount was challenged by two particular persons (theological antinomians), who, like many today, argued against the application of Mosaic Law in government. Anne Hutchinson and Pastor John Wheelwright's antinomian hostility toward applying the Word of God in civil government created factions and discord among the colonial Christian church and their respective government.

The controversy then, just as it continues to divide and weaken the church and their respective nations today, split the colonial Christian community in two disgruntled factions—one that believed Christ was "Lord of all" and should be acknowledged as such, and another that was strangely eager to encourage secularism (despite Christ's strong rejection of the Herodian brand of secularism in His own day). Eventually the antinomians were soundly defeated by the 1637 reelection of Governor Winthrop. Their defeat fostered the eventual creation of Rhode Island providence, which later became the first of the original thirteen colonies to begin retreating from the legal anchor of the Mosaic Decalogue as the basis of their civil laws. (Anne Hutchinson, the "Christian antinomian heretic" and natural advocate of secularism, founded Portsmouth, Rhode Island after Winthrop banished both her and Pastor Wheelwright from the community for what he described as dangerous heresy.)[10]

To parallel with the doctrinal cleansing that happened in Massachusetts Bay Colony back in 1637, I believe the Lord has shown me that we have entered a time in the life, death, and possible resurrection of the America that once was, when the Holy Spirit is calling upon churchgoing believers to leave local churches who refuse to accept the Deuteronomy chapter four mandate of His present-day church, and instead, join forces with those local churches who are already obediently engaging in decentralized political activism. The Holy Spirit is wooing resistant pastors and ecclesiastical powers to repent for their rebellion against the full scope of the Great Commission. Let him that hath ears hear. (But more on this later.)

CHRISTIANITY INSIDE-OUT

The catalyst of the Abrahamic and Mosaic promise to affect the nations of the world sprung forth in the person of Christ, in Palestine 2,000 years ago. *For an obedient modern church, the cases of personal salvation, its assumed effect upon self-government, and the obligatory impact of biblical law upon present-day civil governments, rise and fall together.* While the modern church has done a measurable job instructing society in the inside-out change of the individual heart, it has rejected the application of Mosaic Law upon contemporary governments. This must be remedied by a reformation of doctrine that can only come through a combination of faithful teaching of the Bible (Rom. 10:14),[11] renewal of the Holy Spirit (Jude 1:19–25),[12] followed by the direct, personal intervention of faithful and loving Christians in all arenas of self, family, church, local, state, and federal governments.

Religious antagonists who oppose the truth set forth in this writing have commonly (sometimes angrily) accused me of "trying to save people from the outside-in, instead of from the inside-out." Others have gone so far to say that the application of this doctrine, as it happens to apply to the political and legal world, is "forcing salvation upon the unwilling." This is a curious kind of accusation on several points. First, remember that a spiritual mission—like that demonstrated by Jesus for three and a half years—fed *physical* bread and fish to hungry people and confronted His contemporary *physical* version of the legislative, judicial, and executive branches of Hebrew government regularly. My point here is just to say that Jesus did not espouse the physically useless mysticism that seems to have popularly replaced Christian action in America today. The Book of "Acts" was very properly titled; it was not called the book of "Cultural Retreat."

Recall, again, as has been pointed out throughout this work, that the Grand Sanhedrin operated beneath the auspices of their Roman conquerors as officials of Hebrew government. Speaking directly to government officials, Jesus quipped: "For John came neither eating nor drinking, and [you] say, He hath a devil[!] The Son of man came eating and drinking, and [you] say, Behold a man gluttonous, and a winebibber, a friend of publicans and sinners[!] But wisdom is justified of her children" (Matt. 11:18–19). In other words, the government officials were naturally willing to condemn the righteous works of any godly man, particularly John the Baptist and Jesus, as a means to justify and protect their own decision (both as individuals and as civil rulers, mind you) to reject godly truth. (Recall, there can be no civil justice without truth.) What should be said of preachers—unlike Jesus and John—who are apparently unwilling to confront their own corrupt governments with truth? Do we really love our neighbors when we foster injustice by our absence from the public discourse? Jesus and John did not believe so. We no more love our neighbors when we retreat from politics than we love nearby travelers when we remove warning signs from their highway.

CHRISTIANITY OUTSIDE-IN

To be clear, the emphasis of the church has always been and must remain upon the dimension of *self-government*. (See "the fruits of the Spirit" taught in Galatians 5.) Christianity is a personal relationship that demands personal discipline *empowered* by grace not *excused* by grace. (Sorry habitual sinners and disingenuous repenters.) Unquestionably, souls are saved and discipled one at a time. But please embrace the fact that each self-governed individual soul is, by design of "Nature and Nature's God," unmistakably affected by *exterior* influences. Thus, our Bible explains the absolute necessity for the following:

1. Preacher—*exterior* influence of church government. (See Romans 10:13–14.)

2. Parents—*exterior* influence of family government. (See 1 Timothy 5:8.)

3. Friends—*exterior* influence of social government. (See Matthew 11:19.)

4. Culture—*exterior* influence of civil government. (See Romans 7:7 and Romans 13.)

Apparently, God does not have an aversion to truth-based *outside-in* influences. The Bible does not discourage outside-in influences in any remote way; however, the very opposite is the case.

The priority of the Great Commission is to make self-governed disciples, one at a time. However, what about those who have *already been discipled*? What are they to do? They are to infiltrate, shape, and maintain every exterior influence possible (using the unique grace each disciple is supplied in life) for the sake of the yet lost souls. They are to dutifully place warning signs on the roads leading to destruction.

While it is certainly true that spiritual evangelism must stay out in front of political and legal recovery (else there be no godly man to run for elected office or preside over the courts), it cannot be true that the two issues of *saving souls* and *preserving godly government* could be mutually exclusive. As mentioned earlier in this chapter, according to Paul's instructions given to Timothy on the importance of employing the spiritual influence of prayer upon civil government, those of us who have already been discipled have the responsibility of producing an optimum atmosphere most conducive to successful evangelism! Thus, it is a false dichotomy to suggest that obeying the immutable laws of God *after* one is saved by grace is in any way confusing to the gospel. Specifically, the following actions are required by the Scriptures, with regard to all sectors of human government:

1. A preacher should preach truth and reject lies (good church government).

2. A parent should train in truth and expose lies (good family government).

3. Friends should fellowship around truth and avoid lies (good social government).

4. Civil society should reward good (which cannot occur without justice based upon absolute truth) and punish evil (which emanates from spiritual deception). (This activity produces good civil government.)

We deduce from these truths that when the church refuses to do *anything* beyond simply teaching self-government and they willfully retreat from *all other exterior governments*, evangelism is hindered and Christ's sovereign crown rights over *all* dimensions of government are denied. Focusing *only* upon individuals who are lost (though we acknowledge it is the priority of the church), and simultaneously refusing to do anything about the exterior influences that compete for the hearts of the lost, is nothing short of either ignorance or willful defiance against the sensibilities of the Great Commission. It is a failure to "go [poreuomai] into [eis] all [hapas] the world [kosmos]," which is the original Greek text of Mark 16:15.

At this juncture, it is critical to comprehend the combination of *exterior* as well as *interior* influences that took place in the life of Saul of Tarsus, before and during his conversion to Christ. Looking back upon his own personal salvation, Paul (formerly Saul) said that the particular way he came to Christ was designed by the Holy Spirit to be an example to all people who wish to come to Christ:

> But for that very reason I was shown mercy so that in me, the worst of sinners, Christ Jesus might display his immense patience as an example for those who would believe on him and receive eternal life.
>
> —1 TIMOTHY 1:16, NIV

In Paul's own account of what necessary ingredients were very influential in preparing the soil of his heart to receive Christ, Paul says of the Hebrew civil code:

What shall we say then? Is the law sin? God forbid. Howbeit, I
had not known sin, except through the law: for I had not known
coveting, except the law had said, Thou shalt not covet...So
that the law is holy, and the commandment holy, and righteous,
and good. Did then that which is good become death unto me?
God forbid. But sin, that it might be shown to be sin, by working
death to me through that which is good;—that through the
commandment sin might become exceeding sinful.
                                        —Romans 7:7, 12–13, asv

In other words, Paul clearly shows that the *exterior* civil code of
his nation prepared his heart for the redeeming truth of Jesus Christ,
by placing a righteous standard of justice in his sight (and every other
Hebrew citizen, for that matter). Notice the gravity of the statement:
"I had not known sin, except through the law." Paul's *internal* conviction of sin, which was absolutely necessary for his own true repentance and redemption (and ours as well), was attributed to the public
and *external* civil code of the Hebrew nation. This begs a question:
*What would have happened to Paul if the Hebrew civil code of his
day had practically celebrated and encouraged lust, as America's
system of law does today via "no-fault" divorce and various strands
of pro-sodomite law granting special rights to those who pretend
their sexual fetish is the equivalent of a race?*

My Child Became a Living Epistle

I began this book by sharing one of the most precious experiences of
my entire life—the story of how my child, Jonas, came to Jesus Christ by
the schoolmaster of the law of God, according to Galatians 3:24 (gnv):

Wherefore the Law was our schoolmaster to bring us to Christ,
that we might be made righteous by faith.

But through the Scriptures, we discover that the kingdom from
heaven is here to save more than our individual souls. The kingdom
from heaven is here to save our civilization. As it so happens, individual souls, like man-created governments, are saved the exact same
way. The Mosaic Law is the schoolmaster that leads *both* to Christ.
I would be remiss if I did not remind the Christian world that the
ancient king Josiah's rediscovery of his own national history (his

servants found the forgotten and lost scrolls of Moses) brought a nationwide revival to the people of his generation! A rediscovery of God's law is necessary today if our culture is to enjoy another Great Awakening.

> And the king sent, and they gathered unto him all the elders of Judah and of Jerusalem. And the king went up into the house of the LORD, and all the men of Judah and all the inhabitants of Jerusalem with him, and the priests, and the prophets, and all the people, both small and great: and he read in their ears all the words of the book of the covenant which was found in the house of the LORD. And the king stood by a pillar, and made a covenant before the LORD, to walk after the LORD, and to keep his commandments and his testimonies and his statutes with all their heart and all their soul, to perform the words of this covenant that were written in this book. And all the people stood to the covenant... And like unto him was there no king before him, that turned to the LORD with all his heart, and with all his soul, and with all his might, according to all the law of Moses; neither after him arose there any like him.
>   —2 KINGS 23:1–3, 25

Perhaps our antagonists should weigh the value of this grand story in the scales of their methods of interpretation and application of Scripture? According to Peter, in 2 Peter 2:4–6, the Old Testament was "given as an example" to demonstrate transcendent principles for us today!

In the light of the whole volume of what you have read in this work up to this point, it is abundantly clear that the Deuteronomy chapter four mandate for good government around the globe is directly connected to the need for successful evangelism around the globe. A false standard of truth in the public arena serves to deceive the human soul and hardens his conscience to the transforming potential of the gospel of Jesus Christ! As proof of this, consider that America enjoyed two Great Awakenings in its history, and both occurred in a time of history when our system of law much more closely mirrored the laws of Moses. (This was thoroughly proven in the outlining of America's legal history, which was done for your benefit in chapters seven and eight.)

We've considered the fact that Paul clearly stated his own salvation experience was designed by God as an example for future converts in search of eternal salvation. We've listened to Paul's own testimony of how the Hebrew civil code prepared his heart for repentance by helping him to identify the difference between good and evil. I have shared an example of this precious truth as it unfolded in the life of my beloved Jonas Holland Gordon, who came to Christ for relief from his own knowledge of estrangement from God, at the age of six years old, on Wednesday, May 29, 2013, at approximately 4:30 p.m. We have extrapolated from these points that while government does not have the power to save the human soul, it certainly does have the power to hinder its discernment between good and evil. So we move to view Paul's own tactics when attempting to lead another lost soul to Christ. What did Paul do? What method did he employ to prepare other lost souls for repentance and transformation?

> And when they had appointed him a day, they came to him into his lodging in great number; to whom he expounded the matter, testifying the kingdom of God, and persuading them concerning Jesus, both from the law of Moses and from the prophets, from morning till evening.
> —ACTS 28:23, ASV

In case I have not been clear enough, I present this truth based upon the apostle Paul's testimony: the people of any nation are either redeemable or unredeemable in direct proportion to the degree their culture (systems of law and politics should be assumed) has been preserved (or neglected) by knowledge (or ignorance) of God's immutable and eternal laws. In other words, when the church *increases* the activities of salt and light, they should expect an *increase* of genuine repentances, conversions, and discipleships. When the church *withdraws* and *decreases* salt and light activities, they should expect a corresponding *decrease* of genuine repentances, conversions, and discipleships.

Many antagonists will, at this point in the argument, make the mistake of pretending my hypothesis is a "which came first, the chicken or the egg" scenario, falsely drawing some parallel between Paul's description of the external civil law (as the chicken, we suppose) and the internal drive to repentance before Christ (as the proverbial egg). The argument is, of course, nonsense. It is not a question of which came first—the saved individual or the external legal system that made him feel guilty. It is a question of which came first—the Creator and His law or the creature of clay? The answer is all too obvious, and rejection of it teeters between either ignorance or ineptitude.

Nary a soul could come to Christ without God's law having been *first* introduced to their heart and mind in some way. Furthermore, one must sufficiently determine how *never* reinforcing God's law from an *external* standpoint could be described as "good." God was the *first* to exist! Thus, His *law* came before both the chicken and the egg! As is usually the case, the real intimidating burden of proof rests upon the antagonist. How on earth can he claim that mirroring God's holy law in modern governments will supposedly "hinder" any man's ability to come to Christ? It is a denial of what the Scripture plainly teaches us.

I first discovered one particular antagonist argument (that I later came to understand was quite popular among antagonists of many denominational stripes) while debating the scope of the Great Commission with a particular Reformed pastor residing in the state of Iowa. A few weeks prior to our discussion, I had been discussing the full scope of the Great Commission (in response to a politely hostile caller who didn't feel it was appropriate for me to engage the political world) while on one of the largest and most listened-to radio shows in the state of Iowa. I had been invited onto the show to discuss my controversial stand that had recently garnered national attention with Rev. Barry Lynn of Americans United for Separation of Church and State, particularly screeching that my activities were "the most outrageous attempts to politicize a church that he [had] ever seen."[13] My response to his toothless threats against our church was to further provoke a lawsuit with the IRS by daring them to attack our church's God-given right to defend holy matrimony and speak with First Amendment-protected liberty in the pulpit. I sought to right the wrongs of the IRS violation of free speech in churches, stemming from the old misunderstood and ill-conceived 1954 Johnson Amendment. Apparently, in the process of the interview, my remarks on the Great Commission ruffled some feathers.

Several months after my deliberation with the Reformed antagonist (who took exception to my comments over the radio broadcast), I read the very same antagonist argument published in the book of someone I had at one time considered to be a friend—a minister, oddly enough, of a shared Pentecostal persuasion. The friend's published remarks were particularly interesting, as I discovered them on the heels of a sermon of mine where the author in question had sat noticeably scowling and fidgeting throughout my lecture on the relation between law and salvation. (At the close of that message, the disturbed minister(s) left the pastors' convention prematurely—in a huff.) A few months later, I more or less read the major points of my recent lecture on the biblical role of the modern church "corrected" in their latest book.

The shared paradigm of both the Reformed pastor and the Pentecostal author went something like this: "You are wrong about the Great Commission! Matthew chapter twenty-eight and verse nineteen says 'go therefore and make disciples of all the nations.' The word 'nations' comes from the original Greek word 'ethos,' which means 'races of people.' Clearly this has nothing to do with governments or politics as you have incorrectly claimed!"

My response to this argument is really very simple. We have four Gospels and one particular Book of Acts wherewith we are compelled to understand a comprehensive view of the early church, as well as the meanings of particular commands of Jesus. With respect to the Great Commission, it is recorded by the authors Matthew, Mark, and Luke (in his Book of Acts), and the particular Gospels of Luke and John do not record the discussion at all. We cannot hope to practice any trustworthy and reliably accurate exegesis* of Jesus's Great Commission by exclusively considering the recordings of Matthew and ignoring the writings, in this case, of two additional authors (Mark and Luke) who described the Great Commission.

For example, Matthew does indeed teach us that part of the Great Commission requires that we willingly and obediently "go into all the *races* and preach the gospel." The word Matthew emphasizes is, indeed, the Greek word *ethos*. Yet, in Luke's description (Acts 1:8) of the Great Commission, an emphasis seems to be placed upon the need to (paraphrased) "go into all the *geography* and preach the gospel." Luke quotes Jesus, saying (paraphrased): "you shall be witnesses in Jerusalem, Judea, Samaria, and to the ends of the earth." Those are *physical* locations. But then we get to Mark's rendering of the subject, and he very clearly says: "go into all the social systems." The word he uses is the Greek word *kosmos*.

PIERCE CONTINUALLY EVERY SOCIAL SYSTEM

These three harmonious accounts are complementary to one another. Consolidate the three accounts and you have a complete view of the

---

* Biblical **exegesis** is a systematic process by which a person arrives at a reasonable and coherent sense of the meaning and message of a biblical passage. Ideally, an understanding of the original texts (Greek and Hebrew) is required. In the process of exegesis, a passage must be viewed in its historical and grammatical context with its time/purpose of writing taken into account.

command of Christ. It's as simple as 1-2-3: go into all races, go into all places, go into all social systems. None of these three authors' remarks are mutually exclusive (unless, of course, we foolishly wish to fight against the inerrancy and inspiration of our own Scriptures, to the serendipity of your local humanist professor of religion).

With regard to Mark 16:15, Greek scholar Rick Renner, PhD, describes it thusly: "The word 'world' in this verse is from the Greek word *kosmos*. This is very significant, for the word *kosmos* describes anything that is ordered. In Greek it is often used to denote *a particular political system; a system of fashion; a system found in any part of society, such as a circle of friends; or any sphere where you live and have influence.* [Jesus] expects you to invade every sphere where you have influence and to use your influence to declare the Gospel to people who live, work and function in those places."[14]

The whole passage of Mark 16:15 is rendered "poreuomai eis hapas kosmos." One way of saying it, after careful review of the Greek words in Strong's, could be: "Pierce continually every social system." That is our universal Christian command given in Mark 16:15. Why must we (who are already discipled) "pierce continually the entire social system?" Because the exterior influences can hinder our success if we neglect them and leave a vacuum for evil men to control them!

With regard to church government, retreating from good doctrine does not *help* discipleship. With regard to family government, retreating from teaching family values (by normalizing "gay" lifestyles, for example, or failing to teach the principles of biblical parenting) does not *help* discipleship. With regard to social government, retreating from friendships with the proverbial prostitutes and tax collectors does not *help* discipleship. With regard to civil government, retreating from the arena of law and politics does not *help* discipleship.

Civil law and its template is explained with great detail in the Old Covenant and is acknowledged by all legitimate theologians to be a gift from Father God to this world, according to Romans chapter 13. We have no less responsibility toward its maintenance (the gift from the first person of the Trinity) than we share for the maintenance of the gifts of the third person of the Trinity—whose gifts directly affect our self-government.

Galatians chapter 5 teaches us proper self-government by listing the fruits of the spirit in verses 22 and 23 as love, joy, peace, longsuffering, gentleness, goodness, faith, meekness, and temperance. The same text also clearly warns its readers that failure to walk in this prescribed mode of self-government will result in violation of God's law. Amongst many sins, particular public crimes are listed as the result of failure to biblically self-govern. As Paul describes the "works of the flesh" in verses 19 through 21 he lists "murders, seditions, drunkenness, adultery, and idolatry (which was associated with human sacrifice)." Each of these particular sins rise to the level of requiring criminal prosecution even in today's paganized civil governments. The contrast between good self-government by aid of the Holy Spirit, and the penalties *that remain necessary in the modern world arena of civil government* are described in this verse:

> But if ye be led by the Spirit, ye are not under the law.
> —GALATIANS 5:18

This passage in no way suggests that civil code of the Hebrews was "done away in Christ," as many are accustomed to hearing as an explanation for the previous verse. It expresses what should be common sense. Let the Spirit of God assist you in changing your behavior so that you never fall beneath the punishing powers of righteous civil government. Among other things, the text says to walk in love, and by doing so you won't fall into the sin of hate and end up murdering someone, getting caught, and being punished for the crime of murder.

Beware of the *real* distractions that hinder the gospel...those who build straw men, arguing the unreasonable (I'm being way too kind at this point) premise that "allowing evil men to run and corrupt every dimension of life on earth (except church life, of course) will assist the spread of the gospel." How ludicrous and diabolical can these arguments become and still be believed? This errant plan of retreat is against the plain teaching of 1 Timothy 2:1–4 and denies the worldview and proven fruit of the following great men of history, as it cannot be reconciled with the landslide of biblical examples: Abraham, Joseph, Moses, Joshua, Samuel, David, Gideon, Barak, Daniel, Shadrach, Meshach, Abednego, Ezekiel, Nahum, Jonah, Nathan, John the Baptist, Jesus Christ, Paul, Peter, Luke, and Stephen...(to name only a few). All of the men listed above enjoined some significant engagement within the realm of politics. Daniel, for example, was one of the greatest of prophets, yet he simultaneously served a heathen nation as its prime minister.

History is replete with those who followed that biblical example, like Augustine, John Knox, Wycliffe, Luther, Thompson, Brown, Calvin, Whitfield, Blackstone, Rush, Witherspoon, Finney, Lovejoy, Wilberforce, Haddock, Bonhoeffer, and so many others. They made *extraordinary* contributions to the Christianization of world civilization! These *world-changing* men *preached* and *demonstrated* the moral necessity for Christian engagement in politics—pastoral political engagement, in particular.

So many preachers have bought into this narrow view of their own role in society! They claim: "I'm just called to convert/disciple people into Christianity," and they have taken an either/or mentality—pretending that if they publicly engage in politics, on any level, they suddenly can't preach the message of salvation on Sunday. They deny that Jesus proved otherwise!

Here's a fair question to all these antagonists, who seem convinced that political action will stop evangelism: "Which of you have accomplished the tiniest fraction of discipleship the aforementioned saints accomplished through the very means of cultural engagement you criticize?"

The church, as a whole, has missed the mark. It has been shown through the testimony of historical Christian leaders (mentioned above), and it has been dissected, through the authoritative explanation of Scripture, in this writing. In similar sectors of our world, folks commonly object to Christian political action, asserting: "You are planning to grab the reins of influence through whatever means necessary, usurp the seats of political power, and impose some tyrannical 'theocracy' upon society from the top down with a 'whether you like it or not, it's for your own good' mentality!"[15]

POLITICS: WAR WITHOUT BULLETS

The problem with this particular objection (whether it is made by a "radical Reformed Presbyterian reconstructionist" against a "radical kingdom-now charismatic," or a homosexual activist publishing a screed against my public efforts in 2010 to protect marriage in Iowa and unseat three activist state supreme court judges[16]) is twofold: 1) The person making the accusation is either in private denial or they are being publicly dishonest about what politics actually is (war without bullets)...or both. 2) The person making the accusation intends to do the very thing he criticizes others for trying to do—*win* this particular kind of "war without bullets."

As Christian political strategist Michael Rothfeld once wrote:

> There is absolutely no reason for you to spend your time, talent and money in politics except for this: If you do not, laws will be written and regulations enforced by folks with little or no interest in your well-being.[17] Rothfeld went on in his article to explain that politics is nothing more and nothing less than the adjudication of power:

> Few of the lectures I give on political technology and campaigning make people as agitated as this one. None is more important. Simply put, politics is not about the common good, appealing to men's better angels, nor serving our Lord. These may be your motivations. I pray they are mine. Occasionally, they will be a politician's motivation. Politics is the adjudication of power. It is the process by which people everywhere determine who rules whom... The first mistake most folks make when they set out on a good-faith crusade to do good is to completely misunderstand their targets.[18]

Rothfeld's candid and "agitating" statements are, of course, absolutely true. The threefold reality that 1) no person (or civilization) can enjoy true justice without truth, and 2) there is no truth outside of Christ, and 3) we are required to "love our neighbors as ourselves," explains why Christians should strive to adjudicate power, and therefore, strive to win this political "war without bullets." The *goal* is to righteously adjudicate power—the *motive* is loving our neighbor enough to enter the miserable battlefield where the neighbors' injuries to his conscience and his sensitivity to the convicting power of God's law predominantly occur. This is precisely why Jesus admonished all to love their neighbors as themselves. As He did, He quoted the doctrine of Moses in Leviticus 19:17–18. How did both Moses and Jesus believe true love for our neighbor was to be applied? They taught that godly love rebukes a neighbor and will not allow sin to hold him in bondage. Let's read it.

> Thou shalt not hate thy brother in thine heart, but thou shalt plainly rebuke they neighbor, and suffer him not to sin. Thou shalt not avenge, nor be mindful of wrong against the

> children of thy people, but shalt love thy neighbor as thyself:
> I am the Lord.
>   —LEVITICUS 19:17–18, GNV

To fail to win (or to at least fail to *attempt* a win) is to ensure the enforcement of an ideological incursion *against* truth and reality, thereby making justice impossible. This is harmful to the common good! If we love our neighbors, as we are commanded to love, it is our obligation for the common good to fight against evil and do our very best to *win*! The vacuum must not be filled by wicked humanists who unrighteously adjudicate in the wake of our stubborn absence. I realize we have previously discussed the meaning of Paul's letter to Timothy (recorded in 1 Timothy 2:1–4), but humor me for a moment while I deliberately paraphrase the same verse "upside down" as I believe it may well assist to drive the point home: "First of all, if *your present means of influence* (like, for example, supplications, prayers, intercessions, and giving of thanks) are *not* made for kings, and for all that are in authority; then we will *not* lead a quiet and peaceable life in all godliness and honesty. This *bad* situation would *not* be good, *nor* would it be acceptable in the sight of God our Savior; Because all men *would not* be saved, and *would not* come unto the knowledge of the truth."

History has taught us a lesson on this kind of war without bullets we call "politics and law." If we do not manage this kind of war *without* bullets it will rapidly deteriorate into a war *with* them. Therefore, winning the political and legal battles preserves reasonable peace long enough to save lost souls. To my knowledge, no dead soul ruined by the bullets of war has ever been posthumously evangelized.

With the exception of our defeatist and escapist friends, *winning* is precisely what everyone, every side, every activist, every lawmaker, every voter, every judge, every pundit, every participant, every opinion-holder, every partisan in our kind of representative government intends to do! It is what politics is all about! So much so, that many voters erringly allow other influences to pick the person "who can win" for them, and they rubber-stamp candidates addicted to doublespeak above the candidate who will best secure the common good through principled leadership. We must reject this party-first mentality and always demand that representatives rise to *the standard* given by God in His Word.

Despite our misgivings of party-first corruptions, politics remains to be the adjudication of power! Nothing more! Nothing less! Pretending that it's about anything other than the adjudication of power is nonsensical, and frankly, it is weird. If you have an aversion to "winning" on some wrangled religious grounds, you have doctrinal issues at odds with the demonstration of Christ—our exemplary Champion!

You see, as I pointed out at the outset of this writing, all governments of the world are little more than "theocracies." What differentiates between them is found in answer to the question of "Theo's" identity and character. Once the identity of "Theo" is discovered, we must determine if he, "Theo," is righteous enough to produce authentic justice and liberty. Unfortunately, whether by means of bloody revolutions, rebellions, usurpations, coups d'état, or through an occasional peaceful election, "comrade Theo" always wins! In the wake of each shift of power, once the dust settles, mankind is left whispering (usually so as to avoid being imprisoned for trumped-up allegations of sedition), "Who is this new fellow named Theo?"

THREE CHOICES REMAIN

We only have the same three choices today that were available to the entire world way back in the year of our Lord, 1776.

- 1776 England was a "state-sanctioned religion."
- 1776 America was a "religion-sanctioned state."[19]
- 1789 France was a "secular state."

Which of these three have been most successful during the last 240 years and counting? Our founding fathers "loved" the state-sanctioned religion found in England so much that they risked their lives to flee from it embarking on a perilous journey at sea. England, the archetype of state-sanctioned religion, eventually succumbed to status as "the incredible shrinking empire!"

When asked to describe the difference between the American Revolution and the French Revolution, President Thomas Jefferson replied: "The comparisons of our governments with those of Europe are like a comparison of heaven and hell." George Mason, Father of the Bill of Rights similarly remarked: "I wish America would put her trust only in God and herself and have as little to do with the politics of Europe as possible." France and her magnifique crème de la crème of codified secularism quickly deteriorated into a basket case of what would produce many constitutional "re-dos" across the thread of history. Her first constitution of 1791 lasted only months before it was rendered obsolete. At the time of this writing, France has endured no less than seventeen constitutional "do-overs" since 1789.[20]

In contrast to England's state-sanctioned religion and France's secular state, America's religion-sanctioned state became, in its zenith of the "Roaring Twenties," the most powerful nation in the history of the world. In the crescendo of that thriving decade, just prior to the unforeseen Wall Street crash that would usher in the Great Depression of the 1930s, President Hoover thundered: "We in America today are nearer to the final triumph over poverty than ever before in the history of any land!" Despite the economic catastrophe that took place about one year after President Hoover's celebratory remarks, America managed to survive. At the time of this writing, it has survived these many years under one Constitution—the longest held Constitution in the history of the world! But...who is "Theo" in America right now?

The error of ancient Israel was striving to obey civil law without understanding its implied connection to their personal conscience. Jesus and Paul rebuked such "Judaizers." The error of modern Christianity is striving to obey conscience without understanding its implied connection to civil law.

One ditch produces fruitless obedience (good laws obeyed without faith); the other results in "fruity" disobedience (bad law allowed in the name of grace). Both extremes yield hell for their hoodwinked minions.

If we do not soon return to a place where the average man on the street can tell us who "Theo" really is in America, we will continue our decline into the tomb of lost empires, our steepled churches right along with them. "But God cannot be defeated, brother! He is in control! America is in her current state because it is His will!" proclaims the hyper-Calvinist.

It is not the Lord being defeated that I'm worried about. It is us. Take responsibility for more than only yourselves, my brothers—love your neighbors too.

Jesus, You are Lord of *all*!

CHAPTER 10: REVIEW QUESTIONS

Enjoy this quiz at http://peacemakersinstitute.com/smb-quiz.

1. Why was Moses so aggressively hawkish against idolatry in particular?

2. Is it reasonable to believe that good government was only needed prior to the arrival of our Messiah, but not important prior to the Messiah's millennial reign?

3. Did Christ come to mark the end of Israel's global mission, or did He come to salvage what they had frittered away in disobedience?

4. When the prophet Ezra fought to uphold the jot and tittle of Mosaic Law one thousand years after Moses's death and seventy years into the Babylonian captivity, was it the act of a situationist, an antinomian, or a righteous legalist?

5. Doesn't Ezra's upholding of Mosaic Law one thousand years after Moses's death prove that Mosaic Law was not "temporary" or only for the brief time the Hebrews wandered in the wilderness?

6. Did Jesus tell a rich young ruler that eternal life was found in keeping the commandments?

7. While Jesus cleared the temple in a fit of righteous anger, what Old Testament prophet did He quote?

8. Explain what Jesus meant when He said to Pilate, "My kingdom is not of this world."

9. Explain Christ's three-stage plan to rule the world.

10. Was Governor Winthrop misguided in his view of church and state?

11. What three choices do Americans have for the kind of government they will endure?

12. What did Paul say led him to Christ and therefore became his evangelistic tool for leading others to Christ? What led Jonas Holland Gordon to saving faith in Christ?

Chapter 11

Duverger Is Lord?

*M*AURICE DUVERGER WAS a popular political sociologist (himself a Communist) who became rather famous when he published empirical evidence for what became known as "Duverger's Law." His law concluded that a two-party system will tend to discourage the success of third, fourth, and fifth parties in the political world for a simple, twofold reason: 1) The tendency for alliances to be made by weaker factions seeking to win, and 2) the tendency for voters themselves to gradually abandon the best political choices in favor of a worse choice presumed to be better suited to actually win the contest.

To make it very simple—Duverger correctly identified how the sin-nature of men who ignored God's moral and civic laws would behave on any given day, in an environment where "winning a contest" was more important to them than defending proven truths.

Listen to me, church! For a Christian to submit to Duverger's Law requires him to disobey God's law! Following the way of Duverger's Law is the equivalent of Shadrach, Meshach, and Abednego bowing one knee to Nebuchadnezzar's idol while trying to keep the other leg straight to patronize the God of Abraham. It's the equivalent of Daniel closing his window shutters and curtains and praying in a whisper to avoid the lion's den. It's the equivalent of the Pharisees telling Jesus in the thirteenth chapter of Luke, "We command You in the name of Herod to shut up and get out of our town!," and Jesus replying, "Oh, OK. I'm so sorry. I'll be gone within the hour. I apologize for the misunderstanding."

During elections, when it has been determined by God that something is right, we must do what is right—even when the consequences for doing right causes immediate pain. When something is wrong, we do what is right, even when the consequences of doing wrong brings

immediate pleasure. This is truth, and it is absolute! It is the discipline of Christianity...even on election day! To every Christian in
America who keeps rewarding Republicans because they are alleged
to be the "lesser of two evils" and will supposedly cause less pain
than the Democrat alternative (who is assumed to be "more evil"), I
pose this question:

"What unrepentant sin against Jesus Christ does a Republican have
to commit before you will stop rewarding them with your vote?"

The most common response to this very legitimate question is:
"But, hey! There are only two choices for president. We have to pick
one, and if you don't pick the Republican, you may as well have cast
your vote for the Democrat!"

Three responses:

1. Duverger is Lord? Or was it Jesus Christ?

2. If it was true that by not supporting a dirty Republican
   you are automatically supporting an even dirtier
   Democrat, then it must also be true that by not supporting an even dirtier Democrat, you are automatically
   supporting a dirty Republican.

3. Wait a minute. If either one of those two clichés is true,
   then if you choose to not support either one...wouldn't
   you allegedly be helping both of them at the same time?

Obviously, this argument is silly and illogical. It's actually just propaganda used by the people who act like Duverger is their Lord and
Savior, and winning a dirty contest is more important than cleaning
up the contest. Who is *your* Lord? Duverger...or Jesus?

This whole discussion exposes another fatal problem with the
lesser-of-*two*-evils thinking in American politics. The belief that
every voter is limited to only *two* options on any given ballot is false.
There is always a *third* option. In most states, there is a write-in
blank available, or in the case where a write-in blank is not an option,
then say no to both evils! If Duverger is your Lord, then you are duty-
bound to follow Duverger's Law, and compromising sacred truths is
what you do in order to win, win, win! If Duverger is Lord, then you
must pick between the two evils so you can be a *winner*, even if that
means abandoning the better people running for office in order to

call yourself a winner. This begs another question: When evil people win... is anyone really a winner?

If I ever voted for a candidate of whom I do not approve, simply because others insisted that I should do so, I would cease to really give my voice to the political world. My voice would be silenced behind the voice of group-think, and the entire purpose of a ballot would be cheapened so as to disgrace the dead on history's battle-fields. A write-in blank is equal to or greater than a checkmark, and if Jesus is your Lord (as opposed to Duverger), the value of your vote (or righteous refusal to vote at all) is determined by fixed universal truths beyond human jurisdiction.

Folks, picking which candidate to support is as important as picking which candidate *not* to support. Let the Law of God be your moral anchor, not the popular choice of your party (who is most likely following Duverger's Law while rolling their eyes at the mention of God's law). John Adams said it this way: "Vox populi, vox Dei [the voice of the people is the voice of God] they say, and so it is, sometimes; but it is sometimes the voice of Mahomet, of Caesar, of Catiline, the Pope and the Devil."

You see, when a consecrated Christian rejects a Democrat candidate because he and his party enable evil things like baby-murder (abortion), the murder of the sick, old and infirmed (euthanasia), sexually perverted lifestyles and the theft of private property called "wealth redistribution"... and then spins around in the next moment to support a Republican candidate who is guilty of the *very same crimes against God's law*, he clearly reveals a double-standard, proves he is in idolatry of party and verifies he is an authentic hypocrite.

For example, in the 2012 election cycle, you could hear Barack Obama say things like: "I am committed to *reducing* abortions in America, that's why I am pro-choice." You could also hear Mitt Romney say: "I am committed to *reducing* abortions in America, that's why I am pro-life." The end result of either man in office would have been identical. They both labeled themselves differently for voter appeal, while essentially saying the same thing about "reducing" baby-murder. The truth is, both candidates were simply wordsmithing the exact same pagan situational ethics to garner votes from a targeted audience. Meanwhile, according to the Securities and Exchange Commission, Mitt Romney made around 50 million dollars in profits generated by dead baby body disposals through Stericycle Corporation.[1] We conclude that liberals make their money on the front end of baby-murder, and fake conservatives make theirs on the back end of the for-profit murder-mills. The question is simple and bears repeating: What unrepentant crime against Jesus Christ must a Republican commit before we will stop rewarding them with our votes?

> Don't copy the behavior and customs of this world, but let God transform you into a new person by changing the way you think. Then you will learn to know God's will for you, which is good and pleasing and perfect.
> —ROMANS 12:2, NLT

WHEN COMPROMISE FAILS, TRY MEGA-COMPROMISE?

I sinned by voting for John McCain in 2008. I caved into the pressure of Republican Party propaganda and violated the law of God when that fateful Tuesday of the general election finally arrived. My sin was not one of commission, though. I meant very well to do good and had no intent to do wrong at all when I arrived at my local polling station. I was simply ignorant of my own complicity in the regressive ruin of America and my role in our nation's two-century history of slow anni-hilation. Paul Revere needed not ride through the towns and villages again to warn us the English were coming. Tyranny wasn't *coming* to America... America was *returning* to tyranny. And me? I was caught in the meme trying, however uselessly, to slow it down by rewarding another Republican statist betrayer.

Four years later, in a KGOV broadcast out of Arvada, Colorado (Denver area), on October 31st of 2012, Pastor Bob Enyart of Denver Bible Church explained the tragic foolishness of the Republican Party's attempt to win the 2008 bid for the White House and the pagan GOP establishment's abysmal failure to learn from their grave errors in a second attempt in 2012. Pastor Enyart described what was happening—*again*—during the 2012 elections this way: "The GOP's strategy of compromising in order to win hasn't worked. McCain was pretty liberal and transparent to the fact that he was not a Christian. He was slaughtered. If the GOP was smart, they would have real-ized their compromise strategy was a bad strategy, but instead, they thought they didn't compromise *enough*. So they picked Romney, who's even further left than McCain, and a Mormon, no less. The GOP is testing if *mega-compromise* is the path to victory! If they win, have *we* really won? Of course not! We need to think big picture and long term here. Candidates that run as Christian, pro-life, anti-gay marriage politicians do quite well (Reagan, W. Bush). What message [in the upcoming 2012 elections] do we want to send the GOP? That we stand with their compromising strategy, or that we're more than willing to lose a battle in order to win the war?"

Pastor Enyart accurately described my former ignorance and complicity with the problem of infidelity to God's law on that fateful election Tuesday of 2008. But I learned from my errors and would not repeat them again by voting for Mitt Romney in 2012, no matter how terrible the consequences of a second term for Barack Obama frightened me. Why the change? Not long after Barack Obama (the most un-American president in American history) became the 44th President of the United States in 2008, I realized how Christian people like me were being disingenuously exploited by the Republican Party. I learned how my ignorance had allowed Duverger to masquerade as Lord.

Once McCain became the nominee, I knew he would be the lesser of two evils in a side-by-side evaluation (though not necessarily the "lesser evil" in an unintended consequences contest). I didn't want Barack Obama to destroy Americanism, so I convinced myself I was "voting for Sarah Palin," and I voted for...John McCain. The end of my innocence began on the first day I was mugged by reality. With George Bush out of the White House, Laura Bush launched a nationwide speaking circuit, with her daughter in tow, to promote both of the great evils her husband had claimed to stand against—gay marriage and abortion. I was horrified by such a great betrayal of America's Christian people, even more by the Bush family's unrepentant crimes against common sense, not to mention the laws of God.

Later, after John McCain lost to Barack Obama, I found a video clip of a presidential debate I had apparently missed before the elections had taken place. My revulsion intensified. It seemed a beautiful Florida girl named Terri had gone on a diet to drop a few pounds, and sadly, when she didn't get enough potassium, she passed out on the floor and slipped into a coma. Even though she was eventually back in stable condition and could smile at her parents (though she remained mostly unable to communicate), she was starved to death and denied water in a Florida nursing home. The authorities said it was "the compassionate thing to do." During a Republican primary debate, Romney, Giuliani, and McCain agreed. Republicans...Mitt

Romney, Rudy Giuliani, and John McCain chose to be enablers of Terri Schiavo's perverse euthanasia.

Florida authorities posted armed guards at the nursing home door to keep anyone from sneaking in and trying to put ice chips in Terri Schiavo's mouth. On March 26, in an attempt to take water to Terri, two demonstrators were arrested and taken to jail. They joined another thirty-one God-fearing good Samaritans who also attempted the very same thing to save her life. Terri died after several miserable days of forced starvation. The powers that be wanted her to die from dehydration, because they decided she would likely never completely recover from her dietary mishap. Starvation and dehydration, they claimed, were the more "compassionate" things to do.[2]

IF I WERE THE DEVIL...

When I look back on that horrid day in America, I see the people of Germany in the 1930s, and I hear the argument of "compassion" coming up from the pages of a book called Mein Kampf, written by a man named Adolf Hitler. America has been sliding toward the left for at least the last 100 years. Our nation lunges to the left when a Democrat wins a popular election and it steps to the left when a Republican wins. This is the result of what the political scientists call "Duverger's Law." This is what happens when Christians reject God's law as the final arbiter of their voting-booth decisions and replace His law with Duverger's. This is what happens when God's absolute laws are no longer used as the true anchor on the right, but instead, the position of the hard left (Democrats) becomes the center of gravity, and the soft left (Republicans) calibrates its new position by walking six steps to the right of the hard left. This is what happens when citizens treat politics as if it were a mere sporting event, hoping their favorite team can win the competition. This is what happens when winning is more valued than how the game is played.

But politics isn't really as simple as a fun game of basketball. Political decisions kill people. I'm certain the devil knows that is true too. If I were the devil, I would do three things to destroy America:

1. Get a supermajority of evangelicals to adopt pagan, humanist, situational ethics. (Lesser of two evils pseudo-logic.)

2. Make sure the "hard left" is always "more evil" than the "soft left."

3. Make sure the "soft left" figured out that evangelicals would always reward them with support, no matter *what* they did, so long as they took care to be the "lesser of two evils."

(That way, the soft left would *never* have *any* reason to conform to absolute truths the church still accidentally possessed and repent. And they would remain free to continually move to the left with no pesky absolutes.)

Voilà!

Evangelicals would become my unwitting secret weapons to guarantee America always moved *left*, always grew *further* away from God and eventually collapsed. Brilliant, ain't it? If I were the devil I'd deserve...like...an honorary doctorate in political science or something! Fame! Fortune! A "seat at the table"! Oh, and I'd crush anyone smart enough to figure out the way to ruin my plan was a *revolt* against the *soft left* and enlarge the influence of those who couldn't figure that out. I'd make the smart ones as socially and religiously popular as...Noah.

So how do we stop America from continuing its leftward lemming-march over the deadly cliffs of moral and fiscal insanity? We reanchor our political system on the right (opposite the cliff of insanity) with the only chains strong enough to stop the momentum we've built while heading in that wrong direction for so long...God's immutable laws. By choosing to do so, we refuse to go along with Duverger anymore. We let him know that he is *not* our Lord and that his humanist pagan law has now been replaced with God's law in our lives. We would like very much to win, but we aren't willing to violate God's law to do it ever again. Why? Because we now understand that every time an individual candidate or a whole political party wins a contest by trampling against the law of God, America loses.

This is where things get interesting. Are you worried that obeying God's law, without compromise, "won't work in the real world of politics"? Boy, are you in for a surprise! Want to know why it *will* work?

A FRESH PLUMB LINE FOR CHRIST-HONORING VOTERS

Do you know what happens to a child that is never told "no" and is never punished for terrible behavior? Any psychiatrist worth his salt will tell you that if you reward a child for bad behavior, they will eventually become a monster.

A political party is a lot like a child, because a political party is simply a group of human beings merging into a larger group, bringing all of their own childhood penchants (good and bad) with them. What happens to a child who is never told "no" and is never punished for terrible behavior? Or, worse yet, what happens when a child is *rewarded* for terrible behavior? The result is the same outcome the Republican Party has "enjoyed" over the last many years.

Every time the Republican Party betrays its faithful Christian base by ignoring God's law, we Christians have historically responded by grumbling down to the local polling station and *rewarding* them with our vote. Christians almost *never* punish the Republican Party for their continual transgressions against God's law. As a result, the Republican establishment does not care if we grumble about the bad choices they keep making and the bad candidates they keep conjuring up, so long as we grumble down to the voting booth and reward them, yet again, with more power.

Did you know that the Republican establishment despises you and makes jokes about your faith when you aren't around to hear them? It's true. You are to them like "Mikey" in those old cereal commercials. They think you are too picky. They believe you are nearly impossible to please. But they also know something else about you. They understand from past experience that once they slide that bowl full of fresh political victory across the table and you take your first bite, they will celebrate shouting, "He likes it! He likes it!" They can always depend on you to march down to the polls, like a good boy, and vote for their filthy, hollow souls.

The reason they continue to act this way is entirely your own fault!

That's right! Just like a parent with a spoiled brat for a child, it's time that Christians take responsibility for the monsters they have created. Here's a hard cold fact of political science few would dare dispute: so long as a politician (or a political party, for that matter) knows that at the end of the day you are going to vote for them, no matter what they do, as long as the alternative is "worse" than them...they *will never have any reason* to care what you believe, how you think or why you believe it! So long as you allow them to assume they will *win* with your vote, whether or not you even like them, they won't care!

Now you may finally understand why the honest right of the Republican Party and the honest left of the Democrat Party are continually annoyed with their candidate choices. The candidates are far more concerned with what the Independent voters think than what their own party faithful think... because the candidates know that they have to win the majority vote in order to defeat their opponent... and... if... (read slowly)... Independent voters don't like them more than the other guy *they will not vote for them*!

Get it? If a candidate who conforms to Duverger's Law (or a political party that conforms to Duverger's Law) believes you will also conform to Duverger's Law and vote for them, they will *never* care what you think, they will never change nor will they consider the possibility they might actually be wrong. As long as they know you believe they are the "lesser of two evils" and you have a desperate desire to win, they will always care more about pleasing the Independent voter than you. Why? They know the Independent *will not vote for them* if he is too put off by their positions; *he does not neatly and faithfully obey Duverger's Law*!

Remember, Republicans and Democrats alike live by one law in the political world... Duverger's Law! They only seek to win. The party, to them, is like a favorite sports team in an exciting contest. Being the "winner" is the goal. They don't see politics for what it really is—a tool of death and destruction in the wrong hands—where *how the "game" is played is every bit as important as winning*. They are so used to abortion, they are numb to its evil. They use it as a tool of disingenuous manipulation every election cycle, because they know it's important to you. As long as you cooperate with Duverger's Law yourself, allowing Duverger to masquerade as Lord by abandoning good candidates and noble principles for whoever is "most likely to win," then the "lesser" bad guys will remain the "winners."

So the little-known secret to saving America is simple. Christian evangelical voters, who have all the real solutions for the peace of the entire world neatly organized into a book they call the "Holy Bible," must actually obey that Bible, reject Duverger's Law, and instead, obey God's law. It's time for the bad parent of the spoiled child to lay down some tough love. Here's what this means: When a Republican doesn't abide by the following *four common-sense laws of God*, we must all, with solidarity in the body of Christ, *refuse* to vote for the Republican candidate! We must refuse to vote for him *no matter how rotten the alternative!*

Let me be very clear. We are no longer moved by consequences of obedience. We embrace God's law and reject the false way of Duverger's Law and this culture's situational ethics. Therefore, if the Republican in our district is running against the unholy avatar of Satan himself, we refuse to listen to the abusive false-morality produced by Duverger's Law, shouting: "If Satan gets elected it will be *your* fault, because you didn't vote for me instead!" We inform the candidate that Satan's coming election victory is quite naturally *their* fault because they chose to be a candidate we could not support in good conscience (for the same reasons we can't support their opponent).

Then, because we reject the proverbial satanic incarnation of the far left for the same or similar reasons that we reject the Republican nitwit (which means we are consistent and fair in our basis for rejection), we use our write-in blank and put down someone's name that is more honorable than the pathetic Republican, the pagan worshippers of Duverger's Law, vomited up as our supposed "only choice" during the last primary battle.

God's law makes something very, very clear! Sometimes Republicans, like Democrats...deserve to lose!

The next points are critical to understand! After enough pain and loss, the soulless pagan Republicans can only do one of the following three things:

1. Remain rebelliously and cultishly loyal to the mind-set described by Duverger's Law and realize that if he wishes to *win*, he must force himself to handle power in a way that will enable and rally the ongoing powerful support of "strict and unreasonable" evangelical voters, even though he privately loathes them.

2. Finally have a personal epiphany about what making Jesus "Lord" of his own life actually means. He repents, and now desires with all of his heart, mind, and soul, to please our Creator by running for office, and giving God glory through his life, "whether therefore [he] eat

or drink, or whatsoever [he] do." He rejects Duverger's Law and replaces it with God's law.

3. Keep losing every attempted election like an idiot who never learns, until he finally gives up and goes away.

In each of these three cases, the candidate notwithstanding, America is better off.

Some will make the patronizing and condescending charge: "You Christian voters are so unreasonable and impractical! You have all these lofty purity tests, and you won't support people unless they are pure enough." The truth is, if a candidate can't meet the following "purity test," they are too stupid and dangerous to *ever* be trusted with an ounce of political power, and they most definitely deserve to lose any attempt to obtain it.

In review, the first four of the Ten Commandments logically fall into the realm of our self-government and cannot be made true through any external force. The keeping of these four commandments stems from a choice of our own human will to submit: 1) Do not worship other gods; 2) Do not worship idols; 3) Do not misuse God's name; 4) Keep the Sabbath holy. These are four items of God's law that fall under the logical jurisdiction of self-government, as they take on a vertical relationship between man and God. The remaining six, however, deal with man-to-man relationships. They are foundational to all good civil government and should be the plumb line of political involvement for all professing Christians today.

So without further ado, Mr. Would-be Politician, here's the fresh plumb-line for Christian voters. It's not Duverger's Law for us ... it's God's law. If you cannot abide by these simple and reasonable requirements (six of God's horizontal laws listed in the second table of the law), don't bother asking for our vote, because we won't give it to you under *any* circumstances.

1. The 5th and 7th Commandments: Honor thy father and thy mother! Do not commit adultery!

   Explanation: Whether by your own bad example, or by your own bad decisions as a legislator, stop threatening the institution of the traditional family! Adultery is wrong. Among its many victims, it is a form of abuse that particularly harms children. Along similar lines, homosexuality is wrong, it is against nature and nature's God, it is harmful to those who engage in it, and it is absurd to attempt to redefine marriage to accommodate it.

2. The 6th Commandment: Thou shalt do no murder!

Explanation: Stop enabling the murder of children, you idiot! (Yes, I know it isn't politically correct to say so, and the "nicer than Jesus people" will be offended by it, but I do think it is perfectly moral to call someone complicit in the murder of children an "idiot.") Abortion is to be outlawed—there are no exceptions! The circumstances by which children are conceived are not the children's fault. Punish the criminal guilty of rape and incest, not the innocent child created by it. Do not allow this culture to begin the vile and sick practice of murdering the elderly and infirmed. Euthanasia is demonic and barbaric—there are no exceptions!

3. The 8th and 10th Commandments: Thou shalt not steal! Thou shalt not covet!

Explanation: Wealth redistribution is theft of personal property; it is motivated by covetousness! Stop converting the instrument designed to punish theft (government) into an instrument that performs the theft.

If an individual coveted his neighbor's property and tried to steal it by prying open a locked door with a crowbar, the government would put him in jail. If an individual covets his neighbor's property and sets out to steal it by prying open his neighbor's wallet with a ballot (on any given election day), it is still evil in the eyes of God. *stop raising taxes* and allowing yourself to be a part of this rebellious criminal scam!

God required no more of his own people than 10 percent, so any tax rate above that suggests that you believe you and the government you epitomize are equal to or greater than God Himself. This is evil. Lower taxes! No excuses will be tolerated!

4. The 9th Commandment: Thou shalt not lie! (I predict this will be the most difficult of the laws for politicians to honor. No further explanation should be needed.)

It seems fitting at this juncture to close with something stated by the 40th President of the United States, on May 6, 1983, at the annual banquet of the National Rifle Association, in Phoenix, Arizona:

> Standing up for America also means standing up for the God who has blessed this land. If we could just keep remembering that Moses brought down from the mountain the Ten Commandments, not ten suggestions – and if those of us who live for the Lord could remember that He wants us to love our Lord and our neighbor, then there's no limit to the problems we could solve or the mountains we could conquer together as a mighty force for good.[3]
>
> —PRESIDENT RONALD REAGAN

CHAPTER 11: REVIEW QUESTIONS

Enjoy this quiz at http://peacemakersinstitute.com/smb-quiz.

1. To make it very simple, Duverger correctly identified how part of the human psyche of men who ignored God's moral and civil laws would behave in an environment where "winning a contest" was more important than defending truth. To which part was he referring?

2. Does the discipline of truth change on Election Day?

3. Are Christians commanded to exclusively base moral decisions upon a study of consequences?

4. What unrepentant sin against Jesus Christ does a Republican have to commit before you will stop rewarding them with your vote?

5. If you don't support one bad candidate, is it true that you are automatically supporting another bad candidate by default?

6. Is a voter ever really limited to only two options in most American elections?

7. Is an alleged commitment to reducing abortions in America a necessarily godly commitment worthy of support?

8. What three things has Satan employed to destroy America using unwitting evangelicals as his secret weapon?

9. What system of law is the only system powerful enough to resurrect a dead nation fallen from grace?

10. Explain the fresh plumb line for Christ-honoring voters.

11. What are the only three responses politicians can give to those Christians who make God's law their plumb line, in each case leaving America better off?

12. What American president believed that embracing the Decalogue made America a limitless force for good on earth?

Chapter 12

How to Defend Your Nation by Winning Your City

EFORMED PRESBYTERIAN POSTMILLENNIAL "reconstructionist," Lutheran Two-Kingdoms advocates, Charismatic Kingdom Now postmillennialists, Methodist-Episcopal dominionists (after the fashion of the middle 1800s Rev. Haddock), Anglican devotees of Saint Polycarp (AD 64–155), Dutch-Reformed Calvinist advocates of old world Puritan Covenant Theology, Catholic confessors of the Catechism of the Social Reign of Christ the King and Pentecostal premillennialists, like me, who can't seem to neatly fit into *any* of the previous categories: If you simply believe that Jesus Christ is Lord of *all* the earth, and you believe it literally, regardless of the time the Father has chosen for His return to earth, then this final chapter is for you.

Whether you are a Southern Baptist "mid-tribulationalist" or some yet unnamed denominational amillennialist; whether you be a Calvinist, an Arminian or a Pelagian, you have now traversed this book, and you surely agree that the "ivory tower" is to the university what the steeple has become to the church. Knowing the rich truths of the biblical Great Commission do this world no good at all, if left (as Marcion would have left them) slathered in otherworldly and unfruitful mysticism.

If you have made it this far in my book, despite your Christian background, you simply must agree with me in two ways: 1) You believe the modern church is in error when it teaches a shrunken down version of Jesus's Great Commission—what has become a very small and narrow not-so-great mission of... getting people ready to die! 2) You believe there is an unmistakable difference between being saved by grace and being paralyzed by it! So in this final chapter I will share a plan of action you can emulate as best as you are able within your own community, for the sake of the greater good of the lost.

What I am prepared to share are the high spots of what we have been doing in Sioux City, Iowa, for several years. As we have applied the principles you are about to read, the hard work of our church family has paid dividends that have now begun to impact more than our own city and state, but America on a federal level. In fact, some of our successes are in process, and so vital to the future of this nation, I simply cannot risk sharing them in a book. Revealing too much would be like Solomon showing his entire treasury to a foreign emissary—a decision that later proved to be unhelpful. Nevertheless, I can share a simple skeleton of all you need to know to get started in your own hometown. And, for what it's worth, we Christians in Sioux City hope you get started real soon, because we know we can't save America by ourselves. We need your help!

With that said, the implementation of the strategy I now propose merges the doctrinal understanding of the Great Commission by which you are authorized with a plan of execution that can create an unstoppable force for good within the workings of your local government. Here are five specific things I hope to accomplish in the remaining portion of this book:

1. Direct you toward resources showing how to educate your church with a proper biblical worldview!

2. Show how to successfully uproot the secularist stronghold in your city government!

3. Show how to train your people to take positions of authority in your community!

4. Unlock the long term potential for successful evangelism and church growth like you've never seen!

5. Help pastors discover and experience the difference between pastoring a city and merely pastoring *in* a city!

As conservative Christians, we *should* understand the difference between what is called "decentralized" and "centralized" government. While many parachurch political organizations do support the "decentralized" structure of American politics in theory, the actual implementation of their own political philosophy/strategy to defend Christian moral values is nearly always, ironically, a "centralized" approach to implementation. This is a great tragedy and likely one of the primary reasons for the evangelical political movement's failure to secure lasting cultural change at the close of Ronald Reagan's presidency.

A VICTIM OF OUR OWN SUCCESS

The election of Ronald Reagan was something providential and exciting. Without the "centralized" approach to para-church ministry (that raises funds and uses activism at the highest profile levels of politics), I acknowledge we would most probably have never elected Ronald Reagan as our president. His election, however, and the approach of the "moral majority" ultimately failed. Why? Because American politics, contrary to popular rage and media focus, are built from the bottom up, not the top down. We started equating the term "grassroots politics" with the idea that you rally local citizens to fight the culture war at the national level. Well, it worked once... and only once.

It's time for a new plan.

We need to change the definition of the term "grassroots politics" in our heads so that when we speak and hear that term it reminds us of the idea that we must rally the *local* citizens to fight the culture battles at the *local* level, as opposed to the more commonly held idea that we rally *local* citizens to fight a political war at the *federal* level.

The great mistake of prior conservative Christian political movements and most, if not all current Christian political organizations, is that we have failed to apply our own beliefs of decentralized government to our own plan to rescue America from radical secular humanism. Here's what I mean: we raise money for our "non-profit corporations" much easier by following and accentuating the higher profile issues occurring in politics rather than capitalizing upon the media's lack of attention at the local school board and city council levels.

Christian conservatives need a twenty-year plan. We have to stop applying a fast-food mentality to Christian reconstruction. We have to bankroll low profile, inexpensive candidates at the lowest and most uninteresting levels of American government if we ever wish to affect lasting positive cultural change in America. Why? Because one Ronald Reagan wasn't good enough for this country! We need a constant flow of prospective Reagans to be seeded into every local township in our nation—*where the bad guys aren't usually paying enough attention!*

Citizen "Nobody"

There is a lot of talk about "protecting our foundations," but most of our political activity couldn't be further away. We're sensationalizing national problems at the tip of the proverbial steeple and pretty well ignoring the foundation. Meanwhile, in Gotham City, citizen "Nobody" (who wants to run for the local school board but can't find any valuable advice or financing to run an effective campaign) keeps losing. Every time citizen "Nobody" loses, his like-minded brethren hang their heads in defeat, telling themselves and any other would-be victim of hope: "It isn't worth the effort and sacrifice. Jesus will be back soon. The apocalypse is surely near." (If you don't believe that's true, you haven't tried to recruit a local candidate lately.) Christian conservatives are rapidly becoming defeatists, biding their time until the Rapture. That's pathetic! And it isn't how Paul taught us to face the last days either!

Christian political organizations put lots of time, money, effort, direct mail, DirecTV and Dish Network's newest option of "addressable TV ads," online options and energy into staging prayer rallies on capital lawns and picketing parties in front of courthouses. Meanwhile, the people sitting at the table where the decisions are actually made, know that they arrived at that level of government because, long ago, someone helped them with their first local election.

Decentralized Activism

A core group of my church seems to "get it." Oh there will always be a ratio of persons in any congregation that tend to think church life is a spectator sport, but much of my church family has worked very hard and made great personal and financial sacrifices to apply the teachings contained in this book to their respective towns and cities. (Our congregational members reside in several towns and cities among three states.) That's the secret of our "success," I guess. I hesitate to use that word because when you look at it through my eyes, "success" won't be declared, in its most literal sense, for at least twelve more years. You see, we're eight years into our plan of action right now. But we do know this for sure: Our plan works! The proof is in the pudding. This does not mean we have never been frustrated by an election loss or maligned by the local media either. Quite the opposite is the case. But consider the answer to the following questions:

Why is our city the only one we know of in the US to have produced a Human Rights Commission that voted against gay marriage? Why is our city the only one we know of to have passed a resolution against gay marriage at the city council level? Why did our city change its election laws regarding the formerly flawed method of "appointing" a mayor instead of electing one? Why did we successfully bankroll an unapologetic Christian man's campaign and see him win eighty votes short of the highest margin of victory in our city's history? How did we create synergy across the state of Iowa, linking with hundreds of other churches in a successful bid to forcibly remove three state Supreme Court judges who used judicial fiat to create counterfeit gay marriage out of thin air? Why have several presidential candidates asked to address my congregation and invited little ol' me to join them for a private breakfast or called my cell phone to wish me a happy birthday? (Yes, that one blew me away too!) Part of it is because some of the candidates are exceptionally shrewd campaigners, but it is mostly because the faithful Christians of my congregation have positively applied the Christian principle of decentralized activism! Our priorities are correct, because we model the precise priorities of the Great Commission, particularly those described in Acts 1:8. Here is the order of evangelistic priorities from whence we also see the principle of decentralized activism:

> ...and ye shall be witnesses unto me both in Jerusalem, and in all Judaea, and in Samaria, and unto the uttermost part of the earth.
>
> —Acts 1:8

Here is what we learn from Luke's version of the Great Commission, as it should relate to both evangelistic and political priorities:

- Priority #1: Jerusalem (your own city)

- Priority #2: Judaea (your own state)

- Priority #3: Samaria (your own region)

- Priority #4: The uttermost part of the earth (your nation as it impacts other nations)

This decentralized strategy is most powerful because it is supported by natural law. Think of it for a moment. How did the nations form? Well, the Bible tells us that this whole international community began with earth's first married couple, Adam and Eve. The couple became a family. The family became a village. The village became a town. The town became a city. The city became a state. The state became a region. The region became a nation, etc. Then God had to send a flood to wipe out evil and the whole thing began again with Noah's family. After a great host of people evolved from Noah, Nimrod decided to defy God at the tower of Babel, and God intervened and the entire process started over again. Then, in 1492, Columbus sailed the ocean blue, and the colonial American experience (the decentralized evolution of a nation) recurred in history yet again. We started small, we grew, we spread out, we expanded, and we self-governed. The whole American experience was and remains decentralized. So you see, our activism and our evangelism work in harmony with the laws of nature and nature's God, when we obey the immutable principle written by Luke in Acts 1:8. Start in the city where you live! Your prayers for help will be answered when you cooperate with God's original plan!

While the rest of the political blizzard buzzes down the interstate following the national campaign bus with a paparazzi-like cavalcade of satellite uplink vans and reporter-owned jalopies, we're doing what works! We're applying a decentralized twenty-year plan to American politics. We have other plans, too! Someday, our local candidates will blossom at the highest levels of American government! (We just need more help and more money, naturally!)

As Michael Rothfeld wrote: "... a fight to really make a difference may take years. This is especially true the further from local politics you get."[1] Michael is right, but I want to say it a different way: if you want to really create excitement in politics, you need to garner victories as soon as possible! *the fastest place you can do that is at the local level!*

Don't misunderstand what I'm writing, though. I'm not suggesting that we neglect state and federal issues! To be clear, we need to completely flip our paradigm on how to win this culture war! Christian activists must stop spending 80 percent of their time at the state and federal levels, leaving a lucky 20 percent (or usually less) where it really matters—the local government! We need to put a minimum of 80 percent of our time and resources into small towns, moderately sized cities and other forms of local politics, while the remaining 15 percent of our resources can be used for state and 5 percent for federal issues (or some similar balance). Decentralized activism has a "trickle-up" effect that will eventually pave the way for federal level successes.

Consider gay marriage. Where have Christian politicos and activists been most successful in recent years? If you contrast state and federal success, the state level wins. Why is that? Because the *closer you get to the local level*, the better activism works! My conclusion? If we don't make the necessary adjustment, becoming a *proactive* political force in the United States, we will continue *reactionary* politics at the federal level and everything we love will inevitably be lost. It's that simple.

A POPULATION POOL

In order to implement our plan and properly reconstruct America as it was intended by the founders, one must pull "soldiers" from a population pool. The most powerful and most capable institution on this fallen earth to win the culture war is the true church of the Living God! There is no better place from which to draw upon passionate culture warriors. In order to clearly understand the absolute necessity of pastoral involvement in our strategy, please invest the time to carefully listen to the sermon entitled "The Great Omission" provided freely by Cornerstone World Outreach. (Go to http://www.cornerstoneworld.org/services/pastor_cary_preaches_in_midland_michigan_the_great_omission to enjoy this helpful teaching.) The passion that is necessary for long term success can only come from the inspiration and strength of the Holy Spirit. This kind of inspiration, by heavenly design, comes from an anointed pulpit where the infallible Word of God is preached with boldness!

The unmovable foundation of a biblically accurate worldview is an absolute necessity for all soldiers before they join any culture battles. While the church is the most ideal place for that kind of foundation to be built, we are aware that most modern churches are wholly deficient due to bad doctrine or no doctrine at all. For those unable to locate a strong local church where such is taught, PeaceMakers Institute offers several different educational options for building a biblical worldview. Our most exhaustive training course is a two-year theological study. The theological school is where we enlist "soldiers." It is our "population pool" used for recruitment. Another great tool is the PeaceMakers Institute website. It is packed with teachings, articles, and issue-based treatises that explain biblical positions and offer practical solutions to American troubles. In terms of studying and learning the rationale for Christ-centered politics, this book would be an excellent source of inexpensive theological instruction.

In the case of my city, I particularly wait for PeaceMakers School of Theology students to reach a certain level of study before recruitment. Once a student has successfully passed the test on the theological origins and purposes of government (encountered twenty-six weeks into our two-year program) we invite them (by invitation only) to join PeaceMakers Fellowship™. PeaceMakers Fellowship™ is the source of our local political and legal operations. Willing, trained, and qualified new members are introduced to seven stages of operations used to apply our approach to cultural victory. I will share this with you, momentarily. Without completely delineating the entire program, suffice it to say that what we do is primarily inspired by the words of the Lord in Jeremiah chapter one and verse ten. The Fellowship practices principles shown by the Lord to His prophet Jeremiah: 1) Root out; 2) Pull down; 3) Destroy; 4) Throw down; 5) Build; and 6) Plant.

The Seven Stages of Political Recovery

As I mentioned a moment ago, our population pool is made up of alumni and current students. They are invited to participate in the following seven stages of political and legal action. After a member has shown proficiency and faithfulness in a general layer, they may be invited to increase to a deeper layer, based upon their performance and recognized gifting. The seven stages are as follows:

Stage 1: A local pastor must decide to stop pastoring *in* his city, and begin pastoring his city. Here is one example using social media: http://www.cornerstoneworld.org/sermon_series/five_steps _to_a_political_epiphany

Stage 2: Defending Christianity and the Constitution by contributing to public dialogue. Here are some ideas:

   a. Letters to the editor are written by two or three gifted
      writers and distributed to the entire Fellowship to be
      published under each respective name. This ensures
      strategic, targeted talking points and timely exchange of
      ideas that can apply necessary pressure to public officials

while simultaneously educating the public. Letters vary from "diplomatic" to "outraged," from "highly critical" to "complimentary." The possibilities here are almost limitless. The style of the writing is deliberately varied by each writer to keep the media off balance. Members' names are placed on an unidentifiable rotation for security. This is a very similar strategy to that as described by Alexander Hamilton, who died before his vision of a "Christian Constitutional Society" could be realized. This is also done in an organized effort to defend and support our own fellow-elected officials who are either seeking office or currently hold an office in politics.

b. Online blogging beneath local news articles on popular websites of local interest. An alias is sometimes used to disguise one's identity and a free exchange takes place where intense discussion can transpire without fear of repercussion. (This can be brutal—it is often a place to experience the brunt of the writer's version of "road rage" and participants must have thick skin.) This has also proven to be *very* effective with elected officials who read the blogs. This follows the tradition of the founders who, when writing the Federalist Papers, often signed with an alias like "Publius" or some similar name.

c. Lobbying City Hall or the State Capitol is also done during important meetings. Talking points and/or speeches are prewritten by the Fellowship writers and assigned to different members as deemed necessary. Those who will address the council and/or other elected officials are encouraged to put the talking points in their own words to avoid being flagged as "an organized activist." (It makes no sense, but, apparently some politicians believe it is OK to ignore the message of an activist if they associate with a large group of like-minded voters.)

Stage 3: Infiltrating the social layers of the city.

Members are encouraged to join all social clubs where "movers and shakers" are present. The following are examples: Lion's Club, Rotary Club, Cosmopolitan Club, Chamber of Commerce, Garden Club. They are encouraged to "let their light shine" when a discussion concerning social/moral/political exchange begins. Members who feel they may wish to move to the next level are encouraged to "be friendly" but to maintain the understanding that friendship is not the goal; the acquisition and adjudication of power—politics—is the goal. Those who show no desire to move deeper can remain at this level and simply enjoy newfound friendships.

Stage 4: Infiltrate government boards and commissions at the local level.

Apply for such positions, achieve such positions, and take control of such positions (in sheer numbers, when necessary) to ensure that proper policy recommendations and family-friendly decisions are dispersed as often as possible, and in as many venues as possible. Members who acquire positions on the same commission or board are encouraged to assume a detached interaction with one another when first entering a board or commission. This tactic is important to keep the enemy off balance and protect the righteous political agenda. Note: This is the most vital political position a citizen can possess without having to labor through an extensive and expensive campaign and election!

Stage 5: Infiltrate the political realm at the local level.

Fellowship members are geographically selected (by respective precinct) to infiltrate every possible position within the local Republican Party County Central Committee. By sheer numbers, RINOs* can be routed and the conservative tradition can be preserved and protected. IMPORTANT NOTE: This stage may not take priority, initially, when implementing our "scorched-earth" strategy. It is often necessary to temporarily bypass this stage until later, if one finds himself with a completely dysfunctional central committee that has become skilled at losing elections.

Stage 6: Infiltrate and capture elected office by using the full force of PeaceMakers Political Action donations.

   a. Seek elections at all levels of government with strong
      emphasis and highest priority to always remain at the
      local level with first-time candidates. The continual

---

* **RINO** is an acronym for Republican in name only.

reproduction of grassroots first-time candidates is *essential* to the twenty-year plan! School Boards, City Councils, County Supervisors, Auditors, Sheriffs, County Attorneys, State and Federal offices...

b. Positioning and posturing for judicial appointments by qualified persons is also invaluable.

Stage 7: Export the teaching and applicable plan explained by this book—our "scorched-earth" strategy—to like-minded churches in other villages, towns, cities, and states across America! Let the sharing of these truths be as it was said by the psalmist:

He established a testimony in Jacob and appointed a law in Israel, which he commanded our fathers to teach to their children, that the next generation might know them, the children yet unborn, and arise and tell them to their children, so that they should set their hope in God and not forget the works of God, but keep his commandments.

—Psalm 78:5–7, esv

Chapter 12: Review Questions

Enjoy this quiz at http://peacemakersinstitute.com/smb-quiz.

1. Is the Great Commission more than merely getting people ready to die?

2. In what way have Christian activists become a victim of their own past success?

3. Why is decentralized activism so critical to restoring the life of our once great and godly nation?

4. What are the four priorities revealed in the Great Commission as described in Acts 1:8?

5. Is there any other organization more empowered and authorized than the local church to successfully employ the seven steps of political recovery?

6. Explain the difference between a pastor in a city and a pastor of a city.

7. At what level of activism does one experience the benefit of moral, ethical, and legal victories the soonest?

8. Has the American church been politically proactive or reactive?

9. Has the American church succeeded or failed?

10. Does Christian activism do any good when the Christian activist has not been taught a theonomic worldview?

11. Name the six commands of God to Jeremiah with regard to his charge to reform national politics, and compare what ratio of those six commands were negative and which were positive.

12. Is the mandate of the full scope of the Great Commission limited to only some churches?

Epilogue

Share Your Treasure

IN HIS JOURNAL at sea, Christopher Columbus, that legendary explorer and discoverer of America who faced the rages of nature and the possible loss of his great discoveries from the "new world," described his horrors as follows:

> For nine days I was as one lost, without hope of life. Eyes never beheld the sea so angry, so high, so covered with foam. The wind not only prevented our progress, but offered no opportunity to run behind any headland for shelter; hence we were forced to keep out in this bloody ocean, seething like a pot on a hot fire. Never did the sky look more terrible; for one whole day and night it blazed like a furnace, and the lightning broke with such violence that each time I wondered if it had carried off my spars and sails; the flashes came with such fury and frightfulness that we all thought that the ship would be blasted. All this time the water never ceased to fall from the sky; I do not say it rained, for it was like another deluge. The men were so worn out that they longed for death to end their dreadful suffering.*

At the end of his first voyage, while trying to get home to Spain, he was forced by another dangerous storm to retreat for around ten days off the shores of Portugal. Before fleeing that particular deadly storm, one account records, "Christopher Columbus's ship entered a severe storm. Columbus threw a report of his discovery along with a note asking it to be passed on to the Queen of [Spain], in a sealed cask into the sea, hoping the news would make it back even if he did not

---

* Samuel Eliot Morison, *Admiral of the Ocean Sea: A Life of Christopher Columbus* (Boston: Little, Brown and Company, 1942), 617.

survive. In fact, Columbus survived and the sealed report was never found, or at least, its discovery never reported."[*]

A message in a bottle is a very precious thing indeed. Columbus would not risk dying without passing on what he had learned about the location of what would someday be called "America." Similarly, the tales of legend tell us that some unknown fellow once put a map in a bottle and cast it into the sea. He too could not bear the thought of leaving riches buried in some obscure and watery eternal grave. He wished to share his knowledge with any stranger so richly blessed of heaven to stumble upon his floating bottle.

My message is more purposely aimed than the buoyant cask of Christopher Columbus, but it is with similar passion as he that I hurl it into the current flowing your way. It is written amidst a great storm designed by hell to keep mankind from finding his true home in heaven. Storms that threaten to bury the deepest treasures of the gospel beneath the sands of a paralyzing theory of grace, sealed in a padlocked trunk that might as well be called "The Great Omission."

But I am not afraid!

You did not give in to the opposing elements of those who came before you! You will not have to live with regrets! You have discovered the treasure of His divine kingdom, and you now understand you are necessary, empowered and authorized to accomplish what must be done. As you find your place within His plan, remember to share *your* treasure with the next generation!

There are some beautiful words sung to a famous melody of 1858 that seem to roll within me as I prepare to cork this bottle and pitch it in your direction:

> Stand up, stand up for Jesus! The trumpet call obey: Forth to the mighty conflict, in this His glorious day; Ye that are men now serve Him against unnumbered foes; Let courage rise with danger, and strength to strength oppose. Stand up, stand up for Jesus, Stand in His strength alone. The arm of flesh will fail you, ye dare not trust your own. Put on the gospel armour, each piece put on in prayer. Where duty calls or danger, be never wanting there!

Join me in this solemn prayer for America and the world!

---

* *Wikipedia*, s.v. "Message in a Bottle," http://en.wikipedia.org/wiki/Message_in_a_bottle#cite_ref-2.

Blessed Father of heaven! In the wholesome spirit of nationalism first demonstrated by the apostle Paul, when in Romans 9:1–5 he offered to willingly assume a place in the fires of hell in the stead of his beloved nation of Israel, if by his own damnation, they might be saved, I ask this petition of You. Grant my nation, America, along with the nations of the world, bold pastors with eyes to see once again! Keep us from these ditches! In Jesus's holy name. Amen!

I sincerely pray this work has helped you. I pray that, while reading it, God has been able to stir up something precious within your very soul and spirit. I look forward to seeing you someday in the Golden City, where the patriarchs now await our arrival—the same city which once captured the faith and imagination of our Father Abraham, who "looked for a city whose builder and maker was God"!

—Rev. Cary K. Gordon

Appendix of Biblical Law

I. LAWS OF THE SELF-INTERPRETING BIBLE

1. Scripture interprets scripture (Matt. 4:6–7).

2. Yield to the influence of the Holy Spirit. (2 Pet. 1:20–21).

3. The Bible is a progressive revelation—a successive unfolding of a continuous theme to its consummation (John 5:39).

4. Scripture is to be interpreted literally (2 Cor. 1:20; Luke 4:32; Ps. 138:2; Lam. 2:17).

5. Interpret understanding culture and history (i.e., Matt. 19:7–8). When doing so, there are three considerations:
   a. Political background
   b. Economic background
   c. Religious background

6. Interpret in the light of audience and stated conditions (2 Tim. 2:15). When doing so, there are five considerations:
   a. Who is doing the talking?
   b. Who are they talking to?
   c. What is the subject under discussion?
   d. In what dispensation is the discussion taking place?
   e. Why is the discussion taking place?

7. Interpret in the light of the language gap. The modern meaning of a word may not be consistent with the meaning back then. When doing so, you must consider the three divisions of scriptural language style:
   a. Prose writings (ordinary language)
   b. Poetic writings (composition of language expressed using rhythm and/or rhyme)
   c. Apocalyptic writings (composition of expressed language that is highly symbolic and predictive in nature)

273

8. Interpret in the light of devotional study (Josh. 1:8; Ps. 119:11–13).

9. Interpret the implicit by the explicit (i.e., Matt. 13:10–11, 18–23).

10. Know the difference between the "letter of the law" and the "Spirit of the law" (Mark 7:7–9, Matt. 23:23–26, Matt. 9:13).

11. Interpret understanding the law of applications (2 Tim. 3:16–17). As a general rule, there is one meaning for each verse. However, the truth may have several applications.

12. What Scripture condemns, we must condemn, and we have the right to condemn (John 18:19–23; Ps. 119:13; Matt. 7:28–29).

13. Interpret according to the dispensation in which the scripture is contained (Heb. 8:5–13).

14. Never interpret based upon human experience and personal conviction only (Matt. 15:9).

15. Interpret understanding the law of conscience (1 Cor. 8:7–13; Acts 24:16).
    a. We have no authority to maintain doctrines or to set moral standards on issues that are not specifically addressed in Scripture.
    b. When the Scripture is silent in *specifics* we must revert to scriptural *principles*.
    c. Scriptural principles must be honored by personal conviction.
    d. Personal conviction cannot be enforced upon other Christians.

16. Never force a New Testament standard of morality or doctrine upon an Old Testament passage (Heb. 8:5–13).

17. Never force an Old Testament standard of morality or doctrine upon a New Testament passage (Heb. 8:5–13).

18. Know that all scripture is truly stated, but not all scriptures are statements of truth (i.e., Job 12:6; Job 11:4–5).

19. The Bible should never be studied as merely a textbook (2 Pet. 1:20–21).

20. Inerrancy does not mean exactness of detail (Josh. 10:13).

21. There is not one single doctrine in the Bible that is the key to the Christian life (Eph. 3:17–19).

22. All Bible promises are both selective and conditional (Heb. 6:12).

23. Only use a Bible commentary as a last resort when studying Scripture (1 Cor. 13:12; Matt. 7:29).

24. Know the difference between parabolic and symbolic Scripture:

    a. Parabolic Scripture contains an underlying moral message intended for practical and personal application. It is intended for disclosing information to the saint and hiding information from the heathen (Matt. 16:11; Matt. 13:10–16).

    b. Symbolic Scripture deals with apocalyptic and/or predictive prophecy (Matt. 21:42–45).

25. Interpret symbolic Scripture understanding types and shadows.

    a. A type and shadow is a visible object lesson in the Scriptures by which God taught His people about His grace and saving power—figuratively pointing to a literal redemptive truth (John 3:14–16).

    b. An anti-type is a redemptive truth in the literal sense (John 3:14–16).

    c. Old Testament types point toward New Testament anti-types (John 3:14–16).

    d. New Testament types point toward the anti-types of the ages that succeed the age of grace (i.e., tribulation, millennium) (i.e., John 19:30, Rev. 16:17)

26. Interpret symbolic Scripture understanding the law of types and anti-types (Matt. 12:40; John 3:14; John 13:18–19; Rom. 15:8).

    a. If there is a type, there must be an anti-type.

b. If there is an anti-type, there must be a type.

27. Interpret understanding the guidelines for disclosing types:
    a. Search the New Testament for anti-types (John 3:14; Matt. 12:40).
    b. Avoid trying to be original or clever (Acts 17:21).
    c. Locate points of similarity between types and their fulfillment.
    d. Do not build doctrines on types, unless the New Testament gives the authority to do so (Matt. 12:40; John 3:14).

28. Types and shadows are categorized in six divisions:
    a. Symbolic persons such as Jonah, Moses, Isaac (i.e., Matt. 12:39–40).
    b. Symbolic institutions such as sacrifices (i.e., Eph. 5:2; Rom. 12:1).
    c. Symbolic offices such as the prophet, priest, or king (i.e., Heb. 5:5–10; Rev. 1:6; Heb. 8:1–5; Matt. 23:30–39).
    d. Symbolic events such as Canaan (i.e., Heb. 11:9–10).
    e. Symbolic actions such as the brazen serpent (i.e., John 3:14).
    f. Symbolic things such as the articles of the tabernacle (Heb. 8:1–5; John 6:31–33).

29. When developing doctrine concerning scriptures of a symbolic nature, begin with the anti-type and then apply the type (First, Rev. 21:9–10, the "New Jerusalem"; and then the "Bride of Christ" in Eph. 5:31–33.) See also Matt. 12:40; John 3:14; John 5:39.

30. Develop all doctrines by beginning with the authoritative statements of Jesus first. Second, apply the Epistles. Thirdly, apply the Old Testament passages. When applying the Old Testament passages, never filter doctrinal development through the false way of seeing the New Covenant *replacing* the Old Covenant, but rather see the New Covenant expanding upon the perfectly

inspired and eternal foundation of the Old Covenant (John 5:39; 2 Tim. 3:16).

II. Laws of Biblical Worldview

Sociological Law

All Humans Are Born Evil and Remain So Until Christ

- Romans 7:15–24
- Romans 8:7–8
- Psalm 51:5
- Psalm 39:5
- Jeremiah 17:9
- Romans 3:9–12
- 2 Timothy 3:1–7
- Ecclesiastes 9:3
- Ephesians 4:17–18
- 1 Corinthians 2:14
- Romans 1:18–22
- Romans 12:2

The Age of the Earth Is Unknown—The Age of Humanity Is Known

- Genesis 1 and 2
- The human genealogies in Scripture totaled back to Adam add up to about 6,000 years.
  - From Adam to Abraham, roughly 2,000 years (Gen. 5; 7:6, 11; Exod. 12:40).
  - From Abraham to Christ, roughly 2,000 years (Joshua 14:7 + Judges + Kings + Babylonian captivity + restoration of Jerusalem + Daniel 9:24–27).
  - From Christ to present, roughly 2,000 years

The Inborn Sin-Nature Is Root of All Trouble

- Matthew 13:15
- Hebrews 4:2
- Hebrews 3:12–13

War Is Sometimes Unavoidable

- Acts 5:29
- Joshua 11:20, 23
- Deuteronomy 7:16
- 1 Samuel 15:3
- Judges 2:1–3
- Exodus 22:2
- Genesis 9:6
- Mark 12:1–9
- Romans 13:1–4
- Revelation 19:11

Personal Sin Necessitates Personal Responsibility

- Romans 14:11–12
- 2 Corinthians 5:10
- Revelation 20:11–15
- Matthew 16:27
- 1 Corinthians 3:13–15

Social Reform Poor Substitute for Personal Transformation

- 1 Timothy 5:8
- Matthew 25:14–30
- Matthew 20:16
- Matthew 26:11
- 1 Timothy 5:18

The Laws of Nature and Nature's God Defined Family

- Hebrews 13:4
- Genesis 2:23–24
- Genesis 3:16
- 1 Corinthians 6:13–7:40
- Matthew 19:3–9
- Proverbs 5:15–19

Life Begins At Conception

- Psalm 127:3
- Psalm 139:13
- Isaiah 49:1
- Jeremiah 1:5
- Luke 1:44

Family Government Is Basis of Civil Government

- Genesis 18:18–19
- Genesis 35:11
- 1 Kings 14:22
- 2 Kings 15:9
- Nehemiah 9:2
- Daniel 9:16

Capital Punishment Is Necessary

- Genesis 6:13
- Genesis 9:6
- Genesis 19:13
- Exodus 22:2
- Deuteronomy 7:16
- Mark 12:1–9

- Romans 13:1-4
- Revelation 19:11

An Outward Act of Sexual Perversion Is a Criminal Offense Against Society

- Leviticus 20:13
- Leviticus 18:22
- Romans 1:20-27
- 1 Corinthians 6:9-10
- Genesis 19:1-9
- Jude 6-7
- 1 Timothy 1:9-10
- 2 Peter 2:6, 10
- Ephesians 5:3, 5
- Colossians 3:5

Proper Roles of Males and Females

- Titus 2:2-8
- 1 Timothy 5:1-2
- Matthew 19:4
- 1 Timothy 3:8-15
- 1 Peter 3:7

Premarital Sex Is Forbidden by God

- Hebrews 13:4
- 1 Corinthians 6:13-7:2
- 1 Corinthians 7:7-28, 32-38
- Proverbs 5:15-19
- Proverbs 7:5-27

POLITICAL LAW

Republic v. Democracy

- John 6:38
- Jeremiah 17:9
- Exodus 32:1

Proper Role of Government

- Leviticus 19:35–36
- Deuteronomy 8:17–18
- Job 34:10–12
- Proverbs 28:20
- Ecclesiastes 5:10
- Matthew 25:29
- Matthew 26:11
- Luke 19:26
- Romans 13:7
- Hebrews 11:6
- 2 Thessalonians 3:10
- 1 Timothy 5:8–16

Free Speech

- Matthew 12:36
- Ephesians 4:29
- Exodus 11:7
- Psalm 12:3–4
- Psalm 39:1
- James 1:26
- Ecclesiastes 5:2
- Titus 1:10–11

Decentralized v. Centralized

- Deuteronomy 1:12–15
- Acts 6:2–4
- Proverbs 27:10
- Numbers 16:1–7
- 2 Samuel 15:1–6
- 1 Peter 2:6–8

Globalism v. Nationalism

- 2 Corinthians 6:14–18
- Psalm 74:17
- Acts 17:26
- 1 Samuel 8:5–7
- Judges 2:1–3
- Revelation 13:7

Biblical Law for Nations

- 2 Timothy 3:16–17
- Romans 13:1–2
- Proverbs 14:34
- Isaiah 58:2

Self-Government (Self-Discipline)

- Genesis 2:15–17
- Genesis 9:5
- Romans 13:1–5
- Luke 19:11–27

Population Control

- Genesis 1:28
- Deuteronomy 6:6–7

ECONOMIC LAW

True Causes of Unemployment and Poverty

- Ecclesiastes 5:19
- Proverbs 13:11
- 1 Corinthians 3:8
- Proverbs 20:13
- Proverbs 11:24–26
- Proverbs 28:19–20
- Proverbs 28:22
- Proverbs 23:20–21

True Cause of Employment and Prosperity

- Nehemiah 4:6
- Matthew 25:14–30

Fractional Reserve Banking Rejected

- Deuteronomy 24:12
- Leviticus 19:36
- Proverbs 11:1
- Proverbs 11:15
- Exodus 22:26

Capitalism and Liberty

- Leviticus 25:15
- Deuteronomy 2:6
- Jeremiah 32:44
- Jeremiah 32:10–12
- Acts 5:1–4

Savings and Retirement Plans Are Personal Responsibilities

- 1 Timothy 5:3, 8, 16

- Matthew 25:29
- 2 Thessalonians 3:10
- 1 Timothy 5:17–18
- Deuteronomy 8:18
- Proverbs 13:11

Private Property

- Exodus 20:15
- Matthew 20:15

International Trade v. National Currency

- Judges 2:1–3
- 2 Corinthians 6:14–18
- Daniel 11:23

Just Taxation

- Exodus 20:15
- Exodus 30:15
- Proverbs 11:1
- Leviticus 19:36
- Matthew 22:17–21

Capitalism v. Socialism

- Exodus 20:15
- Leviticus 19:36
- Deuteronomy 25:4
- Exodus 20:17
- Proverbs 14:12
- Psalm 19:7
- Psalm 111:7

Role of Church Government

- 1 Timothy 5:3–16

Self-Regulating Individuals v. Economic-Regulating Government

- Matthew 20:1–16
- Proverbs 11:1
- Luke 10:7
- Leviticus 19:36

Financial Progress

- Proverbs 28:22
- Proverbs 28:20

EDUCATIONAL LAW

Truth Is Absolute and Should Be Taught as Such

- John 14:6
- Deuteronomy 6:6–7
- Galatians 1:8
- Ephesians 6:4
- 1 Corinthians 4:15
- Deuteronomy 4:9
- Hebrews 13:8–9
- Malachi 3:6
- James 1:17

Family Government Is Sovereign

- Deuteronomy 6:6–7
- Deuteronomy 4:9
- Proverbs 1:7–9
- Proverbs 13:24
- Proverbs 22:6–7

- Proverbs 27:10
- Joshua 24:15
- Matthew 22:21
- Ephesians 6:4

Education Must Glorify God

- Deuteronomy 6:6–7
- Proverbs 1:7–9
- Hosea 4:6
- Proverbs 9:10
- Job 28:27–28
- 2 Timothy 3:16
- 2 Corinthians 10:5
- Colossians 2:8

Virtue of Bridled Speech to Be Learned

- 2 Timothy 3:16–17
- James 3:1–2
- Titus 1:10–11
- 2 Kings 2:23
- 2 Timothy 2:14–17, 23
- Colossians 2:8
- 1 Corinthians 1:10

Teacher Must Distinguish Truths and Deceptions for the Student

- 1 Timothy 1:4
- Colossians 2:8
- 2 Timothy 3:6–9
- Galatians 1:8
- Proverbs 1:7

- Hebrews 13:9

No Philosophy or Study of Nature Has Merit Outside the Authority of God's Word

- 2 Timothy 3:16–17

- Proverbs 1:7

- Psalm 19:7

- 2 Corinthians 10:5

- Colossians 2:8

Decentralized Education Is Wise

- Proverbs 27:10

- Psalm 74:17

- Judges 2:1–3

- Acts 17:26

- 2 Corinthians 6:16–18

Jesus's Impact on Politics and Law in 55 Parables

* = Direct Political Implications

** = Indirect Political Implications

No Asterisk = No Political Reference

FOUR YEARS OF careful expository study and research on the fifty-five major parables of Jesus Christ, reveal the following data about His public addresses:

- 52.73 percent of Christ's public teachings had deliberate, direct and/or indirect political/legal connotations that were unmistakable to his contemporary audiences. These were teachings where Christ related self-governing principles to issues of civil society.*

- 47.27 percent of Christ's remaining public teachings focused upon issues of self-government and its relation to the governance of the spiritual world.

The old cliché "Jesus didn't talk about politics" is a popular fallacy stemming from our cultural decline and its unfortunate impact upon modern church doctrine. (Some call this "spiritual blindness.")

- 12 of Christ's parables had *direct* political impact on His contemporary audiences.

- 17 of Christ's parables had *indirect* political impact on His contemporary audiences.

- 26 of Christ's parables had no correlation with political/ legal issues.

- 29 out of 55 parables (52.73 percent) had a tangible impact on political issues of His day.

1. Wise and foolish builders *

- Matthew 7:24–27: Jesus teaches on murder, adultery, divorce, oaths, retaliation, jurisprudence, love and hate, dealing with enemies, hypocrisy, charitable donations in public, prayer and fasting, righteous judgment, criticism, devotion, and the golden rule.

2. Children of the bride chamber **

- Matthew 9:15: Jesus gives this parable for the benefit of the "politically incorrect" prophet—John the Baptist's— heartbroken disciples, who mourn his beheading by Herod's abusive and corrupt exercise of civil authority. Why was he beheaded? For publicly confronting wickedness in government.

3. New cloth and old garment **

- Matthew 9:16: Jesus tells John's broken disciples that they have gone through more than His own inexperienced disciples could yet bear to experience (if they were told what the future held for them as well—at the hands of an abusive Hebrew and Roman government).

4. New wine and old bottles **

- Matthew 9:17: Jesus informs John's broken disciples... "you are older and more experienced than My disciples. They have not yet endured the kind of suffering you now know, but they eventually will. But you can't expect new, young disciples to be able to handle the prediction of coming pain until they are ready."

5. Unclean spirit *

- Matthew 12:43: Jesus teaches on "kingdom" principles. The word "kingdom," of course, is a synonym for "government." Jesus discusses repentance on the levels of 1) self-government; 2) family government; 3) city government; 4) national government.

The seven parables of the present-day kingdom of the absent king:

6. Sower

- Matthew 13:3–23
- Luke 8:5–15

7. Tares

- Matthew 13:24–30
- Matthew 13:36–43

8. Mustard-seed

- Matthew 13:31–32
- Luke 13:19

9. Leaven

- Matthew 13:33

10. Treasure hid in a field

- Matthew 13:44

11. Pearl of great price

- Matthew 13:45–46

12. Net cast into the sea

- Matthew 13:47-50

13. Meats defiling not *

- Matthew 15:10–15: Jesus battles the inappropriate cultural belief of His day, suggesting that the oral traditions (Mishnah) was superior to the written Laws of

Moses (Torah). Jesus reminds the legislators (Sanhedrin) that Levitical law required the death penalty for adult children who abuse their elderly parents. This, in contrast to His present company's use of "Mishnah" traditions to create convenient loopholes that allow abuse of the elderly. He further pronounces coming national judgment upon the whole nation for rejection of the "Living" Word.

14. Unmerciful servant **

- Matthew 18:23–35: Within this teaching, Jesus endorsed the *right* of civil government to severely punish all criminal activity.

15. Laborers hired

- Matthew 20:1–16

16. Two sons

- Matthew 21:28–32: The discussion takes place in the context of the question to Jesus, "By what authority to you do these things?"

17. Wicked husbandmen **

- Matthew 21:33–45: Jesus endorses the right of a family to seek and obtain justice (capital punishment) in the wake of pre-meditated murder.

18. Marriage-feast

- Matthew 22:2–14

Seven parables of the future kingdom when the King returns:

19. Fig-tree leafing

- Matthew 24:32–34

20. As in the days of Noah

- Matthew 24:37–42

21. Man of the house watching **

- Matthew 24:43: As a good servant takes precautions against theft and crime, so doth the diligent ambassador of God's kingdom keep watch in the society (where he lives) against the spiritual causation of corporeal theft and crime—which can ultimately rob men of their eternal abode. Heavenly citizenship creates diligent earthly citizenship and stewardship!

22. Faithful, and evil servants **

- Matthew 24:45–51: As a good servant practices a diligent work ethic in the absence of His master, so doth the diligent ambassador of God's kingdom avoid the dangerous temptation to enjoy distractions, justified by the warped mentality that says "My Lord delayeth His return." Heavenly citizenship requires diligent earthly citizenship/stewardship!

23. Ten virgins

- Matthew 25:1–13

24. Talents **

- Matthew 25:14–30: Jesus explains the concept of a delayed kingdom…a kingdom of ambassadors who are warned by the words given to would-be doctrinal escapists who do not engage the present world, "thou wicked and slothful servants"! In contrast, the Lord says to the faithful, "I will make thee ruler over many things"! This is a parable delegating authority and jurisdiction to His ambassadors in His physical absence. Heavenly citizenship requires diligent earthly citizenship/stewardship!

Four parables to address the conflicts between all present governments, visible and invisible:

25. Sheep and Goats *

- Matthew 25:31–46: Jesus promises to someday return and overthrow all wicked human governments across the globe.

26. Kingdom, divided against itself *

- Mark 3:24: A teaching on the subject of conflict in governing authority as it relates to other jurisdictions (visible government)

27. House, divided against itself **

- Mark 3:25: A teaching on the subject of conflict in family government as it relates to other jurisdictions (visible government)

28. Satan, divided against himself **

- Mark 3:26: A teaching on the subject of conflict in spiritual government as it relates to other jurisdictions (invisible government)

29. Strong man armed *

- Mark 3:27

- Luke 11:21: A teaching on the subject of self-government as it relates to other jurisdictions (invisible government)

30. Lighted candle

- Mark 4:21

- Luke 11:33–36

31. Seed growing secretly

- Mark 4:26–29

32. Man taking a far journey **

- Mark 13:34–37: Jesus explains the concept of a delayed kingdom—a kingdom of ambassadors who are charged with the orders, "occupy until I return," delegating authority and jurisdiction to the ambassadors in His physical absence.

Three parables of righteous judgment, illustrating forbearance and forgiveness:

33. Blind leading the blind **

- Luke 6:39

34. Beam and mote **

- Luke 6:41–42

35. Tree and its fruit **

- Luke 6:43–45: Indirect law and political impact as
  it serves for the self-governing justification of men
  judging men and provides the doctrinal New Testament
  rationale (in perfect harmony with the same expressed
  in the Old Testament) for human courts, jurisdictions,
  and civil authorities in general.

36. Creditor and debtors *

- Luke 7:41–47: Jesus approaches the city gates (city hall)
  with a triumphant crowd following Him. Jesus speaks
  with ignorant civil rulers and praises John the Baptist
  while directly confronting the evil leaders who killed
  John and who also criticized Christ. In their presence,
  He forgives a sinner and justifies His act with this parable. Criticism against men of God will bring judgment
  against cities, states, and nations.

37. Good Samaritan **

- Luke 10:30–37: A lawyer asks Jesus a legal question to
  test Him. Jesus responds with a parable that references
  personal responsibility with regard to station in life and
  governing powers of men who enjoy official positions as
  it relates to both criminal activity and human charity.

38. Importunate friend

- Luke 11:5–9

39. Rich fool

- Luke 12:16–21 (Verse 9: *Take thine ease, eat, drink, and
  be merry.* This was exactly the creed of the ancient

Atheists and Epicureans. "*Ede, bibe, lude; post mortem nullavoluptas.*")

40. Cloud and wind *

- Luke 12:54–57: Jesus teaches that national-level trage-dies are often harbingers of a spiritual problem. He used two recent national tragedies to forecast His nation's coming judgment from God. His lesson was to teach that in the wake of national judgment, all men should repent with introspect and not merely assume those most directly affected by a recent tragedy were "greater sin-ners" than those who are less affected. The isolated inci-dent may quickly engulf a whole society if the causation is not corrected.

41. Barren fig tree *

- Luke 13:6–9: Israel was about to receive "uprooting"—national level judgment—because they failed to pro-duce the fruit they were created to produce. They had strayed from their God-ordained legal and political pur-pose—to spread the law of God with the nations of the whole world.

42. Men bidden to a feast

- Luke 14:7–11

43. Builder of a tower **

- Luke 14:28–30

- (Builder of a tower parable cont'd.)

- Luke 14:33: A parable of militant defense: It is critical to finish the work of building a defensive security tower when a known enemy antagonizes your own. He was speaking in strict military or security terms, to an audi-ence who would have immediately known this to be a depiction of a defensive watchtower, something neces-sary to protect life and good.

44. King going to war *

- Luke 14:31–33: A parable of militant offense: In the day
  of a call to arms, a soldier must love his family enough
  to leave them! He must love his King *more* than his wife,
  children, home, and lands! A dead soldier who loved his
  King *more* may fall in the battlefield while protecting his
  family; but he has more value to his family—dead on the
  battlefield—than a man who didn't love his family enough
  to leave them for the fight. Through that man's cowardice
  (the one who wouldn't love His King "more"), his entire
  family and home will be destroyed when the enemy over-
  takes his village.

45. Savour of salt **

- Luke 14:34–35: Salt was used two ways...positive and
  negative. In a positive sense, it was used to preserve food
  from bacteria and rotting. Even though it had a very negative action—that of destroying the bacteria that caused
  decay and rot—Jesus points out it is "good" because its
  negative actions bring positive results! Becoming a war-
  rior can feel like a life filled with negative activities, but
  it's a "good fight of faith."

46. Lost sheep

- Luke 15:3–7

47. Lost piece of silver

- Luke 15:8–10

48. Prodigal son

- Luke 15:11–32

49. Unjust steward

- Luke 16:1–8

50. Rich man and Lazarus

- Luke 16:19–31

51. Importunate widow *

- Luke 18:1–8: The justice of God is contrasted with human government's inefficiency and corrupt judiciaries.

52. Pharisee and Publican

- Luke 18:9–14

53. Pounds *

- Luke 19:12–27: Behavior and faithfulness to care for the King's domain (while He's absent) is critical to receiving commendation or punishment when the King returns. The King is depicted to care about the condition of His kingdom, whether He is present or not. This is demonstrated in the fact that those who do *not* maintain it in His absence are severely rebuked.

54. Good Shepherd

- John 10:1–6

55. Vine and branches

- John 15:1–5

Appendix 3

Troubling Passages Explained

*I*T IS UNDERSTANDABLE how Bible readers who have not carefully and "rightly divided" the Word of Truth might misunderstand the Bible and mistakenly believe the nearly universal myth that "Christ came to do away with the law." They claim He replaced Mosaic Law with the single law of love.

In order to help unscramble these misunderstandings, this section of the appendix is called *Troubling Passages Explained*. The passages themselves are not "troubling." They are inspired, inerrant, and beautifully communicated truths that even children have the capacity to understand. We do not imply that the Word of God is in any way "troubling." Rather, they are referred to as "troubling passages" because they have been so incorrectly taught (nearly universally) that the strength of the incorrect explanations has grown into mental strongholds that must be forcibly shattered.

It is true that Paul condemns Christians in the early church for insisting upon continuing their relationship to the *whole* law *after* Jesus's death, burial, and resurrection, in the same manner that they had related to the *whole* law *before* His arrival. (Apparently, they had not properly understood the relationship of faith and the law in either point of history.) But there is a considerable portion of the Hebrew law that Paul also teaches as necessary and beneficial for our fallen world.

As this section is read, the reader is admonished to consider the style through which the author intends to explain the *troubling passages*. In each case, the entire portion of scripture is printed for the reader to enjoy. This is done up front to provide the proper context. Then, once the context is read fully, each individual passage will be explained in its chronological order by recalling each verse (expository style) so that the stronghold of incorrect interpretation can be broken from the mind of the reader.

TROUBLING PASSAGE NO. 1

GALATIANS 3:1–11

In the following first *troubling passage* of our study, it is incorrectly claimed that Paul suggested Christ abolished the *whole* law—unequivocally. Let's read the following text of Scripture:

> O foolish Galatians, who hath bewitched you, that ye should not obey the truth, before whose eyes Jesus Christ hath been evidently set forth, crucified among you? This only would I learn of you, Received ye the Spirit by the works of the law, or by the hearing of faith? Are ye so foolish? having begun in the Spirit, are ye now made perfect by the flesh? Have ye suffered so many things in vain? if *it be* yet in vain. He therefore that ministereth to you the Spirit, and worketh miracles among you, *doeth he it* by the works of the law, or by the hearing of faith? Even as Abraham believed God, and it was accounted to him for righteousness. Know ye therefore that they which are of faith, the same are the children of Abraham. And the scripture, foreseeing that God would justify the heathen through faith, preached before the gospel unto Abraham, *saying,* In thee shall all nations be blessed. So then they which be of faith are blessed with faithful Abraham. For as many as are of the works of the law are under the curse: for it is written, Cursed *is* every one that continueth not in all things which are written in the book of the law to do them. But that no man is justified by the law in the sight of God, *it is* evident: for, The just shall live by faith.
>
> —GALATIANS 3:1–11

Is this passage any proof text that Christ has abolished the law in its entirety? No, it is not. It remains in perfect harmony with all those truths already explained throughout this book. The first thing the Bible student should acknowledge before reading Galatians 3:1–11 is the reality that everything Paul says in his rebuke to the "foolish Galatians" could have just as properly been said to the children of

Israel more than 1,000 years before this moment in history. Paul asks the frustrated rhetorical question of verse 3:

> Are ye so foolish? having begun in the Spirit, are ye now made perfect by the flesh?

Fleshly works had *never* been adequate to save *any* human being from hell. Fleshly works had *never* been a pathway toward earning entrance to heaven, neither in the Old Testament nor in the New Testament... neither beneath Mount Sinai in the year 1500 BC nor in the Asia Minor province of Galatia at the time of this writing (approximately AD 68).

To make that very argument, Paul wisely points out to his readers that mere obedience to laws had *never* been the plan of God for man. The proof of this as an Old Covenant truth is illustrated here by Paul. He refers to Abraham, who set the precedent of the basis for all human beings' relationship with God nearly 500 years *before* Moses established the inspired Hebrew civil code. In approximately 2000 BC, what example was set as the only valid pathway toward heaven? Paul reveals the answer in verses 6, 7 and 8:

> Even as Abraham believed God, and it was accounted to him for righteousness. Know ye therefore that they which are of faith, the same are the children of Abraham. And the scripture, foreseeing that God would justify the heathen through faith, preached before the gospel unto Abraham, *saying*, In thee shall all nations be blessed.

Five hundred years after Abraham demonstrated faith as the only way of salvation for all men in all times and dispensations, Moses understood it too. Paul deliberately points this out by reminding the Galatians that Moses wrote a similar warning to his own nation, which had acted as foolishly as the Galatians themselves were now acting... again. Recall verses 10 and 11:

> For as many as are of the works of the law are under the curse: for it is written, Cursed *is* every one that continueth not in all things which are written in the book of the law to do them. But that no man is justified by the law in the sight of God, *it is* evident: for, The just shall live by faith.

Paul says that in the reading of the Old Testament scriptures, the fact that faith (and not works) was necessary for salvation was evident. Recall verse 11:

> But that no man is justified by the law in the sight of God, it is evident.

Paul says further, "it is written." He reminds the Galatians what the Old Testament said about the "good, perfect, pure, clean, true, righteous, sweeter than honeycomb" (see Psalm 19:7–11) laws of God. Moses wrote in his own Book of Deuteronomy chapter 27 and verse 26:

> Cursed *be* he that confirmeth not *all* the words of this law to do them. And all the people shall say, Amen.

But then Paul also reminds the Galatians of something else their own Old Covenant prophet Habakkuk had written as a warning to the tribe of Judah. As Judah faced the severe judgment of God because they were not properly conforming to the Ten Commandments, Habakkuk reminded them in his letter of rebuke, in Habakkuk 2:4:

> Behold, his soul *which* is lifted up is not upright in him: but the just shall live by his faith.

In summary, the fact that heaven could not be gained by works, but that men were justified by faith alone, was "evident" and was "written," according to Paul, in the reading of the Old Testament scriptures. Today's Christians are very familiar with this phrase: "the just shall live by faith." Many think Martin Luther wrote it. Others think of it as an exclusively New Testament revelation that was untrue before Christ arrived. They are both wrong. It is correct that the phrase is found three times in the New Testament, and Martin Luther did make the phrase particularly famous when he nailed his thesis to the door of the Catholic Church. But Romans 1:17, Galatians 3:11, and Hebrews 10:38 are only quoting the Old Testament truth given to the tribe of Judah, who needed to repent in order to avoid destruction.

It was true in the Old Testament that "the just shall live by faith." It stood to reason, then, that if the Galatians believed they could be justified by their fleshly works, they would perish in the New Covenant as painfully as Judah did in the Old.

This *troubling passage* of Galatians 3:1–11 in no way supports the errant teaching that Christ abolished the *entire* law of Moses through His creation of a New Covenant. This much is very clear.

TROUBLING PASSAGE NO. 2

GALATIANS 5:1–6

Stand fast therefore in the liberty wherewith Christ hath made us free, and be not entangled again with the yoke of bondage. Behold, I Paul say unto you, that if ye be circumcised, Christ shall profit you nothing. For I testify again to every man that is circumcised, that he is a debtor to do the whole law. Christ is become of no effect unto you, whosoever of you are justified by the law; ye are fallen from grace. For we through the Spirit wait for the hope of righteousness by faith. For in Jesus Christ neither circumcision availeth anything, nor uncircumcision; but faith which worketh by love.

—GALATIANS 5:1–6

The children of Israel had experienced the greatest liberty of all nations upon the earth because of the civil code God Himself described as "righteous statutes" that would someday be the envy of world-wide nations, according to Deuteronomy 4:8. When Jesus referred to God's law, He said, "My yoke is easy and my burden is light." In other words, "My laws are easy, and my expectations for you to obey them are only reasonable." The antinomians insist that Jesus had "different laws" than His Father. This is completely false, as we have proven throughout this book. Love has always been the chief law, and God has always been the Chief Law-Giver, for He is Love. Jesus continually claimed to be in perfect unity and agreement with His Father in heaven. He could not have made such a claim while simultaneously teaching a whole different behavioral code at odds with that which His Father had already established in the earth for the purpose of clearly distinguishing good from evil.

Even a pagan has expectations in a reasonable friendship. God providing man with the Ten Commandments as the foundation of all righteous government was an invitation to divine friendship. Not even a pagan would endure hanging out with a consummate liar. (Thou shalt not bear false witness.) Not even a pagan would keep a companion that he knew was continually lusting after his wife, secretly hoping to have sex with her behind his back. (Thou shalt not commit adultery.) No pagan would invite a friend over to enjoy dinner if he feared that he couldn't let the guest out of his sight long enough to use the bathroom, for fear his guest would steal his favorite painting off the wall. (Thou shalt not steal.) Not even a pagan would keep a friend that was never truly happy for him when he obtained a new piece of property. (Thou shalt not covet.) So it is true that God's laws are easy to accept and only reasonable to keep. Even the pagans instinctively apply such standards to regular friendships on a daily basis. Recall verse 1:

> Stand fast therefore in the liberty wherewith Christ hath made us free, and be not entangled again with the yoke of bondage.

These things are important to say *before* properly defining the phrase "yoke of bondage" in the first verse. A "yoke of bondage" in the Old Covenant is still a "yoke of bondage" in the New. This "bondage" cannot be the laws that fall into the category of the foundational command, "Thou shalt not murder." Otherwise we are forced to admit that what Paul calls "liberty in Christ" is the freedom to kill others. This "bondage" cannot be the laws that include the command, "Thou shalt not bear false witness." If bearing false witness is bondage, then we are forced to claim that liberty in Christ is the freedom to lie when it is convenient. There are eight more examples I should need not explain to the levelheaded Bible student.

What is the yoke of bondage, then? It is the attempt to be justified by outward acts of compliance with the Mosaic Law, instead of being justified internally by the act of Christ's substitutionary work at Calvary. As it was with the Mosaic Law, it is now with Christ. In order to enter heaven, God demanded repentance from sin, faith, and a change of heart thousands of years before Christ came to Earth. Recall verse 2:

> Behold, I Paul say unto you, that if ye be circumcised, Christ shall profit you nothing.

Without faith in the Redeemer (promised in Genesis 3:15) to come in the future, the outward acts of compliance to the Mosaic Law were damnable to God, particularly the rite of circumcision. If the heart and soul of the man being circumcised did not accept redemption from his sins by faith, then his compliance to Mosaic Law was in vain.

> Therefore circumcise the foreskin of your *heart* and be stiffnecked no longer.
>   —DEUTERONOMY 10:16, EMPHASIS ADDED

> And the Lord your God will circumcise your *heart* and the *heart* of your descendants, to *love* the Lord your God with all your heart and with all your soul, that you may *live*.
>   —DEUTERONOMY 30:6, EMPHASIS ADDED.

After Calvary, without faith in the Redeemer who lived, died, resurrected, and ascended back into heaven, outward acts of compliance to the Mosaic Law were damnable to God. Any attempt for a man to justify himself by his own works, in either the Old Testament or the New Testament, were contemptible to God at all times and in all places. The apostle Paul agreed with the doctrine of Moses with regard to redemption and its proper relationship to the rite of circumcision.

> But he is a Jew, which is one inwardly; and circumcision is that of the heart...
>   —ROMANS 2:29

> In whom also ye are circumcised with the circumcision made without hands...
>   —COLOSSIANS 2:11

Recall verse 3:

> For I testify again to every man that is circumcised, that he is a debtor to do the *whole* law.
>   —GALATIANS 5:3, EMPHASIS ADDED

Notice that Paul's objection is that by insisting upon continuing in the ritual law of circumcision, which was logically done away in Christ, the Judaizers fell from grace by insisting upon Mosaic Law as a *whole*, disregarding the fact that the portions they insisted upon keeping had been done away in Christ. This was objectionable because it ignored the impacting global accomplishments of Christ. For more understanding of why circumcision was done away in Christ, we have already covered the subject on page 170 of Chapter 8.

Recall verse 5:

> For we through the Spirit wait for the hope of righteousness by faith.

This was true in both the Old Testament and the New Testament, so the antagonist's habit of using a passage to pit the New Testament against the Old is a habit of doctrinal error. All men in all times, both before and after the Cross, waited for the hope of righteousness by faith. How does the apostle teach us all the patriarchs of faith gained heaven in the Old Testament? After listing the chronological high spots throughout many different covenants of history that took place before Christ was born, he writes:

> These all died in faith, not having received the promises, but having seen them afar off, and were persuaded of them, and embraced them, and confessed that they were strangers and pilgrims on the earth.
>
> —HEBREWS 11:13

And again, the author of Hebrews restates the only path to heaven in all covenants at all times and in all places of world history:

> And these all, having obtained a good report through faith, received not the promise: God having provided some better thing for us, that *they without us* should not be made perfect.
>
> —HEBREWS 11:39–40, EMPHASIS ADDED

Who were these people who achieved heaven by faith *before* the Cross and await our arrival by faith *after* the Cross? Hebrews 11 tells that the following persons were saved from their sins and justified by faith (not works) so that they could see heaven: Abel, Enoch, Noah, Abraham, Sarah, Isaac, Jacob, Esau, Joseph, Moses, Joshua, Rahab, Gideon, Barak, Samson, Jephthae, David, Samuel, and many others.

Of these men and women, justified and saved by faith in God's redemption through a coming Messiah, the Bible says that "they without us" are incomplete. In Hebrews 12:2, he rightly reminds all Christians that Jesus is the Author and Finisher of our faith, and it is understood, in the context, that Jesus was *also* the Author and Finisher of *theirs*, *before* the Cross.

Recall verse 6:

> For in Jesus Christ neither circumcision availeth any thing, nor uncircumcision; but faith which worketh by love.
>
> —GALATIANS 5:6

And faith worked by love to save lost souls both before and after the Cross of Calvary. There has never been any way to heaven other than the redemptive path made by Father God through His Son, Jesus Christ. Faith transcends the limitations of the time dimension. Faith for a Redeemer to *come* and faith for a Redeemer who *already came* accomplishes the same purpose: forgiveness, remission of sins, and entrance to heaven.

This *troubling passage* of Galatians 5:1–6 in no way supports the errant teaching that claims Christ abolished the *entire* law of Moses through His creation of a New Covenant. This much is very clear.

TROUBLING PASSAGE NO. 3

2 CORINTHIANS 3:1–18

Saul of Tarsus (later Paul) had a tough start in ministry. He had killed Jewish believers who accepted Christ as their long-awaited Messiah and had publicly encouraged their ongoing violent persecution. After a supernatural confrontation with Jesus, Saul was struck blind and sent to submit himself to other Jews who had believed upon Jesus Christ. Naturally, his evil reputation preceded him, and the Jewish believers were initially very reluctant to accept his testimony of repentance and conversion.

In such times of conflict, it became necessary for traveling ministers of the first century church to offer letters of recommendation from other reputable Christian leaders before being accepted into fellowship or allowed to teach doctrine in a local church. Paul was, initially, no exception to this wise practice, and later, he wrote the same kinds of letters of recommendation on behalf of his own apprentices who launched out into their own ministries.

The issue of reputation and credibility in ministry is the backdrop of the discussion that takes place in this next *troubling passage*:

Do we begin again to commend ourselves? or need we, as some others, epistles of commendation to you, or letters of commendation from you? Ye are our epistle written in our hearts, known and read of all men: Forasmuch as ye are manifestly declared to be the epistle of Christ ministered by us, written not with ink, but with the Spirit of the living God; not in tables of stone, but in fleshy tables of the heart. And such trust have we through Christ to God-ward: Not that we are sufficient of ourselves to think any thing as of ourselves; but our sufficiency is of God; Who also hath made us able ministers of the new testament; not of the letter, but of the spirit: for the letter killeth, but the spirit giveth life. But if the ministration of death, written and engraven in stones, was glorious, so that the children of Israel could not stedfastly behold the face of Moses for the glory of his countenance; which glory was to be done away: How shall not the ministration of the spirit be rather glorious? For if the ministration of condemnation be glory, much more doth the ministration of righteousness exceed in glory. For even that which was made glorious had no glory in this respect, by reason of the glory that excelleth. For if that which is done away was glorious, much more that which remaineth is glorious. Seeing then that we have such hope, we use great plainness of speech: And not as Moses, which put a veil over his face, that the children of Israel could not stedfastly look to the end of that which is abolished: But their minds were blinded: for until this day remaineth the same veil untaken away in the reading of the old testament; which veil is done away in Christ. But even unto this day, when Moses is read, the veil is upon their heart. Nevertheless when it shall turn to the Lord, the veil shall be taken away. Now the Lord is that Spirit: and where the Spirit of the Lord is, there is liberty. But we all, with open face beholding as in a glass the glory of the Lord, are changed into the same image from glory to glory, even as by the Spirit of the Lord.

—2 Corinthians 3:1–18

Recall verse 1:

Do we begin again to commend ourselves? or need we, as
some others, epistles of commendation to you, or letters of
commendation from you?

Although letters of recommendation were typically read before
the individual carrying the letter was welcomed by a local church to
teach or receive food, lodging, and financial support, they were only
necessary when the minister who offered his services was unknown
to that particular fellowship. Letters were introductory. They were
written as a means to pave the way for the actual person on the other
end of the letter, who was hopefully awaiting a hospitable reception.
The rationale of such introductions and recommendations were so
the local church would be protected from infiltration and confusion
created by false teachers.

Recall verse 2:

Ye are our epistle written in our hearts, known and read of
all men.

Paul makes the point that he does not need a letter of recommendation in order to accept the ministry of someone he already knows
and dearly loves. He does not need to be reminded of what he already
intimately understands. Paul states that he knows the Corinthians
well, their goodness is clearly written upon his own heart, and others
who meet with him during his many travels read of the Corinthians'
reputation wherever he shows his heart. In other words, Paul praises
them everywhere.

Recall verse 3:

Forasmuch as ye are manifestly declared to be the epistle of
Christ ministered by us, written not with ink, but with the
Spirit of the living God; not in tables of stone, but in fleshy
tables of the heart.

Paul uses figurative language to illustrate his spiritual discernment
of their authenticity as members of the body of Christ. He explains
that the Corinthians' reputation is as though it were literally written
upon his own heart by the pen and ink of Jesus Christ. The fruit that
was produced when the Corinthians were saved and redeemed by the
power of Jesus Christ is as much the "signature of God" as a literal

letter dictated by Jesus and handwritten with ink on parchment by a careful scribe. Paul portrays the Corinthians as what is written, Jesus Christ as the author who is dictating a message, and Paul as the listener with pen in hand. Christ spoke, Paul wrote what Christ said, and the born-again Corinthian people were the story Christ told.

Paul expands the metaphorical language by saying that this beautiful story dictated by Christ was not written with mere ink, but it was written by the Holy Spirit. It was not written upon mere paper, but it was written upon Paul's very heart. It was not merely a public contract or memorial carved in a table of stone (a common practice in that culture), but rather an eternal covenantal memorial enshrined by God in a spiritual and everlasting way.

Recall verse 4:

> And such trust have we through Christ to God-ward.

Just as Paul has logically justified that he does not need a letter of recommendation in order to accept the Corinthians (because he knows them well enough to write a letter about them himself), he now uses the same logic to point out that he has no need of a literal letter of recommendation from other ministerial authorities to present to *them*, in order for his own ministry to be accepted.

Instead, his proverbial letter of recommendation is the demonstration of power by the Holy Spirit. God's approval of Paul's ministry is evident in the miraculous fruit of his prayers and efforts. And the evidence of the power of the Holy Spirit is of so much higher value than a mere piece of paper signed by a man recommending his ministry.

Recall verses 5 and 6:

> Not that we are sufficient of ourselves to think any thing as of ourselves; but our sufficiency is of God; Who also hath made us able ministers of the new testament; not of the letter, but of the spirit: for the letter killeth, but the spirit giveth life.

God gets all the glory for what He has done through both the teacher and pupils by His Spirit. As ink-written letters and stone-carved contracts are created in Palestinian culture to testify to the authenticity and evidence of any legal claim to arise in the future, the Corinthians' conversion and salvation through Paul's ministry is proof enough that Paul is an authentic minister of God. Thus, the Corinthian people are Paul's proverbial "letter of recommendation" to the people of the whole world.

Those who are transformed by the power of Christ are as bona fide as a legal parchment with Christ's own signature. They are as authentic as a stone memorial carved by the finger of God (as was done with the Ten Commandments given to Moses), but they are sealed with something greater than mere ink or stone-chiseled tablets; they are attested to by the Holy Spirit, alive and in person.

Just as a legal covenant signed in ink or carved in stone is necessary as proof of contract after a testator dies, the documented evidence that such a covenant has been agreed upon is *not* necessary if both parties are alive and in the same place reaffirming their covenant together. It was true in both the Old Testament and the New Testament. To ignore a living testator in preference to paper, ink, or stone-carved contracts was to act as if the testator was dead, when, in this case, the Testator was God, who could not die (excepting the temporary kenosis* of Christ). Both the living teacher and the living learner are monuments of God's grace and saving power.

Recall verses 7, 8, and 9:

> But if the ministration of death, written and engraven in stones, was glorious, so that the children of Israel could not stedfastly behold the face of Moses for the glory of his countenance; which glory was to be done away: How shall not the ministration of the spirit be rather glorious? For if the ministration of condemnation be glory, much more doth the ministration of righteousness exceed in glory.

The erroneous temptation to pit the New Testament text against the Old Testament text is apparently insatiable with many Bible teachers today when the above verse is read and often poorly explained. But Paul had no intention of being misread in such a way. Consider first that no such "New Testament" compilation of canonized letters existed at the time this passage was written to the Corinthians. (Let

---

* Philippians 2:7 states: "But made himself of no reputation, and took upon him the form of a servant, and was made in the likeness of men." The phrase "made himself of no reputation" means to *empty* and comes from the Greek word *keno,* from whence is derived the term *kenosis.* Christ emptied Himself of the prerogative of deity. He made Himself vulnerable to physical death, and did so by His own choice. Ironically, His death inaugurated the New Testament. As with the death of a testator, a will and testament is empowered by death to the force of law.

what I just said soak in for a moment. Reread it a time or two. It will protect you from the false paradigm that imagines the right half of our particular Holy Book replaced the left half of our Holy Book, since no such Holy Book with two divided portions existed.) The recipients of these remarks of Paul could not have imagined the pitting of one section of sacred text against another, so to believe such is the meaning now is quite preposterous and unreasonable.

Adam Clarke laments: "The apostle does not mean here, as some have imagined, that he states himself to be a minister of the New Testament, in opposition to the Old; and that it is the Old Testament that kills, and the New that gives life; but that the New Testament gives the proper meaning of the Old; for the old covenant had its letter and its spirit, its literal and its spiritual meaning. The law was founded on the very supposition of the Gospel; and all its sacrifices, types and ceremonies refer to the Gospel."[1]

As has been thoroughly proven throughout this book, but bears repeating, the saints who lived before the Cross were required in every way to place their faith in a coming Redeemer. No person in the Old Covenant was saved by attempts to justify himself by mere external obedience to reasonable religious and/or civil statutes. The same is true now of Christians concerning their own relationship to the New Testament text. Paul's remarks are intended to warn would-be Judaizers that many Jews perished in the Old Covenant for staring at the letters of the sacred text and failing to come to faith and love in the Author of that same text. That is all that is meant. Nothing less. Nothing more.

A modern self-described "Christian" requires this same warning repeated right now. Stare at the chilly physical water of your "Christian baptism" with no faith in the spiritual purpose for the completed work of baptism, and you will reemerge from a religious ceremony with only one small change. Before the ceremony began, you were a dry sinner on your way to hell. After the ceremony, you were a cold and wet sinner on your way to hell. This is an example of the "letter that killeth."

The same can be said of partaking of the Communion table. Hold the dry and unleavened bread in your hand. Eat it. Think only of how it has taken on the unpleasant flavor of the refrigerator where it must have been stored a very long while, and then drink the small cup of juice when given the cue to do so by the pastor. Do so without any true faith in the meaning of the sacred institution of the Communion table, and perish in your sins. This is another example of "the letter that killeth."

Light a candle. Repeat after me. Stand up. Sit down. Turn to page 342 in your hymnal and sing the very most glorious hymns without any heart connection to the meaning of that song, but only a robotic and passive enjoyment in the recognized melody, and find hell when you die. This is "the letter that killeth."

Moses warned all men in Deuteronomy 6:4-6:

> Hear, O Israel: The LORD our God *is* one LORD: And thou shalt love the LORD thy God with all thine heart, and with all thy soul, and with all thy might. And these words, which I command thee this day, shall be in thine heart.

Moses taught men the path toward salvation exactly the same as Jesus. When Jesus was asked by a doctor of the Mosaic Law (see Luke 10:25-28) how a man could gain eternal life, Jesus had the lawyer quote what Moses said in Deuteronomy 6:4-6 (above), and Jesus responded to the words of Moses, saying, "Thou hast answered right. This do, and thou shalt [eternally] live."

Paul uses the phrase "ministration of death" in the text. The word "ministration" refers to the lower implementation of Mosaic Law. It was the purpose of the law of God to describe the behavioral duties of mankind and to assign punishments against any violation of those obligations. This was and remains necessary until the physical reign of Jesus Christ on a perfected Earth. Men needed to know what God expected of them—then and now. How does the New Testament tell us we are able to determine what is and is not a sin that requires repentance and forgiveness? Sin is "transgression of the law."

> Whosoever committeth sin transgresseth also the law: for sin is the transgression of the law. And ye know that he was manifested to take away our sins; and in him is no sin.
>
> —1 JOHN 3:4-5

Paul uses the phrase "which glory was to be done away" in reference to the "ministration of death" contrasted to the "ministration of the spirit." Some have tripped over this to believe the phrase implies the wholesale abolishment of all the law of God. It cannot mean this on many points of evidence. The first is that the same author, Paul, writes plainly in another letter that "The law is good if it is used lawfully" (1 Tim. 1:8), proving that the eternal attitude of God, expressed in His law, is very much in play during our New Testament. What it does refer to is illustrated in overwhelming light of the noonday sun when contrasted with the former reflective light of the moon. The spirit of the law overwhelms the letter of the law with the same ferocity as the sun does the moon at daybreak.

The satirical question must be asked: "How on earth can a man transgress a law that is supposedly abolished completely in Christ?" If it is true that the whole law is completely abolished in Christ, then it is no longer possible for any human to sin anymore, because nothing exists that can be transgressed! By simply taking what is argued to its logical conclusion, it is not difficult to expose the fallacies.

The atonement for sin in the Old Testament was not found in the blood of sacrificial animals, it was in the Redeemer's blood to be shed someday in their future for all their sins. The animal blood pointed toward the coming Messiah. Remission of sins during an animal sacrifice *only* came when the sinner who offered the bulls, goats, lambs, and turtledoves exercised *faith* in divine redemption by a divine Redeemer! Approximately 1,845 years before Christ was born, Job declared:

> For I know *that* my redeemer liveth, and *that* he shall stand at the latter *day* upon the earth.
>
> —JOB 19:25

Approximately 800 years before Christ was born, Isaiah the prophet declared that a personal Redeemer was coming to earth:

> And the Redeemer shall come to Zion, and unto them that turn from transgression in Jacob, saith the LORD.
>
> —ISAIAH 59:20

In the Old Testament, to fail to use faith in a coming Redeemer was to fail to obtain spiritual justification. Failure to obtain justification was an eternal death sentence. Habakkuk, the Old Testament prophet, declared it very plainly when he said in Habakkuk 2:4: "The just shall live by faith." Failure to obtain justification was to fail to embrace the *spirit* of the law, and the only thing left when the *spirit* of the law was neglected, was the *letter*... the *text*... that killeth. It was then, and it is today, the *spirit* that giveth life!

To directly correlate with his use of the phrase "ministration of death," the apostle also uses the phrase "ministration of the spirit" to describe the issue of honoring the *spirit* of the law precisely the same as the Old Testament prophets taught it should be honored. The word *ministration*, in this case, refers to the *higher* operation of Mosaic Law. In contrast to the purpose of the lower *letter* of the law, described above as bringing "death" and "condemnation" (albeit in a glorious way), it was the purpose of the higher *spirit* of the law of God to make a faith-filled, loving relationship possible between God and man and to assign tremendous blessings upon fulfillment of those obligations. The lower *letter* of the law was "glorious," but how much more was (and is) the higher *spirit* of the law, which Paul reminds the Corinthian believers was the motivation for the law in the first place.

The apostle means to contrast the *letter* of the law against the *spirit* of the law. He does not intend to pit the New Testament against the Old Testament. The lower "ministration of death" by the law represents the glorious *justice* of God, as it is properly and righteously unleashed against unrepentant evil men. The higher "ministration of the spirit" represents the glorious *justification* of man, by God, through a Redeemer, as it is richly poured upon humble and contrite men of faith.

Though it would have been without the benefit of a recent encounter with Christ's earth-shaking ministry, which gloriously interrupted world history only a few years prior to this letter to the Corinthians... nothing said in this particular *troubling passage,* so far, could not also have been taught a thousand years before Christ was born. Notice the confrontations of Micah, Samuel, Solomon, Jeremiah, and Hosea, who warned of neglecting the *spirit* of the law in exchange for what Paul described as "the letter that killeth":

> Wherewith shall I come before the LORD, *and* bow myself before the high God? shall I come before him with burnt offerings, with calves of a year old? Will the LORD be pleased with thousands of rams, *or* with ten thousands of rivers of oil? shall I give my firstborn *for* my transgression, the fruit of my body *for* the sin of my soul? He hath shewed thee, O man, what *is*

good; and what doth the LORD require of thee, but to do justly, and to love mercy, and to walk humbly with thy God?

—MICAH 6:6–8

And Samuel said, Hath the LORD *as great* delight in burnt offerings and sacrifices, as in obeying the voice of the LORD? Behold, to obey *is* better than sacrifice, *and* to hearken than the fat of rams.

—1 SAMUEL 15:22

To do justice and judgment *is* more acceptable to the LORD than sacrifice.

—PROVERBS 21:3

Thus saith the LORD of hosts, the God of Israel; 'Put your burnt offerings unto your sacrifices, and eat flesh. For I spake not unto your fathers, nor commanded them in the day that I brought them out of the land of Egypt, concerning burnt offerings or sacrifices: But this thing commanded I them, saying, Obey my voice, and I will be your God, and ye shall be my people: and walk ye in all the ways that I have commanded you, that it may be well unto you.' But they hearkened not, nor inclined their ear, but walked in the counsels *and* in the imagination of their evil heart, and went backward, and not forward.

—JEREMIAH 7:21–24

For I desired mercy, and not sacrifice; and the knowledge of God more than burnt offerings.

—HOSEA 6:6

Recall verses 10 and 11:

For even that which was made glorious had no glory in this respect, by reason of the glory that excelleth. For if that which is done away was glorious, much more that which remaineth is glorious.

—2 CORINTHIANS 3:10–11

As mentioned earlier, the moon shines beautifully at night, but it is good to remember the moon is only reflecting the *greater* light of the sun. The sun's light is temporarily blocked by the cycle of time. As time moves forward, the sun eventually emerges from the darkness, and its greater brilliance so overpowers the moon that it pales in comparison to the light of day. And yet, the moon and the sun did not give different light! No, they gave the very same light.

The Marcionite would claim this *troubling passage* pits the proverbial sun *against* the moon, as if they are in some kind of competition. But this misses the point entirely. They are in no competition. They each shine with the same light, only one was the *source,* and the other a mere *reflection* of that same source. So it is between the glorious light of the "ministration of death" that revealed the *justice* of God against sin, and the "ministration of the spirit" that revealed the *justification* of man, by God. The letter was a mere reflection of the *greater* power and desire of God to redeem the sinner, rather than be forced, through man's faithless rebellion, to grant him the just desserts of eternal death.

Recall verses 12 through 14:

> Seeing then that we have such hope, we use great plainness of speech: And not as Moses, which put a veil over his face, that the children of Israel could not stedfastly look to the end of that which is abolished: But their minds were blinded: for until this day remaineth the same veil untaken away in the reading of the old testament; which veil is done away in Christ.

Some mistake the above verse as a carte blanche rule that *all* who lived in the Old Testament times (particularly all who lived under the administration of Moses), were men of incurably blind minds. This is obviously untrue, since the same man who wrote the passage above also declared that the salvation of innumerable masses who died before Christ had been born were eternally saved by faith in a coming Redeemer.

> For this reason Christ is the mediator of a new covenant, that those who are called may receive the promised eternal inheritance—now that he has died as a ransom to set them free from the sins committed under the first covenant.
>
> —HEBREWS 9:15, NIV

The Scriptures are replete with hundreds, perhaps thousands of examples of Old Testament saints who completely embraced God by faith in His promised redemption, given in Genesis 3:15. As was stated earlier, Hebrews 11 reveals that the following persons were saved from their sins and justified by faith (not works) so that they could see heaven: Abel, Enoch, Noah, Abraham, Sarah, Isaac, Jacob, Esau, Joseph, Moses, Joshua, Rahab, Gideon, Barak, Samson, Jephthae, David, Samuel, and many others.

Clearly the apostle does not characterize *all* men of past ages as blind and unable to come to faith in a promised redemption. He speaks exclusively of those who rebelled in past times as a warning to his present Corinthian hearers that they, too, should beware of this hazard. Jesus declared plainly of Abraham, who had lived approximately 2,000 years before He was born:

> Your father Abraham rejoiced to see My day, and he saw it, and was glad.
>
> —JOHN 8:56

Clearly, Abraham was not spiritually blind. The false teaching of universal spiritual blindness and salvation by works for all who lived under the various covenants revealed throughout the Old Testament is a violation of sound biblical scholarship.

Recall verse 15:

> But even unto this day, when Moses is read, the veil is upon their heart.
>
> —2 CORINTHIANS 3:15

When Moses was alive and speaking publicly, he had to cover the reflection of God's glory because the people's eyes were unable to cope with even the *reflection* of God's own glorious light. And around 1,500 years later, after Moses had been long dead and buried, when the law of Moses (the lower "ministration of death") was read aloud, those who were, at the time of this letter to the Corinthians, refusing to come to faith and love for God, still had a veil (metaphorically speaking) of hardhearted rebellion blocking the light of the higher "ministration of the spirit" of the law. The Jews blocked their eyes from the light of God when merely reflected from the face of Moses. How much more then did the same sinners resist the direct light of

the very Son of God, for the Son of God shone brighter than Moses as
does the sun when compared to the moon!

Recall verses 16 through 18:

> Nevertheless when it shall turn to the Lord, the veil shall be
> taken away. Now the Lord is that Spirit: and where the Spirit
> of the Lord is, there is liberty. But we all, with open face
> beholding as in a glass the glory of the Lord, are changed into
> the same image from glory to glory, even as by the Spirit of
> the Lord.

The solution for ending spiritual blindness has always been the
same. Man must come to faith in God's promise of blood-spilt redemption. This was as possible for men in the Old Testament times as it is
today. Particularly at the time of Paul's writing, as the Corinthians
possessed direct access to the remarkable witnesses of Christ's recent
earthly ministry, it could be argued that they, above all generations of
history, had less of an excuse than those who lived thousands of years
before or *after* the Cross.

This *troubling passage* of 2 Corinthians 3:1–18 in no way supports
the errant teaching that claims Christ abolished the *entire* law of
Moses through His creation of a New Covenant. This much is very
clear.

TROUBLING PASSAGE NO. 4

COLOSSIANS 2:14–17

This *troubling passage* is fully explained in Chapter 4, *Moses: Father
of Fascism?*, beginning on page 79.

TROUBLING PASSAGE NO. 5

HEBREWS 7:1–8, 13

First, it is of utmost importance to provide this statement of fact: Every
whit of law discussed as having been done away in Christ throughout
the entire Book of Hebrews falls beneath the category of *ritual/cer-
emonial* Mosaic Law. At no single point throughout the book is any
solitary portion of Mosaic *civil* law or the foundational eternal truths
shown forth in the *Decalogue* (the Ten Commandments) described as

having been done away by the ministry, death, burial, or resurrection of Jesus Christ. No further explanation should be required, in the light of the work of this book, but for the sake of going beyond the call of duty, I will traverse through the text of Hebrews and provide clarion reproof of God's eternal law and its unimaginable value for the modern systems of governments around the globe.

Second, the author is authoritatively attributed to have been the apostle Paul by all notable church authorities during the first five centuries of Christendom. This is important to note because the same author clearly writes that Christ did *not* do away with the divine foundations of self-government and civil government shown by the two tables of Mosaic Law (the Ten Commandments) in his first letter to Timothy chapter 1, verses 5–11.

The issue at the heart of this letter was helping a predominantly (98 percent) Jewish church, who had recently come to accept Christ as the long-awaited Messiah. The goal of the author was to explain their immediate need to respond appropriately to a new covenant brought to Earth through the Messiah's sacrifice. The author makes it clear that the new covenant is not to be viewed as a cavalier replacement of their sacred Jewish faith, but rather an improved and amended extension of the Mosaic covenant they had known all their lives. This overwhelmingly Jewish church needed to discover Holy Spirit-directed conclusions corresponding to the finished work of Mosaic ceremonial pageantry, and those conclusions were clearly expressed by the conclusion of the book. Throughout the writing, the ceremonial/ritual division of Mosaic Law is clearly and emphatically described as having been completed through Christ's ministry, death, burial, and resurrection.

The Jewish believers are the audience who is addressed. They who have not yet in history been called "Christians" and in no way imagine themselves to be any other than who they truly are—an extension of that historic remnant of obedient Jews who have accepted the One Messiah of the whole world and are required by the apostle to comport their weekly worship practices with the new covenant changes brought by Christ. This is important to note, because it ruins the modern reader's errant tendency to pit the right side of their Bibles against the left side of their Bibles (pages in our present-day Bible that had not even been compiled and canonized into a book called the "New Testament" at the time of this letter from Paul).

Paul's audience is assumed to understand Hebrew covenant theology. They must have possessed sufficient knowledge of the pattern of covenant making with man that had begun in Genesis, because Paul takes the readers of his letter throughout the redemption story from the beginning of time to the present moment of his writing.

With the exception of the "New Covenant" to which they were being introduced, they likely already understood the prior fourteen covenants that grew throughout history as God revealed, in each new covenant, more information about Himself, and greater and deeper invitation to enhanced and improved relationship with Him, at each upgrade. They also likely understood that the nature of each covenantal shift throughout history was always, without exception, an improvement upon man's relationship to God building upon the eternal insight provided by the former covenant, not *replacing* and *destroying* all eternal insight provided by the former.

The following biblical covenants show these historic truths and establish this pattern of ever-growing and improving covenants between God and man:

1. The "Solaric Covenant" is described in Genesis 1:14–18.

2. The "Edenic Covenant" is described in Genesis 1:26–3:24.

3. The "Adamic Covenant" is described in Genesis 3:14–19.

4. The "Cainic Covenant" is described in Genesis 4:11–15.

5. The "Noahic Covenant" is described in Genesis 8:20–9:29.

6. The "Abrahamic Covenant" is described in Genesis 12:1–3.

7. The "Hagaric Covenant" is described in Genesis 16:7–14.

8. The "Sarahic Covenant" is described in Genesis 17:15–19; 18:9–15.

9. The "Mosaic Covenant" is described in Exodus 19:1, 3, 11; and Exodus 24:4–8.

10. The "Healing Covenant" is described in Exodus 15:6; 23:25.

11. The "Palestinian Covenant" is described in Deuteronomy 27:1–30:20.

12. The "Covenant of Levi" is described in Numbers 25:10–14.

13. The "Covenant of Salt" is described in Leviticus 2:13; Numbers 18:19.

14. The "Davidic Covenant" is described in 2 Samuel 7:1–17.

15. The "New Covenant" and its ramifications upon persons crossing into it from a practice of faith previously tied to those lessons from the past is the goal of the writer of the book called *Hebrews*.

Persons who lived within nearly every covenantal period listed above are at some point mentioned by the writer of the Book of Hebrews. Generational ministry is emphasized. Passing the baton of faith from the aged and dying to the young and living is paramount. Learning from the past for a better future is insisted upon. Never forgetting the goal of a city whose *Builder and Maker is God*, is championed. The writer particularly paints an epic portrait of covenant theology and generational ministry in Hebrews 11. The Genesis story of Creation, the lives of Abel and Enoch, and so forth, are chronicled with the deliberate goal of establishing one single truth for all covenants since the first moments of Creation. That single truth is this: No man who lived at any time of history, in any covenant of history, has ever gone to heaven who did not accept the work of Christ's redemption by faith!

As a sophomore is thought to build upon those foundational truths he first learned in kindergarten, and not for a moment led to believe that in order to become a sophomore he must denounce all that was learned in his previous grade levels prior to his sophomore year, so it is with covenantal dealings between God and man. The rationale for every covenant made in world history is God's work progressively restoring all of creation to its former glory before it was originally contaminated by sin in Eden. Since this is the rationale for all covenants in world history, it is understood that each covenant will contain greater degrees of wisdom through which those who cooperate will grow in fresh grace. It must also be understood that with the introduction of each new covenant there will be necessary annulments and

adjustments made from the previous, but *never* an absolute annul-
ment of all *eternal laws of God* introduced during the former.

As the reader reaches Hebrews 7, a particular emphasis is placed
upon the ministry of a certain priest called Melchizedek, who lived
on the tail end of the *Noahic* covenant and whose ministry positively
impacted the life of Abram, with whom God would soon make the
transition to what we call the *Abrahamic* covenant. This is important
as an illustration to the readers of Paul's letter (the Hebrews living in
approximately AD 68) because they, too, are a generation of people
whose lives are in the process of bridging across two great covenants.
They must learn to let go of those good and beautiful parts of their
former covenant, and embrace the new enhancements given by Christ,
through whom a New Covenant has been made during their generation's time on Earth. What specific adjustments must they make, and
why? Paul explains:

> For this Melchisedec, king of Salem, priest of the most high God,
> who met Abraham returning from the slaughter of the kings,
> and blessed him; To whom also Abraham gave a tenth part
> of all; first being by interpretation King of righteousness, and
> after that also King of Salem, which is, King of peace; Without
> father, without mother, without descent, having neither begin-
> ning of days, nor end of life; but made like unto the Son of God;
> abideth a priest continually. Now consider how great this man
> *was*, unto whom even the patriarch Abraham gave the tenth
> of the spoils. And verily they that are of the sons of Levi, who
> receive the office of the priesthood, have a commandment to
> take tithes of the people according to the law, that is, of their
> brethren, though they come out of the loins of Abraham: But
> he whose descent is not counted from them received tithes of
> Abraham, and blessed him that had the promises. And without
> all contradiction the less is blessed of the better. And here men
> that die receive tithes; but there he *receiveth them*, of whom
> it is witnessed that he liveth. And as I may so say, Levi also,
> who receiveth tithes, payed tithes in Abraham. For he was yet
> in the loins of his father, when Melchisedec met him. If there-
> fore perfection were by the Levitical priesthood (for under
> it the people received the law), what further need *was there*
> that another priest should rise after the order of Melchisedec,

and not be called after the order of Aaron? For the priesthood being changed, there is made of necessity a change also of the law. For he of whom these things are spoken pertaineth to another tribe, of which no man gave attendance at the altar. For *it is* evident that our Lord sprang out of Juda; of which tribe Moses spake nothing concerning priesthood. And it is yet far more evident: for that after the similitude of Melchisedec there ariseth another priest, Who is made, not after the law of a carnal commandment, but after the power of an endless life. For he testifieth, Thou *art* a priest for ever after the order of Melchisedec. For there is verily a disannulling of the commandment going before for the weakness and unprofitableness thereof. For the law made nothing perfect, but the bringing in of a better hope *did*; by the which we draw nigh unto God. And inasmuch as not without an oath *he was made priest*: (For those priests were made without an oath; but this with an oath by him that said unto him, The Lord sware and will not repent, Thou *art* a priest for ever after the order of Melchisedec:) By so much was Jesus made a surety of a better testament. And they truly were many priests, because they were not suffered to continue by reason of death: But this *man*, because he continueth ever, hath an unchangeable priesthood. Wherefore he is able also to save them to the uttermost that come unto God by him, seeing he ever liveth to make intercession for them. For such an high priest became us, *who is* holy, harmless, undefiled, separate from sinners, and made higher than the heavens; Who needeth not daily, as those high priests, to offer up sacrifice, first for his own sins, and then for the people's: for this he did once, when he offered up himself. For the law maketh men high priests which have infirmity; but the word of the oath, which was since the law, *maketh* the Son, who is consecrated for evermore.

—Hebrews 7:1–28

Chapter 8:1–13:

Now of the things which we have spoken *this is* the sum: We have such an high priest, who is set on the right hand of the throne of the Majesty in the heavens; A minister of the sanctuary, and of the true tabernacle, which the Lord pitched, and not man. For every high priest is ordained to offer gifts and sacrifices: wherefore *it is* of necessity that this man have somewhat also to offer. For if he were on earth, he should not be a priest, seeing that there are priests that offer gifts according to the law: Who serve unto the example and shadow of heavenly things, as Moses was admonished of God when he was about to make the tabernacle: for, See, saith he, *that* thou make all things according to the pattern shewed to thee in the mount. But now hath he obtained a more excellent ministry, by how much also he is the mediator of a better covenant, which was established upon better promises. For if that first *covenant* had been faultless, then should no place have been sought for the second. For finding fault with them, he saith, Behold, the days come, saith the Lord, when I will make a new covenant with the house of Israel and with the house of Judah: Not according to the covenant that I made with their fathers in the day when I took them by the hand to lead them out of the land of Egypt; because they continued not in my covenant, and I regarded them not, saith the Lord. For this *is* the covenant that I will make with the house of Israel after those days, saith the Lord; I will put my laws into their mind, and write them in their hearts: and I will be to them a God, and they shall be to me a people: And they shall not teach every man his neighbour, and every man his brother, saying, Know the Lord: for all shall know me, from the least to the greatest. For I will be merciful to their unrighteousness, and their sins and their iniquities will I remember no more. In that he saith, A new *covenant*, he hath made the first old. Now that which decayeth and waxeth old *is* ready to vanish away.

Recall verse 3:

Without father, without mother, without descent, having neither beginning of days, nor end of life; but made like unto the Son of God; abideth a priest continually.

—Hebrews 7:3

One translation (The Emphasized New Testament) describes Melchizedek as "without pedigree," another (Translation of Monsignor Ronald Knox) as having "no date of birth or of death" and another

(The New Translation of Olaf Norlie) as "a true symbol of the Son of God." Why is this fact about Melchizedek pointed out to be prophetic of Christ by the apostle Paul? Because Christ is the Redeemer pointed toward in every covenant since the Genesis story. Christ, without beginning or end. Christ from all eternity. Christ is the Redeemer of all men in all times, and therefore, all men in all covenants, regardless of the calendar year in which they lived, were, are, and will be required to accept redemption and justification by faith in the anointed Christ. The possibility of redemption in the Noahic covenant (Melchizedek), which was before the Abrahamic covenant, which was before the Mosaic covenant, remained consistent through all; redemption in each covenant came by faith.

Along with the theme of bettering covenants as time progresses is dealt a startling feature by the apostle. Something unusual is mentioned about Melchizedek, the type of Christ. Melchizedek, though existing during the tail end of the Noahic covenant, was greater than the patriarch who would usher in the greater Abrahamic covenant. A reverse of the covenantal trend is noted in history. Why?

Recall verses 5–7:

> And verily they that are of the sons of Levi, who receive the office of the priesthood, have a commandment to take tithes of the people according to the law, that is, of their brethren, though they come out of the loins of Abraham: But he whose descent is not counted from them received tithes of Abraham, and blessed him that had the promises. And without all contradiction the less is blessed of the better.
>
> —HEBREWS 7:5–7

"The less is blessed of the better," which is to say that Melchizedek was a greater man than Abram, because he was capable of blessing Abram as his subordinate. So Abram ushers in a greater covenant than that past Noahic covenant, in which the majority of Melchizedek's ministry had existed, but the lesser covenant does not necessarily a lesser man make.

This is extremely important for the heretical Marcionites to remember. None of them have ever parted a sea and walked on dry land. None of them have ever outrun an enemy chariot. None of them have made an ax head float. None of them have smashed flower pots in the night and watched the enemy armies below kill themselves.

None of them have lived so anointed that after their burial the dead were raised to life again by merely falling upon their dry bones. Just because one has lived in an inferior covenant does not make the *faith* of the men living in that prior period inferior to the men living in the next. *Faith is the constant thread throughout them all!* Redemption from sin by repentance is the crown of grace men must receive from God at all times in world history if they are to enter heaven after they die. Abram was a great man, but Melchizedek was a greater man! *Melchizedek was a type of Christ.* The message is clear to all covenants of history broached throughout this letter to the Hebrews: Christ is superior to every man who cut a covenant with God in history, because Christ is the *center* of every covenant cut between God and man throughout history. Christ is the Redeemer of all mankind from the foundations of the world.

Paul reminds the Hebrews of his day from whence the Mosaic Law of tithing, received by the Levitical priesthood, came. It had its beginning in the tradition of Abraham around 430 years *before* Moses was born to codify the Decalogue. From whence came the legal example of receiving the tithe of Abraham? It stemmed from the code of Melchizedek, who was a priest after the doctrines of the Noahic covenant. The Noahic covenant had begun around 427 years before Melchizedek was born to teach the doctrines of Noah. Noah influenced Melchizedek, who influenced Abraham, who influenced Moses.

What is to be learned by this illustration of a divine law, such as tithing, passing through three separate covenants without interruption? If something as fundamental as financial contributions remains constant throughout covenants, what might we expect for such principles as "have no other gods before me"? What should we expect to change about "honor your father and mother" or "thou shalt not covet"? This message is certainly clear. Eternal principles of blessing granted by a preacher in response to those who tithe to a divine institution carry through all covenants. Why? They travel through all covenants because they are connected to the timelessness of Christ—the Great *Giver* of eternal life. He is Christ—Giver of His *own* life—before the foundations of the world were laid. Christ, the Redeemer, is seated at the focal point of all divine covenants from Eden until today. For God so loved... He gave. Giving is a part of the eternal nature of God. The tithe is the beginning point for a spirit of generosity that reflects divine love without measure.

The tithe was a human expression of love and gratitude responding to a man's faith in his redemption. The tithe was motivated by love and gratitude in the Noahic covenant. The tithe was motivated by love and gratitude in the Abrahamic covenant. The tithe was motivated by love and gratitude in the Mosaic covenant, and it must as well be motivated by love and gratitude today. Marcionites who teach that "people *were forced* to tithe under the Old Covenant but we are set free from such *bondage* today" butcher the wholesome doctrines of Noah, Melchizedek, Abraham, Moses, Jesus, and Paul in one single ridiculous sentence. They do not comprehend the God of covenant any more than they do the men who were privileged to live under their loving and gracious protections.

Covenants can change. Covenants always improve. Covenants certainly grow in glory and in the impartation of wisdom, but a covenant referred to as "*inferior*" in the past, in contrast with the *superior* of the next, is *never inferior* because of the immutable and everlasting truths it once taught. It is *only inferior* because of the immutable and everlasting truths it was *not* designed to teach.

This is so incredibly important to grasp that it needs to be restated a second time. A covenant referred to as "*inferior*" in the past, in contrast with the *superior* of the next, is *never inferior* because of the immutable and everlasting truths it once taught. It is *only inferior* because of the immutable and everlasting truths it was not designed to teach.

To emphasize this critical truth a third time I will say it another way. A child could attend the very finest private school kindergarten class that money can buy. During the following first-grade year, the parents could describe the previous kindergarten year as having been *inferior* to the curriculum now supplied in the first-grade class, but this would *not* be meant as a poor reflection upon the excellent program taught during the previous year of kindergarten. It would *only* mean that kindergarten was *inferior* in the sense of what it was not yet supposed to teach.

A step further, one might argue that only a very poor school with a terrible lack of discernment would recklessly attempt to teach kindergartners a first-grade curriculum when they had not yet been properly prepared with the foundational essentials kindergarten curriculum was designed to provide. Further yet, one would be a special kind of imbecile who directly taught his newly enrolled first-grader to forget about everything he learned the previous kindergarten year on opening day of the first grade.

Along these same lines of thought Jesus proclaims His disapproval for all schemers of the New Covenant who might think themselves clever to ignore the present validity of the former *inferior* Mosaic covenant's eternal code of behavior:

> For verily I say unto you, Till heaven and earth pass, one jot or one tittle shall in no wise pass from the law, till all be fulfilled. Whosoever therefore shall break one of these least commandments, and shall teach men so, he shall be called the least in the kingdom of heaven...
>
> —MATTHEW 5:18–19

The Marcionite sees the word *inferior* in the letter to the Hebrews and claims a divine covenant from past ages to be "flawed" as if some wisdom it gave was error. This is absurd! It is an outrage! It is a lie! The truth remains that all covenants with God are beautiful and brimming with goodness, mercy, grace, and greatest of all—agape love!

Recall verse 8:

> And here men that die receive tithes; but there He *receiveth them*, of whom it is witnessed that He liveth.
>
> —HEBREWS 7:8

All men in all covenants past and present tense, including but not limited to the Noahic, Abrahamic, Mosaic, and the New Covenant (being explained to the Jews by way of this letter to the Hebrews) receive tithes from men who express their love and gratitude in response to their great redemption. All preachers in all these covenants also share another similarity. They all die as mortal men, despite carrying a great anointing that is capable of responding to the tithe, pronouncing spiritual blessings that cannot be bestowed upon others in any other way or by any other means than the proclamation of an anointed and mortal man of God.

But what of Christ? Christ, who was typified in the priestly ministry of a particular man named Melchizedek, is ever living (past, present, and future) and has always received the spirit of love behind the tithe of men who were grateful for their redemption, whether they paid tithes during the Noahic, the Abrahamic, the Mosaic, or the

New Covenant enjoyed today! To be clear, mere mortal men, who represented God on the earth, received the physical goods of the tithe, but all the while they were giving and receiving them down on Earth, Christ was receiving the spirit of faith in redemption that motivated their earthly tithes! Christ—without beginning or ending, typified by Melchizedek, who had "no date of birth or of death" listed in the ancient scrolls—Christ received the gratitude of men, who, by giving a minimum of ten percent of their profit, expressed faith in their Redeemer!

It is important at this juncture to insist that a reader of the letter to the Hebrews not err by forcing the writing into a narrow dispensational box. It should be obvious by now that the letter to the Hebrews does not *only* describe the church age. The opposite is the case. It explains the eternal truths that flow through all ages without interruption. It points *backward* to the Garden of Eden, reminding us that all men in all covenants of history were required to release faith in divine redemption in order to reach heaven. No man at any time of history was ever "saved by works" from the punishment of hell. The letter to the Hebrews looks *forward* far beyond the church age to a day when the servants of God will never physically die.

This is quite a contrast with what we know and experience as mortals. Ministers of God who have received tithes throughout the Noahic, Abrahamic, Sarahic, Mosaic, Healing, Palestinian, Levi, Salt, Davidic, and the New Covenant of Christ that now rules our day . . . still receive tithes, and they are mortals who still die. It will not always be the way of things.

The Hebrews are being taught the lessons of transitioning covenants, and in thoughtfulness, Paul is preparing them to let go of the portions of the covenant they knew so well (the Mosaic) in order to embrace the new ways of the covenant now made by the blood of Christ. They are also reminded that this new covenant would not be the last one; more was to come.

The eternal laws of God (the rule of tithing is showcased as an example) would pass through those new covenants beyond our view, just as they had passed through all covenants that had come before. It was important for the Hebrews to embrace their own history. Releasing some things from a past covenant was not heresy. It was not disparaging, nor was it disrespectful. It was a part of who they were and how God had related to them throughout their own national history. Should it be so outrageous to expect covenants to change when their own story was filled with such natural changes? No. Paul makes the case that they must embrace the covenant made right in front of them. Things were changing… again, and not for the first time. The Redeemer of all covenants had visited Israel in the flesh. A response to His sacrifice was absolutely demanded by God, and the demands were reasonable and good.

Recall verses 11–21:

> If therefore perfection were by the Levitical priesthood, (for under it the people received the law,) what further need *was there* that another priest should rise after the order of Melchisedec, and not be called after the order of Aaron? For the priesthood being changed, there is made of necessity a change also of the law. For he of whom these things are spoken pertaineth to another tribe, of which no man gave attendance at the altar. For *it is* evident that our Lord sprang out of Juda; of which tribe Moses spake nothing concerning priesthood. And it is yet far more evident: for that after the similitude of Melchisedec there ariseth another priest, Who is made, not after the law of a carnal commandment, but after the power of an endless life. For he testifieth, Thou *art* a priest for ever after the order of Melchisedec. For there is verily a disannulling of the commandment going before for the weakness and unprofitableness thereof. For the law made nothing perfect, but the bringing in of a better hope *did*; by the which we draw nigh unto God. And inasmuch as not without an oath *he was made priest*: (For those priests were made without an oath; but this with an oath by him that said unto him, The Lord sware and will not repent, Thou *art* a priest for ever after the order of Melchisedec:)
>
> —HEBREWS 7:11–21

Paul drives home the issue of covenant theology. In the light of so many covenants that had been built between them and God throughout their national history, why should they pretend that the Mosaic was the perfected summation of all God had to share with earth? The Mosaic was not the last great covenant between God and man! It could not be! Future covenants had been repeatedly predicted by their own revered prophets! They all knew in their hearts that God had more in store, and Paul insisted that the death, burial, and resurrection of Jesus Christ initiated the next great step in the covenantal journey of man toward his Creator.

Paul reminds the Hebrews that their own prophecy given by King David around 1055 BC (in Psalm 110:4) had plainly informed them this covenant change was coming and that it had been fulfilled in Christ right before their very eyes. They only needed to embrace it by faith.

> The LORD hath sworn, and will not repent, Thou *art* a priest for ever after the order of Melchizedek.
>
> —PSALM 110:4

It was important for those who read Paul's letter to the Hebrews to understand that Melchizedek was not a "Levite" and could not have been. Levi wasn't alive when Abram first met Melchizedek at the end of the Noahic covenant. Abraham eventually had a son named Isaac. Isaac had a son named Jacob. Jacob had a son named Levi. Paul points out to the Hebrews something of significant prophetic importance along these lines.

With regard to the DNA that would someday produce a boy called Levi (who would have his own family honored during the Mosaic covenant as the only tribe allowed to serve as priests), that DNA was in the body of Levi's grandfather, father Abram, who had not yet even had his name changed. Yet, Abram was the subordinate of a *greater* man named Melchizedek. In a poetic way, Paul shows the Hebrews that when father Abram paid tithes to Melchizedek, it was as if the entire unborn tribe of Levi, within the seed of Abram (whose wife had not yet become pregnant), was there in the DNA of Abram paying tithes to that higher priesthood.

> Although Levi wasn't born yet, the seed from which he came was in Abraham.
>
> —HEBREWS 7:10, TLL

This alone proved that the Levitical priesthood had *always* only been a temporary portion of the Mosaic covenant. Tithing would continue through all covenants without interruption, but Levitical rites and rituals would not always continue without interruption.

King David understood this exact significance of Melchizedek and prophesied plainly that the Messiah would be a High Priest above all

Levitical high priests. If Melchizedek's priesthood was higher than Abraham, it was also higher than the Levitical priesthood to come generations later. It was time for the Hebrews to embrace a new covenant. Embracing it did not mean they should recklessly throw away the eternal nature of the former, but to accept that *some* things would *carry through* into the new and better covenant, but some things would *not carry through* because they had finished their course. From those laws pertaining specifically to the Levitical priesthood, the New Covenant was released from further observance.

The very most important verse of chapter 7 (verse 22) would point out exactly *who* had saved all men at all times, living in all different covenants, from their sins. An eternal priesthood higher than the Levitical order, had saved Abraham, Isaac, Jacob, Levi, Moses, David, and every other man, woman, and child who had faith in divine redemption during all ages!

Recall verses 22–28:

> By so much was Jesus made a surety of a better testament. And they truly were many priests, because they were not suffered to continue by reason of death: But this *man*, because he continueth ever, hath an unchangeable priesthood. Wherefore he is able also to save them to the uttermost that come unto God by him, seeing he ever liveth to make intercession for them. For such an high priest became us, *who is* holy, harmless, undefiled, separate from sinners, and made higher than the heavens; Who needeth not daily, as those high priests, to offer up sacrifice, first for his own sins, and then for the people's: for this he did once, when he offered up himself. For the law maketh men high priests which have infirmity; but the word of the oath, which was since the law, *maketh* the Son, who is consecrated for evermore.

"Jesus [was] made a surety of a better testament." This phrase in verse 22 is the fulcrum upon which the entire Book of Hebrews pivots. Jesus Christ was the guarantor of eternal redemption, not merely for men who lived after Him in history, but also for those who had lived before Him in history. Paul goes to great pains to emphasize this reality by the type of Melchizedek, who signified the eternity past, present, and future existence of Christ, the anointed One, who was "without beginning." Paul repeats the same thing again to the

Roman church, reminding them that both Abraham and King David understood that their eternal salvation from sin came by faith in a Redeemer God, never by works alone:

> Abraham was, humanly speaking, the founder of our Jewish nation. What were his experiences concerning this question of being saved by faith? Was it because of his good deeds that God accepted him? If so, then he would have something to boast about. But from God's point of view Abraham had no basis at all for pride. For the Scriptures tell us Abraham *believed God,* and that is why God canceled his sins and declared him "not guilty." But didn't he earn his right to heaven by all the good things he did? No, for being saved is a gift; if a person could earn it by being good, then it wouldn't be free – but it is! It is *given* to those who do *not* work for it. For God declares sinners to be good in his sight if they have faith in Christ to save them from God's wrath. King David spoke of this, describing the happiness of an undeserving sinner who is declared 'not guilty' by God. "Blessed and to be envied," he said, "are those whose sins are forgiven and put out of sight. Yes, what joy there is for anyone whose sins are no longer counted against him by the Lord."
>
> —ROMANS 4:1–8, TLB

Recall Hebrews 8:6–7:

> But now hath he obtained a more excellent ministry, by how much also he is the mediator of a better covenant, which was established upon better promises. For if that first *covenant* had been faultless, then should no place have been sought for the second.

The language here is vital to understand. "But now," says Paul. In other words, Christ had an excellent ministry already, before the covenant changed, "but now He obtained a more excellent ministry." Christ was the Redeemer of all men in all covenants. As Paul told the Romans, Abraham was saved (born again) by faith in redemption to come in the future, just as moderns are saved (born again) by faith in redemption that occurred in Christ in the past. "But now," says Paul, something has improved in the making of a new covenant. Christ, symbolized by Melchizedek, was the mediator of all covenants ever made between man and God, because Christ was God in every exchange! Christ mediated the Noahic! Christ mediated the Abrahamic! Christ mediated the Sarahic! Christ mediated the Mosaic and the Healing covenants! Christ mediated the Palestinian and Covenant of Levi! Christ mediated the Salt Covenant! Christ mediated the Davidic Covenant! (Read Hebrews 9:25–28 as Paul continues explaining this theme of timeless redemption through Christ.)

"But now," says Paul, Christ has "also" become the "mediator of a better covenant, which was established upon better promises."

Was the last covenant "inferior" to this new one? Yes, but not because of what it said, did, and accomplished. It was *only* inferior because of what it did not say and was not supposed to accomplish. The King James says, "For if that first covenant had been faultless, then should no place have been sought for the second." Beware the evil teachings of the Marcionite, who thinks in this passage he finds a right to criticize the Mosaic covenant. The previous covenant was not "flawed" or "filled with error" or "untruth" that had to be revised. This is never what is meant by such descriptions in the New Testament. The New Testament in Modern English by J. B. Phillips translates the verse this way:[2]

> If the first agreement had proved satisfactory, then should no
> place have been sought for the second.

The Marcionite (in his false ways) would teach everyone that this new and better covenant was made to *correct* the *errors* of the old— that it was made *in spite of* the old. But we know better from Paul's good teaching that this new and better covenant was made possible *because of* the covenants that had been faithfully made before it, not in spite of them. They had all been made between men of former ages and Christ the eternal God and King!

Recall Hebrews 8:10–13:

> For this *is* the covenant that I will make with the house of
> Israel after those days, saith the Lord; I will put my laws into
> their mind, and write them in their hearts: and I will be to
> them a God, and they shall be to me a people: And they shall
> not teach every man his neighbour, and every man his brother,

saying, Know the Lord: for all shall know me, from the least
to the greatest. For I will be merciful to their unrighteousness,
and their sins and their iniquities will I remember no more. In
that he saith, A new *covenant*, he hath made the first old. Now
that which decayeth and waxeth old *is* ready to vanish away.

Here Paul points forward to an age beyond the present covenant
of the modern church. He points forward to a new covenant that will
someday be made between Christ and the nation of Israel. Though it
does have some similarities with our present covenant, it is important
that the reader not mistake this passage as applying to the present
covenant enjoyed today by all who are born again.

Just as the stubborn Jews in Paul's day needed to be reminded of
God's covenantal dealings with mankind and their ever-changing
and improving trends throughout history, the present-day believer is
admonished to look forward to the recovery of Israel at a time to come
in our own futures. Here is the summary of a coming covenant between
Jesus Christ and Israel based upon what we just read:

1. God will put His complete law inside their minds and
   hearts, giving them total recall of His Law-Word.

2. They shall *not* need to teach their neighbors about
   Christ, because all will already know Him from the least
   to the greatest. (They will have the Bible put into their
   minds and hearts like everyone else.)

3. There will be no more remembrance of the sins and
   iniquities of men on Earth.

Clearly, Bible illiteracy is rampant across the world today. *Access*
to God's Word is unprecedented. More men have *access* to His truth
than ever before in any previous generation, but this passage does not
seem to signify mere *access*, as so many teach. It says God shall *put* the
knowledge in the hearts and minds of men—so much so that neigh-
borly evangelism will be obsolete. Verses 10–13 seem to be describing
the millennial reign of Christ after the great rebellion of the nations
is put down and Christ rules the nations with a rod of iron for 1,000
years. (See Psalm 2:9, Revelation 2:27, Revelation 12:5, Revelation 19:15.)
With that said, we would do well to realize this as a description of our
present goal. It is the next covenant's description that reveals where

God is headed with history today! Revelation of a coming covenant should never be an occasion for defeatism or escapism. We should, as Paul wrote, press on toward *this* mark.

The theme of the book of Hebrews is to show that Christ is not only the Mediator of every single covenant that was ever made in history, He is the Mediator of every covenant between God and man that will yet come in the future. Within that theme and context, Paul makes this statement that has been true during every transition period between covenantal shifts throughout history. It was true when Melchizedek blessed Abram. It was true when Sarah overheard the angel telling Abraham he'd have a son in his old age. It was true when Moses led the Hebrews out of Egypt. It was true when Phinehas, son of Levi, showed zeal for the ways of God and turned away the anger of Jehovah from rebellious Israel. It was true when Nathan prophesied to David the great covenant bestowed upon him from Christ. It was true at this point in history, at the time of Paul's writing, as the Jews faced portions of Mosaic Law being done away in Christ. It will be true of the church age, when Christ returns.

Recall verse 13:

> In that he saith, A new *covenant*, he hath made the first old. Now that which decayeth and waxeth old *is* ready to vanish away.

Ultimately, what things should vanish away as man reaches the culmination of God's plan for the eternal ages? What will eventually vanish away?

1. The frail ministers who die of old age (Heb. 7:8, 28)

2. The inadequacies of all former covenants that could not satisfy God's complete plan (Heb. 7:18–19, 8:7)

3. Spiritually stubborn believers who are uncooperative with God (Heb. 8:8)

4. Divine law illiteracy (Heb. 8:10)

5. Spiritually dead neighbors who need to be taught the laws of God (Heb. 8:11)

6. Symbolic pageantry pointing toward a future reign of Jesus Christ (Heb. 9:1–12:29)

All these things are becoming obsolete, and they are ready to vanish away. What, specifically, has been done away in Christ, according to Paul, the writer of this letter to the Hebrews? Hebrews 9 begins methodically exposing all the ceremonial portions of the law, connected to the Levitical priesthood, that have been done away in Christ. This *troubling passage* of Hebrews 7:1–8:13 in no way supports the errant teaching that claims Christ abolished the *entire* law of Moses through His creation of a New Covenant. This much is very clear.

$$\mathscr{N}otes$$

CHAPTER 1: WHERE SELF-GOVERNMENT
ENDS AND ANOTHER BEGINS

1. John Eidsmoe, *Historical and Theological Foundations of Law* (Powder Springs, GA: Tolle Lege Press, 2011), 431. As an example, the author offers only one of more than 1,100 examples cited in American case law. Consider the finding of the West Virginia Supreme Court in the 1899 case of Moore v. Strickling noting the adultery commandment of the Mosaic Decalogue: "These commandments, which, like a collection of diamonds, bear testimony to their own intrinsic worth, in themselves appeal to us as coming from a superhuman or divine source, and no conscientious or reasonable man has yet been able to find a flaw in them. Absolutely flawless, negative in terms, but positive in meaning, they easily stand at the head of our whole moral system, and no nation or people can long continue a happy existence in open violation of them."

2. Rose Wilder Lane, *The Discovery of Freedom* (New York: The John Day Company, 1943), 10.

3. Bojidar Marinov, "Secular Libertarianism," PeaceMakers Institute, June 21, 2011, http://www.peacemakersinstitute.com/institute/?p=1511.

4. Clarence Manion, *Americanism: The Key to Peace* (Chicago, IL: The Heritage Foundation, Inc., 1951; republished by PeaceMakers Press, 2011), 57; www.peacemakersinstitute.com.

5. Ibid.

6. Ibid.

7. *Wikipedia*, s.v. "Walter Block," http://en.wikipedia.org/wiki/Walter_Block#cite_note-1.

8. Walter Block, "Plumb-Line Libertarianism: A Critique of Hoppe," *Reason Papers,* 29 (Fall 2007): 155.

9. Tom Mullen, "Can Ron Paul Really Be Right About Everything?," June 26, 2011, http://www.tommullen.net/featured/can-ron-paul-be-right-about-everything/.

10. Ibid.

11. Wikipedia, s.v. "Kanun," http://en.wikipedia.org/wiki/Kanuni_i_Lek%C3%AB_Dukagjinit.

12. Lane, *The Discovery of Freedom*, 10.

13. The following compare the types and antitypes of Jesus Christ and Moses:

- Both Moses and Jesus were miraculously saved from infanticide.
- Both Moses and Jesus were born into evil circumstances under evil governmental rulers.

- Both were miraculously commissioned by God; Moses at the burning bush and Jesus in John 8:42.
- Both were discredited by their relatives; Moses in Numbers 12 and Jesus in John 7:1–10.
- Both were rejected by their own Hebrew race.
- Both were willing to forgive those who rejected them.
- Both appeared on the earth after their physical deaths.
- Both fasted for forty days.
- Both demonstrated a supernatural radiance upon their faces; Moses after being on the mountain with God and Jesus on the Mount of Transfiguration.
- Both exercised miraculous control over nature; Moses parted the Red Sea and Jesus calmed the squall at sea.
- Both endured murmurings; Moses in Exodus 16:2 and Jesus in John 7:12.
- Both built a "church," Moses did so according to Acts 7:30–38 and Jesus did so in Matthew 16:18.
- Both were mediators of a covenant; Moses the old and Jesus the new and better.

CHAPTER 2: GENERATIONAL CONSPIRACY

1. John Jeansonne, "Hot Topic: Should Seahawks 'Give It Back'?," *Newsday*, September 26, 2012, http://www.newsday.com/sports/columnists/john -jeansonne/hot-topic-should-seahawks-give-it-back-1.4043066.

2. James Madison, *Memorial and Remonstrance* (Boston: Lincoln and Edmands, 1819), http://religiousfreedom.lib.virginia.edu/sacred/ madison_m&r_1785.html.

3. Ibid.

4. Batsell Barrett Baxter, *I Believe Because...* (Grand Rapids, MI: Baker Book House, 1971), 246.

CHAPTER 3: SITUATIONAL ETHICS: CANCER OF CHRISTIANITY

1. Baxter, *Believe*, 243.

2. Ibid., 244.

3. *Theopedia*, s.v. "Antinomianism," http://www.theopedia.com/ Antinomianism.

4. Ibid.

5. Leonard E. Read, *Clichés of Socialism* (Irvington-on-Hudson, NY: Foundation for Economic Education, Inc. 1962), 46.

6. Ibid.

7. *Theopedia*, s.v. "Marcionism," http://www.theopedia.com/ Marcionism.

8. Baxter, *Because*, 248.

9. *Holocaust Encyclopedia*, "Jewish Councils (Judenraete)," United States Holocaust Memorial Museum, Washington DC, June 20, 2014, http://www.ushmm.org/wlc/en/article.php?ModuleId=10005265.

10. Photo courtesy of Yad Vashem Har Hazikaron, P.O.B. 3477, Jerusalem 9103401 Israel. Used by permission.

11. Photo courtesy of Yad Vashem Har Hazikaron, P.O.B. 3477, Jerusalem 9103401 Israel. Used by permission.

12. Los Angeles Museum of the Holocaust, July 22, 2014, accessed December 3, 2014, http://losangelesmuseumoftheholocaust.blogspot.com /2014/07/this-day-in-history-adam-czerniakow.html#comment-form. Public domain.

13. Photo courtesy of Yad Vashem Har Hazikaron, P.O.B. 3477, Jerusalem 9103401 Israel. Used by permission.

14. Photo courtesy of the United States Holocaust Memorial Museum, Reprinted with Permission. The views or opinions expressed in this book, and the context in which the images are used, do not necessarily reflect the views or policy of, nor imply approval or endorsement by, the United States Holocaust Memorial Museum.

15. Photo courtesy of Yad Vashem Har Hazikaron, P.O.B. 3477, Jerusalem 9103401 Israel. Used by permission.

16. Photo courtesy of Yad Vashem Har Hazikaron, P.O.B. 3477, Jerusalem 9103401 Israel. Used by permission.

17. Mark Nauroth and Garrett Milovich, "The –isms," College Weekend Workshop, accessed December 3, 2014, http://marknauroth.com/the-isms.

CHAPTER 4: MOSES: FATHER OF FASCISM?

1. *Wikipedia*, s.v. "Facism," http://en.wikipedia.org/wiki/Fascism.

2. *Conservapedia*, s.v. "Fascist," http://conservapedia.com/Fascist

3. British Centre for Science Education, "In Extremis—Rousas Rushdoony and His Connections," accessed December 12, 2007, http://www.bcseweb.org.uk/index.php/Main/RousasRushdoony.

4. Bret Hayworth, "Local GOP Chairman Blasts Own Party," *Sioux City Journal*, November 9, 2006, http://www.siouxcityjournal.com/news/article_6ee3e3e1-5e5b-51f0-a30d-bb43d9df8d9e.html#ixzz1Yb97hE51.

5. Bret Hayworth, "Salem Booted from GOP Chairmanship," *Sioux City Journal*, November 21, 2006, http://www.siouxcityjournal.com/news/article_0745cdc0-84e2-5fb1-9e3c-fc6d4c56f12f.html.

6. Thomas Jefferson to Martin Van Buren, 1824. See Paul Leicester Ford, ed., *The Works of Thomas Jefferson, Volume 12* (New York: G.P. Putnam's Sons, 1905), 359.

7. Hayworth, "Salem Booted."

8. Rabbi Yerachmiel D. Fried, "The Prophecy of Moses," *Texas Jewish Post*, February 9, 2012, http://tjpnews.com/?p=4630.

9. Gary North, *Sanctions and Dominion: An Economic Commentary on Numbers* (Dallas, GA: McFarland Publications, 2008), Conclusion, http://www.garynorth.com/freebooks/docs/html/gnsd/conclusion.htm.

10. Phillip D. Yancey, *What's So Amazing About Grace?* (Grand Rapids, MI: Zondervan, 1997), 233.

11. Genesis 25:30–34: "And Esau said to Jacob, Feed me, I pray thee, with that same red pottage; for I am faint: therefore was his name called Edom. And Jacob said, Sell me this day thy birthright. And Esau said, Behold, I am at the point to die: and what profit shall this birthright do to me? And Jacob said, Swear to me this day; and he sware unto him: and he sold his birthright unto Jacob. Then Jacob gave Esau bread and pottage of lentiles; and he did eat and drink, and rose up, and went his way: thus Esau despised his birthright."

12. Matthew 4:8–11: "Again, the devil taketh him up into an exceeding high mountain, and sheweth him all the kingdoms of the world, and the glory of them; And saith unto him, All these things will I give thee, if thou wilt fall down and worship me. Then saith Jesus unto him, Get thee hence, Satan: for it is written, Thou shalt worship the Lord thy God, and him only shalt thou serve. Then the devil leaveth him, and, behold, angels came and ministered unto him."

13. Matthew 8:5–11: "And when Jesus was entered into Capernaum, there came unto him a centurion, beseeching him, And saying, Lord, my servant lieth at home sick of the palsy, grievously tormented. And Jesus saith unto him, I will come and heal him. The centurion answered and said, Lord, I am not worthy that thou shouldest come under my roof: but speak the word only, and my servant shall be healed. For I am a man under authority, having soldiers under me: and I say to this man, Go, and he goeth; and to another, Come, and he cometh; and to my servant, Do this, and he doeth it. When Jesus heard it, he marvelled, and said to them that followed, Verily I say unto you, I have not found so great faith, no, not in Israel. And I say unto you, That many shall come from the east and west, and shall sit down with Abraham, and Isaac, and Jacob, in the kingdom of heaven."

14. Genesis 6:8: "But Noah found grace in the eyes of the LORD."

15. Genesis 39:3–4: "And his master saw that the LORD was with him, and that the LORD made all that he did to prosper in his hand. And Joseph found grace in his sight, and he served him: and he made him overseer over his house, and all that he had he put into his hand."

16. Timothy 1:9: "Who hath saved us, and called us with an holy calling, not according to our works, but according to his own purpose and grace, which was given us in Christ Jesus before the world began."

17. J. Chace Gordon, *Grace Empowerment* (Enumclaw, WA: Pleasant Word Publishing, 2007), 34.

18. Galatians 3:13–14: "Christ hath redeemed us from the curse of the law, being made a curse for us: for it is written, Cursed is every one that hangeth on a tree: That the blessing of Abraham might come on the Gentiles through Jesus Christ; that we might receive the promise of the Spirit through faith." See also 1 John 3:4-5: "Whosoever committeth sin transgresseth also the law: for sin is the transgression of the law. And ye know that he was manifested to take away our sins; and in him is no sin."

19. Mark 7:6–11: "He [Jesus] answered and said unto them, Well hath Esaias prophesied of you hypocrites, as it is written, This people honoureth me with their lips, but their heart is far from me. Howbeit in vain do they worship me, teaching for doctrines the commandments of men. For laying aside the commandment of God, ye hold the tradition of men, as the washing of pots and cups: and many other such like things ye do. And he said unto them, Full well ye reject the commandment of God, that ye may keep your own tradition. For Moses said, Honour thy father and thy mother; and, Whoso curseth father or mother, let him die the death: But ye say, If a man shall say to his father or mother, It is Corban, that is to say, a gift, by whatsoever thou mightest be profited by me; he shall be free."

20. John 14:12 (ASV): "Verily, verily, I say unto you, he that believeth on me, the works that I do shall he do also; and greater works than these shall he do; because I go unto the Father."

21. Gordon, *Grace*, 30.

CHAPTER 5: DIVIDING THE LAW

1. Frank C. Haddock, *The Life of Rev. George C. Haddock* (New York: Funk & Wagnalls, 1887). Public domain.

2. Ibid., 68–69. Republished by PeaceMakers Library, www.peacemakers institute.com.

3. E.C. Wines, *Commentaries on the Laws of the Ancient Hebrews* (New York: Putnam and Co., 1855), 540–541. Digitally Republished by Peace-Makers Library.

4. Ibid., 490.

5. Ibid., 487.

6. Ibid., 490.

7. D. Edmond Hiebert, *First Timothy* (Chicago: Moody Press, 1957), 35.

8. H.B. Clark, *Biblical Law* (Powder Springs, GA: American Vision Press, 2010), xv.

9. Ibid., xii.

10. Note on 1 Timothy 2:1–4: "The Romans permitted subject peoples to worship their own gods, but they had to show their loyalty to Rome by also worshiping the goddess Roma and the spirit of the emperor. Because Jewish people worshiped one God to the exclusion of all others, Rome allowed them to pray and sacrifice for the emperor's health without praying and sacrificing to him. Prayers were offered for him regularly in the synagogues, showing the loyalty of these Jewish institutions to the Roman state. When the Zealots decided to throw off the Roman yoke 'for God,' however, they abolished the sacrifices in the temple. This act in AD 66 constituted a virtual declaration of war against Rome, several years after Paul wrote this letter. Christian public prayers for the emperor and provincial and local officials showed Christians as good citizens of the society in which they lived (Jer. 29:7). Paul's motive is more than keeping peace (1 Tim. 2:2); it is also to proclaim the gospel (1 Tim. 2:3–4). (Craig S.

Keener, *The IVP Bible Background Commentary: New Testament*, 2nd edition, [Downers Grove, IL: InterVarsity Press, 2014], 604.)

11. [Zealots] were Jewish revolutionaries who became prominent by this name especially shortly before the first Jewish war (AD 66–70). Seeking to exonerate his people before the Romans, Josephus marginalized them as robbers and troublemakers, but Zealot sympathizers were almost certainly widespread, apparently even among many Pharisees. Although Zealots technically refers to only one of the resistance groups, modern writers have often used the term as a convenient title for the whole resistance movement. (Keener, *IVP Commentary.*)

12. Kings ruled until the Babylonian captivity in 616 BC—about 513 years. After the captivity of 70 years, Israel had no king but was ruled by the Sanhedrin or body of elders, headed by the high priest or some other individual chosen for the position. This continued until AD 70 [beneath the auspices of the Conquering Romans] when Israel, because of rejecting Christ their Messiah, was destroyed and dispersed as a nation (Matt. 23:37–39; Luke 21:20–24). During all these periods of Israel's history, regardless of the form of government, the elders were always prominent and successfully dictated many things... [Once conquered by the Romans in 63 BC, and finally reduced to a "client state" or "puppet regime" by the Romans (in 37 BC), the Sanhedrin was denied exclusive judicial and executive power over issues of capital punishment.] Only the Romans had the power of life and death. The Sanhedrin... could only imprison and punish short of death. It is true some were killed (Acts 26:10), but this was by Roman permission or by murder, as in the case of Stephen. (Finis J. Dake Sr., *Dake's Annotated Reference Bible* [n.p.: Dake Publishing, 1960].)

13. When Jesus gave His new commandment in John 13:34, it was not the "law of love" that was "new." In fact, Jesus quoted Leviticus 19:18 and Deuteronomy 6:5 when discussing the "greatest" of the Old Testament commands (love). What Christ introduced was a fresh concept of "self-sacrifice," a foreign concept for Jewish culture. Moses and Jesus agreed that the law was designed a harbinger of punishment for those who did not mind their own hearts. Love was always the highest law of the Old Testament. The development of proper conscience was the objective of a righteous legal standard. Jesus defended this truth of Moses by challenging His contemporary rabbis whose doctrines perverted Mosaic Law by emphasizing external obedience without internal repentance. (See Matthew 23:27–28.) Ironically, the same Pharisees who promoted external obedience without proper emphasis on motive also found clever ways to skirt the law through legal loopholes. For this they were also rebuked by Jesus. (See Mark 7:10–11.)

14. See http://www.narcissismepidemic.com/.

15. [With regard to Paul's first letter to Timothy, Chapter 1 and verse 9] [t]here is a moral law as well as a ceremonial law: as the object of the latter is to lead us to Christ; the object of the former is to restrain crimes, and inflict punishment on those that commit them. It was, therefore, not made for the righteous as a restrainer of crimes, and an inflicter of punishments;

for the righteous avoid sin, and by living to the glory of God expose not themselves to its censures. This seems to be the mind of the apostle; he does not say that the law was not Made for a righteous man, but "ουκειται," it does not Lie against a righteous man; because he does not transgress it: but it lies against the wicked; for such as the apostle mentions have broken it, and grievously too, and are condemned by it. The word "κειται," lies, refers to the custom of writing laws on boards, and hanging them up in public places within reach of every man, that they might be read by all; thus all would see against whom the law lay. (Adam Clark, *Clark's Commentary and Critical Notes*, http://www.studylight.org/commentaries/acc/view.cgi?bk=53&ch=1. 1832.)

16. See Leviticus 19:18, Deuteronomy 6:5, and Matthew 22:35.

17. See Acts 21:20–21, where Judaizers became hostile to the message of Christ delivered by Paul.

18. We know from the New Testament that Christ did, in fact, eliminate some limited portions of the old ceremonial Hebrew codex. But on what authority can anyone say, as so many moderns suggest, that He eliminated the entire thing? They cannot do so with biblical authority because only four specific areas of the Law are cited in the New Testament as "done away in Christ" which are as follows:

1) Circumcision (see 1 Corinthians 7:19 and Galatians 6:15).
2) Food Ordinances (see 1 Corinthians 8:8, Galatians 2:10–13, Romans 14:17 and Colossians 2:16).
3) Special Observances of days (holidays) (see Colossians 2:16).
1) Animal Sacrifices (see 1 Corinthians 5:7, Hebrews 2:9, John 1:29 and 1 Peter 2:24).

19. Haddock, *The Life of Rev. George C. Haddock*, 216–217.

CHAPTER 6: THE SIN OF LIBERTARIANISM

1. "Nature, or rather God, has bestowed upon every one of us the right to defend his person, his liberty, and his property, since these are the three constituent or preserving elements of life...Collective right, then, has its principle, its reason for existing, its lawfulness, in individual right; and the common force cannot rationally have any other end, or any other mission, than that of the isolated forces for which it is substituted." (Frédéric Bastiat, *The Law*, 1850. Republished by the Ludwig Von Mises Institute, Auburn, AL, 2007, page 2.)

2. Some have argued that Acts 17:26–27 only refers to individual persons discovering God on a personal level (self-government) within specific geographic boundaries. Clearly, this is incorrect as it ignores part of the truth implied by the text. National borders are neither defended nor maintained by the individual soul, but by a "people"—a "government." This verse clearly refers to both individuals discovering God (on a personal level) and their obvious confederation within divinely predetermined boundaries of government. The connection between the individual and his

government is alluded to as both serving the purpose of God in reaching the sinner.

3. See video archive here: http://belowthebeltway.com/2007/12/09/ john-stossel-interviews-ron-paul-on-legalizing-drugs-and-prostitution/; see also John Stossel and Gena Binkley, "Ron Paul Unplugged," ABC News, December 7, 2007, http://abcnews.go.com/2020/Stossel/ story?id=3970423&page=1.

4. Walter Block, "Open Letter to Ron Paul," LewRockwell.com, December 28, 2007, http://www.lewrockwell.com/block/block94.html.

5. Block, "Plumb Line Libertarianism," 152.

6. Martin Gould and Abigail Walls, "Ron Paul: Let Iran Have the Bomb," August 11, 2011, http://www.newsmax.com/InsideCover/ron-paul-iran bomb/2011/08/11/id/407043.

7. Stephen G. Gey, "Atheism and the Freedom of Religion," in *The Cambridge Companion to Atheism*, ed. Michael Martin (Cambridge: Cambridge University Press, 2007), 250–266.

8. Internet Encyclopedia of Philosophy, A Peer Reviewed Academic Resource, d. Letters on Religious Toleration, "But it is clear that Locke made the exception not for religious reasons but on grounds of state policy...and the atheist was excluded [from political toleration] because, on Locke's view, the existence of the state depends upon a contract, and the obligation of the contract, as of all moral law, depends upon the divine will." http://www.iep.utm.edu/locke/#SH2d. See also J. David Lorenz, "Tradition and Prudence in Locke's Exceptions to Toleration," *American Journal of Political Science* 47, no. 2 (2003): 248–258. "A main threat atheists pose to society, 'in addition to problems with attaining a complete understanding of moral principles,' (Lorenzo, 253) comes from their disbelief in an afterlife, namely the lack of later punishment for earthly blunders. Without the fear of eternal damnation, atheists are 'threats to social order and state security.' Quote attributed to Locke, Page 258.

9. See http://bastiat.org/en/the_law.html.

10. Wilhelm Pauck, ed., *Melanchthon and Bucer*, (Philadelphia: Westminster Press, 1969), 53.

11. Eric Rasmusen, "Divine Law versus Natural Law," Eric Rasmusen's Weblog, November 28, 2008, http://www.rasmusen.org/t/2008/11/divine -law-versus-natural-law.html. Used by permission.

12. Tayler Lewis, LLD, *Plato Against the Atheists* (New York: Harper and Brothers Publishing, 1845), 367.

13. Herbert Schlossberg, *Idols for Destruction*, (Nashville: Thomas Nelson Publishers, 1983), 207.

14. Phillip G. Kayser, *The Flaw of Natural Law* (Omaha, NE: Biblical Blueprints, 1983), 31–32.

15. George Washington, *Address of George Washington, President of the United States, and Late Commander in Chief of the American Army, to the People of the United States, Preparatory to His Declination* (Baltimore: George and Henry S. Keatinge, 1796), 23.

16. Ibid.

17. Adam Clarke's Commentary notes on Genesis chapter fifteen, 1810.

18. Fisher Ames and Seth Ames, "The Dangers of American Liberty," 1805, in Fisher Ames and Seth Ames, *Works of Fisher Ames: With a Selection from His Speeches and Correspondence* (Boston: Little, Brown and Company, 1854), 349.

19. John Stuart Mill, *On Liberty*, 1858; reprinted by Palladium Press, Birmingham, AL, 2002. This specific quote taken from remarks made by Wayne LaPierre on May 14, 2002, in the Introductory Remarks.

20. C.S. Lewis, *The Problem of Pain*, (London: Centenary Press, 1940). Copyright restored 1996 by C.S. Lewis Pte. Ltd., 20.

21. Haddock, *The Life of Rev. George C. Haddock*, 360.

CHAPTER 7: TETHERED: INTERNAL CONSCIENCE AND EXTERNAL LAW

1. Romans 1:19–20: "Because that which may be known of God is manifest in them; for God hath shewed it unto them. For the invisible things of him from the creation of the world are clearly seen, being understood by the things that are made, even his eternal power and Godhead; so that they are without excuse."

Hebrews 10:16: "This is the covenant that I will make with them after those days, saith the Lord, I will put my laws into their hearts, and in their minds will I write them."

Hebrews 8:10: "For this is the covenant that I will make with the house of Israel after those days, saith the Lord; I will put my laws into their mind, and write them in their hearts: and I will be to them a God, and they shall be to me a people."

2. Hebrews 11:13–16.

3. A.A. Hodge, *Evangelical Theology* (Carlisle, PA: The Banner of Truth Trust [1890] 1990), 283–284. See also Clark, *Biblical Law*, xx.

4. Ibid., xxi.

5. Ina Hughs, "Biblical 'Law' Can Produce a Variety of Interpretations," *Knoxville News Sentinel*, June 7, 2000, page A2.

6. Wines, *Laws*, v–vi.

7. Slamweb, "Biblical Illiteracy," October 25, 2010, accessed November 29, 2014, http://slamweb.org/SLAM/biblical-illiteracy-2/.

8. Barna Group, "Barna Studies the Research, Offers a Year-in-Review Perspective," December 18, 2009, http://www.barna.org/barna-update/article/12-faithspirituality/325-barna-studies-the-research-offers-a-year-in-review-perspective.

9. The Jews had scrupulously preserved their genealogical tables till the advent of Christ and the evangelists had recourse to them, and appealed to them in reference to our Lord's descent from the house of David; Matthew taking this genealogy in the descending, Luke in the ascending, line. And whatever difficulties we may now find in these genealogies, they were certainly clear to the Jews; nor did the most determined enemies

of the Gospel attempt to raise one objection to it from the appeal which
the evangelists had made to their own public and accredited tables. All
was then certain; but we are told that Herod destroyed the public regis-
ters; he, being an Idumean, was jealous of the noble origin of the Jews; and,
that none might be able to reproach him with his descent, he ordered the
genealogical tables, which were kept among the archives in the temple, to
be burnt. See Euseb. H.E., lib. i. cap. 8. From this time the Jews could refer
to their genealogies only from memory, or from those imperfect tables
which had been preserved in private hands; and to make out any regular
line from these must have been endless and uncertain. It is probably to
this that the apostle refers; I mean the endless and useless labor which
the attempts to make out these genealogies must produce, the authentic
tables being destroyed... This, were all other proofs wanting, would be an
irresistible argument against the Jews that the Messiah is come; for their
own prophets had distinctly marked out the line by which he was to come;
the genealogies are now all lost; nor is there a Jew in the universe that can
show from what tribe he is descended. There can, therefore, be no Messiah
to come, as none could show, let him have what other pretensions he might,
that he sprang from the house of David. The Jews do not, at present, pretend to have any such tables; and, far from being able to prove the Messiah
from his descent, they are now obliged to say that when the Messiah comes,
he will restore the genealogies by the Holy Spirit that shall rest upon him.
"For," says Maimonides, "in the days of the Messiah, when his kingdom shall
be established, all the Israelites shall be gathered together unto him; and
all shall be classed in their genealogies by his mouth, through the Holy
Spirit that shall rest upon him; as it is written, Malachi 3:3: He shall sit as
a refiner and purifier of silver, and he shall purify the sons of Levi. First he
will purify the Levites, and shall say: 'This man is a descendant from the
priests; and this, of the stock of the Levites;' and he shall cast out those
who are not of the stock of Israel; for behold it is said, Ezra 2:63: And the
Tirshatha said they should not eat of the most holy things, till there stood
up a priest with Urim and Thummim. Thus, by the Holy Spirit, the genealogies are to be revised." (Schoettgen, *A Commentary and Critical Notes.*)

10. Manion, *Americanism.* Also, primary source documentation can
be found in the article "The Truth about the Constitution," published by
Rev. Cary Gordon, July 2010, at http://www.peacemakersinstitute.com/
institute/?p=835.

11. Manion, *Americanism*, 49–50. Republished by PeaceMakers Press,
copyright 2011, Chapter 3.

12. William R. Levesque, "Judge Orders Use of Islamic Law in Tampa
Lawsuit over Mosque Leadership," *Tampa Bay Times*, March 21, 2011,
http://www.tampabay.com/news/courts/civil/judge-orders-use-of-islamic
-law-in-tampa-lawsuit-over-mosque-leadership/1158818.

13. See Sections 1 and 16 of the 1776 Virginia Declaration of Rights,
http://www.constitution.org/bcp/virg_dor.htm.

14. Marinov, "Secular Libertarianism," http://www.peacemakersinstitute .com/institute/?p=1511.

15. Chad Groening, "Perry 'Instrumental' Force Behind Program on Islam," *OneNewsNow*, September 1, 2011, http://onenewsnow.com/education/2011/09/01/perry-instrumental-force-behind-program-on -islam#.VG94J5UtDIU.

16. Amy Sullivan, "The Myth of Sharia Law in America," *Huffington Post*, June 15, 2011, http://www.huffingtonpost.com/amy-sullivan/sharia-myth -america_b_876965.html.

17. See also a footnote at: http://www.qurancomplex.com/Quran/ Targama/Targama.asp?nSora=%202&l=eng&nAya=%20190.

18. Don Boys, PhD, "Jihad: the Sixth Deadly Pillar of Islam!," February 19, 2007, http://www.muslimfact.com/bm/misc-articles-about-islam-and -terror/jihad-the-sixth-deadly-pillar-of-islam.shtml.

19. Wines, *Laws*, 396.

CHAPTER 8: AUTHORIZED: FIFTEEN
CLASSES OF CONDUCT TO FORBID

1. Daniel Botkin, "God's Dietary Laws: Abolished in the New Testament?", *Gates of Eden*, November/December 1997; see also http://www .giveshare.org/Health/dietarylaws.html.

2. The numeric list is based upon notes from *Dake's Annotated Reference Bible*. Commentary inserted within the list is authored by Rev. Cary K. Gordon.

3. Romans 12:18: "If it be possible, as much as lieth in you, live peaceably with all men."

4. Gey, "Atheism,"252.

5. Ibid.

6. See Torasco v. Watkins, 367 U.S. 488 (1961), http://supreme.justia .com/us/367/488/case.html.

7. Texas, Massachusetts, Maryland, Mississippi, Pennsylvania, North Carolina, South Carolina, and Tennessee.

8. Jeffrey M. Jones, "Atheists, Muslims See Most Bias as Presidential Candidates," Gallup, June 21, 2012, http://www.gallup.com/poll/155285/ atheists-muslims-bias-presidential-candidates.aspx.

9. Lawrence v. Texas (2003), (02-102) 539 U.S. 558 (2003), [On-line], URL: http://www.law.cornell.edu/supct/html/02-102.ZD.html.

10. Dave Miller, "Sexual Depravity Continues to Expand," Dave Miller, Ph.D., Copyright 2009 Apologetics Press, Inc. All rights reserved. http:// apologeticspress.org/apcontent.aspx?category=105&article=2691.

11. *Wikipedia*, s.v. "No-Fault Divorce," http://en.wikipedia.org/wiki/No -fault_divorce#cite_note-10.

12. Stephen Baskerville, *Taken Into Custody: The War Against Fathers, Marriage and the Family*, (Nashville: Cumberland House, 2007), 234.

13. Holt v. Holt (1935) 77 F2d (App. D.C.) 538, 541 (Hitz, J).

14. Leo Gozich, "The Dilemma of the Divorce Culture: Can the Local Church Make a Difference?," Enrichment Journal, 2014, http://enrichment journal.ag.org/200002/046_dilemma_divorce.cfm.

15. Centers for Disease Control, *Monthly Vital Statistics Report* 43, no. 9, supplement (March 22, 1995): 2, http://www.cdc.gov/nchs/data/mvsr/supp/mv43_09s.pdf.

16. Rediff.com, s.v. "Hicklin Test," http://pages.rediff.com/hicklin-test /1122578; see also *Wikipedia*, s.v. "Obscenity," http://en.wikipedia.org/wiki/Obscenity.

17. http://www.usdoj.gov/criminal/ceos/prostitution.html.

18. Ibid.

19. Ibid.; see also *Wikipedia*, s.v. "Prostitution in the United States," http://en.wikipedia.org/wiki/Prostitution_in_the_United_States.

20. Andrews v. Vanduzer, N.Y.Sup. 1814 (January Term, 1814). Vanduzer accused Andrews of having had connection with a cow and then a mare and the court understood this to mean that Vanduzer was going around telling others that Andrews had been guilty of the crime against nature with a beast.

21. *Wikipedia*, s.v. "Crime Against Nature," http://en.wikipedia.org/wiki/Crime_against_nature#cite_note-0.

22. See Rose v. Locke, 1975, 96 S.Ct. 243, 423 U.S. 48, 46 L.Ed.2d 185.

23. Walter Wink, "Homosexuality and the Bible," Fellowship of Reconciliation, http://forusa.org/content/homosexuality-bible-walter-wink.

24. Clark, *Biblical Law*, 267.

25. Ibid., 268.

26. Wink, "Homosexuality."

27. W.D. Erickson, N.H. Walbek, R.K. Seely, "Behavior Patterns of Child Molesters," *Archives of Sexual Behavior* 17, no. 1 (1988): 77–86.

28. Peter Sprigg, "Questions and Answers: What's Wrong with Letting Same-Sex Couples 'Marry'?," Family Research Council, http://www.frc.org/get.cfm?i=IF03H01&f=PG03I03.

29. Peter Sprigg and Timothy Dailey, eds., *Getting It Straight: What the Research Shows About Homosexuality*, (Washington DC: Family Research Council, 2004), 28.

30. Rev. William Tvedt, "Homosexuality," http://www.peacemakers institute.com/institute/issues/homosexuality.php.

31. T.G. Sandfort, R. de Graaf, R.V. Bijl, P. Schnabel, "Same-Sex Sexual Behavior and Psychiatric Disorders: Findings from the Netherlands Mental Health Survey and Incidence Study," *Archives of General Psychiatry* 58, vol. 1 (2001): 85–91.

32. E. Goldman, "Psychological Factors Generate HIV Resurgence in Young Gay Men," *Clinical Psychiatry News* (October 1994): 5.

33. "L.A. Studies Show Increase in Risky Sex by Gay Men," *Los Angeles Times*, February 17, 2001, 15. Among homosexual African Americans, the HIV infection rate is one out of three. "Young Gay Black Men Suffer High HIV Rates," Associated Press, February 6, 2001.

34. Four data sets: obituaries from the homosexual press; two 1994 sexuality surveys; homosexual marriage records for Scandinavia; and Colorado medical records. Paul Cameron, Kirk Cameron, and William L. Playfair.

35. Tvedt, "Homosexuality."

36. Materials for history, printed from original manuscripts, *Correspondence of Henry Laurens, of South Carolina* (New York: Zenger Club, 1861), 20, to John Laurens on August 14, 1776, by Frank Moore.

Henry P. Johnston, ed., *The Correspondence and Public Papers of John Jay, Volume III* (New York: G. P. Putnam's Sons, 1891), 342, to the English Anti-Slavery Society in June 1788.

Albert Ellery Bergh, ed., *The Writings of Thomas Jefferson, Volume I* (Washington DC: Thomas Jefferson Memorial Assoc., 1903), 34.

37. Walter E. Williams, "Some Fathers Fought Slavery," Creators Syndicate, Inc., May 26, 1993.

38. Plessy v. Ferguson (No. 210), Supreme Court of the United States, 163 U.S. 537, argued: April 18, 1896 – decided: May 18, 1896.

39. Brown v. Board of Education of Topeka (No. 1.), Warren, C.J., Opinion of the Court, Supreme Court of the United States, 347 U.S. 483, Argued: December 9, 1952, Decided: May 17, 1954.

CHAPTER 9: A GLOBAL COMMONWEALTH OF NATIONS

1. Lee Jefferson, "What Does The Bible Actually Say About Gay Marriage?" *Huffington Post*, September 23, 2011, http://www.huffingtonpost .com/lee-jefferson/bible-gay-marriage_b_886102.html.

2. Ibid.

3. Herodotus (c. 440 BC). The Histories, Book II, 89: "The wives of men of rank when they die are not given at once to be embalmed, nor such women as are very beautiful or of greater regard than others, but on the third or fourth day after their death (and not before) they are delivered to the embalmers. They do so about this matter in order that the embalmers may not abuse their women, for they say that one of them was taken once doing so to the corpse of a woman lately dead, and his fellow-craftsman gave information."

4. Gary DeMar, "Trying to Justify Homosexuality by an Appeal to the Bible," American Vision, June 14, 2011, http://americanvision.org/4656/ trying-to-justify-homosexuality-by-an-appeal-to-the-bible/.

5. Mark 7:9–13: "And he said unto them, Full well ye reject the commandment of God, that ye may keep your own tradition. For Moses said, Honour thy father and thy mother; and, Whoso curseth father or mother, let him die the death: But ye say, If a man shall say to his father or mother, It is Corban, that is to say, a gift, by whatsoever thou mightest be profited by me; he shall be free. And ye suffer him no more to do ought for his father or his mother; Making the word of God of none effect through your tradition, which ye have delivered: and many such like things do ye."

6. Genesis 3:15: "And I will put enmity between thee and the woman, and between thy seed and her seed; it shall bruise thy head, and thou shalt bruise his heel."

7. Isaiah 9:6–7: "For unto us a child is born, unto us a son is given: and the government shall be upon his shoulder: and his name shall be called Wonderful, Counsellor, The mighty God, The everlasting Father, The Prince of Peace. Of the increase of his government and peace there shall be no end, upon the throne of David, and upon his kingdom, to order it, and to establish it with judgment and with justice from henceforth even forever. The zeal of the LORD of hosts will perform this."

8. Deuteronomy 28:1–2: "And it shall come to pass, if thou shalt hearken diligently unto the voice of the LORD thy God, to observe and to do all his commandments which I command thee this day, that the LORD thy God will set thee on high above all nations of the earth: And all these blessings shall come on thee, and overtake thee, if thou shalt hearken unto the voice of the LORD thy God."

9. Exodus 19:3–7: "And Moses went up unto God, and the LORD called unto him out of the mountain, saying, Thus shalt thou say to the house of Jacob, and tell the children of Israel; Ye have seen what I did unto the Egyptians, and how I bare you on eagles' wings, and brought you unto myself. Now therefore, if ye will obey my voice indeed, and keep my covenant, then ye shall be a peculiar treasure unto me above all people: for all the earth is mine: And ye shall be unto me a kingdom of priests, and an holy nation. These are the words which thou shalt speak unto the children of Israel. And Moses came and called for the elders of the people, and laid before their faces all these words which the LORD commanded him."

10. Deuteronomy 28:1–2: "And it shall come to pass, if thou shalt hearken diligently unto the voice of the LORD thy God, to observe and to do all his commandments which I command thee this day, that the LORD thy God will set thee on high above all nations of the earth: 2 And all these blessings shall come on thee, and overtake thee, if thou shalt hearken unto the voice of the LORD thy God."

11. Genesis 12:3: "And I will bless them that bless thee, and curse him that curseth thee: and in thee shall all families of the earth be blessed."

12. Isaiah 9:6–7: (ASV) "For unto us a child is born, unto us a son is given; and the government shall be upon his shoulder: and his name shall be called Wonderful, Counsellor, Mighty God, Everlasting Father, Prince of Peace. Of the increase of his government and of peace there shall be no end, upon the throne of David, and upon his kingdom, to establish it, and to uphold it with justice and with righteousness from henceforth even for ever. The zeal of Jehovah of hosts will perform this."

13. Clark, *Biblical Law*, xxv (Publisher's Introduction).

14. Wines, *Laws*, 303.

15. Ibid., 309.

16. Ibid., 312.

17. Ibid., 313.

18. Ibid.

19. Ibid.

20. Ibid., 315.

21. Petit de Legibus Atticis, in Gale, B. 3 C. 9.

22. Wines, *Laws*, 308.

23. Gardiner Spring, *The Obligations of the World to the Bible* (New York: M.W. Dodd, 1848), 96–97. (Author's emphasis added.)

24. David Pratt, *The Political Thought of King Alfred the Great (Cambridge Studies in Medieval Life and Thought: Fourth Series)* (Cambridge: Cambridge University Press, 2007), 67.

25. Dr. Henry Hart Milman, *The History of the Jews* (New York: Harper and Brothers, 1843), 135.

26. Clark, *Biblical Law*, xxv (Publisher's Introduction).

CHAPTER 10: ART THOU A KING THEN?

1. See Matthew 5:17.

2. Matthew 27:28: "And they stripped him, and put on him a scarlet robe."

3. Matthew 27:29: "And when they had platted a crown of thorns, they put it upon his head, and a reed in his right hand: and they bowed the knee before him, and mocked him, saying, Hail, King of the Jews!"

4. John 10:17–18: "Therefore doth my Father love me, because I lay down my life, that I might take it again. No man taketh it from me, but I lay it down of myself. I have power to lay it down, and I have power to take it again. This commandment have I received of my Father."

5. Matthew 24:35–36: "Heaven and earth shall pass away, but my words shall not pass away. But of that day and hour knoweth no man, no, not the angels of heaven, but my Father only."

6. John 18:36: "Jesus answered, My kingdom is not of this world: if my kingdom were of this world, then would my servants fight, that I should not be delivered to the Jews: but now is my kingdom not from hence."

7. Dr. Greg Bahnsen, "What Is 'Theonomy'?," Covenant Media Foundation, April 1994, http://www.cmfnow.com/articles/pe180.htm

8. Robert C. Winthrop, *Life and Letters of John Winthrop* (Boston: Ticknor and Fields, 1867), 19–20.

9. Paul Copan, *Is God a Moral Monster?* (Grand Rapids, MI: Baker Books, 2011), 73.

10. *Wikipedia*, s.v. "John Winthrop," http://en.wikipedia.org/wiki/John_Winthrop#Religious_controversies. See also http://ox-cam-nyc.blogspot.com/2013/06/john-wheelwright-sidney-sussex.html. See also Anne Hutchison lauded as America's first anarchist by the Ludwig Von Mises Institute: http://mises.org/daily/5967/_"No magistracy whatever was lawful. As Anne's biographer Winifred Rugg put it, "She [Hutchison] was supremely convinced that the Christian held within his own breast the assurance of salvation . . . For such persons magistrates were obviously superfluous. As for the other, they were to be converted, not coerced'."

Winifred K. Rugg, *Unafraid: A Life of Anne Hutchinson* (Boston: Houghton Mifflin, 1930).

11. Romans 10:14: (YLT) "How then shall they call upon him in whom they did not believe? and how shall they believe on him of whom they did not hear? and how shall they hear apart from one preaching?"

12. Jude 1:19–25: (AMP) "It is these who are [agitators] setting up distinctions and causing divisions – merely sensual [creatures, carnal, worldly-minded people], devoid of the [Holy] Spirit and destitute of any higher spiritual life. But you, beloved, build yourselves up [founded] on your most holy faith [make progress, rise like an edifice higher and higher], praying in the Holy Spirit; Guard and keep yourselves in the love of God; expect and patiently wait for the mercy of our Lord Jesus Christ (the Messiah) – [which will bring you] unto life eternal. And refute [so as to] convict some who dispute with you, and on some have mercy who waver and doubt. [Strive to] save others, snatching [them] out of [the] fire; on others take pity [but] with fear, loathing even the garment spotted by the flesh and polluted by their sensuality. Now to Him Who is able to keep you without stumbling or slipping or falling, and to present [you] unblemished (blameless and faultless) before the presence of His glory in triumphant joy and exultation [with unspeakable, ecstatic delight] – To the one only God, our Savior through Jesus Christ our Lord, be glory (splendor), majesty, might and dominion, and power and authority, before all time and now and forever (unto all the ages of eternity). Amen (so be it).

13. Brian Ray, "Iowa Pastor Preaches Politics to Oust Three Justices Who Backed Gay Marriage," USA TODAY, October 13, 2010, http://www.usa-today.com/news/religion/2010-10-14-iowapastor13_ST_N.htm.

14. Rick Renner, *Sparkling Gems from the Greek: 365 Greek Word Studies* (Tulsa, OK: Harrison House, 2003), 467.

15. Dr. Joel McDurmon, "Seven Mountains Domionism: 'Not the Same Brand,'" The American Vision, September 8, 2011, http://americanvision.org/5130/seven-mountains-dominionism-not-the-same-brand/.

16. Grant Schulte, "Iowa Pastor: Churches Will Urge Voters to Remove Three Justices," *The Des Moines Register*, October 10, 2010, http://www.desmoinesregister.com/article/20101011/NEWS09/10110315/Iowa-pastor-Churches-will-urge-voters-remove-3-justices.

17. Michael I. Rothfeld, "The Real Nature of Politics and Politicians," 2009.

18. Ibid.

19. Rev. Cary K. Gordon, "The Truth about the Constitution," Peace-Makers Institute, July 31, 2010, http://www.peacemakersinstitute.com/institute/?p=835.

20. *Wikipedia*, s.v. "Constitution of France," http://en.wikipedia.org/wiki/Constitution_of_France#Past_constitutions.

CHAPTER 11: DUVERGER IS LORD?

1. Dan Amira, "Old Mitt's Investment in a Fetus-Disposal Company Is Not a Great Thing for New Mitt," *New York Magazine*, July 2, 2012, http://

nymag.com/daily/intelligencer/2012/07/romney-invested-in-a-fetus
-disposal-company.html; see also Stericycle Inc. Form S-4, November 30,
1999, http://www.motherjones.com/documents/392936-stericycle
-s4-1999; see also David Corn, "Romney Invested in Medical-Waste Firm
That Disposed of Aborted Fetuses, Government Documents Show," Mother
Jones, July 2, 2012, http://www.motherjones.com/politics/2012/07/
romney-bain-abortion-stericycle-sec; see also MMD Newswire, "Romney Is
Hiding Bain Abortion Profits in His Tax Returns, Says Tampa Foe," Renew
America, August 22, 2012, http://www.renewamerica.com/article/120822.

    2. Oakland Ross, "Schiavo Drifts Towards Death," *Toronto Star,* March
27, 2005, A2.

    3. William J. Federer, *America's God and Country: Encyclopedia of Quo-
tations* (St. Louis, MO: Amerisearch, 2000).

CHAPTER 12: HOW TO DEFEND YOUR
NATION BY WINNING YOUR CITY

    1. Rothfeld, "Politics and Politicians."

APPENDIX III: TROUBLING PASSAGES EXPLAINED

    1. Adam Clarke, *Clarke's Commentary, Vol. III* (London: J. Butterworth &
Son, 1810), 324.

    2. Scripture quotation is from *The New Testament in Modern English,*
Revised Edition. Copyright © 1958, 1960, 1972 by J.B. Phillips. Macmillan
Publishing Co. Used by permission.

About the Author

EV. CARY GORDON currently serves on the pastoral team of Cornerstone World Outreach in Sioux City, Iowa, as Executive Pastor, and resides there with his wife, Molly, his sons Solomon and Jonas, and his daughters, Ella, Rachael, and Caroline. He is most known for his dynamic teaching ministry, particularly in the field of theonomy.

In addition to his pastoral duties, Pastor Cary serves as the President of PeaceMakers Institute: A theological school dedicated to equipping conservative thinkers with the tools necessary to achieve victory in the American culture war. He has made appearances on MSNBC, Fox in the Morning, Fox News, Cavuto, The Ed Shultz Show, and many others. His political commentary has been featured in hundreds of newspapers across America, including USA Today, the New York Times, Atlantic Magazine, World Magazine, and the Los Angeles Times. His radio interviews have been broadcast on thousands of radio stations across America.

On June 5, 1995, Rev. Gordon was ordained as a Minister of the Gospel at Cornerstone World Outreach. He has served the pastorate at Cornerstone over the last twenty years at home and abroad. In addition to his stateside ministry, he has ministered in the nations of Estonia, Israel, Italy, Latvia, and Zimbabwe.

Contact the Author

To contact the author:

CaryG@Cornerstoneworld.org

or write to:

Cornerstone World Outreach
1603 Glen Ellen Road
Sioux City, IA 51106
Office Phone: (712) 274–7572